BVR Legal & Court Case Yearbook 2014

BVR
What It's Worth

1000 SW Broadway, Suite 1200, Portland, OR 97205
(503) 291-7963 • www.bvresources.com

BVR
What It's Worth

Editor: Jan Davis

Publisher: Sarah Andersen

Managing Editor: Janice Prescott

Chair and CEO: David Foster

President: Lucretia Lyons

Vice President of Sales: Lexie Gross

Customer Service Manager: Retta Dodge

ISBN: 978-1-62150-036-0

Table of Contents

Introduction

Where there's a merger, litigation is not far away. A study by Professor Steven M. Davidoff and his colleague Matthew D. Cain showed that 97.5% of takeovers in 2013 with a value over $100 million triggered a shareholder lawsuit. This litigiousness kept the Delaware courts busy and resulted in several noteworthy valuation decisions from the Delaware Court of Chancery, the preeminent arbiter of corporate affairs. *In re Trados Inc.* and *Merion Capital, L.P. v. 3M Cogent, Inc.*, immediately come to mind as must-reads for financial experts. They give invaluable insight into how the court assesses the various methodologies and an expert's technical analysis and understanding of the valuation literature. In somewhat of a surprise, at the end of the year the Court of Chancery issued *Huff Fund Investment Partnership v. CKx, Inc.*, a decision in which it eschewed the DCF analysis, a method it generally prefers, in favor of the merger price. What prompted Vice Chancellor Glasscock to do so makes for a fascinating read.

In contrast, fewer business valuation cases appeared on the Tax Court's docket than in 2012. But *Estate of Koons v. Commissioner* is one opinion that commands attention with its discount for lack of marketability discussion. Another remarkable tax case popped up at the end of the year. In *Estate of Tanenblatt v. Commissioner*, the court considered procedural issues related to expert testimony as well as substantive valuation arguments.

The intellectual property arena saw fewer sensationalistic cases in 2013 than in 2012. But *Apple v. Samsung* reappeared on the scene when in March 2013 Samsung successfully challenged the initial $1 billion award claiming Apple's expert had made irremediable errors in his damages calculation. The retrial on damages later in the year, which Samsung lost, provided for some drama over Apple's lost profits model based on the *Panduit* test. It turned on when Samsung would have begun to avoid infringement of the infringed patents, an issue that is likely to figure prominently in post-trial motions and on appeal, perhaps as early as 2014.

Also attention catching were several IP-*Daubert* cases in which district courts excluded expert testimony based on truncated apportionment. In *Dynetix Design Solutions, Inc. v. Synopsis, Inc.*, the federal district court (N.D. Cal.) acknowledged the difficulty in calculating a royalty base in a product where one component has patent protection, while other components do not, but it still found the expert's reasoning—that he had used the smallest salable unit featuring the patented component—invalid. Plaintiff damages experts increasingly have complained that courts are quick to find their calculations inadmissible, but slower to show what works. Perhaps, in 2014 courts will provide more guidance.

Daubert challenges abounded and several of the numerous 2013 decisions provided extra fodder for thought. Of particular note is *Manpower, Inc. v. Ins. Co. of Pa., LLC,* in which the 7th Circuit found the district court exercised its gatekeeping role "with too much vigor" when it excluded a qualified expert and who had used the proper methodology. Although this is a highly respected court, it remains to be seen whether its note of caution will influence district court *Daubert* rulings in other circuits.

Throughout the year, there also was no shortage of divorce and bankruptcy cases and we reported on many. Predictably, many appeals in marital dispute cases dealt with what method to use and what discounts to apply to value professional practices or other closely held corporations. *McCulloch v. McCulloch,* a decision from the Rhode Island Supreme Court, should head every divorce valuator's reading list, as it addresses the trial court's declining to value assets that by all accounts were worth at least $100 million before assigning a percentage of shares to the wife and making her a minority shareholder in a family business.

This introduction is only able to hint at the abundance and diversity of valuation cases emerging in 2013. Valuation professionals wanting a fuller picture will do well to plunge into the *BVR Legal & Court Case Yearbook 2014.*

Sylvia Golden
Legal Editor, Business Valuation Resources

Court Case Summary Table

Presented in order of State/Jurisdiction, then Case Name

Case Name	Date	State/ Jurisdiction	Court	Summary	Page
Farrell v. Farrell	1/23/13	Arkansas	Court of Appeals	Unclear Valuation of Family Business Interests Requires Remand	95
Russell v. Russell	2/27/13	Arkansas	Court of Appeals	Valuation of Family Business Survives Expert's Deviation From Industry Standards	188
Brocade Communications Systems, Inc. v. A10 Networks, Inc. (I)	1/10/13	California	United States District Court	Expert's Apportionment Cannot Save Flawed Royalty Calculation	41
Charles v. Charles	4/2/13	California	Court of Appeals	Court Reproves Spouse's Efforts to Lower Value of Community Business	52
Goldfarb v. Yelton	6/27/13	California	Court of Appeals	Community Deserves Profits From Separate Business Investment	103
Edgewater Growth Capital Partners, L.P. v. H.I.G. Capital, Inc.	2/28/13	Delaware	Court of Chancery	Expert Uses Irrelevant Basis of Comparison and Sabotages Valuation	74
In re Trados Inc.	8/16/13	Delaware	Court of Chancery	Chancery Trusts DCF to Arrow in on Common Stock Value	215
Koehler v. Netspend Holdings Inc.	5/21/13	Delaware	Court of Chancery	DCF Valuation Meant to Underpin Fairness Opinion Upends It	127
Merion Capital, L.P. v. 3M Cogent, Inc.	7/8/13	Delaware	Court of Chancery	Merger-Related Projections Pass Muster With Delaware Chancery	147
Towerview LLC v. Cox Radio, Inc.	6/28/13	Delaware	Court of Chancery	DE Chancery Court's Appraisal Puts Focus on Precrisis Projections	221
Aries Communications Inc. v. Commissioner	4/10/13	Federal Circuit	United States Tax Court	Tax Court Predicates Bonus on Increasing Asset Sale Price	21
Energy Transp. Group, Inc. v. William Demant Holding A/S	10/12/12	Federal Circuit	United States Court of Appeals	25% Rule Does Not 'Irretrievably Damage' Royalty Analysis	79
Private Letter Ruling 201314002	4/5/13	Federal Circuit	Departement of the Treasury	IRS Gives Hybrid Business Favorable Tax Status	176
Sutardja v. United States	2/27/13	Federal Circuit	United States Court of Federal Claims	Claims Court Rules IRC Section 409A Governs Discounted Stock Option	211
Synqor, Inc. v. Artesyn Technologies, Inc.	3/13/13	Federal Circuit	United States Court of Appeals	Fed. Circuit Affirms $95M Patent Award Based on Price Erosion Theory	213
Davis v. Commissioner	5/16/13	Federal/11th Circuit	United States Court of Appeals	Negotiated Formula for Stock Option Price Obviates DLOM Need	64
Factory Mutual Insurance Co. v. Alon USA	1/23/13	Federal/5th Circuit	Court of Appeals	Court Accepts Cost Approach to Calculate Value of Lost Business	90
Gallagher & Co. v. Babcock	12/18/12	Federal/5th Circuit	United States Court of Appeals	Court Rejects Expert's 'Irrelevant' Theory of Damages	97
Dorrance v. U.S.	3/19/13	Federal/ Arizona	United States District Court	In Demutualization, IPO Share Price Guides Cost Basis Determination	72
Alaska Rent-a-Car, Inc. v. Avis Budget Group, Inc.	6/19/13	Federal/ California	United States Court of Appeals	*Daubert* Tolerates Impeachable Aspects of Expert Testimony	14
Apple, Inc. v. Samsung Electronics Co.	3/1/13	Federal/ California	United States District Court	Expert's 'Aggressive' Damages Theory Necessitates New Trial	19
Brighton Collectibles, Inc. v. RK Texas Leather Mfg.	2/12/13	Federal/ California	United States District Court	Attempt to Base Lost Profits on Infringer's Sales Alone Fails	40

Case Name	Date	State/ Jurisdiction	Court	Summary	Page
Brocade Communications Systems, Inc. v. A10 Networks, Inc. (II)	5/15/13	Federal/ California	United States District Court	Does *Panduit* Lost Profits Theory Require Apportionment?	43
Illinois Tool Works, Inc. v. MOC Products Co, Inc.	8/17/12	Federal/ California	United States District Court	Damages Expert Can Assume But Not Opine as to Market Share	115
In re Novatel Wireless Securities Litigation	12/14/12	Federal/ California	United States District Court	Inclusion of Inflated Purchase Price Does Not Doom Damages Calculation	162
Christou v. Beatport, LLC	1/23/13	Federal/ Colorado	United States District Court	Court Seeks 'Fit' Between Lost Business Value Calculation and Facts	56
Enzo Biochem, Inc. v. Applera Corp.	8/1/13	Federal/ Connecticut	United States District Court	'Murky' Infringement Theory Undercuts Royalty Claim	81
Tyco Healthcare Group LP v. Ethicon Endo-Surgery, Inc.	3/28/13	Federal/ Connecticut	United States District Court	Flawed Market Reconstruction Ends Lost Profits Claim	228
AVM Technologies, LLC v. Intel Corporation (I)	1/4/13	Federal/ Delaware	United States District Court	Difficulty in Calculating Royalty Base No Defense Under *Daubert*	28
AVM Technologies, LLC v. Intel Corporation (II)	2/21/13	Federal/ Delaware	United States District Court	Failure to Analyze Settlement Agreement Dooms Damages Theory	30
Whyte v. C/R Energy Coinvestment II, L.P. (In re SemCrud)	6/10/13	Federal/ Delaware	United States Bankruptcy Court	Bankruptcy Court Wary of Asset Approach in Solvency Analysis	244
Loving v. IRS (I)	1/18/13	Federal/ District of Columbia	United States District Court	Independent Tax Preparers Protest IRS's Regulation Efforts and Prevail	140
Loving v. IRS (II)	2/1/13	Federal/ District of Columbia	United States District Court	Independent Tax Preparers Protest IRS's Regulation Efforts and Prevail	140
Brandeis University v. Keebler Co.	1/18/13	Federal/Illinois	United States District Court	Royalty Calculation Depends on Cost of 'Best Imperfect Substitute'	38
RMD, LLC v. Nitto Americas, Inc.	11/5/12	Federal/ Kansas	United States District Court	Expert's Unconventional Method to Forecast Lost Profits Satisfies *Daubert*	181
Joyce v. Armstrong Teasdale, LLP (I)	8/15/12	Federal/ Missouri	United States District Court	Patent Experts Have Limited Latitude to Comply With New Damages Standards	123
Joyce v. Armstrong Teasdale, LLP (II)	9/26/12	Federal/ Missouri	United States District Court	Patent Experts Have Limited Latitude to Comply With New Damages Standards	123
Samson v. Western Capital Partners LLC (In re Blixseth)	3/28/13	Federal/ Montana	United States Bankruptcy Court	Court Credits Expert's Cash Flow Analysis in Solvency Determination	190
Deseret Management Corp. v. United States	7/31/13	Federal/N/A	United States Court of Federal Claims	IRS Strains to Prove Goodwill in Like-Kind Exchange	67
Microsoft Corp. v. Motorola, Inc. (I)	10/22/12	Federal/N/A	United States District Court	Test Case Considers Proper Framework for RAND Royalty Rates	156
MyGallons LLC v. U.S. Bankcorp	5/31/13	Federal/N/A	United States Court of Appeals	One Expert's Bad Data Undermine Another's Damages Calculation	159
Peek v. Commissioner	5/9/13	Federal/N/A	United States Tax Court	Ignoring Accountant's Advice, Taxpayers Botch Investment Strategy	173
Versata Software, Inc. v. SAP America, Inc.	5/1/13	Federal/N/A	United States Court of Appeals	Fed. Circuit Chides Defendants for 'Improper' Admissibility Challenge	237
Assured Guaranty Municipal Corp. v. Flagstar Bank, FSB	2/6/13	Federal/New York	United States District Court	Damages Calculation Resting on Loan Sampling Is 'Solid'	25
Great Lakes Business Trust v. M/T Orange Sun	4/30/13	Federal/New York	United States Court of Appeals	Expert's Loss-of-Use Computation Holds Up on Appeal	107

Case Name	Date	State/ Jurisdiction	Court	Summary	Page
Liberty Media Corp. v. Vivendi Universal, S.A.	2/12/13	Federal/New York	United States District Court	Expert's 'Aggressively Skeptical' View Does Not Undermine Disaggregation Analysis	134
Securities and Exchange Commission v. Tourre	6/18/13	Federal/New York	United States District Court	Court Upbraids Expert Who Discusses Subject Outside Area of Expertise	194
Estate of Koons v. Commissioner	4/8/13	Federal/Ohio	United States Tax Court	Court Rejects Expert's Regression Equation to Determine DLOM	86
Info-Hold, Inc. v. Muzak LLC	8/20/13	Federal/Ohio	United States District Court	Glaring Unfamiliarity With Patent Law Disqualifies Expert	117
Carnegie Mellon University v. Marvell Technology Group (I)	8/24/12	Federal/ Pennsylvania	United States District Court	In Billion-Dollar IP Case, Expert's Mention of Total Revenue Does Not Violate *Uniloc*	47
Carnegie Mellon University v. Marvell Technology Group (II)	11/6/12	Federal/ Pennsylvania	United States District Court	In Billion-Dollar IP Case, Expert's Mention of Total Revenue Does Not Violate *Uniloc*	47
Carnegie Mellon University v. Marvell Technology Group (III)	12/15/12	Federal/ Pennsylvania	United States District Court	Lack of License Negotiation Experience Does Not Disqualify Expert	50
Pure Earth, Inc. v. Call	7/19/13	Federal/ Pennsylvania	United States Court of Appeals	Court, Not Expert, Misses Mark on Loss Causation	179
Jack Tyler Engineering Co. v. Colfax Corp.	4/10/13	Federal/ Tennessee	United States District Court	Discount Rate Analysis Requires Expert's Subjective Judgments	119
Ericsson Inc. v. D-Link Corp.	5/21/13	Federal/Texas	United States District Court	Prior Standards Licenses Reflect Asserted Patents' 'Real-World' Valuation	84
In Re: LMR, LLC	5/24/13	Federal/Texas	United States Bankruptcy Court	Court Approves Debtor's 'Feasible, But Tight' Plan With 6% Interest Rate	130
SSL Services, LLC v. Citrix Systems, Inc.	4/17/13	Federal/Texas	United States District Court	Assignee's Low Valuation Does Not Control Patent Damages Calculation	205
U.S. Bank N.A. v. Verizon Communications Inc.	1/22/13	Federal/Texas	United States District Court	Expert's 'Unsupportable' Inputs Undermine DCF Analysis and Credibility	232
Versata Software, Inc. v. Internet Brands, Inc.	10/9/12	Federal/Texas	United States District Court	Does Apportionment Rule Extend to Trade Secrets Cases?	236
VirnetX Inc. v. Cisco Systems, Inc.	3/1/13	Federal/Texas	United States District Court	Nash Bargaining Solution Survives *Daubert* Challenge, Royalty Analysis Does Not	247
Hark'n Technologies, Inc. v. Crossover Symmetry	2/21/13	Federal/Utah	United States District Court	Does Use of Full Product Line Data Invalidate Damages Formulation?	113
Electro-Mechanical Corp. v. Power Distribution Products, Inc.	9/10/13	Federal/ Virginia	United States District Court	Invocation of EMVR Subject to Higher Degree of Proof	77
Metamining, Inc. v. Barnette	6/26/13	Federal/ Virginia	United States District Court	Expert's 'Invocation' of Income Approach Does Not Save Valuation	154
Marine Travelift, Inc. v. Marine Lift Systems, Inc.	6/28/13	Federal/ Wisconsin	United States District Court	May Expert Offer Plaintiff's Loss Calculation as His Own?	142
In re Bachrach Clothing, Inc.	10/10/12	Illinois	United States Bankruptcy Court	Bankruptcy Court Discredits DCF as 'Easily Manipulated'	33
Burnett v. Burnett	11/29/12	Indiana	Court of Appeals	Court Affirms Excess Earnings Method for Goodwill Calculation	45
Fancher v. Prudhome	2/27/13	Louisiana	Court of Appeals	Book Value Accurately Reflects FMV of Departing Partner's Interest	93
Alexander v. Alexander	9/10/13	Michigan	Court of Appeals	Low Risk to Business Justifies Expert's Capitalization Rate	16
Loutts v. Loutts	9/20/12	Michigan	Court of Appeals	Michigan Court on Double-Dipping in Divorce: 'It Depends'	139
Keig v. Keig	12/4/12	Nebraska	Court of Appeals	Court Affirms Award for Excluding Value of Farm From Marital Estate	126

Court Case Abstracts

Presented in alphabetical order.

Excess Earnings Method Best Suited to Value NYC Practice

Case name: *A.C. v. J.O.*
Citation: 2013 N.Y. Misc. LEXIS 3524
Date of decision: Aug. 12 2013
Country: US
State or Federal: State
State/Jurisdiction: New York
Court: Supreme Court
Type of action: Marital Dissolution
Experts: Unknown (wife); David Gresen (husband)
Judge: Silber
SIC: 8021 Offices and Clinics of Dentists

Keeping a professional practice in New York City is different. In a recent decision, the New York Supreme Court (Kings County, Brooklyn—a trial court) explained why location mattered when it came to valuing the wife's dental business.

'True' and not 'true' businesses. The husband was a film and television director who also wrote screenplays. His most recent film premiered at the Sundance Film Festival last year and is slated for release soon. He formed his own production company in 1999, one year after he and his wife got married, but had worked in the industry before the marriage, doing the same type of work. He was promoted to first assistant director for work on a major television series during the marriage, but this advancement did not require further education or training. The company was "personal to him and not saleable," he explained. Some film and television companies required crew members to be salaried, whereas others allowed them to bill as a freelancer, that is, to receive payment for work via a business. He went on to say that the latter arrangement permitted him to take business-related deductions.

Moreover, he testified to having copyrighted four scripts. He optioned one and had one made into a film that was sold. Two remained unproduced and unsold. To date, there was no established value for them.

The wife was a partner in a major law firm but resigned before marriage. Once married, the husband and wife agreed that she would pursue dentistry and follow in the footsteps of her father and grandfather. The couple understood that she would earn less as a dentist than she could expect to earn as a law firm partner. After graduation, she initially worked for her father, but when he was ready to retire, she used $130,000 of a home equity loan to purchase his client list and set up her own practice. This amount stemmed from a prior independent appraisal of the value of goodwill of her father's practice. The wife's general practice employed an orthodontist, receptionist, and two dental assistants. She rented space, furniture, and equipment from another dentist.

Although at trial the wife claimed there were no expert appraisals of the two businesses, the husband presented a preliminary report from a financial expert and CPA who had prepared valuations in mid-2011 at the start of the divorce proceedings. Then the wife had cooperated with the expert by providing the requisite financial and personal data that enabled him to value her practice. The expert used the price-to-revenue method, also known as multiple-of-revenue method; it relied on annual revenues and charts of sales of comparable businesses from national reports. This was the appropriate approach for valuing a dental practice, he testified. He concluded that the husband's business was worth $124,000 and the wife's practice $455,000. He explained that he did not have authorization to do work beyond the initial report. Had he prepared a final report, he would have audited the couple's books and records to confirm the accuracy of the information he had received, he said at trial.

He also noted that the wife had zero enhanced earning capacity resulting from her dental degree.

The plaintiffs' attorneys "vigorously" contested the expert's appraisal—its method and conclusions—claiming he provided nothing more than a "calculation report." Subsequently, they procured an alternate valuation for the wife's practice based on the excess earnings method—a "hybrid income approach" that determines net tangible assets and goodwill. (The court's opinion does not specify who prepared it and how.) It indicated the wife's business was worth only $316,000.

The court first found that the CPA's opinion qualified as expert testimony. The fact that his valuation remained preliminary was due to the wife's choice to stop work before the expert could complete his review and should be held against her interests, not the husband's.

The husband's business was little more than "a conduit to receive payment for work he is hired to do." Because the wife did not contribute to the company or the husband's promotion to first assistant director and the company was not a "true" business, the wife had no right to any of the $124,000 value the appraiser had determined.

In contrast, the court found the husband had contributed to the wife's business. For one, he worked during her four-year dental studies. Second, he agreed to the use of part of the home equity loan to purchase her father's client list. This "initial investment," the court said, allowed her to start her business "on the ground running," which, in turn, allowed for the assumption that her income in the first year of practice was "considerably higher than it would have been otherwise." Also, the husband agreed to her using marital property to pay for household help and childcare that enabled her to go to school and build up her practice.

The core issue was which valuation method to use for the practice, the court said. Although there was no uniform approach to computing the value of an ongoing business in the context of an equitable distribution, in this case the excess earnings method was more appropriate. It took into account the absence of tangible assets and the goodwill based on three generations of dentists in the wife's family. The expert's method drew on values that did not adequately consider factors unique to a professional office in New York and to the wife's practice, namely that she did not own the office, an office lease, or any equipment. These factors, the court pointed out, would be part of the "ordinary sale of a dental practice in most of the United States." But given the exorbitant rents in New York, "it is not unusual for a professional to rent an office and the equipment necessary for a business." Because there were no net assets, the $316,000 value derived from the excess earnings method had to represent the goodwill value of the practice, the court concluded.

Next, it determined the percentage of the value to award to the husband. Precedent required consideration of the nonowner spouse's "direct" and "indirect" contributions. The former include that spouse's contribution to the acquisition, maintenance, or increase in the value of the owner spouse's business. The latter referred to the nonowner spouse's taking care of the house and children and thus allowing the owner spouse to focus on the business. The court cited cases that awarded the nonowner spouse 30% or 20% of the business and, in this case, split the difference. It found that 25%, that is, $79,000, appropriately accounted for not only the husband's "minimal direct and indirect contributions" toward the establishment of the business, but also his support during the wife's studies. In addition, he had a right to a $65,000 credit representing half of the home equity loan funds the wife used to buy her father's client list. In a final note, the court pointed out that both partners understood at the outset of the wife's career change that dentistry would be unlikely to enhance her earning capacity, considering she had been an equity partner in a major law firm. Here, regardless of the husband's nonmonetary contributions to the wife's degree, "there can be no distribution of any such value where the value of plaintiff's enhanced earning capacity is zero."

Script valuation proves tricky. The husband's four copyrighted scripts raised a number of questions. Because neither party proved their value at trial, they agreed that there could be no distributive award or credit or offset to the wife at that time. But, said the court, because the husband created these works during the marriage, the wife had a right to "half of such sums paid to the defendant for the sale or use of these works."

But the court attached a caveat to this award: The wife had no right to compensation the husband earned as a result of making future modifications to the works.

In seeming contradiction to this provision in the decision, the court next specified that the wife was to receive "25% of any fees or royalties defendant earns from the four copyrighted scripts, as well as 25% of any sums earned from the sale of all or any part of the copyrights, or any sums paid for the right to make any derivative works from the scripts."

Editor's note: The court's statements create a possibility that any modification to any one of the scripts may diminish if not eliminate the wife's claim to half of a copyright's value. Its order also raises questions as to how to measure the impact of the modification—unless the modification produces a completely new work—considering there is no baseline and no indication as to who gets to quantify it. The court did not set down a procedure.

Daubert Tolerates Impeachable Aspects of Expert Testimony

Case name: *Alaska Rent-a-Car, Inc. v. Avis Budget Group, Inc.*
Citation: 2013 U.S. App. LEXIS 12709
Date of decision: June 19, 2013
Country: US
State or Federal: Federal
State/Jurisdiction: California
Court: United States Court of Appeals
Type of action: Contract
Experts: Unknown
Judge: Kleinfeld
SIC: 7514 Passenger Car Rental

In appealing a $16 million jury award to Alaska Rent-A-Car for the breach of a settlement agreement, Avis claimed the plaintiff's expert made unsupportable assumptions and comparisons regarding the market and other car rental companies that compromised his calculations. The 9th Circuit reviewed the district court's denial of Avis's *Daubert* motion and its motion for judgment as a matter of law (JMOL).

The case arose out of a 1997 settlement agreement Avis made with a number of its licensees after it had bought another rental car company that the licensees claimed would unlawfully compete in their territories. Under the contract, Avis was able to purchase other companies but not use its personnel to steer customers toward the other brand. The plaintiff, Alaska Rent-A-Car, was a longtime Avis licensee and party to the agreement. In 2002, Avis bought Budget Rent-A-Car out of bankruptcy and subsequently centralized its operations. This meant creating a single marketing and sales force that answered calls to both companies' reservation lines. Alaska sued, claiming Avis's actions violated the settlement agreement because they caused Alaska's business to go to Budget, its local competitor.

The district court granted Alaska's pretrial motion and found Avis liable. A jury trial on damages followed. Both sides presented experts, and Avis filed a *Daubert* motion to exclude the damages testimony Alaska's expert gave.

Specifically, Alaska's expert tried to create a hypothetical world in which all elements stayed the same except the breach had not occurred. As a point of comparison, he used the experience of another rental car business, Alamo-National, which was bought out of bankruptcy by another company at around the time Avis bought Budget. He suggested that Alamo and Budget both received an infusion of capital and help from management to compete. But Alamo's buyer had no other car rental company. Therefore, Alamo did not benefit from a centralized sales and marketing force the way Budget did, thanks to Avis's efforts. The expert attributed Budget's faster recovery to Avis's wrongdoing. He also assumed Alamo's national rate of rebound was an indicator for how Budget would have fared but for the breach. Next, he projected how much market share Budget obtained as a result of the breach. The car rental market was a national market and local factors did not distort national rebound rates, he maintained.

After it declared bankruptcy, Alamo saw a 35% drop in market share. It slowly recovered after it was bought. In contrast, Budget was in bankruptcy for a shorter time and recovered faster. The expert estimated that Budget would have lost 32.5% of its market share had Avis bought it but not breached the agreement.

To approximate how much business a revivified Budget took away from Alaska, the expert focused on the Juneau airport. This specificity made it easy to examine the market before and after Budget entered. He found that over the first three years of its entry it claimed an average of 23.3% of the market. Approximately 48% of the gain came from Alaska customers, and the remainder from other companies. To arrive at a statewide figure, he assumed that, after the breach, Budget got roughly half of its customers from Alaska statewide. Based on his assumptions and inferences, he calculated lost profits of roughly $4.1 million from 2003 to 2008 and future lost profits, discounted to present value, of $11.7 million.

Avis's expert critiqued the competing testimony but did not set down any damages figure for the jury. The comparison to Alamo, he said, was invalid given the difference in the companies' duration of bankruptcy and other factors (unspecified). Also, considering how differently the national and the Alaska markets worked, the rival expert was wrong to apply the national market share comparison to Alaska. Similarly, considering the Juneau market only made up 5% of the statewide rental car market, extrapolating from its experience meant ignoring factors specific to the rest of the state. For example, towns across the state relied on roads to link them and doing business more often required a rental car.

In response to Avis's *Daubert* challenge, the trial court allowed Avis to question Alaska's expert. The court subsequently decided to let the testimony in, subject to cross-examination during trial. The jury returned a unanimous $16 million verdict for Alaska, which was slightly more than the figure Alaska's expert had proposed. In a post-trial motion, Avis unsuccessfully argued that Alaska did not prove damages with sufficient certainty. Subsequently, it appealed the district court's prior rulings to the 9th Circuit.

Gatekeeper, but not fact finder. Avis's appeal as to damages evidence drew on federal and state law. It said the calculation of Alaska's expert had three fatal flaws: (1) using Alamo as a comparator;

(2) using the national rather than the Alaska market as a baseline; and (3) extrapolating from the Juneau market to the Alaska market. Under Fed. R. Evid. 702 and *Daubert*, the expert's calculations were unreliable and the district court erred in admitting the testimony.

The appeals court agreed that Avis's arguments might have some merit. But, it said, they all went to impeachability, not admissibility. Although the district court must screen the jury from "unreliable nonsense opinions," it is not supposed to exclude opinions simply because they are impeachable. Here the expert was qualified, and his general methodology was not in dispute. Avis gave the jury good reasons to reject the testimony, but the judge did not err by allowing jury members to hear it. Because the judge is a gatekeeper, not a fact finder, "the gate could not be closed to this relevant opinion," the appeals court concluded.

Avis also repeated its claim that Alaska did not prove damages with reasonable certainty, as the applicable New York law required. The district court erred when it denied its JMOL motion based on that ground.

The 9th Circuit disagreed. New York courts generally reject lost profits if there is a new business venture or the claimant is an existing business projecting future profits when it does not have a past history of profits. Here, Alaska had been operating a successful business "since before statehood." Although a jury might have credited Avis's impeachment testimony, rejected the damage calculations of Alaska's expert, and awarded nothing, it chose not to do so. The jury had the right to decide, said the court, and affirmed the lost profits award.

Low Risk to Business Justifies Expert's Capitalization Rate

Case name: *Alexander v. Alexander*
Citation: 2013 Mich. App. LEXIS 1490
Date of decision: Sept. 10, 2013
Country: US
State or Federal: State
State/Jurisdiction: Michigan
Court: Court of Appeals
Type of action: Marital Dissolution
Experts: Kerry Bean (wife); David Sides (husband); James Gorman (court-appointed)
Judge: Per curiam
SIC: 0762 Farm Management Services

After hearing from the spouses' experts on the value of an agriculture-related business, the trial court brought in a third-party expert and adopted his valuation. The husband appealed the appraisal, claiming it was based on an erroneously low capitalization rate that improperly gauged the viability and risk of the company.

One approach begets three outcomes. In a recent divorce case, the parties contested the value of a small, agriculture-based business that the husband owned and operated during the marriage. The wife's expert said he valued the business under the "holder's interest" standard, using a capitalization of net income approach. Specifically, he considered the net income from the two years prior to the filing for divorce—2008 and 2009—but ignored the years 2005 through 2007. He computed the present value of all future net income by using an 18% capitalization rate, explaining that the rate included a 5.7% equity risk premium (ERP) and a 5% company-specific risk premium.

His capitalization rate indicated a low-risk business, he said, because the agriculture industry was relatively stable and healthy; at the same time, he allowed that another appraiser "could reasonably value the business with a capitalization rate between 11 and 25 percent." He also adjusted for compensation to the husband, saying a reasonable wage would be $140,000.

He originally concluded the company was worth nearly $1.1 million as of December 2009 but subsequently lowered the valuation by "a couple hundred thousand dollars, approximately," based on "new information received the morning of the trial." (The opinion does not specify what the information was and how the expert believed it influenced the valuation.)

The husband's business valuator used the same approach but considered net income from 2005 to 2009. He used a substantially higher capitalization rate of 26.6% because he saw the industry as "relatively unstable" and the company relied on only a few customers. The loss of any one client put its profitability at grave risk, he said. According to him, $110,000 was a reasonable wage for the husband. He concluded that the business's value was a little over $183,100.

The trial court rejected both valuations and appointed a third-party appraiser, who also used the same approach. Like the wife's expert, he considered financial data from 2008 and 2009 alone. He believed certain expenses (e.g., actual meal expenses) were unreasonably high and reduced them, which increased the net income that appeared on the balance sheets.

He arrived at a 13.1% capitalization rate, applying a 5.2% equity risk premium from the *2010 Ibbotson SBBI Valuation Yearbook.* He also found that a 10% size premium was appropriate—it reflected a "lower tiered, more troubled company." He conceded that there was a legitimate argument that the risk factor should be closer to 6% than 10%. In addition, he opted for a company-specific risk premium of 4%, explaining it was "odd to see a company specific risk premium of much out of the range of 3% to 6%." Lastly, he stated $151,600 was a reasonable wage for the husband. All of these considerations yielded a value of $813,000 for the business.

The trial court adopted the third-party appraiser's valuation in its entirety. It specifically noted that the business risk was less than the risk the husband's expert claimed.

The husband challenged the valuation at the Michigan Court of Appeals, claiming the trial court's decision was error: The appointed expert used an improperly low capitalization rate, improperly adjusted the business cash flow for 2008 and 2009, and failed to use financial data for five consecutive years. The appellate court disposed of the arguments quickly.

1. *Capitalization rate.* The husband took issue with several components:

a. *Equity risk premium.* First, he said, the third-party expert claimed to use the 5.2% equity risk premium appearing in the *2010 Ibbotson Yearbook,* when in reality Ibbotson reflected a 6.6% value.

"Presumably [Ibbotson] is a manual used to value businesses, but it is not included in the lower court's record," said the appellate court. Without proof, there was no way to determine whether the trial court erred. Also, the 5.2% rate was comparable to the 5.7% rate the wife's expert used; at the same time, no expert argued for an equity risk premium as high as 6.6%.

b. Size premium. The 10% small-company (or size) premium also was inappropriate, the husband contended, because the *2010 Ibbotson Yearbook* suggested 12.06% would be a more appropriate premium under the circumstances.

Again, the appellate court pointed out that the relevant page from Ibbotson was not on record, and, therefore, the court was unable to decide the validity of the argument.

c. *Company-specific risk premium.* Considering the business did not diversify when it came to risk and he was the only manager there, the husband claimed the 4% rate the third-party expert applied was unjustifiably low.

The appellate court considered the argument an attempt to relitigate an issue that had received extensive attention at trial. Two of the three valuators agreed that the business had a relatively low risk and the appointed expert expressly stated that the range for a company-specific risk premium usually was between 3% and 6%. He opted for a 4% rate, whereas the wife's expert used a 5% rate, the court noted. Accordingly, the 4% figure had support in the evidence.

In sum, the capitalization rate was not erroneously low.

2. Cash flow adjustment. The husband maintained that the third-party expert used an improperly low annual compensation and consequently obtained an erroneously high projected cash flow. Also, there was no justification for normalizing expenses, and he was wrong to use data from fewer than five years to determine business cash flow.

The appointed expert's $151,600 annual wage figure was higher than the $140,000 the wife's expert calculated and the $110,000 the husband's own expert proposed, the appellate court pointed out. In fact, the expert used the most favorable rate.

As to the financial data, the husband failed to provide authority for his arguments. Considering that two of the three experts stated that it was appropriate to rely on data for two years, the trial court did not clearly err when it accepted the third-party expert's choices.

For all these reasons, the appeals court upheld the trial court's valuation.

Editor's note: The 2010 Ibbotson SBBI Valuation Yearbook shows a 5.2% supply-side ERP and a 6.7% historical ERP. It appears that, when the husband referred to a 6.6% ERP, it was the historical rate, which his expert may have used (although the opinion does not expressly say so). This choice would result in the biggest cost of equity and the lowest overall valuation.

Expert's 'Aggressive' Damages Theory Necessitates New Trial

Case name: *Apple, Inc. v. Samsung Electronics Co.*
Citation: 2013 U.S. Dist. LEXIS 29051
Date of decision: March 1, 2013
Country: US
State or Federal: Federal
State/Jurisdiction: California
Court: United States District Court
Type of action: Intellectual Property
Experts: Terry Musika (plaintiff); Michael Wagner (defendant)
Judge: Koh
SIC: 4813 Telephone Communications, Except Radiotelephone (except resellers)

After the plaintiff received one of the largest damages awards of 2012, both sides filed post-trial motions attacking the verdict. The federal court agreed that irremediable errors related to the damages calculation required it to modify the award and order a retrial.

Apple sued Samsung, claiming a range of the defendant's products violated its design and utility patents and some diluted its trade dress. The parties presented a phalanx of experts to speak to patent, technical, and damages issues and filed dueling *Daubert* motions to exclude the competing testimony. (A discussion of the challenges to damages testimony, as well as the court's ruling, appears in the digest in the October 2012 *BVU* and at *BVLaw*.)

In August 2012, a jury found Samsung infringed critical components of Apple's iPhone and iPad. Damages included infringer's profits, lost profits, and reasonable royalties. Specifically, for a wide range of products, the jury awarded exactly 40% of Apple's expert's calculation of Samsung's profits; in some instances, it also added 100% of the expert's calculation of Apple's lost profits. And, for several products, it awarded exactly half of the reasonable royalty award the expert had proposed.

In calculating damages, for all patents, Apple's expert used the earliest date on which the parties discussed infringement.

In total, the jury awarded Apple over $1 billion.

Defendant considers the award excessive. Samsung challenged the verdict on several grounds: 1) Apple's expert made apportionment errors related to design patent infringement; 2) he failed to establish the requisite "but for" causation for lost profits; 3) some of the award was based on "impermissible legal theories"; and 4) the jury based its awards on the wrong notice date that Apple's expert used in his calculations. The court considered each objection as follows.

1) Apportionment. Apple's expert calculated damages for all of Samsung's profits on products that infringed design patents, but Apple never proved that Samsung's infringement was responsible for all of its profits, the defendant claimed. Because the expert failed to apportion, the court should strike every award related to design patent infringement.

The court confirmed its earlier decision (on *Daubert* motions) that holders of design patents may claim the "infringer's entire profits" without having to split damages between the patented design and the product bearing the design.

2) Causation. Samsung claimed Apple had no right to lost profits because it failed to show a causal connection between the infringement and its loss of profits.

Once again, the court disagreed. Apple's damages expert provided detailed evidence as to how the market would likely have behaved "but for" Samsung's infringement. He considered the market share of the largest smartphone manufacturers based on analysis from the International Data Corp., Apple's ability to produce additional phones and tablets, and evidence from expert surveys and fact witness statements related to consumer demand.

3) Impermissible legal theory. Samsung argued that for one of its products that only infringed utility patents, the jury awarded damages that were not a legally permissible form of compensation.

The court agreed. It found that the jury had failed to follow its instructions by improperly awarding 40% of Samsung's profits, amounting to $58 million, when the only remedies available were Apple's lost profits or a reasonable royalty.

"This award cannot stand," it noted, but found it had no way "to reasonably and fairly calculate" the appropriate reduction. Because the court could neither ignore the unlawful nature of the award nor "bend over backwards" to justify the amount, it ordered a new damages trial for this product.

4) Notice dates. Samsung also claimed that numerous awards were excessive because Apple's expert had used an incorrect notice date (that is, the date when the defendant has actual or constructive notice of the patent).

Again, the court sided with the defendant. Three potential dates were in play, it determined. What complicated the issue was that different types of intellectual property allowed for different types of damages awards; for example, utility patent infringement allows for lost profits or a reasonable royalty, whereas damages for design patent infringement may include lost profits, a reasonable royalty, or infringer's profits.

Consequently, it was an error to award infringer's profits for a period during which the defendant only had notice of utility patents. Also, the court noted, under the law, the patentee must give notice of the specific patent the infringer's product violates.

Apple's expert used an Aug. 4, 2010, date, the first time the parties discussed infringement. But, the court said, this date only applied to one patent. Providing a detailed chart that outlined the patents, notice dates, available remedies, and accused products, it found that two subsequent dates applied to six other patents.

For eight phones, the jury awarded 40% of Samsung's profits for the entire period (amounting to some $383 million), even though during some of the time, an award of infringer's profits was not an authorized remedy. Because the court could not readily identify the amount it needed to subtract, the only solution was a new trial as to those items.

Similarly, damages for five phones amounted to exactly half of the expert's reasonable royalty calculations (totaling over $9 million). His numbers were based on incorrect notice dates for several of the patents at issue, the court found. Even though the expert had provided a per-unit royalty rate for each patent and the parties had stated the number of units of each product sold per quarter, the court was not able to calculate the correct number of sales on which to base a reduction.

In total, the court determined that errors related to 14 products required it to reduce the award by over $450 million. It criticized Apple for providing an expert report that used an "aggressive notice date for all of the patents." Had the company taken a more "circumspect" approach and given the jury or court evidence with which to calculate an award for a shorter period of time, the need for a retrial might not exist.

Plaintiff says the award is not enough. In its motion, Apple argued it had a right to additional damages to cover sales that occurred after the trial had concluded.

The law requires that the court make an award for any sale for which the jury did not award damages, the court stated. But it cautioned that the determination of supplemental damages in this case might wait until after the completion of the appeals process, considering the many unresolved issues.

Tax Court Predicates Bonus on Increasing Asset Sale Price

Case name: *Aries Communications Inc. v. Commissioner*
Citation: 2013 Tax Ct. Memo LEXIS 111
Date of decision: April 10, 2013
Country: US
State or Federal: Federal
State/Jurisdiction: Federal Circuit
Court: United States Tax Court
Type of action: Federal Taxation
Experts: Martin Wertlieb (petitioner); Andrew J. Caffrey, Mark R. Lipis (respondent)
Judge: Wherry

What qualifies as a reasonable success fee for the employee who is also the hands-on owner of the company and played a key role in the profitable sale of some of the company's major assets? This was the issue for experts in front of the Tax Court following the IRS's disallowance of most of the compensation the company had claimed as a deduction for the tax year ended (TYE) 2004.

In 1983, the owner/employee incorporated the petitioner in California. He was its sole shareholder and used the company to buy and sell radio stations. He also served as its president, CFO, and general manager for the various stations. The company was a complex enterprise with multiple subsidiaries that each owned stations. Before it sold off some of its major assets in 2003 and 2004, it had gross receipts of over $4.5 million. But records showed that from 1999 to 2002 and immediately after the two years of major asset sales, it was losing money. As early as 2001, the company guaranteed a $20 million Goldman Sachs debt, as did the owner personally. A forbearance agreement required it to sell some of its radio stations to satisfy its obligations under the debt.

In 2003, the owner hired a broker to assist with the sale of one station; specifically, the broker was to find prospective buyers of whom the employee was not aware. But the owner himself procured the first bid, which was in the $18 million-to-$20 million range; subsequently, he managed to persuade the bidder to increase the offer to $28 million. At the owner's suggestion, the broker obtained a rival bid for $33 million, which persuaded the first bidder to agree to a final price of $35 million.

In 2004, the petitioner sold certain assets of another station, including FCC licenses. Before the sale, the prospective buyer offered $12 million for the station, but the owner rejected the bid, making it clear he wanted $18 million. He used the broker to complete the transaction at that price.

For TYE 2004, the petitioner showed a net profit of approximately $4 million and retained earnings of over $12.7 million. It paid the owner nearly $137,000 in salary, $62,500 in commissions, and $6.7 million as a bonus, totaling $6.9 million—all of which it claimed as a tax deduction.

The IRS issued a notice of deficiency, disallowing nearly $6.1 million and finding a deficiency of nearly $2.7 million. At trial, both parties presented expert testimony on reasonable compensation.

Regression analysis 'not useful.' The petitioner's expert had over 40 years of experience in compensation and personnel matters. To render an opinion, he reviewed the financial statements of 10 publicly traded radio broadcasting companies, including Clear Channel. He calculated their pretax revenues and compared them to the petitioner's revenue; similarly, he compared the compensation these companies paid to their CEOs to the amount the petitioner paid to the owner. Because the comparables were publicly traded and the compensation they paid required approval of the boards of directors and state and federal regulators, the expert believed it represented an arm's-length transaction.

In his report, he said that fixed compensation—annual salary and special benefits to the individual—"tended to" correlate to annual company sales or revenues. To show the correlation, he used a linear regression analysis, specifically the trend lines for the correlation of the CEOs' fixed compensation to annual revenues at the 75th percentile to account for the employee's experience in the industry and his status as owner/operator.

Using the same method, the expert also found that variable compensation—annual bonuses and the value of long-term stock awards or long-term incentive payouts during the year—suggested a correlation to the company's profitability. He concluded that, in this case for TYE 2004, reasonable fixed compensation for the owner was approximately $439,000; as for variable compensation, approximately $3.2 million would have been a reasonable bonus for TYE 2003 and $4.7 million for TYE 2004.

The government initially presented an expert to challenge the analysis and conclusions of the petitioner's expert. His rebuttal focused on four major flaws in the expert opinion: (1) It rested on a model analysis that used return on sales as its principal, if not sole, measure of financial performance; (2) given that the comparables the expert had used all had higher revenues than the petitioner, the regressions were used to extrapolate rather than interpolate; (3) on the basis of the p-values, the coefficients were not useful; and (4) on the basis of the R-squareds, the regressions did not explain the variation in either the fixed or the variable compensation. The expert's regression analysis was "not useful" because it did not allow for a "positive conclusion about the reasonableness of the [owner's] compensation," the rebuttal expert stated.

Third expert frames issue differently. Subsequently, the government retained a second expert with long experience in compensation to determine what would be reasonable compensation in this case. He, too, used regression analysis, and scattergrams, to show the correlation between compensation and revenue, net income and profit margin.

Focusing on the position of general manager, he first reviewed data from the National Association of Broadcasters (NAB) and from the Economic Research Institute on executive officer compensation and broadcaster gross income and profitability. Because the employee served as general manager for multiple stations and also as president and CEO, the expert applied a 75% premium to the stated figures. Averaging the resulting total compensation, he arrived at approximately $287,700 and compared it with the employee's actual 2004 compensation. He then discounted the $287,700 backward to compare it with actual compensation in 2003, 2002, and 2001. The results, he stated, showed that for the four years the employee was underpaid by a total of about $173,100, excluding the bonus. If the calculation included the bonus, however, he was overpaid over four years by a total of nearly $8.4 million.

In addition, he compared the actual compensation to data from broadcast company proxies available on the kenexa.com database. But this information included compensation amounts for a number of television and radio companies that, based on revenues, were much large than the petitioner.

As he put it, the question as to the size of the bonus was this: "Assuming the owner acted as a consultant to [the broker], how much were his services worth to improve the $12 million offer to $18 million?" By the expert's calculation, a reasonable bonus for securing the additional $6 million of value was $210,000. When he combined his methods, he found that total reasonable compensation for the owner was approximately $635,450.

By contrast, at trial the petitioner argued that all of the owner's compensation for TYE 2004 was reasonable; it included "catch-up" payments for prior years of underpayment and a justifiable bonus considering the owner had "masterminded and facilitated" the sale of the two radio stations.

'External comparisons are difficult.' Following 9th Circuit law, the Tax Court considered several factors relevant to its reasonableness analysis. They included: (1) the employee's role in the company; and (2) a comparison of the employee's salary with salaries similar companies pay for similar services.

(1) Employee's role in company. At issue was the overall significance of the employee to the company and his general importance to its success.

The government argued that, regardless of the key role the owner played in the company, he was not pivotal to the successful sale of the petitioner's major assets. Rather, the sale was profitable because of the significant appreciation of the FCC licenses.

The Tax Court disagreed. That the licenses were "the principal driving force behind the sale and the key component of the sale price of the subsidiaries" did not diminish his contribution as an employee of the corporation, it said. The owner decided to acquire and maintain the licenses. But the court recognized that his role begged the question of whether he invested in the licenses personally, as a passive owner/investor in the company, or made an investment decision in his capacity as the CEO of the company. If the former, there would be justification for the government's position to disallow the deduction of most of his salary. But since the corporate entities had bought the licenses, the owner had made the decisions to do so in his role as CEO and the corporation should compensate him for his successful strategy, the court determined.

(2) Comparison of salaries. At the outset, the court recognized that the case presented a unique situation. The company was one of a very few in the industry in which the owner was also the operator. Because "external comparisons are difficult," the court said, the parties retained experts to calculate reasonable compensation.

In assessing their "very divergent" opinions, the court referred to the concerns the government's rebuttal expert had expressed about mathematical imprecision.

As to the objection that the petitioner's expert used the regressions to extrapolate rather than interpolate, the court noted that scant financial data were publicly available for companies in the radio industry that were similar in size to the petitioner. Even the government's second expert admitted that his data related to companies much larger than the petitioner, "yet I can still learn from their compensation practice."

The court agreed with the rebuttal expert that the p-values showed that the petitioner expert's regression analysis was not strong but said that these values did not make the analysis completely irrelevant in this case.

As to the R-squared value—"an indicator of the robustness of the regression equation"—the analyses of both government experts produced similar values, which were not strong in describing the mathematical precision of the results of the regression models, the court said. This finding went toward the weight the court would attribute to the experts' conclusions.

In terms of fixed compensation, the petitioner's expert and the government's second expert agreed that the owner was underpaid for four years, the court noted. The former calculated that for that period a total of $1.7 million was reasonable compensation, while the latter said it was $1.1 million. The owner's actual pay was $914,500. Given the R-squared values and p-values of the regression analysis of both experts, the court decided that their opinions deserved equal weight. It averaged their conclusions and found the total should have been approximately $1.4 million. This meant the owner was underpaid by $462,000.

The greatest difference appeared with respect to the bonus, the court pointed out, rejecting both experts' conclusions. Not only was the owner acting as CEO, responsible for increasing the sale from $12 million to $18 million, that is, by 50%, he also was significantly involved in acquiring, managing, and selling the investment. While it was true that, as a shareholder and the chief executive of the company, he had reasons to pursue the highest sale price possible, "his efforts as an employee are still entitled to reasonable compensation for services actually rendered." Based on "our best judgment" and the evidence on record, the court found an appropriate bonus would be one-third of the increase in the sale price, that is, $2 million.

Given these and several other considerations, the Tax Court concluded the petitioner could deduct a total of approximately $2.7 million as reasonable compensation: $462,000 representing four years of underpayment, $199,300 representing the actual fixed salary for TYE 2004, and the $2 million bonus the court found reasonable. It also held the petitioner liable for a section 6662(a) accuracy-related penalty.

Damages Calculation Resting on Loan Sampling Is 'Solid'

Case name: *Assured Guaranty Municipal Corp. v. Flagstar Bank, FSB*
Citation: 2013 U.S. Dist. LEXIS 16682
Date of decision: Feb. 6, 2013
Country: US
State or Federal: Federal
State/Jurisdiction: New York
Court: United States District Court
Type of action: Contract
Experts: Mason (plaintiffs); none (defendants)
Judge: Rakoff

Add to the torrent of lawsuits created by the mortgage loan crisis this breach of contract action in which the defendant contested damages testimony related to allegedly defective home loans that relied on statistical sampling.

The defendant, a federal savings bank that provided residential mortgage loans, contracted with the plaintiff, a financial guaranty insurance company, to provide insurance on its two securitizations, the 2005 and 2006-2 trusts. The first was backed by about 10,000 individual loans, totaling about $600 million; the second by over 5,000 loans, totaling about $300 million. The bank represented to the insurer that all the underlying loans complied with its underwriting guidelines at the time of origination. The insurer guaranteed timely payment of interest and principal to the trusts' investors.

In reality, the plaintiff claimed, many of the loans were materially fraudulent or defective, in violation of the defendant's express representations and warranties. When the bank refused to cure the defects within 90 days of notice or substitute eligible loans, as the contracts required, the plaintiff sued in federal court (S.D.N.Y.) for reimbursement of insurance claims resulting from defaulting loans. A bench trial followed.

It takes a trio of experts. To prove liability and damages, the plaintiff presented three experts whose findings acted upon one another. An expert on statistical sampling created a random sample of 400 loans from each of the securitization pools, totaling 800 loans. He confirmed that the samples were representative of the total loan population by testing the distribution in the samples of seven relevant variables against their distribution in the overall populations. He did not test the representativeness as to loan payment status and original principal balance of the loans.

The plaintiff's origination and underwriting expert reviewed the sample loans for compliance with the contract provisions. She found that 85% of the loans in the 2005 sample and 66.5% in the 2006 sample were defective. Fourteen percent of the loans in 2005 showed signs of fraud, compared to 19.75% in the 2006 sample. The defendant's own underwriting expert countered that most of the alleged defective loans were current or had been repaid. Of the remaining 126 defective loans, only three showed a material breach, he asserted.

The plaintiff's damages expert developed two damages scenarios. For the first, he constructed what he considered "an exact replica" of the two trusts that enabled him to model "the cash flow into [them]" so that he was able to simulate "what would have happened had [the defendant] repurchased the proportion of loans estimated to be defective in the two trusts." To create the model, he relied on the parties' transaction documents, trustee reports for data on actual cash flows, and the underwriting expert's defective loan findings. Although the parties' contracts required the defendant to "repurchase or cure" all defective loans regardless of payment status, his model was "conservative" in that his calculation only considered loans that had defaulted or were more than 120 days delinquent ("charged-off" loans), he stated.

Specifically, for the 2005 sample, he calculated damages based on 47 out of 400 loans, and for the 2006 sample, on 37 out of 400 loans. From there, using the findings of the underwriting expert, he determined what proportion of charged-off loans also were defectively underwritten and then used that percentage to calculate what percentage of the overall losses in the securitization was due to defective loans.

The expert also calculated the percentage of charged-off loans the defendant had to repurchase in terms of the dollar value of the loans, instead of a straight count of loans. This meant dividing the original loan balance of defective, charged-off loans by the total original loan balance of all charged-off loans; he concluded that the defendant should have repurchased 88% of the charged-off loans in the 2005 sample and 76% in the 2006 sample. To simulate the defective loans' effect on the cash flows into the trusts, he extrapolated those rates to the overall pools by multiplying the actual losses by the percentage of defective, charged-off loans.

He based his damages calculation on the assumption that the defendant's repurchase obligations began on the date the plaintiff first made a demand for both trusts, at which point interest applied on the claims the plaintiff paid to bondholders. He stated that if the defendant had met its obligation, sufficient cash would have been flowing into the trusts to meet all obligations to the bondholders; the plaintiff either would not have paid any claims or would have received full reimbursement for the claims it paid, he concluded. Further, had the defendant repurchased the defective loans, there would be excess collateralization of $20.5 million in the 2005 trust and $21 million in the 2006 trust, funds that would insulate the plaintiff against future claims.

Under this scenario, total damages amounted to $111 million, inclusive interest, as of the trial date, he found.

Under a second scenario, he assumed the defendant knew of the breaches as of the offering date of the securities. He calculated the cash that should have come into the trusts from the defendant's repurchases by multiplying the "underwriting defect rate" (the original dollar value of defectively underwritten loans divided by the original pool balance) by the actual gross loss the trusts recorded each month. Based on this altered cash flow, he subtracted what the plaintiff should have paid from what it did pay and determined the net present value of the difference by adding statutory interest, as opposed to contractual interest. The total damages figure was "similar" to that under the first scenario, he found.

Under cross-examination, he admitted to a few calculation errors, including his failure to subtract the $950,000 in reimbursements the defendant had already paid on amounts it owed under the 2005 transaction. Also, he included a few loans that were less than 90 days delinquent in the total of charged-off loans.

Flawed sample design? At two points in the trial, the defendant challenged the testimony of all three of the plaintiff's experts under *Daubert*, but the court reserved a decision until the close of trial.

As to damages, the defendant claimed that a number of flaws in the design of the loan samples made the damage calculations unreliable. Specifically, the expert on sampling failed to test the representativeness of the loan samples against two variables—loan payment status and original principal balance—that were particularly relevant to the damages calculation. The court could not rely on the samples to extrapolate those calculations to the entirety of the loan pools, the defendant argued.

The court disagreed. The plaintiff's expert on sampling convincingly explained that the purpose of using a random sample of sufficient size was precisely to allow for an estimation of the proportion of loans in the overall population exhibiting any characteristic, not just those tested. It found the samples "duly representative of the kind of loan characteristics" the damages expert used in his calculations.

Next, the defendant contended that the damages calculation was based on "too-small of a sample to be extrapolated pool-wide with a sufficient level of confidence in the result." Only a stratified sample—one in which the expert takes a random sample from a subpopulation rather than an overall population—would enable an accurate extrapolation of the damages calculation to the entire population of loans.

Stratification was not necessary, the court found, given the credible testimony of the sampling expert. Further, the damages expert testified the plaintiff would receive reimbursement under a wide range of defects rates. Neither expert's testimony was inadmissible under *Daubert,* the court concluded. (Despite its more serious concerns about the methodology and conclusions of the plaintiff's expert on underwriting, it also found her testimony admissible.)

The court then turned to "the heart of the case," finding: (1) the loans underlying the trusts "pervasively" breached the defendant's contractual representations and warranties; and (2) the defendant breached its contract when it failed to repurchase materially defective loans from the two trusts.

As to damages, it noted that under the contract the plaintiff was not entitled to direct payment of the amounts but to reimbursement of the claims it paid to the bondholders "to the extent that the amounts [the defendant] should have paid into the trust would be sufficient to cover [the plaintiff's] claim payments." The damages model the plaintiff's expert presented proved that the defendant's breach directly and proximately caused the plaintiff to "improperly bear the burden of paying claims on the transaction."

The court accepted the damages expert's calculation but decided to discount "to some small degree" the proposed breach rate, given its concerns related to the underwriting expert's analysis and the calculation errors. Subtracting any amounts the defendant already had paid, it awarded damages for $90.1 million, plus contractual interest.

Difficulty in Calculating Royalty Base No Defense Under *Daubert*

Case name: *AVM Technologies, LLC v. Intel Corporation (I)*
Citation: 2013 U.S. Dist. LEXIS 1165
Date of decision: Jan. 4, 2013
Country: CANADA
State or Federal: Federal
State/Jurisdiction: Delaware
Court: United States District Court
Type of action: Intellectual Property
Experts: Larry Evans (plaintiff); unknown (defendant)
Judge: Andrews
SIC: 3674 Semiconductors and Related Devices

AVM sued for infringement of a single patent, claiming Intel unlawfully used its protected dynamic logic circuit in the company's microprocessors. To show damages, AVM submitted an expert report, which Intel challenged in a pretrial *Daubert* motion in the Delaware District Court.

The expert based his reasonable royalty calculation on Intel's total revenue from the sales of microprocessors. He also drew on four Intel litigation settlement agreements, three of which gave the company rights to patent portfolios that included dozens of patents; the fourth involved only a single patent. Neither his report nor his deposition explained how the value of the technology at issue in the prior licenses compared with that of the patent-in-suit. He concluded that AVM's reasonable royalty damages were between $150 million and $300 million, "or more."

Scope of licenses does not match. Intel sought to exclude the statements for two reasons: 1) The expert violated the entire market value rule (EMVR); and 2) he relied on licenses that were not "truly comparable" to the license the parties would have negotiated for the patent-in-suit.

1. EMVR. Intel claimed that the expert was wrong not to apportion the percentage of revenue for its microprocessor stemming from the unauthorized use of the patent-in-suit.

AVM responded that its expert did not apply EMVR to determine a reasonable royalty rate. But even if he had based his calculation on the value of the entire unit, he had a legitimate reason because the microprocessors were the "smallest saleable patent-practicing units." Therefore, his analysis complied with the general rule of *LaserDynamics v. Quanta Comp., Inc.*, 694 F.3d 51 (Fed. Cir. 2012) (available at *BVLaw*).

On this point, Intel rebutted that the microprocessors included many other components for which the expert had not accounted. Just because a sole feature may have infringed did not mean that the sales of its microprocessors became the royalty base.

The court began its analysis by noting that EMVR represented an exception to the general rule, permitting reliance on the entire market value if the patent holder could show that its protected technology created the "basis for customer demand" or at least "substantially created the value of the component parts." See *Uniloc USA, Inc. v. Microsoft Corp.*, 632 F.3d 1292 (Fed. Cir. 2011) (available at *BVLaw*).

Although it recognized that *LaserDynamics* provided support for both sides, it found Intel had a stronger argument. It likened the case in front of it to *Uniloc*, which centered on Microsoft's Outlook. Even though that program was the smallest saleable unit, Outlook contained too many other components besides the patented tool to make its sales the royalty base. Here, too, the court said it was likely that the microprocessors contained other important parts. "Difficulty in determining a royalty base … is not a reason to accept an unreliable method." What's more, even assuming that the dynamic logic circuit was the most important part, "it is still a long haul to conclude that it drives demand for the entire microprocessor."

2. Prior license agreements. Intel claimed that since most of the agreements the expert considered were portfolio licenses, they lacked the requisite connection to the single-patent license at issue. Also, the expert failed to tie the technology of the prior licenses to the technology of this case.

AVM responded that one of the four licenses did involve only a single patent and its expert chose all the prior licenses specifically because they involved technology similar to the patent-in-suit.

Again, the court agreed with Intel. Since this case concerned a single patent, it stated, "no reasonable juror could consider the prior broad portfolio license agreements to be comparable in scope to a license for AVM's single patent." This left only one "truly comparable" prior agreement for the royalty calculation. But the expert had not analyzed the benefits and value of the underlying technology, the court noted.

Although it favored the exclusion of the opinion, the court postponed a final decision until after the expert's live testimony before the beginning of trial.

Failure to Analyze Settlement Agreement Dooms Damages Theory

Case name: *AVM Technologies, LLC v. Intel Corporation (II)*
Citation: 2013 U.S. Dist. LEXIS 23768
Date of decision: Feb. 21, 2013
Country: US
State or Federal: Federal
State/Jurisdiction: Delaware
Court: United States District Court
Type of action: Intellectual Property
Experts: Larry Evans (plaintiff); unknown (defendant)
Judge: Andrews

This ruling represents the court's final word on Intel's pretrial *Daubert* motion to exclude AVM's expert testimony and raises questions about the plaintiff's ability to support its theory of damages "in excess of $100 million."

AVM sued for infringement of a single patent, contending Intel unlawfully used its protected dynamic logic circuit in the company's microprocessors. To show damages, AVM submitted an expert report that stated that its reasonable royalty damages were between $150 million and $300 million "or more." In its *Daubert* motion in federal court (D. Del.), Intel objected to the expert's use of total accused revenues or overall corporate revenues and profits and his reliance on four Intel settlement agreements.

The court largely agreed with Intel and said it was inclined to exclude the testimony in its entirety, but it reserved a final decision until a hearing that featured the expert in person and subject to cross-examination.

Change in damages theory. At the subsequent *Daubert* hearing, in accordance with the court's earlier finding, AVM's expert relied only on a single 2009 settlement Intel had reached with a third party to support his reasonable royalty calculation.

At the same time, AVM sought to introduce additional testimony from the co-inventor of the patent-in-suit. His opinion, AVM said, was not expert, but it was relevant because it concerned the

Georgia-Pacific factors. By contrast, Intel claimed that this testimony, too, was inadmissible expert testimony under *Daubert*. The court considered both challenges in turn.

Designated expert. In his report, AVM's designated damages expert described Intel's licensing history as "principally the result of patent infringement litigation settlements" and provided seven examples. These included the 2009 agreement, which pertained to a different, single patent that protected technology for improving the speed and efficiency of the microprocessors. Intel paid $110 million to settle the litigation and obtain the license. The expert's report also stated that in 2003, Intel had paid $6.2 million for three different licenses from the same third party.

The expert admitted that he had no background knowledge of any of these agreements "other than their express terms and information from press releases." He determined the range of lump-sum royalties Intel paid for "licenses to practice the claims of micro-processor-related patents comparable to the [the patent-in-suit]" was $110 million to $675 million.

In terms of the 2009 agreement, he suggested that the technology the patent underlying it claimed was less important to "Intel's commercial interests" than that protected by the patent-in-suit and that the royalty base for the former was "far less" than the royalty base for the disputed patent. Consequently, he found that the lump sum Intel had to pay for a license covering the patent-in-suit "should exceed" the payment under the 2009 agreement.

He admitted that his analysis did not consider the circumstances of the litigation and factors that influenced the value of the settlement. For example, it did not explore the reasons for a provision in which the third party agreed to dispute resolution before litigating issues related to its 200 other patents against Intel and its customers and did not compare that provision to other license agreements.

Similarly, in terms of the 2003 agreement, the expert admitted he did not review the underlying three patents or explain why he considered them irrelevant for his current analysis.

AVM claimed that under Federal Circuit precedent damages claims could rest on "a single license agreement, or a single settlement agreement for the patent-in-suit, or a single license agreement for a comparable technology." By extension, damages could also be based on a settlement agreement for a comparable technology, AVM asserted.

The court saw it differently. Even though in its earlier ruling it had found that the 2009 agreement concerned a single patent and was sufficiently comparable in scope to a license the parties in this case would have negotiated, it was concerned that the expert's report lacked the requisite analysis as to the "benefits and value of the technology" the agreement covered.

The hearing did not fill gaps in the report. Simply in terms of the range of royalties the expert suggested, it remained unclear why he did not include the 2003 agreement Intel made with the same third party for $6.2 million, the court said. Moreover, he failed to set out a methodology with which to explain why the 2009 agreement—which related to a different patent—by itself could serve as the basis for an accurate conclusion about a hypothetical negotiation for the patent-in-suit, considering the agreement related to a different patent and came some five years after a hypothetical negotiation would have taken place. "Without analysis of the litigation, the conclusion cannot be based on sound economic and factual predicates," it found.

Such an analysis might have discussed what amount of damages the former plaintiff sought in the litigation and explored the settlement context, including whether there existed a possibility for the plaintiff to pursue treble damages for willfulness. The concern with settlement agreements is that "the coercive environment of patent litigation" is not compatible with a negotiation under *Georgia-Pacific*, which assumes the parties will arrive at a voluntary agreement, the court explained.

It called AVM's proposition that precedent supports basing damages claims on a single settlement agreement for comparable technology a "bridge too far" and noted AVM's failure to cite a single authority. The entire testimony was inadmissible.

Inventor testimony. To bolster its damages evidence, AVM belatedly tried to introduce testimony from the co-inventor of the patent-in-suit and former CEO of the company's predecessor regarding his negotiations with Intel in 2006 and his conduct in a hypothetical negotiation.

In a deposition, the witness discussed the estimated costs "Intel necessarily would have incurred to avoid the patent-in-suit" and the calculation of a "per design technology use" fee. Further, he spoke about the benefits of the patent at issue, legal assignments of the patent, and his actual discussions with Intel in 2006 and 1999. When Intel asked about the amount he would have accepted in exchange for a license of his patent, he replied "no idea" and also stated he had no figure in mind as to the damages AVM should seek from Intel.

Intel argued it was improper expert testimony, it came too late, and it was insufficient evidence to establish AVM's damages. AVM never identified the witness as a person who had knowledge of damages.

The court agreed with Intel, finding that much of the proposed testimony was "the province of expert analysis," including statements about the calculation of design-around costs and "per design technology use" fee. Similarly, only an expert, not a lay witness, was able to address what would have occurred in a hypothetical negotiation.

Also, AVM only disclosed this expert and hypothetical testimony at the eve of trial (February 2013). Admission would prevent Intel from seeking discovery into the witness's damages theory. But, the court said, even if it had been timely, it would have been insufficient to satisfy AVM's burden of proof since the analysis was little more than "a rehash" of the designated expert's testimony. To the extent it was not, AVM failed to show the witness had the qualifications to testify to licensing or had used a reliable methodology.

As a lay witness, he would be able to discuss only facts of which he had personal knowledge. Acknowledging that its decision to exclude all expert damages testimony left AVM in search of evidence to support its damages claim, the court vacated the trial date. But under the law it was unable to grant Intel's motion for summary judgment of no damages "at this time," it said.

Bankruptcy Court Discredits DCF as 'Easily Manipulated'

Case name: *In re Bachrach Clothing, Inc.*
Citation: 2012 Bankr. LEXIS 4807
Date of decision: Oct. 10, 2012
Country: US
State or Federal: State
State/Jurisdiction: Illinois
Court: United States Bankruptcy Court
Type of action: Bankruptcy
Experts: Craig T. Elson (debtor); John D. Ciancanelli, Stan A. Murphy (defendants)
Judge: Hollis
SIC: 5611 Men's and Boys' Clothing and Accessory Stores—Specific categories—

After more than 125 years in business, the owners of a family-run men's apparel business agreed to sell their stock to a private equity firm for $8 million, consisting of $4 million in cash and $4 million in a subordinated note. In connection with the proposed sale, the PE firm's financial advisor (KPMG) reviewed prior audited financials and found the target's historic book value was worth approximately $5 million, "substantially" more than the purchase price, noting in particular its $11 million in excess working capital and over $5.8 million in investment cash. After its own due diligence, the PE firm independently determined that the purchase price was "attractive," in large part due to the company's "strong base of assets" (inventory and accounts receivable), noting, in particular, the target's borrowing capacity of $7 million.

Minimal investment, maximum control. The PE firm structured the sale as a leveraged buyout (LBO), transferring the acquired stock to an affiliated entity, and then immediately replacing the target's board of directors with its own executives. The new entity then effectively caused the company to pay the $4 million cash due to the sellers by: 1) securing a $2 million bank loan, independently guaranteed by the PE firm; and 2) declaring a $2 million dividend. Notably, when they authorized the dividend, the new directors concluded the company was solvent.

Immediately after the acquisition, the PE firm appointed a new CEO, who lacked experience in men's retail but who began making substantial changes. For example, in a single month (May 2005), she marked down the company's inventory by $7 million, or more than 285% of the budgeted amount. Overall, the changes eroded $3 million in working capital, thereby reducing the company's borrowing base from $4.3 million to $1.3 million. At the same time, the company continued to pay the PE firm $400,000 in management fees plus the costs of the purchase, including attorneys' fees of over $800,000, which eventually amounted to over $3 million in extraordinary expenses.

To address the company's liquidity crunch, the PE firm announced it would make an additional $5 million equity investment in early 2006. A few months later, however, the firm began internally discussing the prospect of putting the company into bankruptcy. To effectively convert its investment into a secured claim, the PE firm caused its affiliated entity to execute a $5 million promissory note (including a repurchase of the $2 million bank loan made in connection with the original LBO), and then backdated the note by three months (or beyond the 90-day preference period). A few weeks later, the PE firm withdrew its funding, forcing the company to file for Chapter 11 protection.

According to the bankruptcy court (N.D. Ill.), the debtor "had a strong argument" to recharacterize the PE firm's secured claim as equity, yet for various reasons, it "capitulated" and agreed not to sue its investors or their affiliates (demonstrating the investors' "continued control" over the debtor, the court said). Instead, the debtor sued its former owners to recover the purchase price as a fraudulent conveyance. To prove its claims under federal as well as state law, the debtor had to show the company was insolvent (or rendered insolvent) at the time of sale. To hold the individual sellers liable, it would also have to convince the court to "collapse" the several steps of the LBO into a single transaction as of the sale date.

Accordingly, the debtor's expert evaluated the company in the context of the sale as well as the structured LBO. In his report, he indicated counsel instructed him to rely on the combined action of both the sellers and the PE firm "to determine whether, *as a result of the LBO transaction,* [the company] was rendered insolvent" (emphasis by the court). To rebut these claims, the former owners—now the defendants—retained two experts, working together, to show the debtor was solvent at the time they transferred the company to the PE investors.

To calculate the company's enterprise value, all the experts considered a balance sheet approach, but the debtor's expert ultimately rejected the company's audited, consolidated balance sheet, prepared in connection with the sale, because he believed its reliance on historic book value did not reflect fair market values. By contrast, the defendants' experts used the audited book value as a starting point, and then adjusted it downward by nearly $4.2 million to reflect "known market conditions." Under this analysis, they concluded the debtor was worth $9 million at the time of sale. The debtor's expert criticized this conclusion, saying it did not align with his discounted cash flow (DCF) analysis. In response, the defendants' experts criticized the debtor's expert for not even considering an asset approach.

Ultimately, all of the experts relied primarily on a DCF approach, but with widely divergent results. In particular, the debtor's expert determined the company was worth $1.1 million, but after factoring in the $400,000 management fee to the PE firm, it was worth a *negative* $293,000, he said. Under their DCF analysis, the defendants' experts believed the company was worth just over $6 million. The experts' disagreement largely came down to how each calculated the weighted average cost of capital (WACC) under a CAPM approach, with the debtor's expert reaching a rate of 19.5% compared to the defendants' experts, who derived a 12.3% rate. In turn, this disparity stemmed from the experts' treatment of the following four inputs:

1. *Debt-to-equity ratio.* The debtor's expert chose not to consider the company's actual capital structure, believing this better reflected the view of a hypothetical purchaser. Instead, he used industry standards and the debt structure of comparable companies to establish debt-to-equity ratios for his WACC. However, the defendants' experts "insisted" that ignoring the company's actual capital structure was a mistake, particularly when its actual borrowing capacity at the time of sale made it a valuable prospect and its debt-to-equity ratio was well below that of comparable companies.

2. *Equity risk premium (ERP).* All the experts relied on Ibbotson's *Valuation Yearbook* to derive an equity risk premium, and all applied the arithmetic (rather than geometric) averages of historical data. However, by using Ibbotson's longest data set (going all the way back to 1926), the debtor's expert derived an ERP of 7.2%. By contrast, the defendants' experts believed a shorter time period, going back only 50 years, more appropriately accounted for globalization and its effect on market trends. Using historical data from the prior 50 years, they arrived at a 5.6% ERP.

Notably, in their determination of ERP, all of the experts cited Prof. Aswath Damodaran's treatise on *Investment Valuation* (John Wiley & Sons, 2012), in which he notes that essentially half the users of an historical ERP rely on Ibbotson's entire data set (back to 1926), while the other half use a shorter period. Ultimately—as the defendants' experts pointed out—Damodaran recommends an historical ERP of no more than 5.5%.

3. *Size premium.* Once again, all the experts used Ibbotson's data to derive their respective size premiums. Although the company's market capitalization fit into three size categories—the micro-cap category (deciles 9 and 10), as well as 10 and 10b—the debtor's expert selected the smallest (10b) because the company was smaller than most in that subdecile and Ibbotson's indicated the 10b results were "statistically reliable." This led to a 9.8% size premium.

The defendants' experts believed the micro-cap category was more statistically reliable and a better fit for the company, particularly since Ibbotson's found that smaller apparel and accessory stores performed better than their larger-store counterparts. They also cited Damodaran's recommendation of 4% for small-cap stocks, ultimately arriving at 4.02% size premium for the subject company.

4. *Terminal value.* Using the Gordon growth model, the debtor's expert applied a 3% growth rate to his cash flow projections to reach his terminal value. The defendants' experts, on the other hand, used an exit multiple approach, applying a 6.5 multiple to projected EBITDA. They derived the 6.5 multiple from comparable companies, as well as comparable transactions, and believed the multiple was "conservative" because it fell within the lower quartile of comparable companies and none of the comparable sales involved a lower multiple.

The debtor's expert criticized the "hybrid" exit multiple approach, once again citing Damodaran's treatise and his warning that the use of multiples to calculate terminal value in a DCF results in a "dangerous mix of relative and discounted cash flow valuation." Moreover, the defendants' expert relied on companies with higher revenues and EBITDA margins than the subject, he said. Finally, he used the experts' exit multiple to "back solve" for an implied growth rate of 6.9%, which was more than twice the current economic growth rate.

In response, the defendants' experts explained that the company's lower margin (of 3%) could have yielded a much higher multiple than 6.5, "because there would be more room for growth." For example, one of his comparable companies had an even lower margin than the subject, but reported a multiple of 86. By choosing the more "conservative" multiple of 6.5, the experts actually lowered their terminal value. As for the implied growth rate, by removing the management fees from the calculation, they reached a 5.5% growth rate, which was reasonable, assuming a GDP of 3% and inflation of 2.5%, they said. By comparison, the 3% growth rate that the debtor's expert proposed assumed that the company's future performance—notwithstanding its purchase by the PE investors at an "attractive" price—would lag the economy.

DCF versus 'the real world.' After valuing the company's assets (enterprise value) under the DCF approach, the experts valued its liabilities to reach an ultimate conclusion regarding solvency. Only the debtor's expert subtracted the full face value of the $2 million loan incurred at the time of sale as well as the $4 million repurchase obligation incurred by the PE firm's affiliate. But these contingent debts should have been substantially discounted, the defendants' experts claimed, because the PE firm (or its affiliates) were co-obligors on the loans.

After hearing all the evidence, the court found "no facts or real world evidence" to support the assertion of insolvency. The company had no long-term debt, was current on payables, and held substantial cash in excess of working capital. Moreover, the defendant sellers were not involved in structuring the LBO; nor did they take any part in deciding to take the "massive" inventory markdown after the sale or institute any of the changes that reduced revenues and accelerated liabilities.

In fact, the PE firm and its hand-picked CEO "created [the company's] liquidity crisis," the court said, and the investors' "refusal to provide further capital led to this bankruptcy." The sellers delivered "a solvent and properly capitalized company at closing," the court added, noting as well that any victory in this fraudulent conveyance action would effectively refund the investors their entire outlay. After "loading" the company up with debt and liabilities, the PE firm "brilliantly had two bites at the apple: big profits if it improved [the company's] performance and a refund if it failed."

Based on these facts, the court declined to collapse the sale of the company and the LBO into a single transaction, thereby "ending" the fraudulent conveyance case. Nevertheless (and presumably for purposes of any appeal), it considered the insolvency evidence, first in the context of the DCF method, generally. For example, even though the parties' experts relied on essentially the same data and analysis, the "striking" disparity among their conclusions "lends credibility to the concept that the DCF method is subject to manipulation," the court said, citing *In re Iridium Operating LLC*, 373 B.R. 283 (Bank. S.D. 2007) (available at *BVLaw*). Indeed, the court reiterated *Iridium's* warning that:

> The DCF methodology has been subject to criticism for its flexibility; a skilled practitioner can come up with just about any value he wants. For this reason, it is important to validate conclusions reached using this methodology by comparing the results obtained when other accepted approaches to valuation are used.

In this case, the court found that "each expert generally selected parameters that pushed his valuation in the direction he wanted to go." In particular:

- The court dismissed the negative valuation by the debtor's expert, noting that his inclusion of management fees that were unique to the sale was inconsistent with his valuing the sale from the perspective of a hypothetical buyer.

- The debtor's expert should have used the company's actual capital structure, rather than an industry standard. "Regardless of who purchases a business, a company with actual leverage of 90% has to be worth less than a company with no debt," the court stated.

- In determining the equity risk premium, both experts should have used the geometric mean instead of the arithmetic mean, which the court found (apparently after its own reading) Damodaran used to reach his historic ERP of 5.5%. Further, Damodaran indicates the "arithmetic average return is likely to overstate the premium" and that if "forced to choose" an ERP over the entire historic range of Ibbotson data, he would "go with 4.31%, the geometric average risk premium for stocks over Treasury bonds," but his preferred approach was "market neutral" and less than 3%.

- As a result, both experts overstated the ERP, the court found. However, the 5.6% by the defendants' experts was closer to Damodaran's estimates, while the 7.2% ERP by the debtor's expert was more than double the professor's preferred approach "and just not realistic."

- Regarding the size premium, the debtor's expert "did not pay particular attention to Ibbotson's point that the 10b decile might be less reliable," the court noted. Had he used the micro-cap category, his size premium would have been 4.0%—or less than half his selected rate of 9.8%. The defendants' experts, on the other hand, appropriately factored in industry-specific phenomena to "inform" their decision about the size premium. Their selection of 4.2% also coincided with Damodaran's recommended 4%.

- Similarly, their use of an exit multiple or "hybrid" approach in calculating a terminal value found support in Damodaran's treatise; their use of comparable company data as well as economic growth rates went beyond merely "consulting a book," the court said. "Again, real world information about the performance and sales of [comparable] companies informed [their] valuation of the terminal period," while the debtor's expert continued to "shuffle numbers in and out of formulas to get where he needed to go."

Overall, the defendants' experts provided "better reasoned" explanations for their DCF inputs, and their $6 million enterprise value was "more aligned with real world events or contemporaneous market data," the court held. In support, it cited (among other factors): the due diligence by both the PE firm and its financial advisor; the company's borrowing capacity as well as its working capital reserves; and the adjusted balance sheet test based on audited financials.

The court also found the debtor's expert "exaggerated" the company's liabilities, which he should have discounted due to the PE firm's co-obligation on the various loans. His "more glaring error," however, was to match any contingent liabilities against contingent assets, the court said, citing *Paloian v. LaSalle Bank, N.A.*, 619 F.3d 688 (7th Cir. 2011) (available at *BVLaw*). In this case, for example, the PE investors "could easily pay … and ultimately paid" the bank in full by repurchasing the $2 million loan that the company originally incurred to pay the sellers. Moreover, if the $2 million loan had rendered the company insolvent, it could have pursued a claim against its directors for illegally declaring the $2 million dividend.

In sum, the failure by the debtor's expert to discount the contingent liabilities and his inflated WACC "doomed" his conclusions that the company was insolvent or rendered insolvent by the sale, the court held. The defendants were not required to prove solvency, "but they did so with [their experts'] analysis," and the court dismissed the fraudulent conveyance claims.

Royalty Calculation Depends on Cost of 'Best Imperfect Substitute'

Case name: *Brandeis University v. Keebler Co.*
Citation: 2013 U.S. Dist. LEXIS 18948
Date of decision: Jan. 18, 2013
Country: US
State or Federal: Federal
State/Jurisdiction: Illinois
Court: United States District Court
Type of action: Intellectual Property
Experts: Dr. Anne Layne-Farrar (plaintiffs); Michael Keeley (defendants)
Judge: Posner
SIC: 2052 Cookies and Crackers (except unleavened bread and pretzels)

Although the court (N.D. Ill.) was quick to recognize that the plaintiffs' damages expert had the "general competence to estimate damages," it disapproved of most aspects of her reasonable royalty determination.

No 'cheap, satisfactory' substitute for fat blend. The plaintiffs sued the defendants for infringing a patented fat blend that did not contain trans fats. Both sides offered expert testimony and challenged the competing opinions under *Daubert*.

The plaintiffs' expert primarily considered two factors in her royalty calculation: market share and comparable licenses. Following her conversations with the plaintiffs' biochemistry expert, she concluded that there was no "cheap and satisfactory substitute" for their unique margarine. If the defendants switched to a noninfringing fat blend, they might make soggy cookies; alternatively, if they used butter, which contains no trans fats, the cookies might have a high saturated fat content—both qualities that she believed consumers disfavor. Rather than use a substitute, she claimed, the defendants would pay a substantial royalty for a license. In this regard, she also took into account data from 2002 to 2005 (two to five years before the infringement) that indicated the defendants' loss of market share and the opinion of an industry analyst that linked the loss to the defendants' inability to eliminate trans fats.

Moreover, the expert relied on three license agreements the plaintiffs had with other companies. These included a nonexclusive license they entered into in 2005 with Company A at a (nonstated) flat rate. This rate would be the minimum the plaintiffs would accept, the expert stated. In all likelihood, they would insist on a higher rate, given their stronger position in the market—increased sales and the possibility of business expansion—following a merger. She also considered a settlement agreement arising out of an infringement suit against Company B, which included a license fee and lump-sum payment. She determined the percentage the fee represented of Company B's sales and applied it to the defendants' sales.

Finally, she considered a "complex" settlement agreement with Company C that included multiple components and benefits that went beyond a one-time payment.

Ultimately, her calculation rested on the maximum amount of profits the expert believed the defendants risked if they did not obtain a license. (The court's opinion does not provide any specific amounts.)

The defendants' expert, on the other hand, concluded that a reasonable royalty for use was negligible based on statements from their food scientist that with certain modifications in the manufacturing process, the defendants could produce a noninfringing substitute.

Expert's inquiry misses the point. The court recognized that there might not be a "perfect substitute" for the patented blend, causing the defendants to "court an infringement suit." But the determination of a reasonable royalty depended on costs to the defendants, not maximum profits at risk, the court said, faulting the plaintiffs' expert for failing to provide evidence of the higher production costs and loss of business the defendants would incur if they used the "best imperfect substitute." Her statement that no adequate substitute would satisfy consumer demand lacked support. The biochemist was not a food scientist, and his opinion on sogginess was not conclusive. She should have consulted with a marketing expert or an industrial baker to determine the relationship between consumer demand and the manufacturer's choice of ingredients, the court stated.

It also dismissed the expert's claims about the defendants' loss of market share. There was no basis to assume that a three-year trend would continue for at least another seven years, up to the March 2013 trial date; yet her calculation was based on this assumption. What's more, she failed to test the reliability of the sole analyst's opinion that there was a connection between the loss and the defendants' inability to eliminate trans fat prior to infringing.

Moreover, the court disregarded all but one of the three agreements the expert considered. The Company B license concerned a company "wholly dissimilar" to the defendants (making only two cookies) and did not involve the patents at issue. Also, she had no basis for applying the percentage the fee represented of that company's sales to the defendants' "vast" sales. Likewise, the license with Company C was not comparable, since it included different components the expert failed to value.

The license with Company A was comparable, the court found, because that company's products were similar to those of the defendants. However, it dismissed as "pure conjecture" the expert's statements that then the plaintiffs did not pursue an "economically optimal deal." Even assuming the plaintiffs would have "pressed harder," there was no evidence that the defendants would have agreed to a higher royalty rate. Consequently, the court only allowed testimony that the defendants would have paid as much as Company A did for a license.

With little discussion, it admitted the defendants' expert's testimony.

Attempt to Base Lost Profits on Infringer's Sales Alone Fails

Case name: *Brighton Collectibles, Inc. v. RK Texas Leather Mfg.*
Citation: 2013 U.S. Dist. LEXIS 24644
Date of decision: Feb. 12, 2013
Country: US
State or Federal: Federal
State/Jurisdiction: California
Court: United States District Court
Type of action: Intellectual Property
Experts: Robert Wunderlich (plaintiff); unknown (defendants)
Judge: Curiel

The plaintiff's expert claimed damages from lost sales amounted to $115 million, but the defendants argued the testimony was inadmissible under *Daubert* for a multitude of reasons, including his reliance on a theory that had no grounding in "the real world facts of this case."

The plaintiff manufactured and sold higher-end women's accessories, including expensive handbags, and alleged defendants' knockoffs infringed its trade dress. Under the Copyright Act, it sought actual damages, including the owner's lost profits and damage to goodwill as well as additional profits of the infringer.

Instead of using the plaintiff's sales data—actual sales or forecasts of future sales—the plaintiff's expert proposed to determine lost profits based solely on the number of the defendants' sales. Under this theory, he assumed that one of the defendants' infringing sales correlated with one lost transaction in which the plaintiff's customer would have bought 2.06 authentic items, including handbags, wallets, jewelry, and watches. As all but one of the defendants were wholesale importers and distributors, he counted each transaction in the chain of distribution as a separate sale, disregarding the number of handbags consumers ultimately bought. Even though the defendants' sales amounted to only $8 million, he determined a loss to the plaintiff of $115 million.

His report did not include an economic analysis of the fashion marketplace to support his conclusion of a 1-to-1 ratio or set forth a method with which to arrive at the appropriate scale.

In their pretrial motion, the defendants argued the testimony had no basis in the facts and, therefore, was irrelevant. It was implausible that every customer who bought one of the defendants' imitation handbags, which cost between $20 and $50, would have paid over $200 for one of the plaintiff's handbags. The expert provided no evidence that there was direct competition between the one defendant retailer, which had small Western-style stores, and the plaintiff, which owned upscale boutiques and sold to upmarket department stores.

Moreover, the expert did not use a scientific methodology that others could replicate, simply offering an ipse dixit conclusion. His assumptions were "non-committal and evasive," making his opinion unhelpful to the jury. The expert's math would give the plaintiff a windfall.

The plaintiff contended that a lost profits determination was "inherently imprecise"; its expert simply offered a "framework" that the jury could, but did not have to, use when deciding on a reasonable amount.

Deviating from the 'tried and true method.' At the outset, the court noted with emphasis that the proven method of determining lost profits was "grounded in *plaintiff's* sales data," whereas the expert's theory focused exclusively on the number of the *defendants'* sales. The latter number normally is relevant to a different measure of damages based on a defendant's wrongful gain. The expert failed to show a rational connection between the distinct measures.

To determine the validity of the expert's theory, equating infringing sales with lost profits on a scale of 1-to-1, the court researched case law. In instances where the theory held up, it found, the plaintiff had "convincing evidence from a customer" that she bought the defendant's counterfeit product in place of the plaintiff's. In this case, however, the expert offered no data demonstrating there was a reliable correlation between the defendants' sales and the plaintiff's profits. "The expert has not provided a nexus from the knockoff customer to [the plaintiff's] typical customer who would spend $240 or $400 on one handbag."

The court rejected the suggestion that the opinion could serve as a "framework" for the jury, noting the expert was unable to point to a factual basis for his assumptions or verify that his method was accepted in the field. Given the "analytical gap between the data and the opinion," the testimony was not helpful. For all of these reasons, the court granted the defendants' motion.

Expert's Apportionment Cannot Save Flawed Royalty Calculation

Case name: *Brocade Communications Systems, Inc. v. A10 Networks, Inc. (I)*
Citation: 2013 U.S. Dist. LEXIS 8113
Date of decision: Jan. 10, 2013
Country: US
State or Federal: State
State/Jurisdiction: California
Court: United States District Court
Type of action: Intellectual Property
Experts: James Malackowski (plaintiffs); Elizabeth Dean (defendants)
Judge: Grewal
SIC: 3577 Computer Peripheral Equipment, NEC (except plotter controllers and magnetic tape head cleaners)

The plaintiffs sued the defendants in federal court (N.D. Cal.) for infringing their copyrighted code and patents for technology to improve global server load balancing and store round trip time data for host server switches. The jury awarded $60 million for the copyright violation. Because of conflicting responses on the verdict form, the parties disagreed on the amount of patent damages the jury determined. Specifically, on the "lost profits" line, the jury entered $49 million; on the "total royalty damages" line, it entered $2 million; and on the "total damages" line, which was also the last line on the form, it entered $2 million. The form also indicated a royalty rate of 4%.

The defendants claimed that the jury intended to award only $2 million in total damages, in line with its response to "total damages." The $49 million amount under "lost profits" matched the royalty base the plaintiffs' expert had determined. To this, the defendants argued, the jury applied the 4% royalty rate to arrive at royalty damages. It did not intend to award lost profits.

The plaintiffs contended that they were entitled to both the lost profits and reasonable royalty awards, totaling $51 million. The final line on the form was superfluous; the court should just ignore it.

The defendants challenged both verdicts, claiming they lacked sufficient evidence.

1. Copyright damages. Both sides presented expert testimony. As to copyright damages, the defendants earned $13 million in profit from the products that contained the infringing code, the defendants' expert stated. As she saw it, they were not obligated to apportion the profits, but were only liable for the amount they saved by copying the code instead of generating it on their own. This savings amounted to between $1,500 and $6,700, the cost of paying an engineer to develop a nonprotected code.

Although the plaintiffs did not have to provide evidence of apportionment, they presented an expert who did. On rebuttal, he stated the defendants made $113 million in revenues from the infringing products; after subtracting operating expenses and sales commissions, he calculated a net profit of $93 million.

A different damages standard. At the outset, the defendants argued that copyright damages required the same showing as patent damages: The plaintiffs had to prove that their code drove consumer demand for the infringing products. Also, the defendants claimed that their profit from the products including the code was much less than the $60 million award. Moreover, the plaintiffs' expert calculated profits for five months beyond the applicable infringement period, and the jury failed to award damages based on the established liability.

The defendants overstated the standard, the court said. A copyright plaintiff has to show causation, that is, "but for" the infringement, the defendant would not have made its gross sales. Once the plaintiffs proved causation, the burden shifted to the defendants "to apportion that gross revenue between profit and expenses and among infringing and non-infringing features." The plaintiffs' expert sufficiently explained how he arrived at the $93 million. The court further noted that the jury, in fact, awarded one-third less than the proposed $93 million. Its $60 million figure was within the range the parties' experts set, $13 million and $93 million, respectively. All these facts supported the jury's copyright verdict, the court held.

2. Patent damages. The plaintiffs' expert used "the most common" method to determine a reasonable royalty, proving a royalty base and a royalty rate. Using the entire value of the defendants' smallest articles that included the patented features, he estimated a royalty base of $49 million. He said the patented components were important and the defendants could not have sold their products without them. But he also noted that marketing documents from the defendants on how to prevent losing sales for the products did not refer to the patents, but talked about the "feature generally." He adjusted the royalty rate to apportion the damages between the patented and unpatented components in the products. (The opinion does not provide details about the expert's reasonable royalty or lost profits calculation.)

Truly an exception. The court first addressed the reasonable royalty calculation. Under the general rule, experts must use the "smallest saleable unit" containing the invention to calculate the royalty base, it said, citing *LaserDynamics, Inc. v. Quanta Computer, Inc.*,694 F.3d 51 (Fed. Cir. 2012) (available at *BVLaw*). Only if the infringing feature drives consumer demand for the product may they apply the entire market value rule (EMVR), which is "an exception" to the rule, and use the revenues the defendants received from the entire product as the royalty base. Here, the defendants' products included many parts for which the plaintiffs did not own patents. Also, the plaintiffs failed to provide consumer surveys or customer testimony that proved their technology drove demand. Showing that the defendants could not have sold their products without it was not enough. The expert's statements about the "feature generally," in fact, suggested the opposite.

The expert's apportionment after using EMVR did not save the royalty award, the court concluded. "The Federal Circuit has rejected this methodology. Absent evidence that the patented feature drives demand, the expert should not have used the entire market rule to establish its royalty base." It found that the same flaws invalidated the expert's lost profits analysis. Given the uncertainty surrounding the jury's verdict and the plaintiffs' "problematic reasonable royalty evidence," the court reversed the $51 million patent award and ordered a new trial.

Does *Panduit* Lost Profits Theory Require Apportionment?

Case name: *Brocade Communications Systems, Inc. v. A10 Networks, Inc. (II)*
Citation: 2013 U.S. Dist. LEXIS 69335
Date of decision: May 15, 2013
Country: US
State or Federal: Federal
State/Jurisdiction: California
Court: United States District Court
Type of action: Intellectual Property
Experts: James Malackowski (plaintiffs); Elizabeth Dean (defendants)
Judge: Grewal

Can a plaintiff comply with a court's prior ruling that it may not rely on the entire market value rule (EMVR) theory either in the reasonable royalty or lost profits context and still come up with a viable damages theory on retrial? That was the issue the federal court recently confronted in considering the defendants' motion for a judgment of zero damages.

The plaintiffs sued the defendants in federal court (N.D. Cal.) for infringing their copyrighted code and patents for technology to improve global server load balancing and store round-trip time data for host server switches. The jury awarded $60 million for the copyright violation, which the defendants unsuccessfully challenged in a post-trial motion.

At the same time, the court was receptive to the defendants' attack on the patent damages. To calculate a reasonable royalty, the plaintiffs' damages expert used the entire value of the defendants' smallest products that included the patented features, estimating a royalty base of $49 million. The defendants could not have sold their products without the patented functionalities, he said.

The court found the plaintiff failed to show that the patented functionalities actually drove consumer demand for the infringing products. Therefore, the plaintiffs could not rely on the EMVR and consequently could not rely on the defendants' entire revenue from those products as the royalty base. Further, the plaintiffs failed to show that the infringing products were the "smallest saleable unit" implementing the patented features; this, the court concluded, meant that, when the expert used the entire value of the articles, he did so by improperly relying on an EMVR theory.

Moreover, the court, without doing a full analysis of the plaintiffs' ability to meet the applicable *Panduit* test, decided that they could not rely on the EMVR for purposes of showing lost profits. Based on the defective reasonable royalty calculation and uncertainties surrounding the jury verdict form, the court reversed the $51 million patent award and ordered a new trial.

'Federal Circuit's variety of opinions' leaves opening. Ahead of the new trial, the parties agreed to limit themselves to the evidence and record of the first trial. Subsequently, in a pretrial motion, the defendants tried to exclude all of the plaintiffs' prior damages testimony, saying it conflicted with the court's earlier findings, and they also requested an entry of judgment for zero dollars or, at most, a lump-sum royalty payment (unspecified) based on what their expert had proposed at trial.

Lost profits. Specifically as to lost profits, since the plaintiffs could not rely on the EMVR, they had no theory, but, even assuming the plaintiffs had a theory that did not rely on EMVR, they had to apportion the profits to account for the value of the patented features, the defendants argued. The court dismissed the first argument, noting that its decision regarding reliance on the EMVR did not imply the plaintiffs had failed to substantiate any lost profits theory.

As to their apportionment argument, while "appealing," the defendants failed to cite Supreme Court or Federal Circuit case law that required apportionment when a patentee claims lost profits based on *Panduit,* which the court described as"an alternative theory of establishing lost profits."On the contrary, the court added, the Federal Circuit recently stated that the *Panduit* factors "place no qualitative requirement on the level of demand necessary to show lost profits." See *Versata Software, Inc. v. SAP America, Inc.,* 2013 U.S. App. LEXIS 8838.

This statement, concluded the court, stood for the proposition that "apportionment—at least as consumer demand stands as a way of showing apportionment—is unnecessary under *Panduit.*"

Reasonable royalty. As for the reasonable royalty theory, the plaintiffs maintained that their expert would be able to use the prior evidence and testimony to develop a theory that aligned with Federal Circuit precedent and the court's earlier ruling. The Federal Circuit stated that "the base used in a running royalty calculation can always be the value of the entire commercial embodiment as long as the magnitude of the rate is within an acceptable range (as determined by the evidence). See *Lucent Technologies v. Gateway, Inc.*, 580 F.3d 1301 (Fed. Cir. 2009). This theory, the plaintiffs suggested, did not conflict with the Federal Circuit's other decisions in *Uniloc* and *LaserDynamics* because it would not rely on the EMVR but on evidence that the infringing products were the smallest saleable unit; consequently, the expert could use the entire revenue from the sales of the products as the royalty base.

The court noted that in *Uniloc* and *LaserDynamics*, the Federal Circuit seemed to "disavow" the very language from *Lucent* that the plaintiffs now hoped to rely on. At the same time, it acknowledged that the Federal Circuit never expressly overruled *Lucent*'s holding. Considering the Federal Circuit's "variety of opinions" and the statutory requirement for a reasonable royalty if there is infringement (which there was here), the court refused to exclude the expert's testimony. It summed up its position this way: "The court has its doubts, but it is willing to give [the plaintiffs] an opportunity to present a theory that can survive the Federal Circuit's directives and this court's order."

Court Affirms Excess Earnings Method for Goodwill Calculation

Case name: *Burnett v. Burnett*
Citation: 2012 Ind. App. Unpub. LEXIS 1477
Date of decision: Nov. 29, 2012
Country: US
State or Federal: State
State/Jurisdiction: Indiana
Court: Court of Appeals
Type of action: Marital Dissolution
Experts: R. James Alerding (wife); unknown (husband)
Judge: Bailey
SIC: 8011 Offices and Clinics of Medical Doctors—Specific categories—

The husband was an anesthesiologist in a large practice with 68 partners. The total number of partners had remained fairly stable, with every partner holding an equal ownership interest. However, under an operating agreement, they received unequal distributions based on a formula (which the opinion does not provide). The 32 partners who joined since 2001 had paid $100, and those who left received $100 plus a termination benefit.

Actual earnings versus industry standard. At divorce, the wife presented expert testimony from a credentialed business valuator to quantify the husband's business interest, including its intangible value, that is, goodwill. Because Indiana considers only goodwill attributable to the enterprise community property, the expert eliminated the husband's personal goodwill from his calculation, using a variation of the excess earnings method.

He found the following factors indicated goodwill that inhered in the business:

- The practice was an organization with a formalized structure that required every partner to execute a covenant not to compete;
- The entity, not the individual partners, owned contracts with multiple facilities, and its ability to generate revenue did not depend heavily on the personal services that any one partner performed;
- The business's name did not feature individual partners, and its identity remained unchanged despite the arrival or departure of partners;
- The practice alone determined what partner would provide services at what facility; the husband was able to work at a facility regardless of his personal relationship with patients or surgeons; and
- As a partner in the business, the husband did not need to expend time on nonbillable activities, including finding and scheduling work and billing and collecting for it.

To determine personal goodwill, the expert reviewed industry data from a trade group about the number of billable units that anesthesiologists record annually and the compensation that corresponds with a specific production level. The husband's billable units for 2009 indicated he was slightly below the 90th percentile in terms of productivity. At the same time, his earnings exceeded those of anesthesiologists at the 90th percentile. The expert used the difference between his actual earnings and the industry standards to capitalize the excess earnings.

As to the calculated value of the husband's interest, the expert said it applied under different assumptions, including the sale of the practice, the sale of the husband's interest, and the husband's remaining a partner or leaving the business. He concluded that the investment value was $337,000 and the fair market value was $253,000.

The trial found the expert's methodology properly eliminated personal from enterprise goodwill. The noncompete agreements and the practice's long-standing exclusive contracts with multiple facilities suggested it would continue to have value even if the husband withdrew. "This," the court said, "is indicative of enterprise goodwill." Ultimately, it adopted the appraiser's lower value and found the business interest was worth $253,000.

The husband challenged the valuation in the state Court of Appeals, claiming the trial court failed to separate personal from enterprise goodwill.

No there there. The law is well settled and requires that "goodwill that is based on the personal attributes of the individual is excluded from the marital estate," the appellate court said, citing *Yoon v. Yoon*, 711 N.E.2d 1265 (1999) (available at *BVLaw*). The value that exists in the patient base and would be transferrable to a buyer who does not bring the same attributes to the business as the individual physician is enterprise value, the court continued.

The evidence supported the trial court's valuation based on the expert's calculation. Moreover, the court stated, the lower court's "extensive findings of fact and conclusions of law" made it easy to discern what portion of the expert's aggregate value was attributable to the husband's personal goodwill: "none."

In Billion-Dollar IP Case, Expert's Mention of Total Revenue Does Not Violate *Uniloc*

Case name: *Carnegie Mellon University v. Marvell Technology Group (I)*
Citation: 2012 U.S. Dist. LEXIS 120558
Date of decision: W.D. Pa. Aug. 24, 2012
Country: US
State or Federal: Federal
State/Jurisdiction: Pennsylvania
Court: United States District Court
Type of action: Intellectual Property
Experts: Catherine M. Lawton (plaintiff); Creighton Hoffman (defendants)
Judge: Fischer
SIC: 3674

Case name: *Carnegie Mellon University v. Marvell Technology Group (II)*
Citation: 2012 U.S. Dist. LEXIS 158718
Date of decision: W.D. Pa. Nov. 6, 2012
Country: US
State or Federal: Federal
State/Jurisdiction: Pennsylvania
Court: United States District Court
Type of action: Intellectual Property
Experts: Catherine M. Lawton (plaintiff); Creighton Hoffman (defendants)
Judge: Fischer
SIC: 3674 Semiconductors and Related Devices

This complex patent litigation began in 2009, when the plaintiff claimed the defendants infringed two patents related to high-density magnetic recording technology. The defendants allegedly used the patented method to design and sell chips to customers that, in turn, incorporated the chips in devices (e.g., high density disk drives) for sale to third parties.

At trial before the federal district court, the plaintiff presented an expert who calculated a reasonable royalty rate for the defendant's infringing use after first considering the possibility of an established royalty, but finding none. The defendants offered a rebuttal expert, and both sides filed

Daubert motions plus a supplemental motion, which the court decided in three separate rulings (cited in sequence above).

Could, but did not, use entire market value. In her report, the plaintiff's expert stated that she thought the "entire market value rule" (EMVR) applied to the case. She believed that the defendants considered the technology "must have" and would place great value on the right to use it. "To be conservative," however, she did not use the EMVR of the more than 1.4 billion chips the defendants sold between 2003 and 2010. Rather, she explained, her reasonable royalty analysis was "clearly predicated on the apportioned value" of the chips between the patented and unpatented features. Any reference to the defendants' total operating profit per unit was to show a starting point for her apportionment analysis. In terms of apportioning, she considered some 350,000 chips, accused and nonaccused, and ultimately attributed the entire price premium to the patented methods.

In performing a *Georgia-Pacific* analysis to calculate a reasonable royalty, she considered one of the defendants' internal documents, a PowerPoint slide that proposed a 3% royalty rate on "substantial key functionality" (the opinion does not specify of what). By contrast, she stated, the plaintiff "actually used a 25% or 33% rule in negotiations." She also considered three very broad licensing agreements between the plaintiff and corporate associates from 1992 to 1997 that generated between $150,000 and $250,000 annually. But these contemplated benefits for both sides beyond the licensed use of the patents, including special rights to the inventions for corporate sponsors and the plaintiff's ability to place its students with them. Also, the associates were able to direct one-half of their annual fees to specific research, but in exchange would commit to acknowledging the plaintiff's contributions in their public reports. The expert found these agreements irrelevant to determining a reasonable royalty in this case. Ultimately, she calculated a running royalty of $0.50 per unit for each infringing sale and minimal damages of $734 million or possibly more, depending on the defendants' sales data at trial. (The opinion does not indicate the defendants' total revenue and average price per chip or the expert's total apportioned values.)

In their *Daubert* motion, the defendants asserted that the expert's analysis was flawed for at least five reasons, which the court considered in turn.

1. EMVR. The defendants argued that "any read channel contains a number of components that are unrelated to the patented feature," which the plaintiff's expert acknowledged. Consequently, they said, there was no evidence that the plaintiff's technology drove consumer demand for the chips. Notwithstanding the expert's disavowal of using the entire market value of their chip sales, the defendants maintained she violated the rule.

Under the EMVR, an expert may calculate damages based on the entire market value of an accused product only when the patented feature creates the basis for (or a substantial basis for) customer demand, the court agreed, citing *Uniloc USA, Inc. v. Microsoft Corp.*, 632 F.3d 1292 (Fed. Cir. 2011) (available at *BVLaw*). In this case, the defendants had a legitimate concern, i.e., that the expert would testify that she *could have* applied the rule, but chose not to. To do so might lead to a situation similar to that in *Uniloc*, in which the expert misled the jury by comparing potentially appropriate calculations with much greater revenue figures.

The plaintiff's expert had "steered away" from violating the rule, the court said. Simple reference to average operating profits is acceptable as "long as the testimony does not lapse into statements that tend to show how 'reasonable' a royalty is when compared to a much larger amount." It concluded that, in fact, "some reference to revenues, margins, and values is necessary to formulate a reasonable royalty" and denied exclusion on this ground, but limited the expert's testimony. Except to start her analysis, the expert could not discuss total revenue and could only consider: total sales, total apportioned revenue, average price per chip, operating profit per chip, and apportioned profit per chip.

2. *Apportionment analysis.* The expert extracted the total number of chips sold from too small a subset, the defendants claimed. Also, her attribution of the entire price premium did not take into account that the new, accused chips featured improvements that the older generation did not have. The plaintiff countered that any challenge to the sufficiency of the evidence was a jury question and that the expert had relied "on all available data points." The court agreed that these arguments went to the weight of the evidence and that any attack on the evidence the expert used should take the form of cross-examination at trial.

3. *Irrelevant data.* The defendants challenged the expert's reliance on the PowerPoint slide because it was not a license agreement, had no apparent link to the patents-in-suit, and, even if it were a license, would not have been between "similarly situated" entities, as *Georgia-Pacific* requires. The court agreed, but found the expert only used it as a "starting point" in her hypothetical negotiation analysis, which was "extremely detailed," and declined to exclude her testimony on this basis.

4. *Twenty-five percent rule.* The expert's "reference to a rule that is tied to the facts of the case does not run afoul of *Uniloc*, even if it appears to do so on its face," the court said.

5. *Prior agreements.* "It is not the court's place" to question whether the plaintiff's prior agreements with its affiliates offered its expert sufficient guidance in her analysis. The rules of evidence do not allow for exclusion of an expert because of a dispute over the underlying facts, the court said, and denied the defendants' motion except for limiting the expert's ability to discuss total revenue.

Licenses may 'inaugurate' analysis. Instead of a reasonable royalty rate, the defendants' expert proposed a lump-sum payment based on the plaintiff's three prior agreements with its affiliates. The expert took a two-pronged approach: If the court determined that the agreements demonstrated an established royalty for the patents-in-suit, then a reasonable royalty could not be greater than \$250,000. Even if there were no established royalty, he concluded that a hypothetical negotiation analysis would still lead to the same amount, based on the agreements and "a number of additional factors" (which the court's opinion does not detail).

The plaintiff claimed the agreements were not sufficiently comparable because they benefitted the parties in ways that went beyond the pay-for-use exchange in a hypothetical negotiation analysis.

Examining the agreements, the court found the plaintiff received more than the \$250,000 payment and the associates more than the right to use the patents. Moreover, the three licenses specified different amounts. At the same time, the small number of licenses and their lack of uniformity made it difficult "to see how any general acquiescence ... would result in an established royalty." Accordingly, it precluded the expert's testimony as to an existing established royalty.

As for his proposed reasonable royalty of $250,000 based on the same foundation, the problem was once again comparability, the court found. The expert failed to explain how the three agreements' unique benefits factored into a hypothetical negotiation between the parties in this suit. The expert could appropriately use the prior agreements to "inaugurate" his analysis, the court said, because even though they covered more than royalties, they did transfer rights to the patents-in-suit. Once again, any weaknesses in the expert's opinion were the proper subject for cross-examination, not exclusion, and the court also admitted the defendants' expert's opinion.

In a final, supplemental motion, the defendants claimed the plaintiff's expert had failed to compare the value of the at-issue technology to the next-best alternative, as required under *Apple v. Motorola, Inc.*, 2012 U.S. Dist. LEXIS 105387 (N.D. Ill. May 22, 2012) (available at *BVLaw*). The court found this objection untimely and unfounded and declined to change its *Daubert* ruling.

After trial, on Dec. 27, 2012, a jury awarded the plaintiff $1.17 billion. The defendants immediately announced they would challenge the verdict. Some news sources have agreed the verdict may be in jeopardy, citing "questionable assumptions" by a "hired-gun" expert. See, e.g., www.businessweekl.com/news/2012-12-26/marvell-ordered-to-pay-1-dot-17-billion-for-infringing-patents.

Lack of License Negotiation Experience Does Not Disqualify Expert

Case name: *Carnegie Mellon University v. Marvell Technology Group (III)*
Citation: 2012 U.S. Dist. LEXIS 177647
Date of decision: Dec. 15, 2012
Country: US
State or Federal: Federal
State/Jurisdiction: Pennsylvania
Court: United States District Court
Type of action: Intellectual Property
Experts: Catherine M. Lawton (plaintiff); Creighton Hoffman (defendants)
Judge: Fischer
SIC: 3674 Semiconductors and Related Devices

In 2009 the plaintiff sued the defendants, claiming they infringed two patents related to high-density magnetic recording technology. Specifically, they used the patented method to design and sell chips to customers that, in turn, incorporated the chips in devices (e.g., high-density disk drives) for sale to third parties. Both sides retained experts to calculate damages and filed *Daubert* motions with the federal court (W.D. Penn.) to exclude the competing testimony.

After receiving updated financial and sales information from the defendants, the plaintiff's expert revised her initial report and submitted a supplemental report. In their subsequent *Daubert* challenge, the defendants claimed the plaintiff's expert lacked the qualifications to testify about her reasonable royalty opinion.

The expert worked for an international consulting firm specializing in "strategy issues related to complex litigation." Although she had a bachelor's degree in finance, she had not done post-graduate work, nor was she a CPA or otherwise certified in business or finance. She also lacked experience in engineering, computer science, semiconductors, or patent analysis.

She spent much of her 27-year career as an expert witness, specializing in intellectual property cases that spanned a number of industries and testifying in 16 cases. The valuation methods she used in this case (*Georgia-Pacific* framework) applied similarly across all of the industries, she said. She admitted she had no "real-world" experience negotiating licenses for the kinds of patents or computer chips on which this lawsuit centered.

In this case, she based her damages calculations on the defendants' actual sales and financial data, determining that the price per chip was $4.42 and the operating profit per chip was $2.16. Comments from the defendants' CEO and a marketing executive suggested that their target gross margin for all products was 50%, she stated. She next compared sales of the defendants' chips to two big customers in 2003, when the defendants sold products with and without the infringing devices. The data showed that the defendants received profits from the accused chips in excess of the 50% target margin, between $0.06 and $0.72. This would have been the range the parties would have considered within the context of a hypothetical negotiation, she stated. Ultimately she determined that a reasonable royalty in this case was $0.50 per accused chip, relying on testimony from the plaintiff's technical experts, who described the technology as "industry standard" and "must have" for the defendants. Assuming a violation of both patents-in-suit, she determined a royalty base of over $2.3 billion and a reasonable royalty of $1.17 billion.

Accusations of being a 'hired-gun' expert. The defendants' challenge focused on the expert's lack of actual experience in negotiating patent agreements. Even though she "tried to morph herself into a general financial economic expert ... it's hard to imagine who would pick up the phone and ask for her licensing advice," they argued. Also, her lack of practical experience in accounting, finance, and economics made the expert simply a "hired gun," or professional witness, of whom several courts have disapproved.

The plaintiff responded that the expert had testified and applied the *Georgia-Pacific* factors in several patent cases and withstood a challenge to her credentials.

The court said that the plaintiff "narrowly proffered" the expert to render an opinion on intellectual property damage. True, a person with a post-graduate degree in accounting or finance and experience in actual patent license negotiations on behalf of a nonprofit entity, such as the plaintiff, or a company in the semiconductor industry, such as the defendants, has superior qualifications, it continued. "This theoretical individual may likely be the best qualified." But the 3rd Circuit applied a liberal standard to the qualification of experts, which this expert met, considering her educational background and other experience.

As for the defendants' claim that she lacked the requisite practical negotiation experience, "the flaw in this type of challenge is that the hypothetical negotiation has no application in the real world," the court said, citing *Pulse Medical Instruments, Inc. v. Drug Impairment Detection Service, Inc.* (available at *BVLaw*). It is a legal construct relying on "artificial" assumptions to enable a reasonable royalty calculation.

Also, being a professional witness is but one of a number of factors courts consider when evaluating the proposed expert's qualifications. "For litigants to have access to experts, it may be necessary for some experts to concentrate on litigation," the court noted, agreeing with circuit precedent. Considering the totality of the circumstances, the court admitted the expert's damages testimony.

After trial, on Dec. 27, 2012, a jury awarded the plaintiff $1.17 billion. The defendants immediately announced they would challenge the verdict. Some news sources have agreed that the verdict may be in jeopardy, citing "questionable assumptions" by a "hired-gun" expert. See, e.g., www.businessweek.com/news/2012-12-26/marvell-ordered-to-pay-1-dot-17-billion-for-infringing-patents

Court Reproves Spouse's Efforts to Lower Value of Community Business

Case name: *Charles v. Charles*
Citation: 2013 Cal. App. Unpub. LEXIS 2386
Date of decision: April 2, 2013
Country: US
State or Federal: State
State/Jurisdiction: California
Court: Court of Appeals
Type of action: Marital Dissolution
Experts: Thomas Turk (wife); Alfred Warsavsky (husband); Glenn Mehner (joint)
Judge: Bedsworth

"The subtext of this date-of-valuation-of-a-community-business case," the California Court of Appeal said, "is how a strategy can backfire." The operating spouse of the business counted on its value declining between the date of separation and the date of trial. Instead the company flourished in the five years leading up to trial. After the trial court denied his last-minute request to change the valuation date, the husband appealed the judgment.

Upward revision. The husband was an equal partner in a two-man interior design firm. His interest, including all of goodwill, was community property. In May 2006, the husband and wife separated, and one year later, in May 2007, the trial court declared the marriage dissolved. One month later, both parties retained the same CPA firm to value the marital interest in the business. It calculated a value of $226,000 for the end of 2006.

In 2009, the husband, in a one-sided conversation with the accountants, claimed the company was in grave financial trouble and expected a $100,000 loss for the first quarter of 2009. In response, the appraiser lowered the value to $198,000.

In reality, however, 2009 proved to be a successful year, with gross revenue of about $2.4 million and a profit of $1.3 million before officers' compensation. This yielded a $716,000 value, a revised October 2010 report from the accountants showed.

In September 2010, the wife asked the court to set a trial date, stating that "all discovery has been completed." The court ordered a trial setting conference for November 2010. In December 2010, the husband retained a new lawyer, who, within days, filed a motion to value the community's interest in the firm at the date of separation. The court only heard the motion a week before trial was to begin, in February 2011. The wife successfully objected to a change in valuation date, claiming the motion was untimely. She also persuaded the court to preclude the husband from offering testimony about the valuation closest to the date of separation, showing the $226,000 value. Ultimately, the trial got underway only in late August 2011.

By then, both parties presented competing experts, but the court also heard from the once jointly retained expert. It noted that, at some point, the husband had stopped paying the accounting firm, which "substantially interfered with their on-going work."

A matter of 'reasonable compensation.' The wife's expert was a recognized economist, who valued reasonable compensation for the husband at $649,000 per year, using data from the Risk Management Association. By contrast, the husband's expert, a CPA, set the figure at $1.34 million based on information from the Economic Research Institute. The formerly joint expert gave an in-between figure: $875,000 per year.

Moreover, the husband's expert stated that a $51,530-per-month income for the husband represented the business's cash flow situation as of July 2011, the date nearest to the trial. However, based on data he received from the company's controller, he also projected a lower figure, $41,612, for the whole of 2011.

The business showed a low in gross revenue of $2.3 million in 2006 and an increase to $2.6 million in 2008. Gross revenue in 2009 was about $2.4 million. But in 2010 it was $3.7 million. The wife's expert and the former joint expert, both, averaged income for the years 2006 through and including 2010.

The trial court noted that the critical difference in the valuations was the calculation of goodwill, which, in turn, hinged on how much "reasonable compensation" the experts attributed to the husband. "The more income of the business is attributable to the operating spouse, the less an investor wants to pay to buy the business and replace the operating spouse," it summed up the issue.

It credited the opinion of the wife's expert for two reasons: One, his credentials were "over-the-top impressive"; two, he based his analysis on studies from the Risk Management Association that provided a better comparison sample of firms in terms of asset size and sales. On the other hand, the Economic Research Institute data did not provide the husband's expert with any information as to how closely the sample data lined up with his own criteria, the court found.

To the reasonable compensation figure of $649,000, the court then applied a multiplier of 2 to capture risk, finding that gross revenues for the relevant period never dipped below $2.3 million. (The higher the multiplier, the lower the perceived risk.) It valued goodwill for the entire firm at $1.45 million. Combining this amount with fixed assets of approximately $190,000 and an additional $190,000 in owners' equity, it found the business's total value amounted to $1.8 million, which yielded a community interest of $918,000.

For purposes of spousal support, the court used the $51,530-per-month figure the husband's expert had proposed to reflect cash flow for July 2011, finding there was no corroboration for the data undergirding his lower projection for all of 2011.

Beware 'the chimera of projection.' The husband appealed. arguing first and foremost that the trial court erred by not establishing the value of the business on the date of separation. Secondarily, he objected to the trial court's rejection of his expert's projections for 2011 and the use of "outdated data" in the valuation of the wife's expert.

Valuation date. As the state Court of Appeal put it, the husband's objection to the valuation came in two "permutations." One, he claimed the trial court had no choice but to value the design firm at the date of separation; two, if the court was going to use the date of trial, it had to reduce the value so that it took into consideration the husband's post-separation efforts.

This argument, the court stated, had no traction with it for a simple legal reason: It ignored the standard of review that applied to the lower court's decision. Under state law, the trial court "shall" value assets and liabilities as near as possible to trial; it "may," upon a timely motion and for good cause, switch to valuation as of the date of separation to achieve an equal division. Given the trial court's discretion, the issue on appeal was not whether the trial court erred but whether it acted *reasonably* when it denied the husband's late motion, the appellate court stated with emphasis.

To assess the trial court's decision in this light was an "an easy call," the higher court said. By the time the husband finally brought his motion, discovery was complete. Opening up the issue would have put the wife at a disadvantage. She would have had to redepose the husband as well as obtain depositions from his business partner and other employees. The latter, the appellate court noted, "might be somewhat less inclined to ascribe the entirety of the business's recent success just to [the husband's] efforts." A new valuation date also would have required substantial extra work from the experts, who would have to reconstruct the business environment that existed in 2006 to fix the company's value.

Moreover, policy reasons, such as "the need to deter operating spouses from gamesmanship in the control of community businesses," supported the decision, the appellate court stated. The trial court reasonably questioned the husband's motive for requesting a change in valuation date so close to trial. Had he been serious about his contention that the firm "was fundamentally a two-man show (or maybe even a one-man show)," the appellate court said, he would have filed his motion in 2007, 2008, or even 2009. What's more, as the court pointed out, the company had a website that emphasized "the institutional stability of [the firm] (as distinct from the company simply being a manifestation of [the husband's] own artistic vision)." When questioned by the trial court, the husband said that some of the information on it was not accurate.

The true reason for bringing the motion so late, the appellate court concluded, was that the husband mistakenly thought the firm's value would decline from its date of separation value.

Projections. The husband also claimed that the trial court "improperly discounted" the projections his expert created for 2011. Under the evidence code, there was no need for extra corroboration from the firm's controller or the husband's business partner; the testimony was admissible. Also, the trial court had to consider his expert's projection of reduced income for the balance of 2011 determinative.

The appellate court disagreed. The trial court was not making an evidentiary decision, but one related to the credibility of the experts and their methodologies. On the whole, it simply found the figures the wife's expert proffered "more compelling." The trial court acted reasonably when it preferred "hard historical data to the chimera of projection."

The trial court's decision to base its support calculation on the $51,530 monthly income figure the husband's expert specified when determining cash flow for July 2011 at most was harmless error. That figure worked out to less than half of what the same expert said was reasonable compensation for purposes of determining the company's goodwill ($1.34 million). Had the trial court used the value the husband's own expert claimed as reasonable compensation, his income for support purposes would be more than twice the amount the trial court determined. He "got off easy," the appellate court said, because that figure was lower than the lowest reasonable compensation figure by any of the experts.

Outdated data. Finally, the husband claimed the trial court "had to" reject the valuation from the wife's expert because it relied on data for 2010, when the business had an exceptionally good year. The year 2011, he contended, generated much less income. Because the expert did not exclude the 2010 data but did exclude the 2011 data, his valuation lacked substantial evidence.

Not so, the appellate court found. As to the year 2010, the wife's expert averaged income for 2006 up to and including 2010 and thus obtained a properly representative longitudinal sample. Moreover, the trial court was right to credit an expert who excluded data for the year 2011. Considering trial took place in August 2011, the middle of the third quarter, any decline for that year would at best be a projection based on data from the first two quarters. "The year was still subject to manipulation and uncertainty."

Also, the reviewing court said, given the husband's "track record," that is, his earlier misstatements about the company's health in 2009, the trial court had reason to be skeptical about any negative projections. In its decision, the trial court expressly noted that the projection from the first two quarters of 2011 indicated a gross of $2.57 million, higher than 2006, 2007, and 2009, but a bit lower than 2008.

For all these reasons, the court of appeal affirmed the trial court's determination.

Court Seeks 'Fit' Between Lost Business Value Calculation and Facts

Case name: *Christou v. Beatport, LLC*
Citation: 2013 U.S. Dist. LEXIS 9034
Date of decision: Jan. 23, 2013
Country: US
State or Federal: Federal
State/Jurisdiction: Colorado
Court: United States District Court
Type of action: Antitrust
Experts: Jay Freedberg (plaintiffs); unknown (defendants)
Judge: Jackson
SIC: 5813 Drinking Places (Alcoholic Beverages)

In a suit (D.C. Colo.) involving dueling electronic dance club owners and their businesses, the defendants filed a *Daubert* motion to exclude expert testimony regarding lost profits and lost enterprise value.

The plaintiff owned two nightclubs in Colorado that gained national attention as venues for electronic dance music (EDM), featuring DJs who performed live. The defendant worked for the plaintiff as a "talent buyer," booking "A-List" and other DJs. During his employment, he also developed an "enormously successful" EDM e-commerce site. In 2007, the parties had a falling out, and in 2008, the defendant set up a competing club. In 2010, the plaintiffs sued, alleging various antitrust violations, trade secret theft, and interference with prospective business expectancies. By threatening A-List DJs that he would not feature their work on his online site, the defendant coerced them into performing primarily in his club and was able to take over the relevant market, the plaintiffs claimed.

Lost profits calculation not 'mysterious.' To quantify lost profits and lost enterprise value damages, the plaintiffs presented testimony from a CPA who also held certifications in business valuation and financial forensics.

Lost profits. His methodology for calculating lost profits met the recommendations of the AICPA and the accounting industry, the expert stated. First, he projected revenues that the business probably would have realized had it continued as in the past; next, he accounted for factors unrelated to the case that likely would have affected revenues; finally, he deducted projected expenses.

In this case, he first determined the actual cover charge revenue the plaintiff's two clubs realized in 2006 and 2007 on their respective EDM nights—Thursdays and Saturdays. Assuming "things would stay about the same," he then calculated "expected" cover charge revenue for 2008 through 2010. But cognizant of the economic downturn at that time, he attempted to adjust by using statistics from the North American Industry Classification System specific to Colorado bars, nightclubs, and other drinking establishments during that period. Similarly he calculated the clubs' historical revenue (2006-2007) from food, drinks, and various sales and assumed he could use the average percentage of revenue from those years for his forecasts. These data gave him "total" revenue projections.

He next projected the clubs' variable expenses (cost of goods sold, advertising, bank fees, equipment rental, payroll taxes) from 2006 to 2007 to 2008 through 2010. After subtracting them, he concluded that lost profits for both clubs were about $1.2 million.

The defendants' objections focused on how he applied his methodology.

- He did not consider revenue from other club nights and the plaintiff's other clubs that could have offset the losses specific to Thursday and Saturday nights;
- He failed to consider additional factors that might have reduced revenues, including the entry of a new and strong competitor;
- He omitted 2005 revenue data;
- His conversion of lost sales for Thursday and Saturday nights to lost profits, using a variable cost-to-sales ratio that applied to all nights, was problematic;
- His reliance on information he obtained from the plaintiff's counsel raised questions about his numbers; and
- Cross-examination revealed at least one mistake in his lost profits chart.

There was "nothing mysterious" about the expert's calculation, the court stated. *Daubert* merely requires that an expert's testimony be relevant and reliable. Here, the expert's explanation as to "how he went about" calculating lost profits would be helpful to the jury. Saying that challenges to his assumptions and even mistakes in his calculations were issues for cross-examination, it admitted this part of the testimony.

Lost enterprise value. The expert stated that there were three standard methods to determine the value of a business: 1) calculation of net asset value; 2) comparable sales; and 3) capitalization of earnings (income method). He rejected the first method because it did not account for goodwill, which he considered a significant component of the value of the plaintiff's business. Also, he could not find comparable sales because only three nightclubs were in the relevant area that featured live, top-rated DJs for electronic dance music. This left the third method.

The expert's calculation rested on the assumptions that the plaintiff intended to sell the two clubs around December 2010 and that events occurring after Dec. 31, 2010, would not be relevant. He relied on the plaintiff's deposition testimony that in 2006 or 2007, both parties had conversations to the effect that the defendant might buy one of the plaintiff's clubs and turn the other into a condominium project. "They were pretty close to the numbers," the plaintiff stated. Given the reduction in profitability, the plaintiffs lost $2.1 million in enterprise value, the expert concluded.

The defendants did not challenge the expert's method or his capitalization rate (not specified). But the court found his opinion left too many issues unanswered. The question, it said, is "'fit,' that is, whether there was a logical relationship between his calculation of lost enterprise value and the facts of the case. "Vague" testimony about conversations between the plaintiff and the defendant, before the defendant even left the plaintiff's business, was not necessarily relevant to establishing the value of his clubs at the end of 2010. Even assuming the plaintiff wanted to sell at that time, "is the alleged loss in enterprise value perpetual?" Moreover, the court asked: "What is the value today?" And if the plaintiff prevailed in this action, "would damages for lost enterprise value as of December 31, 2010 permit [him] to have his cake and eat it too?"

The court noted that in their motion to supplement the expert's opinion—which it granted—the plaintiffs argued that under the law, past lost profits and present lost enterprise value were not mutually exclusive. But this proposition still did not answer its basic questions, it said, reserving final judgment as to this part of the testimony for trial.

Can Defendant Disclaim Its Own Projections to Undo Expert's Valuation?

Case name: *Citrin Holdings, LLC v. Minnis*
Citation: 2013 Tex. App. LEXIS 5723
Date of decision: May 9, 2013
Country: US
State or Federal: State
State/Jurisdiction: Texas
Court: Court of Appeals
Type of action: Dissenting Shareholder
Experts: Scott Bayley (plaintiffs); Dr. Flores (defendants)
Judge: McCally
SIC: 6513 Operators of Apartment Buildings

This appeal represents another post-trial attack on an expert's analysis for relying on another source, notably the defendants' own projections, when calculating the present value of the plaintiff's interest in a series of income-producing properties. The trial court erred in overruling its *Daubert* challenge, the defendant contended.

Last minute offer to buy part of portfolio. In 2003, the parties decided to form companies that would buy and develop real estate near air- and seaports. They financed part of the venture with the help of an equity investor. According to the plaintiff (an owner and his business), they had an "overarching partnership" in which he had a 45% interest and the defendant (another owner and his business) held a 55% interest to create single-purpose entities in which each held title to each of the properties.

Disputes arose over the parties' relationship with the equity investor and the majority owner's alleged effort to reduce the plaintiff's minority interest to 25%. In mid-December 2006, the minority owner sued the majority owner in state court, alleging fraud and negligent misrepresentation and requesting an accounting. In late December 2006, the defendant removed the plaintiff as president from one of the companies that had a portfolio of properties slated for development, and in mid-March 2007 he dissolved all the entities. He subsequently formed other companies that took over the old project management agreements.

During litigation, the plaintiff expanded its claims. He said that the defendant usurped opportunities to which he had contributed, including the "MMT" project that the parties pursued while still working together, but from which the plaintiff was forced out in June 2007. Also, he did not receive his share of the proceeds from the post-dissolution sale of one property that the parties bought for $8.5 million and the defendant sold for $13.1 million in 2007, without notifying the plaintiff. And the defendant refused to sell the property during the optimal time. The plaintiff said that, at the time of his ouster in December 2006, the market was at its peak. In contrast, in late 2007, the opportunities were dwindling. Even so, Morgan Stanley offered to buy four of the nine properties in the portfolio for $131 million. The defendant declined because the equity investor considered the offer too low.

Do stabilized values represent present value? The plaintiff retained an expert with extensive experience in valuing real estate similar to that at issue to compute his interest in the companies' income-producing properties as of March 2007. The defendant offered rebuttal expert testimony and challenged the plaintiff's expert under the state equivalent of *Daubert*.

The plaintiff's expert adopted figures, including the capitalization rate, net operating income, and stabilized values, from an investor summary schedule for the first quarter of 2007 that one of the defendant's senior analysts had prepared for the equity investment committee. He said he did so after confirming the defendant "was doing the methodology the same way that I would do." For his computation, the expert used the "direct capitalization" method to determine the income a property produces when it reaches a stable level of operations. He called it the "stabilized income" of the business; in real estate, he added, that point occurred when a project was 95% to 100% leased. Dividing the net operating income by the 6.5% cap rate the defendant had provided for the internal projections yielded the stabilized value, the expert explained.

If a property was not stabilized—not fully leased—he used the same method, but with adjustments, to arrive at a stabilized value. Specifically, he computed the stabilized net operating income, calculated the rental income that was lost during the period of achieving stabilization, and subtracted the latter from the stabilized value. Moreover, he deducted costs for improvements and leasing and advertising. These steps yielded the "as-is" or "present" value, he said. Considering the nine properties in the portfolio, he determined the plaintiff's total interest was worth over $28.2 million, factoring in debt to lenders and the equity company's equity and preferred return.

By his own admission, the defendant's expert had never before valued income-producing real estate properties such as the ones in dispute. He also had never testified as an expert witness to a commercial real estate valuation and had never used the direct capitalization method for valuing a real estate project.

The defendant's expert said he also relied on the defendant's internal projections and investor summary schedules "as being accurate."

His main problem with the competing computation was that the plaintiff's expert assumed the defendant's financial data reflected March 2007 values, when in reality they represented values as of 2009 or 2010. Particularly, the rival expert did not consider factors such as time value of money, and he also failed to apply a discount rate to his values.

The defendant's senior analyst also testified, stating she prepared the schedule to "give us an idea … what [the defendant company's] interest would be at some point in the future." She said she never intended her analysis to reflect "as-is" value and considered it a "mischaracterization" to say it was. She confirmed that the defendant computed the cap rate and that other employees provided other information. The financial models went to the equity investor and lenders, but the latter never used the supplied figures but did their own property appraisals, she said. She stated she was not a valuation expert.

The plaintiff's expert specifically addressed some of the criticisms from the rebuttal expert. "I think it's a lack of understanding of what I did," he said. "I started with the stabilized values and then adjusted the stabilized values." After adjusting for costs, "the result is the as-is value, the value in its current state if … it hasn't reached stabilization yet." In terms of the time value of money, he said, "when those stabilized values are prepared, those are prepared as if the property were stabilized in the first quarter of 2007." Because not all are stabilized, he made adjustments "taking into account the time value of money, discounting those costs to present value, subtracting the present value of those costs from the present value of the stabilized value, which gives you the as-if value for the first quarter of 2007."

He strongly disagreed with the other expert's claim that his analysis lacked a discount rate. That suggestion, he said, implied that his values were future values, which they were not. Under his analysis, he arrived at the present value. "And it's incorrect to believe that the stabilized value is a value in the future."

He also rejected the senior analyst's statements, saying that "she might be a little confused about what she's doing, because you can't project a value in the future by using a current cap rate."

The defendant did not challenge the qualification of the plaintiff's expert or attack his methodology. Rather, it claimed the opinion was inadmissible because the financial data underlying the analysis of the plaintiff's expert did not reflect the March 2007 value of the stabilized values. The trial court was not persuaded and admitted the testimony.

The case went to trial, and the jury found for the plaintiff on each of the 10 legal grounds he stated. It awarded actual damages for over $28.2 million. In April 2011, the trial court entered final judgment in that amount based on the breach of fiduciary duty claim. But it expressly provided that if recovery on that theory became "less favorable," the plaintiff "may recover on any one of the other theories found by the jury."

One key appellate issue. The defendant subsequently appealed to the Texas Court of Appeals on numerous grounds. Because it applied to all claims, the most critical issue was whether the trial court erred in denying the defendant's "reliability challenge" of the plaintiff's damages expert, the appellate court observed.

On appeal, the defendant claimed the expert's calculation was unreliable, and thus inadmissible, because it rested on the defendant's unreliable internal projections. He treated "internal future projections for undeveloped properties as current values of developed properties," the defendant asserted. For example, the expert's valuation for the MMT project as of March 2007 was unreliable because at that time the defendant did not have development rights to the project until April 2007.

The plaintiff objected that the defendant should not be able to discredit the very projections it provided to the equity investor and lenders for financing. Regarding the MMT project, the expert provided a reasonable explanation for his assumption, believing that as of March 2007, "it was pretty clear that they were going to be closing ... and getting those rights," and there was additional evidence that the defendant had spent years and millions of dollars pursuing the rights to the project.

The plaintiff also pointed to independent evidence that supported the expert's conclusions and the damages award, including the Morgan Stanley letter of intent offering to buy four properties for $131 million in late 2007.

The appellate court agreed that the defendant's effort to discredit its own projections "would lack credibility, if those projections are otherwise reliable." At the same time, the fact that they were the defendant's internal figures was not, "standing alone, evidence of reliability," it added.

In this case, the plaintiff failed to show that "the stabilized values [the defendant] placed on the properties were anything more than its hopes for what the property would be worth in the future." After all, the plaintiff's expert rejected the testimony from the defendant's senior analyst about the projections, calling her "confused" about their purpose. "In essence," the court said, the expert "challenged [the analyst's] competence to create the projections." Accordingly, they were not evidence the plaintiff could use to support the damage award against the defendant.

As to the MMT project, the court dismissed the expert's explanation but credited evidence the defendant presented post-*Daubert* hearing, at trial, showing that the rights were to expire at the end of 2010 because construction had not started and that it pursued an extension. There was no guarantee in March 2007 that the defendant would obtain the rights, and, therefore, the plaintiff expert's assumption was based on speculation, the court said.

In terms of the Morgan Stanley offer, it came some eight months after the March 2007 dissolution and it only valued a portion of the overall portfolio. Given these limitations, it was not independent evidence that could support the damages award.

In sum, because the plaintiff expert's analysis rested on an unreliable foundation, the trial court erred in admitting the testimony. Further, because the plaintiff was unable "to cobble together any other reliable evidence" to undergird the award, it could not recover the $28.2 million on any of the 10 claims in the trial court's alternative judgment, the appellate court said, striking down the award.

Late reliability argument prompts dissent. The decision to find error with the trial court's evidentiary ruling triggered a dissent. The majority failed to consider the evidence and arguments the trial court had in front of it at the time of the *Daubert* challenge, not during the trial or post-trial, the dissent said. Nowhere then did either side ever argue that the internal projections or investor summary schedules were incorrect or unreliable. Instead, the dissent observed, the issue the trial court dealt with was whether the data on which the expert relied reflected the present value of the stabilized values. Noting the credentials the plaintiff's expert had and citing to the record of the expert's direct and cross-examination on this issue, the dissent found the trial court had ample evidence to decide that the plaintiff's expert had a valid foundation for his opinion.

In a footnote, it added that the majority opinion addressed arguments, including those related to the MMT project, which the defendant had failed to raise earlier; therefore, the trial court could not be faulted for not considering them. Also, the majority discussed evidence independent of the expert's analysis, including the Morgan Stanley offer, which had nothing to do with the defendant's complaint about the trial court's evidentiary ruling. For all these reasons, the appellate court should overrule the defendant's reliability claim, the dissent concluded.

Buyout Agreement Irrelevant to Valuation of Spouse's Business Interest

Case name: *Colclasure v. Colclasure*
Citation: 2012 Okla. LEXIS 106
Date of decision: Nov. 20, 2012
Country: US
State or Federal: State
State/Jurisdiction: Oklahoma
Court: Supreme Court
Type of action: Marital Dissolution
Experts: Kenneth W. Klingenberg (wife); Ralph E. Blodgett (husband)
Judge: Kauger
SIC: 2426 Hardwood Dimension and Flooring Mills—Specific categories—

The wife owned a hardwood floor business for four years before selling a 49% interest to her fiancé for $5,000. After they were married, the couple executed an operating agreement that contained a buyout clause. This provision stated that in the event of a divorce, the parties would hire an independent appraiser to value the company, but if they failed to agree on one, each would retain an independent appraiser. If these valuations diverged too much, they would hire a third appraiser to calculate an averaging valuation. The valuation date was "the last day of the month immediately prior to the month in which the [triggering] event occurred," according to the agreement. It also allowed each member to compete with the company while working for it.

In December 2009, the parties filed for divorce, but the husband remained working for and receiving income from the business. He also continued to charge expenses to the company and started a competing business using company resources, prompting the wife to obtain a court order restricting these activities.

Instead of following the buy-sell agreement, the parties each retained experts to calculate the value of the business for trial. The wife's expert, a CPA and lawyer, used an income and excess earnings approach and a Dec. 31, 2009, valuation date. The date did not comply with the buy-sell, but it was closest to the divorce filing and the end-of-year financial records were "better," he said. At the same time, he accounted for nearly $300,000 that the husband diverted from the business after the valuation date because "the event was both known and knowable." Based on figures that the wife gave him, he concluded that the diversion caused the total value of the business to drop by $104,000. (The court's opinion does not provide the total value of the business.) Under the buy-sell agreement, he said its value was approximately $216,000.

During cross-examination, the wife's expert acknowledged a $144,000 calculation error. He also stated he used a different date than the buy-sell agreement would otherwise provide and that he didn't apply generally accepted accounting principles; rather, he followed NACVA's professional standards. Under continued questioning, he admitted to using a 36.96% capitalization rate in an earlier report, as opposed to, what he agreed was, a "relatively high" 47.05% in his final valuation and acknowledged using a C corporation tax rate even though the company was an S corp. Finally, he stated that the business grossed over $126,000 in 2003 income from receipts worth $635,000.

By contrast, the husband's expert, a CPA and CVA as well as an attorney, used a capitalized cash flow approach and a Nov. 30, 2009, valuation date per the buy-sell agreement. He made no adjustment due to the husband's competition or diversion of funds because he believed neither was "known or knowable" at the valuation date. He also did not include any enhanced benefits the husband might have received and overall valued the company at $480,000 and the husband's interest at $235,200.

The trial court adopted the husband's value and, after the appellate court affirmed, the wife petitioned the state Supreme Court for review.

Parties 'cherry-pick' agreement. The wife argued the value failed to reflect the husband's direct competition, which provided him income based on diverted funds while he continued to receive income from the marital business.

The husband claimed there were no grounds for reducing the award. His competition occurred after the valuation date, which, under the buy-sell agreement, was "unalterably" Nov. 30, 2009. Moreover, the agreement specifically permitted him to compete with the marital business.

At the outset, the appellate court noted that the parties "cherry-picked" their agreement for the terms most favorable to each. They could have resolved the business valuation based on the buy-sell provision, but once they went to trial, the result turned on the statute's requirement for a "fair and just" disposition of assets. In this case, the husband bought into the business for $5,000 and then received 47 times that amount in the trial court's award, which, on its face, was not equitable, the court held. Further, the trial court should have accounted for the husband's disbursements and his competition with the business, particularly given his status as an insider. Once again, the buy-sell agreement's provisions were irrelevant in this regard; the focus should have been on whether the husband's actions "lowered the company's value."

The court also agreed with the wife that state precedent required addressing the husband's income and diversion of funds during the pending divorce, but it declined to adopt her expert's valuation, which failed "to give a balanced picture" of these amounts, since it relied on the wife's calculations. Accordingly, the court remanded the case for a new determination of the business's value.

Notably, a strong dissent accused the majority of "invading the province of the trial court while rewriting the parties' contract." The wife made a bad business decision by selling a portion of her business to her soon-to-be husband. Their subsequent agreement was unambiguous, permitted direct competition, and provided a valuation formula. Further, the dissent cited the inconsistencies in the valuation by the wife's expert, particularly his "inflated" capitalization rate and his choice of a higher C corp tax rate. For all these reasons, it would have affirmed the trial court's award.

Negotiated Formula for Stock Option Price Obviates DLOM Need

Case name: *Davis v. Commissioner*
Citation: 2013 U.S. App. LEXIS 9850
Date of decision: May 16, 2013
Country: US
State or Federal: Federal
State/Jurisdiction: 11th Circuit
Court: United States Court of Appeals
Type of action: Federal Taxation
Experts: Alex Howard (Petitioner)
Judge: Ripple
SIC: 6141

The petitioner taxpayer contested the Tax Court's finding that his exercise of an option to buy additional shares in a closely held company was taxable income and claimed the court was wrong not to apply a marketability discount in its stock valuation.

The case revolves around a highly profitable subchapter S corporation that operated a payday loan business. Its shareholders included the petitioner, who owned 23%, and his children; all stakes were minority. The petitioner was indispensable to the business, taking an active role in operations and ensuring that key credit agreements remained in effect. A bitter divorce in which the wife, who owned no interest in the company, demanded half of his shares, threatened to upset the configuration. The petitioner rejected any dilution of his interest in the company, telling the others he would pull out if the number of his shares decreased.

Option to pass through wife. He devised a plan, to which all agreed, to reconstitute his ownership interest in the company. In 2002, following his transfer of 188.86 shares to the wife, she granted him an option that allowed him to repurchase the shares for $16 million. But all sides knew that she would not hold on to the stock. Instead, the company immediately redeemed her shares for cash and assumed the obligation under the option. Subsequently, the company and the petitioner negotiated an amendment to the option, including: (1) a cashless exercise that enabled him to give up a number of his shares equaling $16 million, under a specified formula for the exercise price, in exchange for paying nothing; and (2) a requirement that he notify the company in writing if he decided to make a 26 U.S.C. § 83(b) election. This provision allows a person who receives property in connection with the performance of services to choose to treat the property as income in the year received, instead of deferring recognition.

When the petitioner exercised the option in 2004, using the cashless provision, he received 131.8 shares. Under the formula, 57.05 shares were the equivalent of $16 million, making the remainder of shares worth $36.9 million. The company took a deduction for this amount (passed through to the shareholders), stating it gave the option in connection with the petitioner's performance of services under § 83(h). The petitioner did not report the exercise as income nor claim a deduction, believing it had no tax consequences.

The IRS issued dual deficiency notices. In the U.S. Tax Court, the agency argued that exercising the cashless option resulted in gross income for the petitioner and allowed the company to claim a deduction. The company contended it had granted the option to secure the petitioner's continued involvement in the business.

The petitioner claimed that, because he received the option from the wife incident to their divorce, his exercise of it fell under the code's § 1041 nonrecognition provision. As to the value of the stock, he presented an expert who applied a 30% discount for lack of marketability (DLOM) to reflect his minority interest in the corporation.

The Tax Court in essence determined the company granted the option following the petitioner's repeated threats of leaving the company. Also, the amended option expressly referred to the § 83(b) election, which only applies to income from property transferred to secure the performance of services. Consequently, the stock transfer occurred in connection with the performance of services and the value of the shares was taxable income.

In terms of valuing the stock, the court declined to apply a DLOM because the parties had negotiated a formula for determining the shares' value. Based on it, the value of the 131.8 shares the petitioner received was $36.9 million, it concluded. (Find a detailed discussion of the Tax Court proceedings at *BVLaw*.)

'Essentially a different option.' The petitioner then appealed the decision at the 11th Circuit Court of Appeals, resuming many of his earlier arguments.

First, he maintained, the Tax Court erred in ruling he received the option in connection with the performance of services. Even if part of the reason for giving him the option was to ensure his continued presence at the company, there were additional purposes, including stabilizing control of the company and "resolving family strife." Also, because he received the option from the wife, it could not have been related to the performance of services. And, given that it passed through the wife in the context of divorce proceedings, under § 1041, the shares he received were not recognizable income.

The Court of Appeals agreed with the Tax Court that the transaction was subject to § 83 and the petitioner's exercise of the option produced ordinary income. The record showed he was a "key employee," who gave no consideration for the option other than his promise to remain at the company and work hard for it. That he received the option from the wife was not important because he intentionally structured the transaction to avoid a grant directly from the company. The parties knew that the company would immediately cash out the shares the wife acquired and give him an option to buy shares directly from it. The company was the "de facto counter-party" under the original option and, more importantly, the amended option, the appellate court stated. In fact, the latter option included substantially different rights than the former option contemplated, which made it "essentially a different option."

Section 1041 provided no shield in this case, the court continued. It applied only to the transfer of property between spouses or former spouses incident to divorce proceedings, "not to the subsequent disposition of that property by the recipient spouse or former spouse." Exercise, the court said, was distinct from transfer. Even if the petitioner could have exercised the original option, "he still would have had to recognize as ordinary income the difference, if any, between the fair market value of the shares and the option price."

In this case, however, he only could, and did, exercise the option the company granted, which contained new rights. The rights were not incident to divorce.

Second, the petitioner claimed, the Tax Court erred when it failed to reduce the value of the shares from their negotiated price in the amended option agreement.

The 11th Circuit also found this argument without merit. "[T]here is no authority for the proposition that a lack-of-marketability discount is necessarily required." By referencing the number of shares the parties valued at $16 million under their negotiated formula, the Tax Court had a "solid, real-world basis for its valuation of the shares purchased." In essence, in assessing the shares' fair market value, the Tax Court, reasonably, used the parties' own valuation of the shares on the exercise date. The petitioner should have included $36.9 million in ordinary income, and the company had a right to claim that amount as a deduction, the appellate court concluded.

IRS Strains to Prove Goodwill in Like-Kind Exchange

Case name: *Deseret Management Corp. v. United States*
Citation: 2013 U.S. Claims LEXIS 987
Date of decision: July 31, 2013
Country: US
State or Federal: Federal
State/Jurisdiction: N/A
Court: United States Court of Federal Claims
Type of action: Federal Taxation
Experts: BIA Consulting, Inc., Jerry Hausman (respondent); Ms. Flynn (government);
Judge: Allegra
SIC: 4832 Radio Broadcasting Stations (networks)

Can a radio station have goodwill? And if it can, did the plaintiff's station possess goodwill at the time it was swapped for other stations? The U.S. Court of Federal Claims recently explored the legal and valuation dimensions of this question within the context of a tax refund case.

Underachiever. The plaintiff was a holding company for subsidiaries that owned and operated radio stations throughout the country. In 1998, it acquired KZLA, the only country-music FM station in the Los Angeles market. Between 1998 and 2000, the relevant period, the city was the second-largest radio market in the country and growing at a rapid speed, from 13.2 million in 1998 to 13.6 million in 2000. Of the 70 stations, 21 were "viable FMs," that is, with ratings that indicated they were "serious competitors." KZLA had two advantages over other contenders: It was one of 14 licensed to transmit from the highest elevation in the area, and it was authorized to exceed FCC restrictions as to the power stations could use to broadcast signals. Despite these advantages, it was not performing well. While radio market guides showed that revenue for stations in the L.A. market between 1994 and 2000 grew at a compound annual rate of 12.2%, KZLA's revenue between 1998 and 2000 remained fairly flat, at about $16 million per year. In 1998, its adjusted audience share was 2.6, dropping to 2.4 in 1999 and increasing to 2.6 in 2000. Another measure of success, revenue share, confirmed the picture: KZLA's revenue share was 2.6 in 1998, 2.1 in 1999, and 1.8 in 2000.

In late 1999, management retained Coleman Research to perform a "perceptual study" to determine how the audience looked at the station and reveal its "brand image position." The study showed that the station lacked "brand depth" beyond music and that its listenership was "underdeveloped." There was room to grow in the 24-to-54 age group, it said. At the same time, the existing audience was "relatively loyal and committed to the station"; in fact, it was the "absolute favorite" among country-music listeners. There was "unrealized potential," the report concluded.

Appraisal values license. In October 2000, the station owners and a third-party communications company agreed to an asset exchange: The former would swap the assets of KZLA for those of the latter's three or four St. Louis stations. The exchange value of the assets was $185 million. The value of KZLA's tangible assets was approximately $3.4 million, and the value of all intangible assets, excluding the station's FCC license and goodwill, was about $4.8 million. The parties to the swap retained a consulting firm to perform an appraisal of KZLA's assets. The appraiser found the station had a "going concern value" of $156,000 and its FCC license was worth nearly $176.8 million. The firm valued KZLA's going concern as the "cost that would be required to replicate the systems and procedures in place and in use at the station." It calculated the value of the FCC license using the "residual fair market value" method—subtracting the value of the station's other, tangible and intangible, assets from the $185 million exchange value and assigning the difference (the residual) to the FCC license. Importantly, the appraiser assigned no value to goodwill, claiming that: (1) there was legal precedent that held that "broadcast stations do not possess any goodwill"; (2) broadcast stations in general "do not enjoy any goodwill in the sense of either listener or advertiser loyalty"; and (3) KZLA in particular "does not possess any other traditional manifestations of goodwill." KZLA's new owner kept the country format until 2006 and also implemented some of the recommendations Coleman had made earlier to increase brand depth.

For the tax years 2000 through 2002, the plaintiff filed a consolidated federal income tax return for itself and the subsidiaries, including the prior owners of KZLA. It designated the asset exchange as a "like-kind" exchange and recognized gains based on the appraiser's valuation, assigning no value to goodwill. The Internal Revenue Service disagreed with the reporting of gain from the exchange. It determined that the station had a goodwill value of $73.3 million on the transaction date and alleged a deficiency as to the 2000 tax year. Ultimately, the plaintiff sued, stating it had overpaid taxes of nearly $25.6 million. The parties tried the case in 2012 in front of the Court of Claims, with both sides presenting expert valuation testimony.

Why goodwill matters. Under the Internal Revenue Code's section 1031, a taxpayer may defer recognition of gain or loss from qualifying exchanges of like-kind property. Congress recognized that when a taxpayer simply exchanges one investment property for a similar—like-kind—one, he or she "has not cashed in on his [or her] investment but continued that investment, albeit in a different property." At the same time, Treas. Reg. § 1.1031(a)-2(c)(2) provides that a business's goodwill or going concern value is not of a like kind to the goodwill or going concern value of another business. Therefore, the nonrecognition provision does not apply. In qualitative terms, goodwill is "a useful label with which to identify the total of all the imponderables qualities that attract customers to the business." In quantitative terms, it is "the excess of cost over the fair value of the identifiable net assets required."

In this case, the Court of Claims said, the first issue was to determine whether KZLA had any goodwill at the time of exchange. It looked specifically at the $176.8 million residual. The plaintiff argued that the station had no goodwill and all of the residual value belonged to the station's FCC license. Citing an earlier (1969) Court of Claims case, the plaintiff contended that there was a *per se* rule that FCC-licensed stations could never have goodwill because audience loyalty hinged on format and on-air personalities. Changes to these components could prompt listeners to flee. Also, KZLA was underperforming, as the Coleman study showed. In contrast, the government asserted that the value of the FCC license was much less than the amount the plaintiff assigned to it and the remainder represented KZLA's goodwill.

The Court of Claims saw indications of goodwill. The station was the only country-music station in a market of nearly 13 million listeners; some of those followed it closely. For this reason, the new owner retained the format. Also, the Coleman report's references to "brand depth" and "music image" suggested there was "evidence of some degree of goodwill, albeit underdeveloped." Simply because listeners might abandon a station that changed its format or on-air presenters did not mean a station could not have goodwill. By analogy, it asked: "Can it be that nationally-recognized restaurant chains lack goodwill because their customers might flee if they radically changed their menu?" Also, even if there is a connection between the existence of goodwill and a business's ability to generate profit, "goodwill may exist where a firm is unprofitable, or at least not more profitable than the 'norm.'" There simply was no *per se* rule of law against goodwill in radio stations, the court held. It declared this rejection significant because it meant that the appraiser's valuation report rested on a "faulty premise." The appraiser's approach of using the residual basis to allocate the remainder of the purchase price to the station's license was "legally erroneous."

Government values goodwill. The plaintiff stuck to its position and did not offer a valuation of the station's goodwill. But the government did, introducing an expert who used the residual method not to calculate the value of the station's FCC license, but its goodwill. The plaintiff presented expert rebuttal testimony.

Broadly speaking, the IRS expert tried to isolate the income attributable to the FCC license by performing a discounted cash flow (DCF) analysis of the station, treating it as a startup. She created projections for the revenue, operating cash flow, and net free cash flow that KZLA could reasonably be expected to achieve in the market, based on past performance, market operating and financial benchmarks, as well as the performance of other radio stations in the L.A. market. The operating cash flow resulted from subtracting future operating expenses from the revenue flow; the net cash flow resulted from subtracting from the operating cash flow taxes, depreciation, capital expenditures, and additions to working capital. Discounting the net free cash flow to present value, she then extracted the value for KZLA's license. She initially found it was worth $131.4 million, which left a residual value of goodwill of $45.4 million.

Noteworthy components of the DCF analysis included:

- *Market revenue:* Drawing on the appraiser's estimate, the IRS's expert projected $851 million in revenue in 2000, $1.1 billion by 2003, and $1.8 billion by 2009.

- *Taxes:* In calculating the income flows, she computed taxes at a 35% rate after deducting projected depreciation/amortization from operating cash flow. Importantly, to determine the amortization deductible for the FCC license, she assumed the FCC license was worth $80 million and had a 40-year useful life.

- *Discount rate:* She used an 11.7% discount rate to adjust future cash flow, a rate she derived from modifying figures in Ibbotson's *2001 Yearbook.* Specifically, she estimated the cost of equity financing at 14.54% and the after-tax cost of debt financing at 7.48%. She then allocated those percentages, assuming that 60% of the financings were equity and 40% were debt.

- *Terminal value:* She used the Gordon growth formula, assuming a 4.5% perpetuity growth and a discount terminal value back 10 years based on the 11.7% weighted average cost of capital (WAAC).

After correcting for errors in her cash flow projections and working capital calculation, the expert later lowered the goodwill figure to $36.5 million.

The plaintiff's rebuttal experts highlighted three errors that the competing expert had failed to correct by the time of trial. Had she done so, they contended, the license value would have increased to $179.6 million, leaving no portion of the $185 million purchase price to assign to goodwill. The errors centered on:

- *Value of the license:* Instead of using the full value of the FCC license in calculating the amortization deduction owed, the IRS expert used a proxy value of $80 million. She derived this value by looking at 10 comparable radio sales from around the country that took place between 1995 and the spring of 2000.

- *Useful life of the license:* Instead of the 15-year period the Internal Revenue Code prescribed, she used a 40-year period as the useful life of the license. The government admitted this was an error.

- *Starting date:* Instead of starting the amortization of the license on the transaction date, October 2000, she used Jan. 1, 2001.

Moreover, her discount rate was too high, the rebuttal experts said. She based her risk-free rate on the average yield of 20-year U.S. Treasury bonds in the year 2000 (6.8%), when she should have used the yield for the transaction date (6.04%). Also, authoritative literature showed that her claimed 8.1% equity risk premium was too high; it should have been no more than 6%. And the equity-to-debt ratio should have been 58% to 42%, projecting a greater use of debt. All of these adjustments would decrease the discount rate to 9.91%.

The IRS subsequently made two of the three modifications the plaintiff's experts had urged regarding the amortization deduction—changing the useful life and starting point—but adhered to the $80 million proxy value for the license. The government also adopted the proposed 58%-to-42% equity-to-debt ratio. As a result, the claimed goodwill value dropped to about $19.8 million.

DCF a 'double-edged sword.' These corrections notwithstanding, the Court of Claims found the government's goodwill valuation problematic. "Logic suggests that the value of the license employed in determining the amortization deduction must closely approximate its actual value," otherwise the projected income stream will be understated, which, in turn, causes the value of the license to be understated, it said. In a DCF analysis, it made no sense "to simply pick a supposed 'average' license value," as the IRS expert did. In a footnote, the court pointed out specific flaws regarding the comparable radio sales that undergirded the expert's proxy value determination. For one, there was no reason why license values involving stations across the country were comparable to the value of an L.A. license. Also, all but two of the transactions the expert considered were between 1995 and 1997 and as such did not capture the explosion in license values in the L.A. market in 2000.

In terms of calculating the discount rate, the court agreed with the plaintiff that the suggested 6.04% figure was the appropriate starting point for determining the cost of equity a startup radio station would have incurred in October 2000. In fact, this approach matched the approach the government's expert used to determine the debt component, said the court. One of the plaintiff's experts also convincingly testified that at least half a dozen articles indicated that an 8.1% equity risk premium was "too high." The court adopted the plaintiff's proposed 9.91% discount rate.

The Court of Claims provided an exhibit to illustrate the effect of the adjustments on the remainder goodwill value.

Effect of the Adjustments on the Remainder Goodwill Value (Data in Millions of Dollars)

(A)	(B)	(C)	(D)	(E)	(F)
Transaction's Total Value	*Less Tangibles & Intangibles*	*Amortization License Value*	*Equity Rate: Changes to Defendant's Calculations*	*License Value*	*Goodwill Value (Remainder)*
185	8.243	80	No Change	156.999	19.758
			Modified Risk Free Rate	169.088	7.669
			Modified Equity Risk Premium	194.934	-18.177
			Both Modifications	212.954	-36.197
185	8.243	120	No Change	167.298	9.459
			Modified Risk Free Rate	180.031	-3.274
			Modified Equity Risk Premium	207.241	-30.484
			Both Modifications	226.202	-49.445
185	8.243	156.742	No Change	176.757	0.000
			Modified Risk Free Rate	190.083	-13.326
			Modified Equity Risk Premium	218.545	-41.788
			Both Modifications	238.371	-61.614
185	8.243	170	No Change	180.170	- 3.413
			Modified Risk Free Rate	193.710	-16.953
			Modified Equity Risk Premium	222.624	-45.867
			Both Modifications	242.762	-66.005

Even if the court adopted the government's "extraordinarily low" proxy value for the license, the two equity rate adjustments would cause the goodwill value to fall below zero, it said. Alternatively, if it used a license value that was closer to the actual value but retained the IRS expert's proposed 11.7% discount rate, the value of the station's goodwill would fall below zero at an amortization value for the license of around $156.7 million. Therefore, even this understated value resulted in a calculated license value of over $176.7 million. This amount left nothing for goodwill. The plaintiff proved its claim, the Court of Claims concluded. "[T]the use of discount calculations to value goodwill represents a double-edged sword in that the numbers can demonstrate the presence or the absence of goodwill," it cautioned.

In Demutualization, IPO Share Price Guides Cost Basis Determination

Case name: *Dorrance v. U.S.*
Citation: 2013 U.S. Dist. LEXIS 37745
Date of decision: March 19, 2013
Country: US
State or Federal: Federal
State/Jurisdiction: Arizona
Court: United States District Court
Type of action: Federal Taxation
Experts: Unknown
Judge: Snow
SIC: 6311 Life Insurance (life insurers-direct)

In their action for a tax refund, the taxpayers claimed theirs was the "rare and extraordinary" case that required the application of the "open transaction doctrine" because there was no ready market for the mutual rights in their life insurance policies and no practical method to determine the fair market value.

The plaintiffs formed a trust to arrange for survivor coverage for their heirs. It purchased five life insurance policies with mutual insurance companies that provided over $87 million in coverage, as well as an interest in the companies themselves. The policyholders had a right to vote on corporate decisions and a right to receive the companies' surplus should the entities liquidate. The plaintiffs paid premiums, but the companies did not allocate premiums or assign an independent cost to the mutual rights. The plaintiffs described these rights as "ownership" rights, whereas the IRS called them "membership" rights. The court referred to them as "mutual rights."

In the late 1990s, all five mutual life insurance companies demutualized and converted into stock-based companies. Prior to seeking policyholder approval, at least one of the companies promised its policyholders that, if they voted for demutualization, premiums would remain the same, and, in fact, none of the premiums the plaintiffs paid increased after the event.

'Sound' share allocation methods. In exchange for relinquishing their mutual rights, the plaintiffs received shares of stock. When determining how much stock to give policyholders, the companies calculated a "fixed" component to correspond to the policyholders' loss of voting rights and a "variable" component that sought to measure "the policyholders' past and projected future contributions to the surplus of the company." Sixty percent of the variable component was an estimate of each policyholder's past contributions, and 40% was an estimate of future contributions.

The different companies used slightly different methods to calculate the contributions, but all obtained independent expert opinions that the share allocation methods were "sound" and the stock compensation was "fair and equitable." At the time, the companies stated to the IRS that the fair market value of the stock their policyholders would receive during demutualization was equal to the value of the mutual rights. Specifically, the stock the plaintiffs' trust received had a total value of $1,794,771, which they sold some two years later for an aggregate value of $2,248,806.

Following the IRS's traditional position that stock acquired in the demutualization of an insurance company has a cost basis of zero, the plaintiffs paid taxes on the full amount but subsequently sued for a refund, claiming, in a pretrial motion, that "the open transaction doctrine" controlled the case. The doctrine, which courts have found applies only in "rare and exceptional" circumstances, allows a taxpayer to apply gains received from the sale of a portion of a piece of property to the entire original basis without apportioning the basis between the property that was sold and the property that was retained. In a landmark case, the U.S. Court of Federal Claims ruled that demutualization of a mutual insurance company was one of those circumstances. See *Fisher v. United States*, 82 Fed. Cl. 780, 795 (Fed. Cl. 2008) (a digest of the case and the court's opinion are available at *BV Update* and *BVLaw*).

The IRS, in its summary judgment motion, argued that the plaintiffs failed to meet their burden of establishing that they paid anything for the mutual rights. They paid premiums to obtain insurance benefits, not mutual rights.

In its pretrial ruling, the district court (Arizona) disagreed with both parties. Considering the plaintiffs paid premiums for policies that included both policy rights and mutual rights, they proved that they paid *something* for the latter, it stated with emphasis. At the same time, the open transaction doctrine did not apply because the plaintiffs' mutual rights were not "elements of value so speculative in character" that it was impossible to determine their worth. Accordingly, the default rule applied, requiring that the basis in the life insurance policies "be equitably apportioned among the several parts," the court decided, citing Treas. Reg. § 1.161-6(a) and relevant case law.

Cost basis formula. At trial, the focus was on determining an equitable method to "allocate the premiums the plaintiffs paid before demutualization and apply that amount as cost basis to calculate the taxable gain, if any, on the sale of stock."

The court found that when the plaintiffs bought insurance policies they received vested mutual rights. But even though those rights contributed to the value of the policies from the time of purchase, it was not possible to calculate their cost before the demutualization. In other words, the court said, it was not simply a matter of looking at the payment of premiums. Rather, the first valuation of what the plaintiffs paid for the mutual rights was the IPO price of the shares under the demutualization. The insurance companies allocated shares based on: (1) the value of voting rights; (2) past contributions to surplus; and (3) projected future contributions to surplus. Because the plaintiffs had not actually paid for the portion covering the future contributions, those were not part of the basis.

In sum, the court found the basis was a combination of the IPO value of shares the plaintiffs received for the fixed component and 60% of the variable component. In this case, for the fixed shares, the insurers calculated an aggregate IPO value of $3,164. At the same time, 60% of the IPO value of the variable shares yielded $1,074,964. This amounted to a cost basis of $1,078,128, applicable to the sales proceeds of $2,248,806. Considering the plaintiffs paid tax at a 15% capital gains rate, they had a right to a refund of $161,719.20, the court concluded.

Expert Uses Irrelevant Basis of Comparison and Sabotages Valuation

Case name: *Edgewater Growth Capital Partners, L.P. v. H.I.G. Capital, Inc.*
Citation: 2013 Del. Ch. LEXIS 54
Date of decision: Feb. 28, 2013
Country: US
State or Federal: State
State/Jurisdiction: Delaware
Court: Court of Chancery
Type of action: Miscellaneous
Experts: Roy D'Souza (plaintiffs); David Clarke (defendants)
Judge: Strine

The plaintiff contested the foreclosure of a company in the Delaware Court of Chancery, claiming it was not commercially reasonable under the Uniform Commercial Code (UCC) as to the sale process and price, considering its expert's valuation and "real world" indications of value.

Merger proves 'a disaster.' Through debt financing, a private equity firm invested in several businesses that it merged into one company, leaving the new entity heavily leveraged. The Court of Chancery (Chancellor Strine) called the integration "a disaster," noting the firm failed to establish a clear leadership structure for the combined operations. In February 2006, a month after the merger, the company failed to meet its EBITDA requirement. Subsequent default events forced the PE firm to guarantee about $4 million of senior debt. The December 2006 balance sheet showed negative stockholder equity of about $28.7 million. At that time, the firm's executive who was primarily responsible for the investment asked the company director for a $9 million rebate, stating that at the time of the acquisition, the valuation of the combined company was approximately $170 million, but a year later it was closer to $90 million.

In January 2007, the company lost its largest customer, and the PE firm decided to sell it. This plan failed because the company could not procure an unqualified going concern opinion. By mid-2007, the PE firm described the company's cash situation as "dire" and expressed concern about its "deteriorating quality of earnings." A September 2007 internal e-mail cautioned the firm "not to engage any consultant to discuss valuation." Around that time, one of the defendants, the debt purchaser, bought 39% of debt from a senior lender at about 76 cents on the dollar. Some two weeks later, it bought an additional 6% of the same debt for about 72 cents on the dollar and became the largest senior lender.

Eventually the senior lenders "drew a line in the sand": they would not provide another round of short-term relief unless the PE firm agreed to cede control of the company's board or buy them out. The firm chose "to quit." Its directors resigned and appointed experienced restructuring consultants. Ultimately, the lenders decided to sell the company assets under Article 9 of the UCC rather than place it in bankruptcy. Under a foreclosure sale agreement, the debt purchaser gave the company 55 days and funds to hire a qualified investment banker to procure a buyer for its assets. Despite a comprehensive market check and some expressions of interest, ultimately the company did not receive a single bid.

The debt purchaser then arranged for an open auction, and in March 2008, an affiliate (co-defendant) bought the company's assets for $41 million, plus the assumption of $50 million in liabilities. The PE firm did not participate in the bid.

A valuation with 'glaring mistakes.' In its suit, the firm claimed the debt purchaser and its affiliate violated Article 9 of the UCC by staging a sale that was not commercially reasonable in terms of process and price. The defendants argued the firm sued to avoid paying on the $4 million guaranty.

To support its position that the price "bore no relation to the value of the company," the PE firm retained a valuation expert, who performed a discounted cash flow (DCF) analysis to establish its enterprise value. He testified that on the date of sale, the company was worth $110 million. He admitted that he did not use the available actual cash flows but rather projections a company employee had prepared in August 2007 based on the assumption that the company would undergo a "dramatic turn-around" after restructuring of its debt.

The plaintiff's expert also used the guideline company method, deriving an EBITDA multiple for three public companies that operated in the same industry but were in different financial shape.

The defendants' expert noted "some glaring mistakes" in his counterpart's original report. For one, the analysis rested on the wrong basis of comparison. The subject company had no earnings on its revenues, whereas the comparable companies had significant profit margins. In addition, he overstated the EBITDA multiple for at least one of the comparables. The data on which the plaintiff's expert had relied did not reflect a change in company structure—the sale of one division—that reduced the multiple by half, from 12 to 6 times.

In response, the plaintiff's expert revised his report as to the multiple, but, as the defendants' expert pointed out, despite the "pretty significant change," he did not change the overall value he assigned to the company.

The PE firm itself proposed an even higher value than its expert, claiming on the date of the auction, the company was worth $130 million to $150 million because in the prior year, potential bidders had sent an "indication of interest in that range." A top executive responsible for the investment said that "real valuation comes down to what somebody is willing to pay for the company." According to him, a company's value was "not some multiple of EBITDA analysis.... Valuation methodologies employed by third-party valuation analysts ... typically don't really reflect the real world."

By contrast, one of the company's directors stated that the board hoped to obtain a minimum bid of $100 million, including liabilities. He "felt strongly" the resulting bid, at $41 million, was fair and explained that the purchase price dropped from $56 million to $41 million toward the end of negotiations because the debt purchaser agreed to assume additional liabilities, including the company's employment contracts. The director also acknowledged that based on what he knew about the company's operations and performance at that time, he "would not have paid $20 million."

Why did PE firm not bid? The Court of Chancery first reviewed the sale process. The analysis pivoted on whether the way in which the debt purchaser sold the company's assets conformed to "the practices of a financial advisor who sells distressed entities." Considering the defendants funded the company's effort to find a buyer for approximately two months and enabled it to work with an experienced banker who, in turn, marketed it diligently, the court concluded the process was commercially reasonable.

To the firm's objections that the sale period was too short, the court replied: "A going concern that cannot go, because it cannot pay its bills, cannot be compared to Apple, Johnson & Johnson, or DuPont, which can."

As to the price, the Court of Chancery emphasized that a low price did not establish a statutory violation. The law did not require it to look at the "fair value" of the transaction but to "scrutinize carefully all aspects of the disposition" to ensure it conformed to the reasonable commercial practices of sellers of this type of asset.

Considering all the evidence, the court found:

- The valuation the PE firm's expert submitted was unreliable. In terms of the DCF analysis, he used "optimistic cash flow projections" based on a turnaround plan that was never carried out. It remains unclear, the court said, why he relied on "stale, not to mention, unrealistic data" even though he had access to the actual financials until at least October 2007.

- Also, as the defendants' expert showed, he failed to compare the company to other distressed companies, the only relevant point of comparison. Further, it "makes no sense" that he changed a valuation multiple for one company but not his ultimate conclusion as to the overall value.

- If the PE firm could have sold the company for $130 million to $150 million "or even much lower" in 2007, *it would have done so* (emphasis in the opinion). It could not because it could not obtain the requisite going concern opinion and survive buyer's due diligence.

- The firm failed to explain why it did not bid for the company's assets if it believed the subject was worth as much as the firm claimed. Its decision suggested "it did not believe that the company was worth more than the minimum bid."

- The company director's testimony was "highly reliable" as to the value of the deal. As a large equity holder, he had "skin in the game," and he had no material ties to the debt purchaser. He considered the minimum bid "fair."

Because the court concluded the sale was commercially reasonable, the price the buyer paid for the assets was reasonable as well. The company's "poor performance and operational mess under [the equity firm's] own leadership" showed in the value its assets received at the auction. Ruling for the defendants, the Court of Chancery required the PE firm to pay the $4 million it owed under the guaranty.

Invocation of EMVR Subject to Higher Degree of Proof

Case name: *Electro-Mechanical Corp. v. Power Distribution Products, Inc.*
Citation: 2013 U.S. Dist. LEXIS 1288771
Date of decision: Sept. 10, 2013
Country: US
State or Federal: Federal
State/Jurisdiction: Virginia
Court: United States District Court
Type of action: Intellectual Property
Experts: Graham Rogers (plaintiff); Keith Hock (defendants)
Judge: Jones
SIC: 4911 Electric Services (electric power distribution)

Although the entire market value rule (EMVR) applies both in the reasonable royalty and lost profits context, it is more prevalent, and has generated more law, in the former circumstances. A recent case stands out because the court had an opportunity to rule on the defendants' post-trial claim that the jury improperly based a lost profits award on sales of the entire apparatus rather than the infringing device alone.

The plaintiff and the defendants directly competed in a market for power distribution systems applicable to underground coal mining. The plaintiff held a patent that enabled it to develop and bring to market a device to ensure quicker, easier repair of electronic components in the system. Concerned over losing customers, the defendants designed a similar product and sold two power systems to coal mines; the systems embedded the patented feature. The plaintiff sued, alleging infringement and presenting expert testimony on lost profits and, in the alternative, a reasonable royalty. The defendants contended there was no infringement but also offered a counter damages expert.

Customer motivation. Specifically, the plaintiff's expert applied EMVR to calculate lost profits based on the defendants' two sales. He reasoned that the patented functionality was the basis for the customers' purchase of the entire system and the infringing and noninfringing components operated as a single functioning unit and were sold together. Using the plaintiff's traditional profit margins, he calculated lost profits of $624,000. At the same time, he computed a lower lost profits amount of $491,000 based on a cost-plus pricing requirement from one of the coal mine buyers.

If lost profits were not the appropriate measure of damages, he said, the plaintiff had a right to a reasonable royalty of $200,800. He obtained this amount from using a 4.325% royalty rate and multiplying it by the revenues from the entire systems—again applying EMVR.

He admitted that he was not aware of customers that already owned an entire power system without the infringing device but decided to replace it with a new system simply to obtain the patented component. He believed customers first decided to buy the power system and then decided whether it should include the protected feature.

The defendants' expert objected that there was insufficient evidence to justify the application of EMVR and any recovery for lost profits. In terms of a reasonable royalty, he proposed a lower rate of 2.5% to 3%. He found that when sold individually the infringing component cost between $19,000 and $20,000 and that the defendants had sold 25 of them. Consequently, the plaintiff should recover between $9,500 and $16,600 as a reasonable royalty, he concluded.

The jury found the defendants liable and awarded the plaintiff $491,000, in line with the plaintiff's expert's alternate EMVR-based lost profits calculation.

In a post-trial motion, the defendants requested a new damages trial or modification of the award. There was inadequate evidence to support damages based on EMVR, they objected. Also, the plaintiff failed to show it had a right to lost profits; therefore, the jury should have awarded a reasonable royalty.

The court addressed both aspects of the argument. As to lost profits and EMVR, it considered decisions from the Federal Circuit that allow for recovery based on the entire apparatus containing multiple features when the patented feature is the "basis for customer demand." Under the legal test, EMVR applies if: (1) the infringing components form the basis for customer demand for the entire machine, which includes nonpatented features; (2) the infringing and noninfringing components are sold together and form a functional unit; and (3) the individual infringing and noninfringing components are "analogous to a single functioning unit." *Cornell Univ. v. Hewlett-Packard Co.,* 609 F.Supp. 2d 279 (N.D.N.Y. 2009).

Moreover, the court pointed out, the Federal Circuit's *LaserDynamics* decision made it clear that a plaintiff could not simply invoke EMVR by showing that a customer that was in the market for a larger product would choose a version that contained the protected component over one that did not. "Instead, the plaintiff must prove that the customer's decision to buy the larger product in the first place is motivated by the presence of the patented component." *LaserDynamics, Inc. v. Quanta Computer, Inc.,* 2012 U.S. App. LEXIS 18441 (Fed. Cir. 2012).

In this case, the testimony from the plaintiff's expert showed that the patented component was not the primary motivation for the sales of the power systems. The plaintiff failed to provide the "higher degree of proof" that could support its expert's EMVR theory. Because his lost profits calculations rested on EMVR and the jury adopted one of them in awarding damages, the lost profits award was unjustified.

Instead, the court determined that at most the plaintiff had a right to a reasonable royalty using its expert's proposed 4.325% royalty rate and applying it to the defendants' sales of 25 infringing devices at $20,000 per unit. In granting the defendants' motion, the court gave the plaintiff a choice of accepting a reduced award at $21,625 or agreeing to a new trial on damages.

Note: The *LaserDynamics* and *Cornell* opinions are available at *BVLaw.* A discussion of *Cornell* appears in the Oct. 6, 2011, webinar *Patent Damages: The Entire Market Value Rule,* Part 3 of *BVR's Online Symposium on Litigation & Economic Damages,* available at *BVResearch.*

25% Rule Does Not 'Irretrievably Damage' Royalty Analysis

Case name: *Energy Transp. Group, Inc. v. William Demant Holding A/S*
Citation: 2012 U.S. App. LEXIS 21200
Date of decision: Oct. 12, 2012
Country: US
State or Federal: Federal
State/Jurisdiction: Federal Circuit
Court: United States Court of Appeals
Type of action: Intellectual Property
Experts: Terry L. Musika (plaintiff); Jonathan D. Putnam (defendants)
Judge: Rader
SIC: 3842 Orthopedic, Prosthetic, and Surgical Appliances and Supplies

The plaintiff developed technology for reducing acoustic feedback in a digital hearing aid. In 2005, it sued the defendants for infringing two of its patents. At trial before the federal district court in 2007, the plaintiff's expert calculated reasonable royalty damages using at least two different approaches.

Pre-*Uniloc* reference to 25% rule. First, he conducted a *Georgia-Pacific* analysis to determine the rate the parties would have agreed on during a hypothetical negotiation, focusing in particular on factors such as the unique relationship of the parties, the nature of the patented invention, and the nature of the industry. The expert also referenced the 25% rule of thumb, i.e., the presumption that the plaintiff, as licensor, would have expected to receive at least 25% of the defendant's profits from selling the infringing products.

In a separate analysis, he looked to the defendants' average profit margins on the accused products, as set forth in their expert's report. He determined that the infringing products earned 6.4% more in operating profits than industry averages and 9.2% over the defendant's noninfringing devices. The higher figure represented the top end of a range of royalties the parties might have negotiated, he believed. Ultimately, he proposed an 8.4% royalty rate, which amounted to over $65.7 million in damages.

By contrast, the defendants' expert proposed a lump sum of $1 million, or a royalty rate in the 0.25%-to-0.5% range, based in part on license agreements from an industry group that showed a flat 3% royalty for all patents. Applying the top rate to his proposed royalty base, he calculated a maximum of $3.5 million in damages.

In challenging the defendants' royalty rate range, the plaintiff's expert said these rates were "low, industry-friendly, and not probative of market rates." He also referenced a report on cartels from a German regulatory body that found the hearing aid market was highly concentrated and enjoyed "exceedingly high profit margins" due to the lack of competition. The defendant challenged the German report, but the district court admitted it on a limited basis, that is, the plaintiff's expert could refer to the report for background on the market and industry, but could not to use it for inflammatory purposes (e.g., to call the defendants' activities "collusive").

After hearing all the evidence, the jury found for the plaintiff and awarded $31 million in lump-sum damages. The defendants moved for judgment as a matter of law (JMOL), as well as a new trial on damages, in essence claiming that the plaintiff's expert's royalty rate analysis and conclusions were speculative and the award was excessive. Except for reversing a finding of infringement as to one of the two patents, the district court denied the motions. It agreed with the plaintiff that, based on the defendants' sales figures, the award equated to a royalty rate in the range of 4% to 5%, which was "approximately halfway between" the proposed royalty rates by the parties' experts.

***Georgia-Pacific* subject to greater scrutiny.** The defendants appealed to the U.S. Court of Appeals for the Federal Circuit, raising three primary issues concerning damages:

1. *German cartel report.* Following the trial in this case, a German appellate court had overturned the conclusions in the cartel report, finding no restrictions on competition in the related industry. Accordingly, the plaintiff's expert should not have relied on the report to support his royalty rates, the defendants argued.

The Federal Circuit disagreed, finding the trial court's cautionary instructions tempered any prejudice. Moreover, the report contained relevant facts that bolstered the plaintiff's expert's calculations. In particular, its statements about the high profit margins on hearing aids supported the expert's higher royalty rate as compared to the lower rate the defendants' expert proposed.

2. *Twenty-five percent rule.* By using the 25% rule of thumb, the plaintiff's expert rendered his entire reasonable royalty analysis unreliable, the defendants contended, citing *Uniloc USA, Inc. v. Microsoft Corp.*, 632 F.3d 1292 (Fed. Cir. 2011) (available at *BVLaw*).

In response, the Federal Circuit specifically affirmed its finding in *Uniloc*, which declared the rule a "fundamentally flawed tool for determining a baseline royalty rate in a hypothetical negotiation." At the same time, in this case, the expert's discussion of the rule "did not irretrievably damage the reasonableness of his method and result," in large part because (unlike the expert in *Uniloc*), he conducted "an entirely separate analysis" based on his review of industry and the defendants' profit margins. He also conducted a *Georgia-Pacific* analysis, relying prominently on such factors as the parties' relationship and the nature of the invention and the industry.

Notably, the Federal Circuit admonished "once again" that it "does not endorse *Georgia-Pacific* as setting forth a test for royalty calculations, but only as a list of admissible factors informing a reliable economic analysis." (Note: This line appears to be dicta in the opinion, authored by Chief Justice Randall Rader.)

Finally, the Federal Circuit noted (as the district court had) that the jury did not accept either expert's analysis, but awarded lump-sum damages equating to royalty rates in the range of 4% to 5%. Since this rate fell within the plaintiff's expert's alternative profit margins' analysis, the court found sufficient evidence for the award, which was not "outrageous or grossly excessive."

3. *Incorrect royalty base.* The expert's royalty base overstated damages by including sales related to the one patent that the district court, in its JMOL, found was not infringed. The defendants asked the court to apply the jury's effective royalty rate to a base that excluded the noninfringing sales.

But the Federal Circuit declined to reduce the award. For one, the defendants' argument was not timely in the appellate proceeding. Even if it had been, the verdict form did not clearly allocate a sum to the noninfringed patent, and the court could not simply "correct a damages figure by extrapolating a royalty rate from the jury's lump sum damages award and multiplying that royalty rate by a revised sales base." Accordingly, it affirmed the jury's $31 million award in full.

'Murky' Infringement Theory Undercuts Royalty Claim

Case name: *Enzo Biochem, Inc. v. Applera Corp.*
Citation: 2013 U.S. Dist. LEXIS 107990
Date of decision: Aug. 1, 2013
Country: US
State or Federal: Federal
State/Jurisdiction: Connecticut
Court: United States District Court
Type of action: Intellectual Property
Experts: Dr. Gregory Bell (plaintiffs); Brian Napper (defendants)
Judge: Arterton
SIC: 8731 Commercial Physical and Biological Research

In a patent dispute, the plaintiffs requested a retrial on damages, claiming a right to additional damages based on indirect infringement, but the defendants objected on double-dipping grounds. Encouraging someone to buy the infringing product is part of the actual sale of that product, they argued. The U.S. district court (D. Conn.) reviewed the parties' post-trial challenges to the jury verdict.

The plaintiffs (a global company and its wholly owned subsidiaries) were leaders in the field of molecular diagnostics and owned patents covering reagents (chemical substances that are added to chemical systems to bring about a chemical reaction) for labeling and testing of DNA. They claimed the defendants' manufacture, use, and sale of reagent products for DNA sequencing directly infringed one of their patents. There also was indirect infringement because the defendants "encouraged" their customers to use the accused reagent kits with the defendants' own line of DNA sequencing tools. "Encouraging" included providing technical support and software that facilitated the accused products' use in conjunction with the sequencing. The sequencing instruments themselves did not violate the plaintiffs' patents.

The defendants claimed: (1) there was no infringement; and (2) there was no indirect infringement. Considering the plaintiffs admitted the sequencing instruments themselves did not infringe, "there [could] be no separate inducement by the sale of the instruments beyond the sale of the reagent [products]."

At trial, both parties presented expert damages testimony. In terms of direct infringement, experts for both sides used the entire value of the reagent kits to establish a royalty base, which was $845 million. On cross-examination, the plaintiffs' expert explained he had obtained the number from the defendants' financial records and that he and the competing expert agreed on the same base. He also said that there was no need for apportionment since the protected technology underlying the reagent kits enabled the DNA sequencing, which was the "raison d'être" for the kits.

As to the royalty rate, the expert considered an agreement the plaintiffs had made with Yale University in 1981, that is, 14 years before the patent in suit actually issued and 10 years before the defendants introduced their products for DNA sequencing. This early contract specified a 7% rate applied to the reagent products, a 5% rate applied if the products were part of a diagnostic kit, and a 3% royalty applied if they were in the research kit. But as time went by, it became clear that there never was a sale of just reagent products. The only way they became available was in kit form. Consequently, the 3% rate was too low in the context of a hypothetical negotiation between the parties, the expert concluded.

The Yale agreement also gave the plaintiffs a right to sublicense its reagent kits "under the terms and conditions no greater than those acquired by [the plaintiffs]." The head of Yale's cooperative research office testified that he believed this meant charging a rate no less than the 3%—the minimum rate the plaintiffs would have to pay Yale: "Otherwise you have no incentive to sublicense because it costs you money to sublicense."

The plaintiffs' expert also identified later agreements between the defendants and third parties concerning the patented technology, which provided for higher royalty rates. The patented technology was central to driving up the reasonable royalty rate, he said.

The defendants argued that, under the Yale agreement, the plaintiffs would not be allowed to sublicense its reagent kits for more than 3%, given the language in the contract. Specifically, "terms and conditions no greater than those acquired by [the plaintiffs]" included the royalty rates the agreement specified, they argued.

The jury found the defendants liable for direct infringement related to the reagent products and awarded $48.6 million in reasonable royalty. But it awarded $0 damages for indirect infringement related to the sale of the defendants' DNA sequencing instruments. In post-trial motions, both parties objected to different parts of the award and requested a new trial on damages.

Risk of double dipping. The plaintiffs claimed a new trial was needed to determine additional damages stemming from the "induced infringement" by the sales of the sequencing tools. The defendants argued that the jury's award related to the sale of the reagents precluded damages related to the sale of the noninfringing instruments because it meant compensation for the same acts of infringement.

The court agreed with the defendants that additional compensation would have meant double dipping. The plaintiffs' theory as to infringement stemming from the sale of the instruments was a "murky issue" before and throughout the trial, it noted. In fact, during deliberations the jurors specifically asked for clarification as to the relationship between the sale of the reagent products and the sale of the noninfringing instruments that used the products. The court saw no reason to overturn the jury's $0 award, particularly since the plaintiffs wanted damages premised on the same acts of direct infringement.

Also, the plaintiffs' expert admitted there were noninfringing uses involving the sequencing instruments, and the defendants' expert plainly rejected an additional royalty. The plaintiff expert's proposed 4.5% royalty rate related to the sales of the defendants' sequencing tools was inappropriate because he drew on third-party agreements that directly covered the defendants' sequencing instruments, which was not the case here. The jury based its decision on common sense and evidence, the court concluded as it denied the plaintiffs' motion.

The defendants claimed, first, that the award violated the entire market value rule and, second, that the jury's use of a 6% reasonable royalty rate improperly exceeded the 3% kit rate that the plaintiffs' agreement with Yale specified.

The plaintiffs countered that there was sufficient evidence that the sales of the reagent kits formed the proper base for the reasonable royalty calculation.

As to the first argument, the court found the jury properly concluded it should apply its royalty rate to the $845 million base, considering that both experts used the same base, which included the entire value of the kits. Also the plaintiffs' expert had said that the patented technology in the kits enabled the DNA sequencing, which, in turn, was what the kits were meant to do. The jury learned that the technology was a "significant determinant of demand for the kits" and that the protected reagents in the kits were "a critical key component."

As to the 6% royalty rate, the jury had reason to consider the Yale agreement and other agreements the plaintiffs' expert mentioned in determining what royalty rate hypothetical negotiation between the parties would have generated. The plaintiffs' expert explained that, since the Yale agreement, any differentiation in rate between just the reagent products and the reagent products in kit form disappeared because the reagents now are available only in a kit. Therefore, a 3% rate in the context of negotiation between the litigants was too low. Further, testimony from the Yale research office explained why it did not make sense for the plaintiffs to sublicense their technology for a lesser rate than 3%. For all of these reasons, the court upheld the $48.6 million award for direct infringement.

Prior Standards Licenses Reflect Asserted Patents' 'Real-World' Valuation

Case name: *Ericsson Inc. v. D-Link Corp.*
Citation: 2013 U.S. Dist. LEXIS 71564
Date of decision: May 21, 2013
Country: US
State or Federal: Federal
State/Jurisdiction: Texas
Court: United States District Court
Type of action: Intellectual Property
Judge: John R. Bone (plaintiffs); unknown (defendants)
SIC: 4899 Communications Services, NEC (radio broadcasting operated by cab companies)

In a standards case involving wireless technology, the plaintiff alleged infringement of several patents covering two features of the IEEE 802.11n standard, which governs wireless networking transmission methods. Its damages expert derived his reasonable royalty from a per-unit royalty he calculated for each licensed product, but, in a *Daubert* challenge, the defendants in essence contended his opinion was inadmissible because he failed to apportion his proposed royalty base between accused and nonaccused features.

The plaintiff (two related entities) is a leading telecommunications technology company. In 2010, it sued the defendants, a gaggle of networking, electronic, and multinational computer companies, in federal court (E.D. Tex.), claiming they violated six patents of its 802.11 portfolio.

Its expert examined eight of the plaintiffs' previous 802.11 licenses with third parties that involved the claimed patents to determine a per-unit royalty, which he then applied to the defendants' accused products to calculate a reasonable royalty. The expert limited the revenue pool on two levels: He only took into account revenue from the licensing of the company's 802.11 portfolio, and he apportioned the 802.11 licensing revenue to "extract" the value that attached to nonasserted patents.

He further recognized that the six patents in suit did not make up the entirety of the company's portfolio, which includes 18 standard essential patents. Therefore, he "very conservatively assumed that [they] represent at least 50% of the total value of the [company's] 802.11 portfolio," he said, and reduced his per-unit royalty accordingly. The court's opinion states that he supported his 50% apportionment with some 20 pages of analysis but does not provide further detail.

His revenue base was not the market value of the end products, he stated, but the market value of the contribution of the patents at issue to the end products.

Claims of indirect and direct EMVR violations. The defendants objected to the expert's per-unit royalty. His damages model, they claimed, did not apportion his royalty base between the accused and nonaccused features. This lack of apportionment was an attempt "to side-step the requirements of the entire market value rule" (EMVR).

They further alleged it "squarely" violated EMVR because the accused features were only part of a chip set that was one of many components in the end products and they did not drive customer demand for the end products. In sum, the expert could not use the value of the end products but only the value of the chip sets, the smallest salable units that included the patented technology.

The plaintiff countered that the expert's calculation did not invoke EMVR. It rested solely on the number of units sold, not the price of the units sold. In standards licensing, a per-unit royalty based on the number of products sold was common, it pointed out. What's more, the damages model linked the hypothetical negotiation to real world evidence.

Apportionment. The court found that the expert's analysis included two kinds of apportionment that the defendants ignored. On one level, it limited revenue to the value of the plaintiff's 802.11 contribution. Each of the eight licenses undergirding the analysis covered only "the portion of the 802.11 standard the third party licensees believed was covered by [the plaintiff's] portfolio," the court noted. Although the defendants sought to downplay the significance of the licenses, they "reflect a real-world valuation." The licensees would not have paid for a license unless they believed the plaintiff's patents covered at least part of the standard, and they would not have paid for a portion of the standard the plaintiff's patents did not cover. Accordingly, the court said, "the money paid under these licenses represents the market's valuation of the 802.11 contributions of the [plaintiff's] patents."

The expert also reduced his per-unit royalty to 50% given that the plaintiff's six asserted patents were only a subset of its portfolio. In this regard, too, he made a "realistic and thorough attempt to apportion revenue to only the asserted patents," the court concluded, leaving challenges on his apportionment analysis to cross-examination.

EMVR. The court also rejected the defendants' argument that there was lack of proof that the patented features drove customer demand. Under the expert's analysis, the licensing revenue from the plaintiff's portfolio was attributable only to the value the patents added to the licensees' end products, not the end products as a whole. "It goes without saying that the licensees would not have paid value for the portions of the 802.11 standard unrelated to [plaintiff's] patents," the court reiterated.

Also important was that his analysis called for a per-unit royalty on all sales of accused products; as such the royalty rate remained constant regardless of the final sale price of the end product. "This," the court found, "further illustrates that [the expert] does not rely on the value of end products." Therefore, the proposed damages model did not implicate the EMVR.

In concluding, the court noted that the defendants raised an argument that the testimony was excludable because it did not consider the plaintiff's RAND obligation without briefing the issue. For all of these reasons, it denied their motion to exclude.

Court Rejects Expert's Regression Equation to Determine DLOM

Case name: *Estate of Koons v. Commissioner*
Citation: 2013 Tax Ct. Memo LEXIS 98
Date of decision: April 8, 2013
Country: US
State or Federal: Federal
State/Jurisdiction: Ohio
Court: United States Tax Court
Type of action: Estate and Gift Taxation
Experts: Mukesh Bajaj (petitioners); Francis X. Burns (respondent)
Judge: Morrison
SIC: 5962 Automatic Merchandise Machine Operators

In connection with a major asset sale, the decedent formed a limited liability company (LLC) and made a will under which he left the residue of his estate to a revocable trust. At the time of death, the trust owned a 50.50% total interest in the LLC, whose value was over $300 million. When the estate challenged the Internal Revenue's deficiency determination as to estate and generation-skipping transfer taxes, the primary issue was the valuation of the trust's interest in the LLC—which hinged on the magnitude of the applicable marketability discount (DLOM).

The decedent owned a company that was in the vending-machine business and claimed exclusive rights to selling Pepsi beverages in its territories. In 2004, the company agreed with PepsiCo. Inc. to sell its business to a Pepsi affiliate. For this purpose, the company, whose shareholders included the decedent and his four children, transferred all of its assets to a wholly owned subsidiary (the LLC) and the shareholders executed a stock purchase agreement (SPA) with the Pepsi affiliate. Among other things, the SPA specified that the LLC would sell all shares for approximately $340 million, plus working capital (the final purchase price was $352.4 million). Moreover, the LLC assumed certain environmental, health, and safety liabilities related to the company's Florida production facility; and it committed to own liquid assets with an aggregate fair market value of at least $10 million and maintain a positive net worth of at least $40 million until January 2012. Importantly, the four children's agreement to sell their company shares to the LLC was contingent on the latter's offer to redeem their varying membership interests.

By March 2005, the date of the decedent's death, all four children had accepted the redemption offer. At the end of April 2005, the redemptions closed, with the final payments occurring around July 2005. The decedent had contributed his membership interest in the LLC to a revocable trust established some 15 years earlier. He had amended the terms of the trust such that its beneficiaries were no longer the children, but the grandchildren, their lineal descendants and surviving spouses; shortly before his death, he instructed the trustees to vote in favor of amending the LLC's operating agreement such that it: (1) eliminated his children as permitted transferees of membership interests; (2) eliminated the board of advisors, which included his children; and (3) for the first 15 years of the LLC's operations, limited discretionary distributions per year to LLC members to 30% of the difference between distributable cash and income tax distributions.

Only weeks before the decedent died, in February 2005, one son wrote a letter calling the redemption offer "punitive" but expressing gratitude for the "exit vehicle" and stating that the children would "like to be gone." He said the operating agreement "guarantees litigation."

At the time of death, the revocable trust had a 50.50% total percentage interest in the LLC, resulting from a 46.94% voting interest and a 51.59% nonvoting interest. The redemption of the children's interests increased the percentage to 70.93%. The LLC's net asset value was about $317.9 million. At the beginning of 2006, it had over $200 million in highly liquid assets and owned two companies whose combined assets made up only 4% of its total assets.

Besides its interest in the LLC, which was held through the revocable trust, the estate had assets totaling over $26.6 million, which is the amount it reported on the estate tax return. The IRS issued notices to the estate initially claiming a deficiency in estate taxes of nearly $42.8 million and to the revocable trust for a deficiency in generation-skipping transfer tax of nearly $15.9 million.

The agency subsequently increased the deficiencies based on its determination that the trust's interest in the LLC at the time of death was worth over $148.5 million. The estate and the trust challenged the notices and petitioned the federal Tax Court for review. Both sides offered valuations from notable financial experts as to the trust's fair market value.

Gaping DLOM difference. The parties agreed that, assuming the trust had a 50.50% total interest in the LLC and the latter had a value of some $371.9 million, the trust's pro rata asset value was over $160.5 million. They further agreed that its actual value was less because of a lack of marketability but strongly disagreed over the size of the applicable marketability discount.

Estate and trust's expert. The petitioners' expert was Mukesh Bajaj, whose DLOM determination drew on his influential 2001 regression study of 88 companies. (See "Firm Value and Marketability Discounts," 27 *J. Corp. L.* 89 (2001)). There, he used an equation to explain the difference between the price of the publicly traded stock of a company and the price of the same type of stock of the same company sold privately pursuant to a restriction that the buyer must wait before reselling the shares. When Bajaj applied the equation to the trust's 50.50% interest in the LLC, he arrived at a 26.6% "initial marketability discount." But, he said, the differences between the trust's interest and the shares in the 88 companies required further adjustments. He added a second—4%—discount to account for certain limitations that applied to the LLC, including environmental obligations it had assumed under the SPA. Because the LLC was closely held, small, and unknown and selling an interest in it to persons who were not direct descendants required a 75% vote of its members, he applied a third—3%—discount and arrived at a 31.7% DLOM. As a result, he concluded the trust's interest equaled the pro rata net asset value of the LLC's assets minus 31.7%, yielding a value of approximately $110 million.

He also determined that there should be no control premium because the holder of the trust's interest only had a 46.94% voting power and as such had not enough control to obtain "private benefits." Even if the holder obtained a 70.42% voting interest following the redemption of the children's interests, there were no private benefits because the operating agreement and the SPA imposed restrictions on the LLC. He also saw no reason to apply a discount for lack of control.

Government's expert. The IRS's expert was Francis X. Burns. He, too, considered the 2001 Bajaj study but for various reasons declined to perform a regression analysis to predict the marketability discount. As he saw it, the equation resulted from a data set of companies that earned their profits mainly from active business operations; in contrast, the LLC had only two small ones. Also, the equation explained only one-third of the variation in the discounts in the ownership interests in the 88 companies from which Bajaj had generated the equation. Moreover, all 88 transactions involved ownership interests of less than 50.50%. And, the IRS expert said, the Bajaj equation systematically overestimated the relationship between block size and the valuation discount.

Instead, Burns found that a 5% to 10% DLOM was appropriate based on a number of critical factors. Most important, the risk that the redemptions would not go through was small, he found. On the other hand, the SPA imposed obligations on the LLC related to potential environmental, health, and safety liabilities; also, it was reasonable to assume that the LLC would make cash distributions, an owner of the revocable trust's interest would be able to force the LLC to distribute most of its assets once the redemptions closed, and most of the LLC's assets were liquid. For all these reasons, he decided a 7.5% DLOM would be a reasonable accommodation between a hypothetical seller and buyer.

Like the petitioners' expert, he concluded that neither a control premium nor a discount for lack of control was appropriate. Even though the voting interest at the time of death was only 46.94%, the redemption of the children's interests was reasonably foreseeable, he said. Consequently, the voting power would increase to 70.42%. At the same time, the LLC's major assets were cash, not operating assets, and it was unlikely that a controlling member of the LLC "could extract value above its pro-rata claim on company assets." On the other hand, that degree of voting power allowed the owner to control the LLC's board of managers.

Likelihood of redemption. The petitioners and their expert objected that Burns's low discount primarily resulted from the mistaken assumption that the redemption would occur and increase the voting interest of the owner of the trust's interest from 46.94% to 70.42%. Although each of the four children had signed a redemption offer before the decedent's death, the petitioners claimed these were not enforceable under applicable state law because they did not include vital terms, including the price at which the LLC would redeem the interests. Further, the son's February 2005 letter suggested that the children did not intend to sell their interests.

The court agreed that the question of whether the redemptions were likely was pivotal to the valuations. It disagreed with the petitioners and their expert on this point and other points and credited Burns's analysis. The redemption offers, the court said, expressly stated that the interests were redeemable at a price equal to each owner's share of the value of the LLC's assets; since most of the assets were cash, it was easy to establish their value and by extension the redemption price. A state court likely would have enforced the signed letters. Moreover, the LLC successfully could have sued any signer who tried to renege on the contract. What's more, because a critical aspect of the redemption offers was to remove the children from the ownership of the LLC, a court would have ordered specific performance.

The February 2005 letter equally suggested that the children did not want to remain owners of the company; "they wanted cash," said the court. At the same time, the LLC's managers wanted them removed as owners. Accordingly, both sides had incentives to effect the redemptions. The petitioners tried "to create a smokescreen of uncertainty around the redemptions which did not in fact exist as of the valuation date," concluded the court.

Burns's assumption that the owner of a 70.42% voting interest in the LLC could order the latter to distribute most of its assets also had traction with the court. Despite the SPA's provisions regarding liquid assets, it did not bar the LLC from distributing most of its assets. And even if the board of managers were reluctant to do so because the decedent had preferred that the LLC invest its assets in operating businesses after his death, the key was that hypothetical buyers and sellers of the trust's interest would proceed from the knowledge that the LLC could be forced to distribute most of its assets, the court pointed out. "A majority member who could force the LLC to distribute most of its assets would not sell its interest for less than the member's share of such a distribution," said the court.

In this case, if the LLC's total assets valued almost $318 million and it had to retain $40 million of the assets, per the SPA, it could distribute approximately $278 million to members. Assuming a 50.50% interest in the LLC, the holder could expect to receive about $140 million in a distribution. This amount, said the court, was the minimum sale price of the interest. Therefore, it rejected Bajaj's $110 million valuation and adopted Burns's—and the government's—$148.5 million valuation.

Balloon interest payments. A secondary issue concerned a $10.75 million loan the LLC had made to the revocable trust in February 2006 to pay estate and generation-skipping transfer taxes and for which the estate claimed an interest expense deduction of over $71.4 million. The terms of the loan provided that repayment would be in installments from 2024 through 2031—a deferment that caused the interest to swell and meant the estate would have to remain active throughout the repayment of the loan. Once more, the court agreed with the IRS's position and did not allow the deduction. There was no need to borrow the money because in 2006 the trust had a 70.42% voting interest in the LLC and the LLC had over $200 million in highly liquid assets. The trust had the power to force the LLC to make a pro rata distribution to its members, including the trust, said the court.

Court Accepts Cost Approach to Calculate Value of Lost Business

Case name: *Factory Mutual Insurance Co. v. Alon USA*
Citation: 2013 U.S. App. LEXIS 1481
Date of decision: Jan. 23, 2013
Country: US
State or Federal: Federal
State/Jurisdiction: 5th Circuit
Court: Court of Appeals
Type of action: Damages (incl. Lost Profits)
Experts: Leslie H. Miles (plaintiff); Dean Harris (defendants)
Judge: Prado

How to measure damages for a facility for which no market exists was one of the issues confronting the 5th Circuit Court of Appeals when it reviewed the district court's $3.8 million award to the plaintiff related to a destroyed waste treatment plant.

The defendants owned and operated an oil refinery in Texas that contained a third party's waste treatment plant. After an explosion destroyed the plant, its owner filed an insurance claim with the plaintiff and received payment of $6.1 million. Subsequently, the insurance company sued the oil refinery owners to recover damages, and the latter stipulated to liability. At a bench trial, both parties agreed that damages should be the fair market value (FMV) of the plant before the explosion but disagreed over how to determine FMV in this context.

The crux of the plaintiff's argument was that there was no market for the type of facility that existed before the accident that could provide a measure of value. Its industry expert stated that it would be "unwise" and "highly uncommon" to build a plant such as the one destroyed "completely out of used equipment." Therefore, it sought the adjusted replacement cost.

The defendants claimed they were only liable for the cost of the plant's components and that used versions of those were available from vendors.

Value of whole exceeds value of parts. Both sides presented damages experts. For his calculation, the plaintiff's appraiser considered the remaining life of the original plant at the time of the explosion. Without this adjustment to the replacement costs, he said, the plaintiff would receive a windfall. Since the original equipment was no longer available, he met with plant employees who were familiar with it, explained to them "what depreciation is made up of and how to calculate it," and adopted their estimate. This, he stated, was the method he had used in the past. He expressed surprise at the employees' "aggressive" estimate that the facility only had 65% of its remaining life, which he thought was low, considering his experience with various chemical processing plants. But having observed the employees' discussions, he believed that they competently applied the considerations (unstated) he had proposed and concluded the depreciation number was reliable.

He also considered statements from an employee who identified nearly three-quarters of the equipment that was at the plant and tried to obtain quotes from vendors regarding the price. The expert said that this was the type of information—estimates and opinions from others—experts reasonably rely on to solve valuation questions.

The plaintiff's industry expert spoke to the multiplier that should apply to the underlying cost figure to account for anticipated costs related to the construction, including installation, startup, overhead, and testing. There are different ways to look at multipliers, he said: either take a percentage of value, "say a hundred percent of cost increase," or think of it as two times the original amount. Also, multipliers were not ideal but appropriate here where there was no better information available. He initially recommended a 2.0 multiplier but later increased the figure to 2.5. In the past, multipliers ranging from 1.8 to 3.2 when building the type of plant that was at issue applied. Based on their experts' calculations, the plaintiff sought $6.1 million—or precisely the amount the plaintiffs had already paid out for lost value.

The calculation of the defendant's expert consisted of determining the cost of the plant's component parts. He admitted he did not account for installation, on-site engineering, or startup. Rather, he said, his damages figure covered equipment that was "sitting on the ground, not assembled." He noted that experts generally disfavor the use of multipliers "for their inaccuracy" and that they were only appropriate "for broad cost estimates." The use of a multiplier was inappropriate in this case, he concluded. Total damages were no more than $878,000.

The district court found that although there was a market for the components that made up the plant, there was none for the company's used waste treatment system. Since the market value of a fully operational plant was greater than the sum of the components, the measure of value was the adjusted replacement cost. It estimated that new equipment, including taxes and shipping, costs approximately $2.3 million. The court added 10% as a contingency. It then multiplied the combined amount by 2.25 and multiplied the result by 0.65 to account for the 35% depreciation the plaintiff's expert had proposed. It arrived at a total of $3.8 million in damages.

Expert's valuation bolsters claim. The defendants appealed on three grounds, stating the district court erred: (1) when it used replacement cost to determine the market value of the plant; (2) when it admitted the plaintiff's expert testimony regarding the 35% depreciation; and (3) when it used a 2.25 multiplier that lacked a factual basis. The Court of Appeals considered the objections in turn.

1. Replacement cost. Prior case law stood for the proposition that "evidence of replacement cost is no evidence of market value damages," the defendants claimed. The district court should have measured the plant's market value by pricing the individual components that were likely present at the facility before the accident.

At the outset, the appellate court noted that the defendants read a much broader meaning into the cited case, which concerned a totaled car and the plaintiff's attempt to use the insurance company's payment as proof of damages, than it supported. At most, that case held that an insurance payment was not sufficient evidence to prove damages. In this case, the Court of Appeals pointed out, the plaintiff offered much more proof when it "utilized the services of an appraiser to determine the value of [the facility]."

Also, the destroyed plant was not like a totaled car, whose market value emerges by looking at comparable sales in a specific geographic area. In this case, each facility had proprietary components, and the plant's underlying process was patented. Further, in their appeal, the defendants failed to address the finding that no market exists, insisting instead that their ability to price out components precluded the use of replacement cost as a measure of damages. The district court had discretion to consider the countervailing arguments, and its decision duly considered the labor, layout, and installation of the plant. Replacement cost was the appropriate measure of damages, the Court of Appeals stated.

2. *Inadmissible expert testimony.* Beyond relying on the employees' estimate as to how much life the plant had left before the explosion, the plaintiff's expert did nothing to calculate the depreciation, the defendants claimed. This uncritical adoption made his testimony inadmissible under Rule 703 of the Federal Rules of Evidence, which requires an expert to bring his professional judgment to the use of data he receives from external sources. The plaintiff countered that the expert had explained how he had arrived at the factors he had used to determine the plant's depreciated value.

The Court of Appeals agreed with the defendants that the depreciation aspect of the testimony was problematic. Although he "clearly articulated what depreciation means and how it is usually calculated," he did not describe the particular experience he brought to the process of evaluating the number the employees provided. At the same time, there was no way to verify whether they acted in accordance with his instructions. That said, the court continued, "insofar as he educated and interviewed [the employees], [the expert] did more than just repeat information gleaned from external sources." Also, he showed that he was familiar with appraising heavy industrial plants "broadly," if not the type of plant at issue.

Finally, it was important to consider what was "feasible," the court said. Although he could have developed a more accurate estimate "by inspecting records or the equipment itself," neither was available. He consulted one of the few sources of information to which he had access: the employees. Under the circumstances, the district court was in the best position to assess the admissibility of his testimony.

3. *Multiplier.* There was no basis for the plaintiff's proffered 2.5 multiplier and the district court's 2.25 figure, the defendants claimed.

The appellate court disagreed. There were few records to estimate the cost of rebuilding the plants, a situation which "counsels in favor of using a multiplier," it stated. The district court received two permissible views on multipliers and used one that was well within the range the experts proposed and that was consistent with experience as to those plants. For all these reasons, the Court of Appeals upheld the award.

Book Value Accurately Reflects FMV of Departing Partner's Interest

Case name: *Fancher v. Prudhome*
Citation: 2013 La. App. LEXIS 318
Date of decision: Feb. 27, 2013
Country: US
State or Federal: State
State/Jurisdiction: Louisiana
Court: Court of Appeals
Type of action: Judicial Dissolution (incl. Withdrawal, Buy Out)
Experts: Ben Woods (plaintiff); unknown (defendants)
Judge: Williams
SIC: 7359 Equipment Rental and Leasing, NEC (appliances; TVs, VCRs, and other consumer electronic equipment rental)

A withdrawing member of a limited liability company unsuccessfully appealed the trial court's decision to use the book value of the company's assets, rather than rely on his expert's going concern analysis, to capture the fair market value (FMV) of his share.

The plaintiff owned a one-third interest in the LLC. When he joined the company in 2008, he brought with him critical business from his earlier work as a consultant. When he fell out with the other two partners approximately one year later, he filed for withdrawal and a determination of the value of his interest. At that time, his contact was the company's primary source of business.

The trial court allowed the withdrawal as of May 2009, but the remaining issue was how to determine the FMV of his interest on that date. At trial, he presented expert testimony from a CPA, who based his valuation on company tax returns and year-end financial statements for 2008 and 2009.

'Exclusive source of business.' There were three ways to value a business—the income, asset, or market approach—the expert stated. The income, or discounted cash flow, method involved projecting future company earnings and applying a discount to arrive at the present value, he went on to say. In this case, he performed a going concern analysis, assuming the company would continue its operations, and computed an FMV of $2 million. Accordingly, the plaintiff's share was worth $666,666. The expert did not apply discounts.

But he also stated that the company's unadjusted book value was approximately $37,800 as of December 2008. He said he did not receive information about the assets the company owned on May 2009. To compute the adjusted, or fair market, value of the assets, he used estimates of the company's inventory and accounts receivable based on published IRS ratio data and arrived at a total value of $636,400.

The market approach required data of prior sales of comparable companies in the same industry, he noted.

The company's accountant also testified, saying he had prepared year-end financial statements and federal tax returns for the company for 2008, 2009, and 2010. In 2009, the company showed a loss of nearly $98,000 because of declining business in the second half of the year. At the same time, there was "a lot of money in the bank" in May 2009 and June 2009, he stated, which led him to recommend a salary increase for the remaining members.

The trial court rejected the income approach in this situation. Considering the plaintiff provided "almost the exclusive source of business" to the company, his leaving meant one could not assume the company's future cash flow. The market approach did not apply because the business was a small, closely held company whose profits depended on the skills of its members. Holding a minority interest in the company meant the plaintiff could not make business decisions nor require distributions, the court found. Also, his interest was not marketable "because its value was indistinguishable from plaintiff himself."

Therefore, the trial court determined, the book value of all company equity best reflected its FMV. Adopting the expert's $37,800 value, it found the plaintiff's share was worth approximately $12,500.

Incorrect use of minority discount? The plaintiff contested the valuation at the Louisiana Court of Appeals. The trial court erred because it failed to consider all of the company's assets at the time of the withdrawal. Specifically, the court incorrectly applied a minority discount and failed to take into account that, at the date of his withdrawal, the company's bank account showed an additional $500,000 in cash. At a minimum, the trial court should have credited his expert's testimony that the adjusted book value was $636,400.

The appellate court found no merit in the arguments. The trial court made the requisite factual findings before deciding on the asset approach. Although it discussed discounts when it described the nature of the plaintiff's interest in the company, it did not apply a discount when it used the book value. Even though the company accountant testified to there being "a lot of money in the bank" in May 2009, he did not say it was $500,000 precisely.

As to the adjusted book value, the appellate court pointed out that the trial court specifically noted that there was no evidence that the inventory amount the plaintiff's expert proposed was accurate considering the company leased most of its equipment and provided services. It did not need to keep an inventory of goods. Also, the expert failed to show that the IRS data corresponded to the company's actual account receivable. Accordingly, the trial court did not err in discrediting his adjusted book value. For all of these reasons, the appellate court upheld the $12,500 valuation of the plaintiff's share.

Unclear Valuation of Family Business Interests Requires Remand

Case name: *Farrell v. Farrell*
Citation: 2013 Ark. App. LEXIS 33
Date of decision: Jan. 23, 2013
Country: US
State or Federal: State
State/Jurisdiction: Arkansas
Court: Court of Appeals
Type of action: Malpractice (Appraisal)
Experts: Alan Stagg, John Langham (wife); Mike Johnson (husband)
Judge: Gladwin
SIC: 1241 Coal Mining Services (except site preparation and related construction activities on a contract basis)

The wife appealed the trial court's decision to assign all interest in the family businesses to the husband, which, she claimed, left her with a shortfall of $4.4 million.

The husband owned a 19.4% interest in two sets of closely held family businesses. The first entity included mining and land companies; the second was called the "Texas ventures." At trial, the husband requested that she receive one-half of all the business interests. However, she asked the court to value the companies and award money instead. Both parties presented experts to provide valuations.

As to the first entity, the wife's expert stated that, in general, the value of a coal mine lay in its reserves—the coal in the ground—and that the value of the particular company was $13.2 million. He did not value the Texas ventures, but the wife's CPA determined they were worth $3.2 million.

The husband provided several valuations for the first business, including one from the company's controller that stated book value (not specified). One of the experts cautioned that any valuation had to account for the costs of extracting the coal as well as bonding and permitting. (The opinion does not provide further details.)

The husband's CPA initially stated the Texas entities were worth $1.6 million, but said he revised his opinion after talking with the wife's CPA. Subsequently, he assigned a negative value of $536,000. If his client could sell these companies for anything, "he would do it in a heartbeat," he said.

Division of assets deviates from valuation. The trial court initially issued a letter opinion stating it had considered the various valuations, but noted some had deficiencies and limitations "too numerous for a lengthy discussion." The statute referred to "fair market value," the court said. But this standard was of no consequence, since the business was a closely held family corporation and the shares were not for sale. The issue was: What was "the value long term to the owners or to someone who would buy the entire operation?" As to the mining business, the court credited the wife's expert's valuation, but applied a 25% discount "for mining costs and contingencies." It determined a total value of $10.2 million. Adding this amount to the remainder of the valued estate, it found the total marital assets were worth $11.2 million and each party's share was $5.6 million.

The court gave numerous reasons not to make the wife a minority shareholder, among them the concern that the wife or her representative would impede business operations. Therefore, it awarded all the shares to the husband, along with the accompanying corporate debt, and the rest of the marital estate, valuing $979,000, to the wife. Because the court recognized that this resulted "in an extremely uneven division of assets" in the husband's favor, it also ordered the husband to pay the wife $10,000 per month for life in alimony. These payments would make the division equal.

The trial court did not incorporate its letter opinion in its subsequent divorce decree. Although it agreed with the wife that there had to be valuations for all assets, it did not expressly value the Texas ventures. In assessing the mining business, it again expressly adopted the valuation of the wife's expert. However, it lowered the value to $9.9 million, noting it had considered the business-related debt. At the same time, it reduced the wife's share of the marital estate to $964,000.

The wife asked the court to reconsider its unequal division. She requested that it place a value on the Texas businesses. She also stated that even if their value were zero, the marital estate would still be worth about $11 million. As it stood, her award was only 9.7% of the assets. To remedy the shortfall, the court should increase the monthly alimony payments to $33,000 or order the husband to pay a $4.4 million lump sum.

After the trial court denied the motion, she appealed, making ostensibly the same arguments. The husband, in turn, contended that the trial court in fact had valued the Texas entity. It had lumped all the values into its calculation and incorrectly attributed the supporting evidence to the wife's expert, whose $13.2 million valuation referred only to the mining business.

The Court of Appeals agreed with the wife that the lower court's decision was problematic. The opinion left it unclear whether the trial court meant to include the Texas entities in the valuation it adopted. Although the court's value for the first business was within the range of expert testimony, the law required it to state expressly the value of the property. And even though the court explained its decision to award all business interests to the husband in its letter opinion, it failed to incorporate the latter in the official divorce decree. This failure was in violation of the statute. On remand, the lower court also might reconsider its alimony award, the appellate court noted.

Court Rejects Expert's 'Irrelevant' Theory of Damages

Case name: *Gallagher & Co. v. Babcock*
Citation: 2012 U.S. App. LEXIS 25761
Date of decision: Dec. 18, 2012
Country: US
State or Federal: Federal
State/Jurisdiction: 5th Circuit
Court: United States Court of Appeals
Type of action: Contract
Experts: John Caraher (plaintiffs); unknown (defendants)
Judge: Higginbotham
SIC: 6411 Insurance Agents, Brokers, and Service (insurance agents and brokers)

The plaintiffs provided insurance services nationwide and sued the defendants for breach of employment agreements and lost profits damages. When they bought a defendant's consulting business in 2003, he agreed to work as vice president for their New Orleans office and brought on board former employees. All signed noncompete and nonsolicitation agreements, but broke them when leaving in late 2007 and early 2008 to work for one of the plaintiffs' competitors. Of the 19 clients who subsequently left the plaintiffs, 13 followed the defendants to their new workplace.

The jury heard damages testimony from the plaintiffs' CFO, who was also a CPA, and whom the district court (E.D. La.) qualified as an "expert in the field of accounting."

He presented two different damages estimates, proceeding from the premise that there is a direct link between the value of a business and the profits it will generate. First, he calculated lost profits based on what the fair selling price of the plaintiffs' partial book of business would have been if the defendants had tried to rebuy the client relationships the plaintiffs lost due to their breach. He considered the average annual profits the defendants earned during the three years prior to their departure, then subtracted the profits resulting from the clients that remained with the plaintiffs after the defendants left. The remainder, he said, was the annual average profits the plaintiffs earned from the lost clients. He multiplied that number by 6.5, the approximate number of years a client stayed with the plaintiffs, and calculated a total of $2.7 million in lost profits.

His second estimate focused on calculating the investment return the plaintiffs expected to obtain in 2003 when they bought the defendant's book of business. Given that the plaintiffs generally retained clients for 10 to 15 years following a merger, the expert considered expected profit margins over a 10-, 13-, and 15-year period. He assumed that profits from existing clients generally diminished over time as they gradually went elsewhere. He subtracted the plaintiffs' actual profits from 2003 to 2008 and the expected profits on the business after the defendants' departure. To project what profits the plaintiffs would have made after 2008 if there had been no breach, he used the 2007 profit margin for the New Orleans office, which was 38.9%.

He determined that over a 15-year period, lost profits would amount to $2.8 million; over a 13-year period, to $1.9 million; and over a 10-year period, to $1.3 million.

The jury form only asked for the amount the jury believed would "fairly and adequately" compensate the plaintiffs for the damages they incurred. It did not require the jury to identify the part of damages related to loss of clients to other brokers. Ultimately, the plaintiffs secured a $1.2 million lost profits award.

Six 'spooked' clients. The defendants contested the outcome in the 5th Circuit Court of Appeals, challenging primarily the expert's second approach for several reasons:

- He should have based his calculation on the amount of net profits the competitor actually earned from the 13 clients who followed the defendants to their new employer, instead of the amount of profits the plaintiffs expected to earn from these clients;
- He based his calculation on the 2007 profit margin of the New Orleans office, which was 38.9%, instead of the much lower 2008 rate, which was 13.1%;
- He used the plaintiffs' historical client retention rates, instead of the lower actual rates after the defendants' departure; and
- His calculation "reduced" the lost-profit projection to clients who left the plaintiffs after the breach without considering that the group of 19 was not the same as the group of 13 clients who switched to the defendants.

The plaintiffs countered that, in general, the amount of profits plaintiffs lose need not equal the profits defendants make as a result of the breach. Also, the expert did not use the 2008 profit margin or post-retention rate because the defendants' wrongdoing deflated the numbers. As to the six clients who went elsewhere, the defendants' breach "spooked" them in that they may have been afraid of being drawn into the litigation. Therefore, the defendants were responsible for the loss of business from all clients who left the plaintiffs.

Based on the $1.2 million figure, the Court of Appeals found that the jury likely adopted the expert's 10-year calculation in his second estimate, with some downward adjustments. Therefore, the defendants' critique of that calculation was appropriate.

But the appellate court quickly disposed of the defendants' first few arguments, finding that if the plaintiffs are able to obtain greater profits absent a breach than the defendants actually do owing to the breach, they have a right to those larger profits. It also agreed that the 13.1% profit margin rate and post-departure retention rate "likely" did not reflect what the plaintiffs would have made in the absence of a breach.

However, the court said with emphasis, the defendants' remaining argument revealed a critical flaw in the expert's methodology. "The group of clients who *chose to leave* is not the same as the group of clients *who followed the defendants*" to their new employer. The expert himself testified that the plaintiffs expected to lose clients every year, but provided no explanation why these six went to other competitors after the defendants had left. To say these clients feared "the specter of litigation" was "too speculative and conjectural."

The defendants' breach was not leaving the plaintiffs, but accepting work from clients who went with them; therefore, they were not responsible for the other lost clients. Finding the lower court erred when it admitted the expert's "irrelevant" theory of damages, the Court of Appeals vacated the $1.2 million award and remanded for further proceedings.

Court Affirms FMV Determination for S Corp Medical Practice

Case name: *Gentile v. Gentile*
Citation: 2013 Ohio App. LEXIS 1251
Date of decision: April 4, 2013
Country: US
State or Federal: State
State/Jurisdiction: Ohio
Court: Court of Appeals
Type of action: Marital Dissolution
Experts: Bernard Agin (wife); Steve Steer (husband)
Judge: Kilbane

In appealing the fair market value determination of his medical practice, the husband claimed that the trial court erred when it included goodwill as a divisible asset and that its conclusion had no support in the record.

The husband, a successful plastic surgeon, was the sole owner of a medical practice that had a main office and two smaller offices. In addition, he had two personal service contracts with two aesthetic laser companies. Both the husband and wife retained experts to compute the value of the practice—one of numerous areas of contention.

Gaps and inconsistencies. At trial, at the end of 2011, the husband testified that he earned approximately $143,500 per annum from the practice but also had income from the service contracts. The latter income, he said, went into his personal accounts because these proceeds were not related to his practice but were personal payments to him. Various official court documents revealed inconsistent statements as to his income. For example, in a document from October 2011, he stated his income as $455,000 per year. He admitted that his tax returns indicated his gross income in 2007 was about $1.1 million, in contrast to $673,000 in 2008 and $564,000 in 2009.

He also stated that the corporation repaid substantial loans to him arising out of the purchase of equipment and expenses. He admitted that his corporate receipts book contained at least a six-month gap and that he had taken "at least a couple thousand" from the practice's cash proceeds.

Experts for both parties used the net asset approach to determine the business's fair market value. The husband's expert said he considered financial information from the practice, including depreciation schedules, payables, long-term debts, and equipment values. Further, he researched the values of comparable practices and visited the main office. And he considered depreciation expenses, tax effect of the income, receivables, which he put at 30%, and the value of inventory on hand. In his computation, he made several deductions related to the $220,000 the practice owed to the husband, a $67,650 bill for website development, a $40,000 debt to another company, as well as taxes. He determined there was no value for the practice's goodwill and concluded the FMV was $16,300. (Elsewhere the opinion states the value as $16,500.)

On cross-examination, the husband's expert acknowledged that financial data for plastic surgeries suggested a global upward trend in performance. He also believed the husband's income had increased from 2007 to 2008. He admitted he had not investigated whether the husband voluntarily understated his income during the divorce proceedings or had hidden assets. Similarly, regarding the value of equipment, he did not procure an independent valuation but used the figures the husband provided.

Moreover, he admitted that, although the husband had told him that there were no corporate distributions in 2010 and 2011, he knew the husband received payment in 2010. He further acknowledged that he excluded the husband's consulting income from the laser companies, and finally he stated that the IRS would consider the family's lifestyle in its determination of whether there had been full disclosure of all reportable income.

The husband's accountant also testified, verifying that the business was an S corporation. In 2010, it had gross receipts of nearly $1.1 million and listed deductions of $404,000 and net income of $155,000. The corporation paid some of the husband's expenses, which either were charged to it or reclassified as personal distributions to him.

The wife's expert served both to critique the rivaling opinion and undertake a valuation. One area of his criticism related to the deductions the other expert made for loans and debts. While the husband's expert listed the $220,000 loan as a corporate liability, he should have considered it an asset for the sole shareholder, that is, the husband. As for the $40,000, it was a three-year debt that the creditor had not tried to collect. It was a mistake not to assign a value for goodwill, the wife's expert said. The Goodwill Registry, an accepted standard, provided a value for the type of practice at issue, which was $171,000, he concluded.

He also noted that the husband realized or collected about 70% of his receivables, not 30% as the husband's expert claimed. Moreover, his conversations with the wife and former employees of the husband showed the practice took in some $200,000 in cash each year that did not appear on the books. When he combined these findings with the assets of the practice, the wife's expert calculated the business's total assets amounted to nearly $694,000.

After deducting for liabilities, he concluded the FMV of the practice was $679,000. But he also stated that if one excluded the imputed unreported additional cash revenue, the FMV was $486,000.

The trial court's valuation found pros and cons as to both computations. Regarding the $220,000 loan, the court subtracted that sum from the value of the practice but included it as an additional asset of the parties. It agreed with the wife's expert that the $40,000 debt was not a true liability considering that in three years the creditor had made no attempt to collect it. The court credited the wife's expert regarding the value of goodwill but dismissed that expert's claim of there being $200,000 annually in unreported cash.

The court found the practice had $333,000 in assets, $171,000 in goodwill, $204,000 in debt, and $73,000 in liabilities. Accordingly, the total value was approximately $227,000, a figure roughly in the middle of the experts' valuations.

In appealing the divorce decree to the Court of Appeals of Ohio, both parties objected to the value the trial court had assigned to the practice. The husband specifically challenged the inclusion of goodwill as a divisible asset. The reviewing court briskly rejected the challenge. In deriving its calculations, the trial court carefully considered the evidence on record, the appellate court concluded, and it upheld the FMV determination of the practice.

NY Court Ratifies DLOM in Fair Value of Real Estate Companies

Case name: *Giaimo v. Vitale*
Citation: 2012 N.Y. App. Div. LEXIS 8706
Date of decision: Dec. 20, 2012 (slip op.)
Country: US
State or Federal: State
State/Jurisdiction: New York
Court: Court of Appeals
Type of action: Dissenting Shareholder
Experts: Z. Christopher Mercer (petitioner); Joan Lipton and Jeffery Baliban (respondent)
Judge: Panel
SIC: 6513 Operators of Apartment Buildings

A brother and sister held roughly equal shares in two companies that owned 19 Manhattan residential properties. When they couldn't agree on managing the company, the brother claimed shareholder oppression and sought judicial dissolution; the company, through the sister, elected to buy his shares.

To determine the statutory fair value of his interest, the court appointed a special referee who, after an extensive hearing, published his findings in a 180-page report. Both parties accepted the value he had determined for the corporations' properties under the net asset value (NAV) approach, but disagreed with aspects of his valuation of the companies. Specifically, agreeing with the dissenting shareholder's expert, he declined to apply a discount for lack of marketability (DLOM). However, disagreeing with both sides' experts, he did apply a present value discount for built-in capital gains (BIG) tax liability to the corporations' realty assets, assuming a 10-year holding period. In response, the parties asked the New York Supreme Court (trial court) for review of his findings on discounts. (The court's opinion does not discuss any of the amounts at issue.)

New York courts should consider the illiquidity of the shares at issue, the court noted. In the leading case, *Friedman v. Beway Realty*, 87 N.Y.2d 161 (1995) (available at *BVLaw*), the Court of Appeals upheld the application of an "unmarketability discount" in fair value proceedings involving a real estate holding company. The referee's attempt to distinguish *Beway* from this case was not persuasive, the court found. But even though it disagreed with his reasoning, the court affirmed the referee's finding based on the facts of the case: The record showed a limited availability of similar properties, which made it likely that a buyer would purchase the assets through the corporation.

It also adopted his present-value BIG discount, rejecting the parties' respective arguments—that it should be dollar-for-dollar (the company) or zero (the dissenting shareholder). (For a complete digest of the opinion, including the court's reasoning on the discounts and leading cases, see the July 2011 *Business Valuation Update*.)

Difference in marketability exists. On appeal, both parties in essence reiterated their earlier arguments regarding New York law.

DLOM. Beway and similar cases addressing valuation of shares in real estate holding companies required the application of DLOM, the company maintained. Based on the build-up method and restricted stock and other studies, its expert determined an applicable DLOM range of 8% to 30% and recommended 20% for this case.

The shareholder asserted that there was no evidence that the corporate shares were less marketable than the underlying real estate assets. Moreover, in a prior case, *Vick v. Albert*, 47 A.D.3d 482 (1st Dept. 2008) (available at *BVLaw*), the court specifically declined to apply DLOM to a real estate partnership. Because there should be no DLOM, the company's expert's calculation was of no consequence.

The appellate court affirmed the lower court's finding that *Vick* did not govern the case. But, it said, the lower court erred "in assessing that the marketability of the corporations' real property assets was exactly the same as the marketability of the corporations' shares." Notwithstanding shared factors, corporate ownership of the real estate entails risks that outright ownership does not. These risks and the costs of liquidation require consideration, the appellate court found. Because neither the lower court nor the referee broached the issue of how much of a DLOM to apply and because it had the record in front of it, the appellate court decided that a 16% rate against the corporations' assets was appropriate. "We find that the build up method … best captures the DLOM applicable in this particular case," it concluded.

BIG. Like the lower court, the appellate court rejected both sides' arguments. New York law recognizes "that embedded capital gains taxes in assets held by C corporations will affect what a hypothetical willing purchaser … will pay for the corporate stock," the court stated. On the other hand, a 100% discount implies there would be an immediate liquidation of the acquired assets, a scenario that contradicts the basic assumption underlying the fair value standard, "that the business will continue as an ongoing concern."

The lower court's reduction of BIG to present value, assuming a 10-year holding period, on the other hand, "appropriately adjusts for embedded capital gains taxes that will not be paid until some time in the future," the appellate court concluded and affirmed the finding.

Community Deserves Profits From Separate Business Investment

Case name: *Goldfarb v. Yelton*
Citation: 2013 Cal. App. Unpubl. LEXIS 4629
Date of decision: June 27, 2013
Country: US
State or Federal: State
State/Jurisdiction: California
Court: Court of Appeals
Type of action: Marital Dissolution
Experts: Dana Grigg (wife); Michael Thompson (husband); Sally White (court-appointed)
Judge: Lambden

A recent appeal in a California divorce case considered whether there was any community interest in the proceeds from the sale of stock during marriage of a company the husband had formed before marriage and what the appropriate method was for apportioning business profits.

Two years before marriage in 1982, the husband, with a partner, founded an agricultural biotech company and bought 400,000 shares of common stock for $4,000. He conceived and developed the company's business plan, arranged for two third-party investments—via stock purchases—and recruited scientific talent. From the beginning and for the first two years of his marriage, he was responsible for managing the company by serving as president, CEO, and chairman of the board. As he continued to implement his strategy and attract new investments during the marriage, it grew substantially; after about five years it took a product to market that proved highly successful. For five or six years, he worked more than five days a week but gradually surrendered control to a designated successor, who had joined the company a year after the husband's marriage and was at the center of a successful change in business plan. The husband also held a controlling interest in the company and was the highest compensated officer or director, receiving $92,000 in 1985. In July 1986, the company undertook an initial public offering (IPO). By 1988, the husband sold all of the stock, netting over $3 million.

Two methods of apportionment. Under California law, when community endeavor increases the value of a separate property business, it is necessary to "quantify the contributions of the separate capital and community effort" to ensure the community receives adequate compensation. "Accordingly, courts must apportion profits derived from community effort to the community, and profits derived from separate capital are apportioned to separate property." Courts have used two approaches to apportion business profits: (1) under the *Pereira* method, they allocate a fair return to the separate property investment and the balance of the increased value to community property;

(2) under the *Van Camp* method, they determine the reasonable value of the community's services, allocate it to community property, and designate the remainder as separate property. Broadly speaking, *Pereira* applies when business profits are the result of the community's efforts. *Van Camp* comes into play when the community is "more than minimally involved in a separate business, yet the business profits accrued are attributed to the character of a separate asset."

Driving force or passive investor? At divorce, the parties presented experts to assess the husband's role in the company to determine to what extent the community contributed to the business's profits, suggest the appropriate apportionment method, and present a valuation of the founder's stock at the time of the marriage.

According to the husband's expert, the company's 1986 IPO prospectus suggested that it was the co-founder, not the husband, who, in 1981, recruited the company's scientific advisory board, which, in turn, attracted accomplished scientists to it. Also, given the husband's young age, investors did not consider him the "primary attraction, and probably expected to replace him with a more mature executive." Instead, they trusted the co-founder's reputation, the advisory board members, and the research team. He claimed the husband's successor deserved primary credit for securing certain financing and making the company profitable after the husband resigned.

He also proposed that this case called for the *Van Camp* rather than the *Pereira* approach because the business was scientific in character and the husband had no scientific skills, did not work as a scientist, and had "very limited" management, sales, finance, and other relevant experience.

In terms of the stock valuation, he stated that the most appropriate indicator of the stock's value at the date of marriage was the price a third-party investor paid for the company's preferred stock at the end of 1981, two months before the marriage. Specifically, it paid $1.50 per share for Series B preferred stock but later exchanged five of those shares for one share of series C preferred stock; this reverse split, the expert said, increased the value to $7.50 at the date of marriage. He added that "a company like this is either going to hit a home run, or they're not going to be worth anything. So the distinction between preferred and common [stock] really only is a small distinction."

Factoring in long-term interest, he estimated the husband's stock was worth over $5.3 million on the date of sale. Since this amount was higher than the actual proceeds, there was no community interest under either apportionment method, he stated.

The wife's expert "did not offer much of any opinion" about the husband's compensation in the trial court's words. He suggested that approximately 12% of separate funds and 85% of community funds accounted for the purchase price of the stock in the husband's name but provided no evidence. He contended that using the third investor's stock purchase as an indicator of the fair market value of the founder's stock was improper because it differed from the stock the husband owned. Further, the transaction was not an arm's-length sale since the investor was not a disinterested party but had strategic reasons for buying it.

Third expert weighs in. The court decided it needed assistance and appointed its own expert to review the material and analysis the husband's expert had provided, as well as perform a compensation survey of the adequacy of the husband's pay at the company.

As to the husband's role, this expert noted that the husband founded the company, worked there, invested his own and family money, brought in outside investors, and, as president and chairman of the board, was integral to the company. Also, she thought that, at the time of marriage, the company was still in startup mode and not "fully operational," going through rounds of financing and cultivating vital business contacts. For these reasons, she believed *Pereira* rather than *Van Camp* should apply.

In terms of compensation, she stated that, if the court were to use the *Van Camp* approach, the community had been undercompensated by a total present value of $473,253.

Regarding the stock value, she agreed that the founder's stock was not equal to the preferred stock the third-party investor bought since the former did not afford voting rights or preferences. Quoting a 1986 pre-IPO prospectus, she said that historically, under the company's 1981 stock option plan, the company granted stock at much lower exercise prices than the $7.50 the husband's expert claimed. "The exercise price of each stock option granted on the Option Plan must be at least equal to the fair market value of the underlying shares on the date of grant." Exercise prices ranged from $0.39 to $1.53 per option, starting from 1981 through May 1986. For mid-May 1986, vested and exercised options averaged $0.39 per share; during the fiscal year ending September 1983, the exercise price was $0.30 per share, and the following year it ranged from $0.25 to $0.30 per share. Further, she found that in 1982-1983, the company repurchased 50,000 shares of common stock at $0.30 per share.

Accordingly, she concluded that the value of the founder's common stock at the date of marriage was $0.39 per share and the total value of the husband's stock was $156,000. Applying an interest rate equal to the 10-year Treasury bond yield, she determined the value of the stock that represented separate property was almost $275,400.

The court's expert acknowledged that, at the relevant time, the company did not make any money, lost substantial amounts for the first few years, and "maybe didn't have any value whatsoever." What counted, in her opinion, was that the board of directors then set a value that it believed was a fair market value. How it arrived at a value, however, was not clear to her.

In response, the husband's expert insisted that the 1981 third-party investor's acquisition of preferred stock was the best indicator of the husband's stock value. Even if the latter theoretically had a lower value, he said, it was wrong to ignore that transaction and not "quantify the value of the supposed preferences given these preferred shares." Also, the company's stock option grants were not arm's-length transactions, he said, since there was no public market for the common shares at the relevant period. Moreover, he stated with emphasis, the language in the prospectus "was *not* truthful; it was common 'boilerplate' used at the time to avoid employee taxable income when options were exercised." Like other startups, the company then did not obtain a third-party appraisal "in order to give its Board the freedom to price stock options as it saw fit," he said.

The trial court said the record showed the husband "had a serious and major impact on" the company's success during the marriage and applied the *Pereira* method of apportionment. He was in charge from inception, and the designated successor did not even join the company until a year after the marriage; even then he was only a vice president responsible for marketing and only assumed CEO responsibilities at the end of 1985, three years after the marriage. On the date of marriage, the company was "by no means" self-sustaining; it only sent a product to market in 1984 and did not turn a profit until 1986.

In deciding on the value of the husband's stock, the court credited its appointed expert, noting that the 1981 stock option plan required that each option have at least the fair market value of the underlying shares, that employees in fact received options with an exercise price ranging between $0.39 and $1.53 per share, and that $0.39 was the average price for shares exercised through May 15, 1986. Based on the court expert's recommendation, it adopted $0.39. Consequently, it concluded that of the approximately $3 million in sale proceeds almost $2.8 million was community property.

'Chief contributing factor' in company's success. The husband appealed, in essence claiming the trial court erred both in its choice of apportionment method and its stock valuation. The wife cross-appealed for unrelated reasons. The California Court of Appeals considered the two arguments in turn.

1. Apportionment method. The husband said there was not a "scintilla" of evidence that supported the court's decision to use the *Pereira* method for apportioning proceeds between community and separate property. The *Van Camp* approach was appropriate because the record made it clear that during the marriage the husband was not the principal reason for the company's growth and attendant profit. And it would be the proper measure of community allocation if there were an adjustment based on the undercompensation the court's expert claimed as to the value of the husband's services.

The appellate court found the argument problematic. For one, it assumed *Pereira* only applied if he was "principally" responsible for company growth following the marriage. But case law did not indicate that others could not also be involved in the successful business efforts. According to the appellate court, the issue was whether his efforts were "a very significant reason for the company's profitability." Also, the husband overstated the significance of factors that favored his position, relying on assertions of his expert regarding the importance of the co-founder, the advisory board, and the designated successor that either had no support in the documents he cited or no support at all. In sum, there was ample evidence to conclude that he was the "chief contributing factor" in the company's success.

2. Stock value. The husband argued the trial court improperly adopted its expert's determination that the stock was worth only $0.39 per share at the date of marriage, the husband argued; however, the expert did not in fact value the stock but simply relied on company pre-IPO statements regarding its stock option plan. Therefore, as a matter of law, there was no valuation that calculated the fair market value of the stock.

The fair market value determination may rely on the "use of recent sales of the unlisted stock, which were made in good faith and at arm's length, within a reasonable period either before or after the valuation date," the husband stated. This was the method his expert used and which the court should have considered.

The appellate court viewed the issue differently. Although the husband did not expressly claim that the pre-IPO document misstated anything, he "ultimately argues that the court could not rely on [the company's] own representation of fair market value in the stock option plan," it said. But the husband failed to cite authority that the trial court could not rely on its expert's determination and the bases for it. There was no question of law here, it stated. Further, despite the husband's contention that the court's expert based her valuation on conjecture, her testimony showed that she considered his expert's valuation, the differences in the nature of the stock, and the state of the company at the date of marriage. The trial court had discretion to disbelieve the statements from the husband's expert that the stock option exercise prices were too low to reflect fair market value.

For all of these reasons, the Court of Appeals affirmed the trial court's decision to apportion most of the stock sale proceeds to the community.

Expert's Loss-of-Use Computation Holds Up on Appeal

Case name: *Great Lakes Business Trust v. M/T Orange Sun*
Citation: 2013 U.S. App. LEXIS 8689
Date of decision: April 30, 2013
Country: US
State or Federal: Federal
State/Jurisdiction: New York
Court: United States Court of Appeals
Type of action: Damages (incl. Lost Profits)
Experts: Samuel Goldfarb (plaintiffs); Louis Magnan (defendants)
Judge: Panel

In March last year, a federal court in New York awarded the plaintiffs over $11.7 million for the loss of use of their dredge, a unique—in size and capability—backhoe excavator, after the defendants' ocean-going cargo vessel had rammed it. The defendants subsequently appealed.

In 2008, an allision (which the appellate court defines as "a collision between a moving vessel and a stationary object") involving the defendants' vessel and the plaintiffs' dredge put the excavator out of use for 194 days due to extensive repairs. In addition, there was reduced use during an approximately 24-day startup period. The defendants admitted liability and paid between $5 million and $6 million to settle the matter. But the plaintiffs pursued consequential damages, including loss of use or lost profits. The main issues at a three-day bench trial were: (1) whether the plaintiffs proved their damages claim with reasonable certainty; and, if so, (2) what was the period of loss?

Both sides presented damages testimony. The most impactful factors for the calculation of the plaintiffs' expert were that there was a strong national and international market for the type of dredging the plaintiff's machinery could perform and that the dredge posted a 92% utilization rate for the 85 days before the accident and was able to sustain that rate after it resumed activity up to the trial date. Also, in early 2007, another dredge that was the only serious competitor was lost at sea. At the time of the allision, the plaintiffs' dredge was working on two contracts the U.S. Army Corps of Engineers had awarded to the plaintiffs as part of its New York Harbor Project. Because it was in repairs when the plaintiffs won a third contract, they had to employ less-capable dredges.

The expert performed a "contribution margin analysis" to compute losses on a per-day basis and also determined the revenue lost during the startup period when the dredge worked at less than full capacity. By his calculation, damages amounted to $11,736,645 and broke down as follows:

- $58,843 per day @ 92.19% = $54,248 x 194 days = approximately $10.5 million for repair period, plus
- $54,248 for 24.3 days = $1.318 million less $105,633 in startup profits = approximately $1.2 million for startup period.

The defendants' expert proposed zero lost profits damages.

The court found the plaintiffs proved that there was a "robust" national and international market for the type of work the dredge could perform. It credited the plaintiff's expert's methodology and adopted his repair period and utilization rate. In conclusion, it accepted his damages figure in full. (Find an extended discussion of the district court's decision and the opinion in *BV Update* and at *BVLaw*.)

The defendants appealed to the Court of Appeals of the 2nd Circuit, which affirmed in a non-precedential summary order "[f]or substantially the reasons stated by the District Court in its thorough and well-reasoned opinion." Contrary to the defendants' claim, the appellate court said, the plaintiffs did not have to show that the dredge had lost a specific contract to recover damages. Under the district court's factual finding, there was "an active market," both in New York City and other areas in the country, at the time of the accident, immediately afterward, and into the foreseeable future. Accordingly, the lower court properly determined that, "if not" for the allision, the dredge would have found work or moved on sooner to additional work.

As for the lost profits calculation, the defendants argued the 92% utilization rate was the result of an unusually busy period in the dredge's work history. It created a distorted basis for damages. The appellate court disagreed, stating that the lower court considered the market in which the dredge would have operated but for the incident. And it properly rejected the testimony from the defendants' expert. His lower rate had excluded certain contracts and failed to account for the increase in use since 2007. "We see no reason to disturb these findings," the appellate court concluded.

Court's Discount Rates Don't Overvalue Business Interests

Case name: *Halliday v Halliday*
Citation: 2012 Tenn. App. LEXIS 856
Date of decision: Dec. 6, 2012
Country: US
State or Federal: State
State/Jurisdiction: Tennessee
Court: Court of Appeals
Type of action: Marital Dissolution
Experts: Robert E. Yates, II (husband); David C. Wood (wife)
Judge: Dinkins
SIC: 6500 Real Estate

The husband held varying interests in six companies that owned real estate. At divorce, he and the wife presented expert testimony about the value of the businesses and his interest in each. Both experts used the net asset method, but disagreed on the appropriateness and percentage of discounts for lack of control (DLOC) and lack of marketability (DLOM).

When is a DLOM appropriate? The husband's expert explained that, generally speaking, the DLOC recognized that a minority interest was worth less "than a proportionate share of the value of the total entity" and applied to partnerships in which a "partner did not enjoy the full rights of ownership." A discount for lack of marketability dealt with how quickly an owner could turn his interest into cash "if [he] chooses to sell," the expert said.

He reviewed case law that addressed discounts, "various factors" (unspecified) that related to the husband's business interests, and a study from a national business valuation firm. Ultimately he found that a 36.1% DLOM was appropriate for five of the six entities.

The wife's expert said that the DLOC measured "the decremental effect on an equity investment's pro rata value" when an owner did not have complete control over "the entity's financial operation and legal decisions." It was contingent on the size of the interest and whether there were "multiple types of ownership." He believed applying a DLOM was inappropriate "if the business is not for sale." This was the situation for all businesses here, he concluded.

Turning to the particulars, the experts and the trial court made the following valuations:

1. His expert valued the husband's 100% interest in a subchapter S corporation at $430,000, to which he applied a 36.1% DLOM to arrive at $275,500. The wife's expert determined his interest was nearly $680,000, using no DLOM. Both agreed that a DLOC was not appropriate given the husband's complete ownership.

The trial court valued the business at $560,000, with no discount.

2. The husband owned a 50% interest in a general partnership that his expert valued at $4.2 million. Applying a 35% DLOC and 36.1% DLOM, he calculated a $880,000 value for the husband's interest.

The wife's expert agreed to the total value, but found the husband's interest was $1.9 million, applying only an 8.46% DLOC.

The court valued the husband's interest at $1.8 million, using a 15% DLOC, but no DLOM.

3. The husband also held a 50% interest in a limited liability corporation, which his expert valued at over $3.1 million. Applying a 35% DLOC and 36.1% DLOM, he determined his interest was worth $640,000. The wife's expert agreed as to the value of the company, but applied only an 8.46% DLOC and found the husband's interest totaled $1.4 million.

The court valued the husband's interest at $1.3 million, using a 15% DLOC.

4. Moreover, the husband held a 17.5% interest in a partnership whose asset was a 16-acre tract of undeveloped land near a highway connector. His expert valued the company at $400,000 and the husband's interest at $28,000, applying a 37.7% DLOC and a 36.1% DLOM. Her expert determined the husband's interest was worth $61,500, applying a 12.2% DLOC.

The court adopted the specified value of the real property, $400,000, and valued his interest at over $70,000. After applying a 20% DLOC and a 10% DLOM, it arrived at a total value of $50,000.

5. The husband owned a 33.33% interest in a company his expert valued at $565,000; applying a 37.7% DLOC and a 36.1% DLOM, he determined the husband's interest was $75,000. The wife's expert valued the company at $620,000. Applying an 11.48% DLOC, he concluded the husband's interest was worth $183,000.

The court, using a 15% DLOC and 10% DLOM, determined the husband's interest was $144.000.

6. The husband's expert valued his 50% interest in a sixth business at negative $83,000, but the wife's expert calculated it was worth $52,000. Neither applied discounts.

The court found the business in general had a negative value, and the husband's "negative value [was] $83,000."

Undersized discounts, oversized alimony award? The trial court then used the calculated values to determine a $1.1 million alimony in solido award for the wife, which the husband contested in the Tennessee Court of Appeals. It resulted from the lower court's overvaluation of his business interests, he argued. The court should have applied larger discounts.

The appellate court affirmed the valuations with little discussion. It noted that the trial court applied a discount for lack of control where the husband did not have a 100% interest in the company and a discount for lack of marketability as "appropriate." The lower court's amounts of discounts fell within the range of the experts' testimonies.

Did Patent Expert 'Supercharge' the 25% Rule of Thumb?

Case name: *Halo Electronics, Inc. v. Pulse Electronics, Inc.*
Citation: 2012 U.S. Dist. LEXIS 153334
Date of decision: Oct. 25, 2012
Country: US
State or Federal: State
State/Jurisdiction: Nevada
Court: United States District Court
Type of action: Intellectual Property
Experts: John Hanson (plaintiff); unknown (defendants)
Judge: Pro
SIC: 3677

In 2007, the plaintiff, a manufacturer of communication magnetics, sued the defendants, suppliers of global electronics components, for patent infringement. Its claims included direct as well as induced infringement due to the nature of the defendants' business. Specifically, in addition to making direct sales into the U.S., the defendants also sold infringing components to customers outside the country. In turn, several of these customers sold the parts to manufacturers that incorporated them into end products—such as servers, computers, switchers, and routers—for resale back into the U.S.

Before trial, the defendants moved to dismiss the claims of induced infringement related to any accused products that third parties imported into the U.S. They also tried to limit the damages period by claiming they didn't have notice of infringement until 2003 (rather than 2002, as the plaintiff asserted). After losing both motions, the defendants challenged the plaintiff's expert under *Daubert*, claiming the expert's calculation of a royalty base and royalty rate were unreliable.

As a preliminary matter, the defendant argued the expert incorrectly incorporated non-U.S. sales into his calculations and incorrectly calculated losses beginning in 2002. Since the court had already determined these issues in its pretrial rulings, however, it declined to relitigate the defendants' claims in the guise of a *Daubert* motion and held that the expert used the correct damages period and relevant sales.

Estimation 'necessary' for indirect sales. As for determining the indirect sales (i.e., the amount of accused products that the defendant sold to third parties for U.S. import), neither the defendants nor their customers kept any specific records of these sales except for general investment disclosures. Given this lack of statistical evidence, the expert approximated indirect sales as follows:

- He identified generally the type of end products that could contain the accused products (such as servers, computers, etc.);

- He used the worldwide sales figures for these end products to determine their percentage of sales into the U.S.; and

- He looked at the worldwide sales figures for the defendants' third-party sellers, focused primarily on those to whom the defendants sold a high percentage of the infringing products.

Based on this evidence, the expert assumed that at least 30% of the defendant's infringing components became incorporated into end products that were eventually imported into the U.S. This 30% royalty base was reasonable, he believed, given that a prior licensing agreement between the plaintiff and one of the defendants' competitors suggested a higher rate. In addition, the plaintiff's vice president estimated the rate could be higher.

To determine a reasonable royalty, the expert applied each of the 15 *Georgia-Pacific* factors in a hypothetical negotiation between the parties, ultimately estimating a range of 10% to 15%. In the context of this analysis, he considered a patent use license that the defendants inherited after acquiring another company, asserting the license covered comparable technology to the patents in suit.

In their *Daubert* motion, the defendants objected to the expert's use of general statistical evidence to calculate his royalty base. The court disagreed, however. Given the lack of direct sales evidence in this case, the expert "narrowed his inquiry to the end-products that could contain the accused products" and specifically tailored his estimate "to the potential amount of the defendants' accused products imported back into the U.S.," the court stated and admitted the expert's 30% royalty base.

As for his royalty rate, the defendants claimed it represented a "supercharged" 50% version of the recently discredited 25% rule of thumb. (See *Uniloc USA, Inc. v. Microsoft Corp.*, 632 F.3d 1292 (Fed. Cir. 2011) available at *BVLaw*.) In essence, the expert obtained his 10%-to-15% range simply by dividing the plaintiff's and defendants' profit margins in half and using the two figures as the upper and lower limits for the range. Moreover, the "acquired" license on which he also relied was not sufficiently comparable because the defendants did not negotiate it.

Once again, the court disagreed with both arguments. Finding no evidence that the expert proceeded from a "50% rule of thumb" assumption, it admitted his royalty rate analysis based on a proper application of the *Georgia-Pacific* factors. Also, it found the acquired licensing agreement was relevant, because, following the acquisition, the defendants paid royalties under it and renegotiated its terms. Overall, the district court declined to exclude any part of the expert's analysis and directed the parties to proceed to trial.

Editor's note: According to the plaintiff's attorneys, on November 26, the jury found the defendants liable for infringement and awarded $1.5 million. See www.fr.com/HALO-Electronics/.

Does Use of Full Product Line Data Invalidate Damages Formulation?

Case name: *Hark'n Technologies, Inc. v. Crossover Symmetry*
Citation: 2013 U.S. Dist. LEXIS 24644
Date of decision: Feb. 21, 2013
Country: US
State or Federal: Federal
State/Jurisdiction: Utah
Court: United States District Court
Type of action: Intellectual Property
Experts: Mark E. Elwood (plaintiff); unknown (defendants)
Judge: Stewart

In a trade dress infringement suit, the defendants challenged the qualifications of the plaintiff's damages expert and the completeness and methodology of his lost profits determination. Both parties retained experts to compute the damages the plaintiff allegedly sustained from the defendants' sale of infringing sheathed, elastic resistance bands.

'He didn't do the actual math.' The plaintiff's expert had nearly 30 years of experience as an auditor, financial controller, and CPA. He did not provide an actual damages figure because, he said, he lacked the defendants' most recent sales figures. Instead he set out a "simple" formula with which to calculate damages. He assumed that "but for" the defendants' wrongful conduct, all of their sales would have gone to the plaintiff. The calculation required multiplying the average sales price of the plaintiff's product by the number of infringing units the defendants sold and subsequently multiplying the result by the incremental profit percentage on the plaintiff's products.

The latter, he found, was instrumental in arriving at a damages figure. To compute it, he first determined the plaintiff's fixed and variable costs, noting that only variable costs affected the production of additional units and, therefore, the profit arising from the sale of those units. As he recognized that variable costs might be difficult to identify, he "judgmentally" added 2.5%, to arrive at a total variable cost percentage. This adjustment, he said, ensured "that the variable profit rate is not overstated." Moreover, he relied on data for the plaintiff's entire product line rather than that for the products at issue.

The defendants' expert agreed with the formula as such because it was generally applicable in trade dress infringement cases. But instead of assuming the plaintiff would have obtained all of the infringing sales the defendants made, he proposed factors (unspecified) to reduce the number of lost sales.

In their pretrial *Daubert* motion, the defendants claimed the plaintiff's expert's testimony was inadmissible for three reasons: (1) he lacked experience in the requisite roles or fields; (2) his expert report was incomplete; and (3) his data and methodology related to the incremental profit percentage were unreliable. The court considered the objections in that order.

1. *Experience.* The expert lacked experience in valuing intellectual property or analyzing lost profits in infringement cases and, therefore, was unqualified, the defendants alleged.

The court disagreed. Given his nearly 30 years of working in the accounting industry, he was capable of analyzing the plaintiff's financial data and making conclusions about profitability. His report did not attempt to value intellectual property but to identify a method for determining lost profits from the sale of goods.

2. *Incomplete report.* Because the expert's report failed to provide an actual damages figure and did not include a methodology, it violated Rule 26 of the Federal Rules of Civil Procedure, which requires a complete statement, the defendants claimed. As to the damages figure, even if he lacked the most recent sales data, he should have calculated damages through 2011. In terms of the methodology, he did not explain the origin of his formula or provide evidence that it had undergone peer review or was accepted in the industry.

The plaintiff countered that a damages figure based on incomplete sales data would have been inaccurate. Concerning the methodology, the defendants' expert had proposed the same formula, albeit with adjustments. Also, its expert's assumption that all the infringing sales would have gone to the plaintiff was valid; in any event, as the fact-finder, the jury, not the expert, would decide the number of sales the plaintiff lost due to infringement. The court agreed that the plaintiff's expert had information to make a preliminary damages calculation. But his failure to do so did not prejudice the defendants. Although he "did not do the actual math," he provided the formula with which the defendants could have performed the calculation themselves. Also, the defendants' objection to the methodology had no traction considering their expert used the same formula.

3. *Incremental profit percentage.* The defendants also attacked the reliability of the expert's methodology for developing the incremental profit percentage. Both his variable cost estimate and his use of the entire product line, instead of the products at issue, made the computed figure unreliable.

The plaintiff argued the incremental profitability for the infringed products actually was higher than the number the expert proposed and the aggregation of data, in fact, was a windfall to the defendants, as its evidence at trial would show.

The court found the plaintiff failed to support its assertion of a windfall and noted that aspects of the expert's computation of the incremental profit percentage were indeed "troubling." On the one hand, the defendants' concerns about the variable cost estimate went to the weight of the testimony and were the subject of cross-examination and competing expert testimony.

But using the wrong data as the basis for the damages conclusion represents "a more serious deficiency." Different products generate different profitability, depending on cost and the manufacturer's strategy, and "lumping all of the costs together" may distort the profitability number of the products at issue, the court noted. What's more, here, the incremental profit percentage was a "key component" of the expert's damages formulation and "the primary reason" his testimony would be helpful to the jury. Ultimately, however, the court decided this issue also went more toward weight than admissibility and should be challenged at trial.

In admitting the testimony, the court dismissed the plaintiff's suggestion that the expert might discuss evidence at trial that he did not include in his report to support the argument that the use of the full product line did not prejudice the defendants. "This will not be permitted," the court said, because it would deny the defendants the opportunity to prepare.

Damages Expert Can Assume But Not Opine as to Market Share

Case name: *Illinois Tool Works, Inc. v. MOC Products Co, Inc.*
Citation: 2012 U.S. Dist. LEXIS 116471
Date of decision: August 17, 2012
Country: US
State or Federal: Federal
State/Jurisdiction: California
Court: United States District Court
Type of action: Intellectual Property
Experts: Christopher Barry (plaintiff)
Judge: Sammartino
SIC: 5013 Motor Vehicle Supplies and New Parts

The plaintiff, which owns patented technology for cleaning automotive intake systems, filed infringement claims against the defendant, which sells products for automotive maintenance and cleaning. Before trial in federal district court, the defendant challenged the plaintiff's expert under *Daubert*—in particular, his first and primary report regarding lost profits and his second, supplemental report on a reasonable royalty.

Lost profits turned on market share theory. As a preliminary matter, the defendant claimed the expert's lost profits calculations were unreliable—in particular, his calculations that the plaintiff held a 50% market share of the patented products, and thus, "but for" the defendant's infringement, the plaintiff would have been entitled to 50% of its net sales. The expert based his 50% market share assumption on discussions with the plaintiff's employees, including its director of technology. In addition, his report stated that, to his knowledge, the plaintiff and defendant were the only manufacturers of the patented product and that in a "but for" scenario, it was likely that all of the defendant's customers would have bought the plaintiff's product. However, to keep his assumptions (and calculations) "conservative," he elected to adopt a 50%, rather than a 100%, market share estimate.

At the same time, in his report as well as his deposition, the expert conceded that he did not conduct any additional research or investigation to evaluate the 50% market share estimate. Under these circumstances, "not one single iota of economic evidence" supported the expert's estimate, the defendant claimed, and asked the court to strike his entire lost profits opinion.

After hearing all the evidence, the court "was inclined to agree" with the defendant, but only to a degree. That is, to the extent the expert's lost profits damages testimony was "based on an underlying factual assumption that [the plaintiff] held 50% of the market share" and "assuming that the information provided to the damages expert by the technical experts is supported by proper factual predicates," his testimony was admissible, the court held. The defendant was free to challenge the expert's assumption on cross-examination and through the testimony of its own experts.

At the same time, the expert could not state an *opinion* as to the plaintiff's market share. "Bare reliance on a 'rough estimate'" by the plaintiff's technology director did not rise to the level of reliability "that *Daubert* envisioned," the court observed and permitted the expert to testify to only those portions of his lost profits damages arising from the factual assumption of a 50% market share.

Accommodating an aberrant pricing scheme. In its second challenge, the defendant claimed the expert "inflated" his lost profits calculations by using the defendant's selling price, but then subtracting the *plaintiff's* costs. "Commingling" or "mixing and matching" the inputs was improper and warranted exclusion, it said, particularly since the defendant charged a price that was 30% higher than the plaintiff did for the patented products.

In his report, the expert explained that he used the defendant's average sale price with the plaintiff's costs "to reflect [the defendant's] market pricing and channel mix, but as manufactured under [the plaintiff's] cost structure." This was also the way he "did it in virtually every case," he said. Moreover, additional evidence suggested the defendant may have manipulated its pricing structure for related products to boost sales of the patented product, creating an aberration the expert sought to accommodate in his mixed/matched inputs.

In general, the measure of lost profits is the difference between the patent owner's cost of production and the price at which it would have sold the product, absent the defendant's infringement, the court explained. However, estimating the two variables of "cost" and "price" can be done in "any number of ways." In this case, the court did not find any case law supporting the expert's methodology—but neither did it find any discrediting his choice of variables. As a result, his calculations were admissible, the court ruled, subject to "vigorous" cross-examination at trial.

The defendant's third and final challenge went to the expert's supplemental report, which he disclosed eight months after his initial lost profits report. Not only was the second report untimely, the defendant claimed, but it was also prejudicial because it introduced "a new theory of calculating damages" (i.e., a reasonable royalty analysis) and should be disallowed. The plaintiff defended the report by saying it was an appropriate and timely, supplemental response to the defendant's challenge of its main theory of damages (i.e., lost profits).

The court "doubted the veracity" of this defense. Nevertheless (and without specifying why the plaintiff's expert might have failed to disclose his reasonable royalty analysis within the original discovery deadlines), the court permitted the expert to present this alternative theory of damages at trial, subject to the plaintiff making him available for deposition by the defendant and assuming all costs.

Glaring Unfamiliarity With Patent Law Disqualifies Expert

Case name: *Info-Hold, Inc. v. Muzak LLC*
Citation: 2013 U.S. Dist. LEXIS 117953
Date of decision: Aug. 20, 2013
Country: US
State or Federal: Federal
State/Jurisdiction: Ohio
Court: United States District Court
Type of action: Intellectual Property
Experts: Robert L. White (plaintiff); David Paris (defendant)
Judge: Black
SIC: 7389 Miscellaneous Business Services (bail bonding)

Daubert is a forgiving standard when it comes to the admission of expert testimony. When a party does succeed in excluding an expert, it is likely to be because the expert's opinion is irrelevant or his or her methodology unreliable, or both. Exclusion based on the expert's lack of qualifications is less common, which makes a recent patent infringement case in which the court found that the damages expert failed all the *Daubert* requirements most noteworthy.

The plaintiff was a production company that recorded on-hold messages and developed a patented system for remote control of the message delivery system. The defendant provided music programming to businesses and purported to hold the most extensive program catalog in the industry. The plaintiff filed suit (S.D. Ohio), accusing the defendant of direct, contributory, and induced infringement and offered expert testimony as to a reasonable royalty. In a pretrial motion, the defendant argued that the expert was inadmissible under *Daubert;* also, because the plaintiff would be unable to prove damages without that testimony, the court should dismiss the action.

Invoking the discredited 25% rule. The plaintiff's expert had done tax and audit work for some 15 years for the plaintiff. However, he had no prior experience or exposure to patent cases and patent law. For example, he did not know about the *Georgia-Pacific* factors or about patent licenses and he was unaware of the Federal Circuit's 2011 *Uniloc* decision in which the court repudiated the 25% rule of thumb (*Uniloc USA, Inc. v. Microsoft Corp.*, 632 F.3d 1292 (Fed. Cir. 2011)) (available at *BVLaw*). To educate himself, he said he reviewed two Federal Circuit cases, from 1996 and 1983, respectively, and he read a treatise by Alexander Poltorak, a scholar, writer, and commentator on intellectual property issues.

For his reasonable royalty calculation, the expert said he considered a 2009 settlement agreement and a license linked to the company's CEO. But in his deposition he admitted the agreement was irrelevant because it came about in 2009, one year after any hypothetical negotiation would have taken place. He also claimed that he considered the franchise royalty rates of 10% of the defendant's billings for music service that appeared in a document on the Securities and Exchange Commission website. But he admitted that he did not rely on published royalty rate standards by industry. He conceded that one of the cases he had mentioned was "not pertinent" since it did not concern the same industry and was decided long before any hypothetical negotiation would have taken place.

Ultimately, he admitted that all of this evidence was inconsequential as far as his royalty rate determination was concerned.

Instead, he used the 25% rule as a starting point to get to a 15% royalty rate on which he based his *Georgia-Pacific* analysis. He described this approach as an "alternative method" to calculate reasonable royalty damages, but he did not provide another methodology that would lead him to the 15% royalty rate. Finally, he stated that the "appropriate royalty base is comprised of all the revenue generated by [the defendant] on related client sales" and thus included revenue from collateral sales in the royalty rate.

He based his calculation on the information and assumptions the plaintiff and its attorney wanted him to use, without independent analysis. Moreover, he used data from the defendant's expert's report without performing his own investigation or verification.

Multiple deficiencies. Under *Daubert,* the court found the testimony inadmissible on numerous grounds. The expert's total acceptance of the discredited 25% rule of thumb demonstrated his utter lack of understanding of the issues that dominate patent cases and the legal principles that underlie a patent damages calculation, it said. Without this knowledge, he was unqualified to assist the jury in understanding the evidence or deciding facts in dispute.

His reasonable royalty calculation also was irrelevant and unreliable since he simply applied an improper legal standard—the 25% rule of thumb—rather than developed it based on the facts of the case. His attempt to justify the use of the 25% rule by calling it a starting point to which he then applied the legitimate *Georgia-Pacific* factors ran afoul of *Uniloc,* said the court. There, the Federal Circuit expressly stated that a calculation that started with a fundamentally flawed premise resulted in fundamentally flawed conclusions even if there were adjustments to the premise based on legitimate considerations. And, although the expert called this approach an "alternate method," he did not set forth another approach with which to calculate the royalty rate and did not deviate from the 15% rate he obtained using the 25% rule of thumb. In fact, he admitted that all the other evidence he mentioned—the prior settlement agreement, the two cases, and the treatise—were not "pertinent" to his computation.

What's more, he was unaware of the entire market value rule (EMVR) and simply used all the revenue the defendant generated from collateral sales as the royalty base. Accordingly, he provided no analysis of the facts to determine whether "the patented feature creates the basis for customer demand," as EMVR required.

Finally, he did not test any of the information or assumptions the plaintiff gave him, which makes his opinion "more advocacy for Plaintiff than expert testimony." At the same time, his relying on the facts and numbers that appeared in the rival expert's report without testing that information also was improper under the Federal Rules of Evidence.

All these flaws rendered the expert's testimony inadmissible, concluded the court. At the same time, it found that the plaintiff had no right to damages. But for procedural reasons, it declined to dismiss the case just yet.

Discount Rate Analysis Requires Expert's Subjective Judgments

Case name: *Jack Tyler Engineering Co. v. Colfax Corp.*
Citation: 2013 U.S. Dist. LEXIS 51603
Date of decision: April 10, 2013
Country: US
State or Federal: Federal
State/Jurisdiction: Tennessee
Court: United States District Court
Type of action: Contract
Experts: Dr. Ralph Scott (plaintiff); Z. Christopher Mercer (defendant)
Judge: Cleland

In a contract dispute, the plaintiff's expert used the discounted cash flow method (DCF) to calculate lost profits. In its *Daubert* motion, the defendant took no issue with the method as such, but contended the expert's reliance on numerous unfounded assumptions rendered the analysis unreliable.

In 2001, the plaintiff received exclusive distributorship rights to sell the defendant's industrial and construction products in designated parts of the country. Although the defendant promised a contract by the end of 2004, the parties never formalized their arrangement. Instead, in October 2007, the defendant unilaterally terminated the agreement. In 2010, the plaintiff sued in federal court (W.D. Tenn.), alleging a violation of the state's Repurchase of Terminated Franchise Inventory Act, breach of contract, and unjust enrichment.

The plaintiff retained an economist to determine lost profits, and the defendant presented a credentialed business valuator to rebut the testimony. Both parties filed pretrial *Daubert* challenges.

No variable costs, no mitigation. The plaintiff's expert used the DCF method to compute damages. He calculated the plaintiff's base annual sales of the defendant's products based on the plaintiff's average sales of those products from 2004 though 2006, while it was a distributor. At his deposition, he explained he developed his discount rate of 6.0% by applying a 2.5% real rate of return, 2.35% equity risk premium, 3.1% size premium, and a -2% adjustment for analyzing only "one product line instead of a business valuation to account for possible real growth." He identified the sources (not specified in the opinion) that were the basis for his analysis and explained certain judgments he made based on his experience to arrive at the final numbers.

Because the plaintiff's owner and CEO told him that there were no variable costs in connection with the sale of the defendant's products, he did not include them in his analysis. But in his deposition, he acknowledged that these costs could exist. In the same vein, based on his conversations with the owner, he assumed the plaintiff did not mitigate. "I have no way of knowing what [the plaintiff's] mitigation opportunities are," he said, adding that the owner was the expert in this regard.

He calculated lost profits into perpetuity. Specifically, his analysis began with a year-by-year calculation of past losses for five years, followed by a year-by-year calculation of projected future losses for 15 years, and an assignment of a capitalized terminal value. By calculating damages into perpetuity, he maintained, his analysis assumed the defendant's product line was part of a business that could go on forever. Even if the plaintiff's owner could not stay in the company indefinitely, he could sell the company; in case of sale, the plaintiff's value would be contingent on the product lines it had at that time. Moreover, the expert used ex-post discounting, that is, he discounted damages to the date of judgment. (The opinion does not give the expert's damages figure.)

The defendant's rebuttal expert disagreed with several aspects of this analysis. For one, he preferred ex-ante discounting, discounting damages to the date of the breach; this approach was appropriate for businesses with an uneven earnings history or historical losses. His review of the plaintiff's profit history since 2000 indicated significant losses and financial problems, he said.

He also criticized the competing expert's failure to include variable costs and mitigation in his analysis. His experience showed that it was "unreasonable" to assume that all of the plaintiff's costs related to the sale of the defendant's products were fixed. As he saw it, "there are marginal costs associated with marginal activity." As for mitigation, the plaintiff showed an increase in gross sales in 2007, which suggested that it was successful in mitigating any damages resulting from the defendant's conduct.

Further, the plaintiff's expert failed to prepare the requisite analysis of "local, regional or national economic outlooks as of the date of termination or subsequent to termination." These aspects, the rebuttal expert stated, were important considerations when computing lost profits; for this reason, his opinion included a discussion of industry trends as well as the defendant's performance. As he put it, the plaintiff's expert made no "attempt to ascertain why [the plaintiff] was experiencing sharply declining sales of the defendant's products and sharply lower gross margins throughout the business."

Speculative base for annual sales figure. The defendant agreed that the DCF approach to calculating lost profits was valid but claimed the plaintiff's expert used numerous baseless assumptions that made his analysis unreliable. The court considered the objections in turn.

The expert's base annual sales figure was speculation because he did not analyze the plaintiff's historic overall profitability or consider sales of the defendant's products outside the three-year period, the defendant argued.

The court noted the plaintiff's expert did not arrive at the base annual sales "by merely guessing" but used "reasonable facts." Specifically, he derived the figure from the plaintiff's actual sales of the defendant's products. As for his not analyzing the plaintiff's overall sales or considering additional sales, the defendant did not show that the DCF method required this type of analysis. Concerns that the calculation failed to include all the relevant facts were best addressed at trial.

Two, the discount rate was speculative, the defendant stated. The expert failed to consider all of the relevant risk factors and external market forces. He did not probe into the plaintiff's financial health, the potential loss of a product line, an industry premium, industry trends, the defendant's sales trends, and future economic conditions.

The court saw it differently. The expert developed his 6.0% discount factor from identified source material and judgments based on his expertise. Choosing a discount rate is not a "purely mechanical calculation," the court pointed out; rather, it "is a decision that requires a number of subjective judgments." Whether the analysis incorrectly disregarded additional considerations was a matter of weight, not admissibility.

Three, the analysis failed to include variable costs and account for mitigation, the defendant objected. The expert's admission at his deposition that there could be variable costs was proof that he should have taken those costs into account. Also, the plaintiff "clearly" mitigated its damages considering it earned higher profits in 2007 and 2008, after the defendant's termination of the contract, rather than earlier when it was still a distributor.

The court noted that, the defendant's objections notwithstanding, it did not identify variable costs or mitigation opportunities. Its claims were just as speculative, resting on nothing more than the expert's statement as to variable costs and the plaintiff's realization of higher profits following the termination of the contract. Even if not based on substantial evidence, the plaintiff's expert's assumptions were not "so unrealistic and contradictory as to suggest bad faith."

Four, there was no justification for calculating lost profits into perpetuity. The defendant claimed the expert improperly assumed that the parties would be doing business into eternity, even though manufacturers frequently terminated sales agreements with representatives. Also, the defendant had a right to end the contract upon giving proper notice, and it would have done so much before the 20-year period following the contract's end.

The court pointed out that the defendant's own expert agreed that "when determining the value of a portion of a business, the discounted cash flow method provides a forecast for a finite number of years at which point a terminal value is calculated." The defendant did not really contest the methodology but only the length of time for calculating lost profits, the court concluded.

Ex-ante versus ex-post discounting. For its part, the plaintiff agreed it was appropriate to present the rebuttal expert's report to the jury, barring three topics.

First, the plaintiff objected to the rebuttal expert's ex-ante discounting. It claimed that the Federal Circuit had "soundly rejected" this methodology, citing *Energy Capital Corp. v. United States,* 302 F.3d 1314 (Fed. Cir. 2002) (available at *BVLaw*).

The court disagreed. For one, *Energy Capital* did not hold that ex-ante discounting always required exclusion under Rule 702. In any event, that case did not explain why ex-ante discounting was an inappropriate methodology for calculating lost profits in all circumstances. Other authority made it clear that the answer as to what type of discounting applied depended on "the facts of the case," the court noted. Here, the rebuttal expert reasoned that the method was appropriate because of the plaintiff's history of losses and financial trouble. This method was reliable, the court found.

Second, the plaintiff argued, the rebuttal expert's criticism of its expert's failure to consider variable costs and mitigation was unwarranted. That he, himself, could not identify any such costs or prove mitigation made his critique speculative. What's more, the plaintiff expert's decision was firmly "rooted in the evidence of the record."

The court stated the rebuttal expert based his critique on the defendant's tax returns and his own expertise, both of which provided a reliable basis for his argument.

Finally, the plaintiff objected to the rebuttal expert's discussion of industry trends and the defendant's economic performance. These statements, it argued, were not rebutting the testimony of its expert; rather, they were an attempt to bolster the defendant's anticipated theory that it terminated the contract for cause, based on the plaintiff's low sales.

The court also dismissed this argument, finding the expert's discussion of these points was relevant to his critique of the competing opinion. And even if its only purpose were to strengthen the defendant's defense, this testimony was admissible because it was relevant, the court concluded. In sum, the court denied both parties' *Daubert* motions.

Patent Experts Have Limited Latitude to Comply With New Damages Standards

Case name: *Joyce v. Armstrong Teasdale, LLP (I)*
Citation: 2012 U.S. Dist. LEXIS 114847
Date of decision: August 15, 2012
Country: US
State or Federal: Federal
State/Jurisdiction: Missouri
Court: United States District Court
Type of action: Intellectual Property
Experts: Stephen Weeks (plaintiff)
Judge: Jackson
SIC: 7372

Case name: *Joyce v. Armstrong Teasdale, LLP (II)*
Citation: 2012 U.S. Dist. LEXIS 137905
Date of decision: Sept. 26, 2012
Country: US
State or Federal: Federal
State/Jurisdiction: Missouri
Court: United States District Court
Type of action: Intellectual Property
Experts: Stephen Weeks (plaintiff)
Judge: Jackson
SIC: 7372

The first decision in this malpractice case concerns the defendant's *Daubert* motion against the plaintiff's damages expert; the second involves a follow-up motion to dismiss all claims based on the same alleged flaws in the expert evidence.

Attorney advises patentee *and* his company. The large Missouri law firm Armstrong Teasdale represented the plaintiff, James Joyce, in his application for a patent related to software firewall technology. In 2000, the same attorneys also helped the plaintiff form a company, with his wife and another couple, and prepared an exclusive, royalty-free license for the company to sell the patented software for its remaining life.

Several years later, the plaintiff divorced and gave up a 50% interest in the patent to his wife; their co-owned company also terminated his employment and reduced his ownership interest to 7%. The plaintiff sued the law firm for malpractice, alleging the attorneys acted in conflict with his interest by representing the company and its economic exploitation of the firewall technology. Had this conflict not existed, he said, his former company's exclusive license would have included a minimum royalty or "anti-shelving" provision in the event he lost his employment.

The plaintiff retained a damages expert to assess the value of the patent as of the trial (2009). Applying a relief from royalty approach, the expert estimated the amount of licensing fees that the plaintiff's firewall software would have generated in the computer security industry but for the defendant's malpractice. Even though the industry was "quite competitive," he believed that 10% of existing security products could use the patented technology. Assuming that major licensees "aggressively" pursued this potential, another 10% of the products would actually use the software, resulting in a net royalty base of 1% of the entire market.

The risk that the patent would achieve such penetration amounted to 30%, he said—a "moderate" risk, given the industry condition and competition. This 30% "risk factor" was also the discount rate, he explained, which incorporated both the discount to present value as well as the risk of market failure or displacement of the technology. The expert also estimated that the patent would achieve commercialization by the end of 2010, with a five-year "ramp-up" period in which it would penetrate an additional 20% of the market annually, remaining at this utilization rate until the patent expired in 2020.

Finally, the expert looked at computer software licenses from general industry sources and derived a reasonable royalty rate of 10%. Applying all of his estimates to the entire computer security products market—which was expected to generate revenues of $13.5 billion in 2009 and annual growth rates of 5% to 9%—he believed the plaintiff's patent had a present value of $37 million.

Post-valuation case law tightens standards. In its *Daubert* motion, the defendant criticized the expert's methods and conclusions on several grounds. First, in valuing the patent, the expert did not account for the 50% ownership interest now belonging to the plaintiff's ex-wife and the exclusive licensing rights belonging to his former company.

More importantly, the expert based his market segmentation and penetration estimates on generalizations about the computer security products industry without any quantitative analysis to demonstrate how those rates would be reasonable as compared to related technologies. For instance, in his deposition, the expert admitted that he did not "calculate" his segmentation and penetration rates so much as base them on "his experience." This speculation rendered his opinions inadmissible, the defendant argued, citing *IP Innovation LLC v. Red Hat, Inc.*, 705 F. Supp. 2d 687 (E.D. Tex. 2010) (available at *BVLaw*).

Second, in deriving his 10% royalty rate, the expert relied on sources that estimated average rates for the entire computer software industry without attempting to analyze whether those licenses were truly comparable to the technology at issue, as required by *ResQNet.com v. Lansa, Inc.*, 594 F.3d 860 (Fed. Cir. 2010) (available at *BVLaw*). In addition, the Federal Circuit's 2010 decision in *Uniloc USA v. Microsoft Corp.*, 632 F.3d 1292 (also at *BVLaw*), disallowed any "general or theoretical" royalty rates as running afoul of *Daubert*.

Finally, the expert used the entire market value of the computer security products industry to calculate damages without any showing that the patented firewall drove the demand for such products, as *Uniloc* also requires. Without any "sound economic and factual predicates" for his calculations, the defendant said, the expert's present value calculations, including his reasonable royalty rates, were inadmissible.

After reviewing all the evidence and arguments, the court agreed that the expert's methods were speculative and failed to use any reliable, quantitative methodology to support his damages estimates. Moreover, his analysis contravened recent Federal Circuit precedent as well as its pronouncements on the entire market value rule in *Uniloc*. Exclusion would be appropriate, the court said, but it would also make it "impossible for the plaintiff to prove damages at trial." Because the plaintiff relied so heavily on its expert report and testimony to support his claim—and because the *ResQNet.com* and *Uniloc* cases came out after the expert's report and deposition—the court granted him an extension of time to "repair" his opinion and testimony.

But not enough time? In less than a month, the expert prepared a supplemental report, and this time the defendant moved for summary judgment based on the lack of sufficient proof of actual damages. The expert still had not cured the three substantial flaws in his analysis, the defendant maintained; namely:

1. *Market utilization and penetration rates.* To support these estimates, the expert's supplemental report included information that "five leading players" in the data security market offered product lines that used a firewall heuristic similar to the one that the plaintiff's patented software used. Moreover, "no fewer than 132 subsequently issued U.S. patents cite" the plaintiff's patent, he said, which sufficiently supported his 10% estimate for both rates.

Although this information was more specific than any in his original report, the defendant said, the expert still did not identify "what products and what percentage of the products use heuristics; what revenues flow from such products; and how the 132 citations correlate to an estimate the patent would penetrate 10% of the market."

2. *Average royalty rate.* In his supplemental report, the expert asserted that 10% was the "average royalty rate for software patents" that get into production, and he expected royalty rates for data security products to be even higher than the average, "due to their high value in protecting the licensee's customers from losses due to computer threats." His report did not identify any specific sources for these statements, however, above the general industry sources cited in his original report.

3. *Entire market value.* To support his use of the entire market value of the industry, the expert maintained that "all constituent parts of an integrated data security product could benefit" from the patented method. But this statement also suffered from any link to reliable evidence of consumer use and demand, the defendant claimed.

Once again, the court agreed with the defendant's arguments. The expert's supplemental report "failed to include any sort of qualitative analysis" to support his market utilization rates, and his royalty rate estimate relied on the same published sources that the court previously determined were insufficient, without directly linking these licenses to the technology at issue. Lastly, without any reliable evidence that the plaintiff's patented software would create the basis for consumer demand, his use of the entire market value of the industry failed to comply with *Uniloc*.

For all these reasons, the court found the plaintiff's evidence failed to establish a material factual dispute regarding whether damages were reasonably ascertainable, an "essential element of [the] plaintiff's claim," the court held, and dismissed the case.

Court Affirms Award for Excluding Value of Farm From Marital Estate

Case name: *Keig v. Keig*
Citation: 2012 Neb. App. LEXIS 224
Date of decision: Dec. 4, 2012
Country: US
State or Federal: State
State/Jurisdiction: Nebraska
Court: Court of Appeals
Type of action: Marital Dissolution
Experts: Bryan Robertson (husband); unknown (wife)
Judge: Inbody
SIC: 0191 General Farms, Primarily Crop

At divorce, the husband and wife disagreed over the distribution of assets connected to the family farm, which the husband had acquired through gift and inheritance before the marriage. Specifically, he held a personal 30.9% interest in the business; the remainder was in two trusts, including an irrevocable trust in which he had a life interest and which, at trial, showed a balance of over $1.4 million.

When the family set up the LLC for the farm, they decided that the husband would be responsible for its day-to-day operations and receive a guaranteed annual payment of $24,000; the wife took care of the house and children, helping on the farm as needed. The husband said he reinvested all the capital he earned from the business to keep it going. Therefore, there were few marital assets.

Ability to liquidate is a 'big deal.' The husband's expert determined his direct interest in the farm using the evaluation date, trial balance, income tax returns, 1065 tax documents for the LLC from 2004 through 2010, amended and restated operating agreement, guaranteed payment agreement, articles of organization, depreciation schedules, yield reports, and an appraisal from a certified real estate appraiser that valued the farm at $3.5 million, not including its grain inventory.

The expert calculated a total value of $4.2 million for the farm, which he multiplied by the husband's 30.9% interest. The interest holder's ability to liquidate was a "big deal," he noted. Here, the husband did not have a controlling interest, and his interest in the trust was only a life interest; also the property was "land rich and cash poor." For all these reasons, he applied a 25% discount for lack of control and a 35% discount for lack of marketability, arriving at a fair market value of $637,000 for the husband's share.

The trial court, which did not adopt the valuations for the farm or state a valuation in the divorce decree, awarded the business and related assets to the husband. At the same time, it ordered him to pay the wife a $250,000 "*Grace* award."

In a motion for a new trial, which the trial court denied, the husband claimed the award was excessive. Subsequently he appealed to the Nebraska Court of Appeals.

Appellate court performs valuation. The gist of the husband's argument was that the farm and everything connected with it represented premarital property; therefore, the lower court had no authority to perform a valuation or distribution of it. Also, the *Grace* award was excessive, in that it meant the wife would receive 39.25% of his total interest in the farm.

A *Grace* award was a cash payment to a wife when gifted family farm and ranch corporation stock was excluded from the marital estate, the appellate court explained, referencing *Grace v. Grace,* 380 N.W.2d 280 (1986) (available at *BVLaw*). To determine whether the size of the award was appropriate, the appellate court performed its own valuation.

The assets the couple acquired during the seven years for the business were "substantial," more than $1.1 million, it found. The husband failed to mention that the farm's investments and capital amounted to over $4 million and were steadily increasing and that his premarital trust accounts were in excess of $1 million and represented a continuous, significant source of income, even accepting a discount for lack of control and recognizing his limited interest in the trust.

The court concluded his interest in the business was about $1 million; measured against it, the $250,000 *Grace* award was not excessive.

DCF Valuation Meant to Underpin Fairness Opinion Upends It

Case name: *Koehler v. Netspend Holdings Inc.*
Citation: 2013 Del. Ch. LEXIS 131
Date of decision: May 21, 2013
Country: US
State or Federal: State
State/Jurisdiction: Delaware
Court: Court of Chancery
Type of action: Dissenting Shareholder
Experts: Unknown (plaintiff); unknown (defendants)
Judge: Glasscock
SIC: 6153 Short-Term Business Credit Institutions, Except Agricultural (credit card service)

A dissenting shareholder sought a preliminary injunction to stop the merger and acquisition of the target company, claiming the sale process was not reasonably designed to maximize the sale price, because of the board's reliance on a weak fairness opinion resting on multiple problematic valuations.

The plaintiff held stock in a publicly traded corporation that provided reloadable prepaid debit cards and financial services to consumers who did not have traditional bank accounts. The defendants were the company, its eight directors (the board), and the intended buyer. Organized in 2004, the company was private until it conducted an IPO in late 2010 at $11.00 per share. In 2011, the market price for its stock fell drastically, reaching a low of $3.90 per share in the third quarter of that year. The board believed the market undervalued the company and repurchased stock in fall 2011 and early 2012. As a consequence, company shares traded in the $7-to-$9-per-share range, which, as the board saw it, still did not reflect the company's long-term potential value.

No market check. Throughout 2011 and 2012, several entities expressed interest in pursuing a merger, including two private equity (PE) firms and the defendant buyer. One of the PE firms proposed to buy a minority stake in the company for $12.00 per share. In contrast, the defendant buyer made a cash tender offer for the entire company at $14.50 per share based on certain conditions. The trading day before the board received the buyer's indication of interest (IOI), the stock closed at $11.65.

In light of the offer, the company began to negotiate exclusively with the buyer. The board retained Bank of America (BofA) as a financial advisor for the transaction, which drew up a list of nine potential purchasers. The board declined to contact any of them, ostensibly to minimize the risk of leaks and rumors regarding a potential sale. But after the parties had drafted a merger agreement, the company, concerned about meeting its legal obligations, briefly reached out to one company in late December 2012. When its gesture was met with silence, it concluded there was a lack of interest in the market in general in the company.

In early January 2013, the buyer made another offer, increasing the price to $15.25. The board's counteroffer was for $16.75, including other conditions, which the buyer rejected, suggesting instead that the board shop the company around to other potential bidders. The board declined, deciding an auction would not generate bona fide bidders. In late January, the parties' negotiations led to agreement on the key terms of the deal, including a price of $16.00 per share in cash; a 3.9% termination fee, amounting to $53 million; and a no-shop provision. In February, the board approved the agreement and decided to recommend the transaction to the company's stockholders.

On Feb. 19, 2013, BofA presented a fairness opinion to the board judging the deal fair. As a result, the parties executed the agreement. The $16.00-per-share price represented a 45% premium over the company's stock price one week before the deal. But after the company released favorable earnings on February 13, its stock price increased; this meant a significant cut in the premium to 25%. The total value of the transaction was approximately $1.4 billion. Following the announcement, shareholders swiftly filed two separate suits, including this one in the Delaware Court of Chancery, challenging the transaction.

The gist of the plaintiff's request for an injunction was that the sale process was not conducive to maximizing the price. The board breached its duty of care when it decided not to seek alternative bidders and relied on the weak fairness opinion from BofA.

'Not good' indicators of value. In assessing the board's single-bidder strategy, the Court of Chancery found the directors had "several indicia" as to how the market valued the company. In 2012, its stock price hovered around $8.00 per share even after share repurchases to boost its "true" value. A PE company's bid for a minority interest was for $12.00 per share. When the board did approach a third party that previously had indicated an interest in the company, it made no offer. Within this context, the court said, the board's decision to engage in the single-bidder process was not per se unreasonable.

This finding, however, was not the end of the analysis. Rather, the issue was whether, in light of the board's decision, its actions as a whole produced a "process reasonably designed to maximize price." For that determination, the court looked closely at the board's reliance on the fairness opinion.

The BofA opinion rested on several valuations, which the court reviewed in turn.

1. Two valuations that were based on the price of company stock found the transaction fair because the buyer's offer represented a premium over the stock price.

The court was not persuaded. Considering the volatility of the company stock since it went public in 2010 and the board's open views that the market undervalued the company, the stock price was "not a good indicator" of its value, it said.

2. Next, the opinion relied on comparable companies and transactions analyses, both of which were problematic, the court stated. As to the former, BofA's lead banker on the deal admitted that 14 of the 15 comparables were dissimilar to the target company.

As to the latter, the board itself acknowledged in the proxy that most of the comparables were "quite old," predating the financial crisis, and the targets of the comparables were not "particularly similar" to the company at issue. The court concluded that neither of these analyses was "a strong indication" of the company's value.

3. Lastly, the bank conducted a discounted cash flow analysis (DCF). It, in effect, showed that the $16.00-per-share price was below the valuation it produced. Specifically, the DCF found a reasonable price range that was between $19.22 and $25.52 per share. Also, the analysis was based on five-year financial projections, whereas management customarily projected no more than three years into the future.

In his deposition, the CEO used the latter fact to distance himself from the valuation. The DCF method, he said, "really has no commercial reality in terms of valuing a business … where you take five years of forecasted cash flows and discount them back at some sort of arbitrary discounted rates." This was not a good prediction of how a company would deal with "the next 9/11 or the next fiscal cliff."

The Court of Chancery zeroed in on these points, finding that an "anomalous DCF valuation" made the fairness opinion a less reliable substitute for a market check. The $16.00-per-share merger price was "20% below the *bottom* range of values implied by the DCF," it pointed out with emphasis. In the end, the defendants themselves were "reduced to arguing that the DCF valuation is unreliable here," the court said. The fairness opinion in this case was a "particularly poor simulacrum of a market check."

The court concluded that the lack of market check and reliance on a weak fairness opinion, among other factors, indicated the sale process was unreasonable. But even though the plaintiff showed that she faced the threat of irreparable harm without an injunction, the court was "reticent ... to enjoin a transaction that affords stockholders a premium in the absence of a competing offer." In the gap between the parties' agreement and the closing, the market likely became aware that the company was for sale, but no suitor appeared, the court pointed out. If it imposed an injunction and a material change caused the deal to fail, the harm to stockholders could be "quite large."

In denying the plaintiff's request, the Court of Chancery observed that it was unlikely the directors could meet their burden at trial to prove they acted reasonably, but it made no findings as to whether the $16.00-per-share price was adequate or there was another buyer willing to pay more.

Court Approves Debtor's 'Feasible, But Tight' Plan With 6% Interest Rate

Case name: *In Re: LMR, LLC*
Citation: 2013 Bankr. LEXIS 2127
Date of decision: May 24, 2013
Country: US
State or Federal: Federal
State/Jurisdiction: Texas
Court: United States Bankruptcy Court
Type of action: Bankruptcy
Experts: None (debtor); Byron Hinton (creditor)
Judge: Mott
SIC: 7011 Hotels and Motels (hotels, except casino hotels, and motels)

The debtor, a hotel owner and operator, slid into bankruptcy, but it subsequently achieved what the court called "a remarkable turnaround" thanks to the burgeoning local hotel market. As a result, it asked the Bankruptcy Court for permission to "cramdown" its reorganization plan on the objecting creditor.

Revenue increase throughout bankruptcy. The debtor was a limited liability company that in 2007 purchased a hotel in Austin, Texas. Besides cash equity contributions from its four members, it used a bank loan to finance the remaining $3.9 million of the purchase price. The hotel secured the loan. The loss of its Best Western franchise in 2010, the protracted conversion to another franchise, and the lingering national recession led to a severe decline in revenue. The creditor, a private equity distressed debt investor, acquired the loan in mid-2012 and posted the hotel for foreclosure as soon as it matured in September 2012. To preserve the hotel, the debtor filed Chapter 11 bankruptcy a month later.

Since then, the business's circumstances have improved markedly. Gross income was at a low, $919,000, in 2010 but increased to $1.12 million in 2011 and $1.14 million in 2012. The debtor projected net revenue (after occupancy taxes) of about $1.25 million in 2013. It credited the upturn to the improving local economy and Austin's ability to stage well-known cultural and sports events, including South by Southwest, that attract leisure travelers on a budget, in addition to businesspeople—both of whom were target customers for the debtor.

One of the debtor's witnesses, a hotel broker and consultant with experience in selling and financing hotel real estate, testified to the connection between the strength of the local economy and the hotel market, citing the *Texas Hotel Performance Factbook*. The latter provided statistics for the ZIP code in which the hotel operated that confirmed that, in the last quarter of 2012, the debtor's revenue increased 19.1% and its room occupancy by 12.5% compared with the same quarter of 2011. This witness also said that the hotel's 2013 revenues year-to-date compared to 2012 were up 16.5% and its revenue per available room per day (RevPar) was up by 8%.

No 'true interest rate expert.' In January 2013, the debtor, wanting to continue hotel operations, proposed a plan for reorganization to which the creditor objected. All other creditors and interest holders were in favor of approval. A plan confirmation hearing followed. The debtor showed it had made three adequate protection payments of $23,750 each and was prepared to make the impending fourth one. Its members also planned to make a $200,000 equity infusion, providing the business with nearly $474,000 in cash on hand and $70,600 in escrow for upgrades and repairs, as well as payment of the annual property taxes.

Assuming the creditor had a secured claim of $3.2 million, the debtor planned to make 59 monthly payments amortized over 25 years at 6% interest, with a balloon payment of the remaining amount of the secured claim in the 60th month, in five years. To the extent the creditor had an unsecured claim, the debtor planned to pay it in 60 equal monthly installments, also with a 6% interest. The creditor would retain its lien on the hotel, as well as other collateral to ensure payment of its secured and unsecured claims. The debtor projected to have at least $118,000 cash on hand at the end of the plan's five-year term.

The creditor contended, among other things, that the plan was not feasible because the debtor could not meet its projections, the $200,000 in member contributions was speculative, and it lacked the funds to make upgrades and repairs. Importantly, the proposed 6% interest rate was below market interest rate and failed to meet the Bankruptcy Code's § 1129(b)(2) "cramdown provisions."

It presented a licensed real estate appraiser (the only one testifying at the hearing), who used both the comparable sales and income approaches to value the hotel at $3.2 million as of October 2012, the bankruptcy filing date. Specifically, in terms of comparables, he considered one sale from 2010, three sales from 2011, and one sale from 2012. He used $358,400 as net operating income. Institutional investors, he said, would not be interested in the hotel; smaller investors that might consider acquiring it would not be interested in the restaurants' business. Consequently, he excluded any rental income the debtor was receiving from the two restaurants on its property. He recognized there currently was a "good" market for Austin hotels but claimed there was no major change that made him reconsider his earlier appraisal. Yet, when pressed at the hearing, he admitted that hotels in the city had risen in value during the past seven months.

The court noted that neither side presented a "true interest rate expert." The debtor's hotel broker and financing witness said that loans that had an 80% debt-to-100% value ratio (80/20 loans) currently had an interest rate between 4.5% and 5.25%. The debtor's proposed 6% rate was a "premium" over the market, he maintained. He admitted there were no loans with a 100% debt-to-100% value ratio (1/1 loans) or greater in the current market.

The creditor's appraiser confirmed both of those statements. He added that any loans with a 1-to-1 ratio or greater would only be from a high-risk lender that would charge more than 6% interest.

A representative of the creditor who had financing experience confirmed that there was "absolutely no market for income producing real property." He added that obtaining such a loan would require tiered financing from a hard money lender, which would consist of a "mezzanine" debt with a 15%-to-17% return and/or an equity participation requiring a percentage return in the mid-to-high-20% range.

Same interest rate for secured and unsecured claims. The U.S. Bankruptcy Court (W.D. Tex.) first determined the value and amount of the creditor's secured and unsecured claims. As to the value of the collateral, i.e., the hotel, it noted that the only probative evidence was the real estate appraiser's $3.2 million valuation, dated October 2012. But this value did not reflect the improved market and the corresponding increase in the value of the hotel. Normally, it said, a court would reduce the value of the secured claim by the amount of outstanding property taxes on the hotel—$68,000—but in this instance it decided not to do so because "there can be no real dispute based on the record" that the value of the hotel had increased by at least that amount since the appraisal. Therefore, the secured claim was for $3.2 million and the unsecured claim for a little over $520,000, considering the debtor's protection payments.

Secured claim. Next the court considered the plan's feasibility under Sect. 1129(b)(2), which was known as a "cramdown" in bankruptcy parlance, it said. The provision applied here because the creditor, which held both secured and unsecured claims, rejected the plan. Specifically, the issue became whether the debtor's proposed 6% interest rate was sufficiently high to yield the creditor at least the "present value" of its secured claim.

The court first looked to the U.S. Supreme Court's decision in *Till v. SCS Credit Corp.*, 541 U.S. 465 (2004), a Chapter 13 bankruptcy case that nevertheless has guided most bankruptcy courts in their feasibility analysis under Sect. 1129. Under the "*Till* formula approach," the court looks to the national prime rate and then adds a supplemental "risk adjustment." In this context, the court dismissed the creditor's suggestion that the debtor had the burden of presenting a "true interest rate expert" to prove a cramdown interest rate.

"It is fair to say," it stated, that "courts almost invariably conclude that efficient markets are absent in a Chapter 11 case." Based on the opinions of the parties' financial consultants and the appraiser, this was certainly the case here, it concluded. All agreed there was no 1/1 loan to be had in the current market, "which is what the Debtor's Plan effectively proposes." To obtain this type of loan required "the kind of tiered financing that have led other courts to conclude that no efficient market exists for the cramdown loan."

The national prime rate, which had not changed in years, was 3.25% at the time of the hearing, the court found. For the upward risk adjustment, courts typically consider factors such as the circumstances of the bankruptcy estate, the nature of the security, and the duration and feasibility of the reorganization plan and generally have approved of an upward adjustment of 1% to 3%, the Bankruptcy Court remarked.

In this case, the circumstances of the estate had "dramatically improved" since the bankruptcy filing, "as the Debtor started with a negative cash position that has now grown to over $300,000 in cash on hand." At the same time, the creditor's collateral, the hotel, was appreciating in value as independent statistics and credible testimony about Austin's hotel market and economy and the excellent location of the hotel showed. Its value would rise through the plan, the court concluded, considering the owners' cash equity infusion for upgrading the property. The owners also personally guaranteed the debt, and there was insurance for the hotel.

The debtors' plan was "feasible, but tight," particularly when it came to the balloon payment due in five years, the court stated. Its revenue projections were conservative and the projected expenses were "realistic and reasonable," aspects that further reduced the risk. In an earlier hotel case, the same circuit had approved a plan with a 5% cramdown interest rate. Given the circumstances of this case, a 2.75% upward adjustment was sufficient to ensure at least the "present value" of the secured claim. If anything, the court said, this rate was "on the higher side of the 1% to 3% general range."

Unsecured claim. Because the objecting creditor also had an unsecured claim, the court scrutinized the debtor's plan for repayment of that debt using the same formula approach. That the debtor's plan provided the creditor with the same risk adjustment—6% interest rate—for both types of claims "may, on its face, appear to ignore that unsecured debt may be inherently riskier than secured debt," the court observed. It added that an unsecured creditor often had a better chance of repayment if the debtor survived rather than its being forced to liquidate. If there were liquidation, the creditor likely would foreclose on the hotel and receive no more than the $3.2 million value its own appraiser determined for the hotel—meaning little or nothing of the $520,000 unsecured claim.

For various reasons, in this case the unsecured claim had "less risk and more protection than most unsecured claims." The court pointed out that the debtor did not try to "strip down" the lien to secure only the secured claim, although courts have permitted lien stripping in Chapter 11 cases. Also, if the debtor defaulted in its payments of the secured or unsecured claim, the creditor had state law remedies to enforce its lien rights. Further, the creditor actually benefited from having an unsecured claim. Total monthly payments on both claims would be approximately $30,700. If the creditor only had a secured claim of $3.8 million, it would receive only about $24,600 a month because of the 25-year amortization. All the factors suggested there was not enough risk to require a cramdown interest above 6%.

Finally, the court observed that the formula's starting point, the national 3.25% prime rate, already accounted for some degree of risk. "Although this Court will not go [as far as] starting its upward risk adjustment from the Treasury Bill rate, it merely serves to demonstrate that [the creditor] is receiving over a 5% upward risk above a truly riskless rate on its unsecured claim. Because the debtor also met the other plan confirmation requirements, in this instance it "actually succeeded" in its unusual attempt to cramdown both secured and unsecured claims, the Bankruptcy Court concluded.

Expert's 'Aggressively Skeptical' View Does Not Undermine Disaggregation Analysis

Case name: *Liberty Media Corp. v. Vivendi Universal, S.A.*
Citation: 2013 U.S. Dist. LEXIS 19485
Date of decision: Feb. 12, 2013
Country: US
State or Federal: Federal
State/Jurisdiction: New York
Court: United States District Court
Type of action: Securities
Experts: Dr. Blaine Nye (plaintiffs); Dr. William Silber (defendants)
Judge: Scheindlin

In the latest installment of this decade-old securities litigation, the defendants filed a post-trial motion claiming expert testimony on loss causation and damages was fatally flawed and asking the federal court (S.D.N.Y.) to overturn the jury's €765 million award.

The dispute has its roots in the late 1990s, when top executives planned to transform Vivendi, S.A., from a small, publicly traded French water utility into an international telecommunications conglomerate. In the course of various acquisitions and a merger involving two large U.S. companies (Seagram's and Universal), Vivendi's debt swelled. During this time, the company and two former executives allegedly made material misstatements about the conglomerate's finances that caused company stock to trade at inflated levels between 2000 and 2002.

Lawsuits followed, including a class action by U.S. and foreign shareholders. A trial in January 2010 resulted in a jury verdict that found Vivendi liable for violating Section 10(b) of the Securities and Exchange Act and Rule 10b-5 based on 57 misstatements.

The case at issue involved individual plaintiffs, Liberty and certain subsidiaries, and revolved around a Dec. 16, 2001, merger agreement that required the plaintiffs to exchange some of Liberty's shares for Vivendi securities. Liberty also alleged Section 10(b) violations as well as breach of four warranties in the merger agreement based on 25 misstatements or omissions. Liberty retained the same loss causation and damages expert who earlier had testified on behalf of the class-action plaintiffs.

In June 2012, the jury found Vivendi liable on all claims and awarded Liberty €765 million in economic damages.

Vivendi sought to upset the verdict by renewing its motion for judgment as a matter of law (JMOL) or a new trial, arguing that no jury "should have been permitted to base a verdict" on the unreliable testimony Liberty's expert provided on loss causation and damages. (Find a discussion of Vivendi's pretrial challenges to the expert's regression analysis and event study in the June 2009 *BVUpdate* and at *BVLaw*.)

Nine materialization days. Vivendi challenged several aspects of the expert's analysis, such as disaggregation, one-day event window, Moody's downgrade, maximum inflation date, the inflation amount, and the damages amount. The court considered the issues in turn.

1. Disaggregation. Loss causation is the bedrock of proving damages in complex securities claims. Under the law, Liberty could only claim damages for declines in Vivendi's stock price that resulted from events representing materializations of Vivendi's previously concealed liquidity risk.

Liberty's expert tried to disaggregate the effects materialization events had on the stock price from the effects non-fraud-related "confounding" events produced. He examined 166 trading days, starting with the date the parties signed the merger agreement to the date when the last claimed materialization event took place, August 2002, to determine whether there was a statistically significant decline in price after removing market and industry effects. Further, he eliminated company-specific effects that were not related to the disclosure of the concealed liquidity risk. He reviewed 16,000 news releases and thousands of analyst reports, he said, and isolated nine days on which there were negative returns that linked to the materializations of the concealed liquidity risk. "In those days, ... everything had to do with the fraud," he stated on cross-examination.

On the other hand, Vivendi's expert claimed that on several of the nine materialization days, there was competing bad news that could have influenced the stock price. He pointed to the fourth day, when there were news reports that News Corp. was not going to buy an entity Vivendi tried to sell, but on cross-examination, he conceded that this event did not seem to affect the stock price. Moreover, Liberty's expert showed that the market perceived Vivendi's effort to sell this company as related to its liquidity risk.

In its JMOL motion, Vivendi disputed the validity of the disaggregation analysis. Liberty's expert claimed to have excluded non-fraud-related, company-specific events from his damages calculation but failed to disaggregate a single event on any of the nine materialization days.

The court found the expert addressed the issue at trial when he stated that there were no confounding events during the nine materialization days. The absence of those events might stem from his having excluded days with non-fraud-related declines prior to selecting the nine materialization events windows, the court suggested. But, it added, the testimony was not clear on that point. Also, the jury could have found that none of the confounding events Vivendi proposed were non-fraud-related and at the same time affected Vivendi's share price. Liberty's expert's testimony was not inadmissible simply "because it took an aggressively skeptical view of the significance of non-fraud-related news" on the nine days.

2. *One-day event window.* Liberty's expert used a "one-day event window" to measure the share price decline in response to the materialization events. Specifically, he assessed the change over the course of one trading day, from market close to market close. He believed this short window was appropriate because "over a day the market becomes more and more efficient"; relevant public information becomes "fully absorbed and reflected in the market price." He also stated that the current academic standard was "to extend the event period to the close of … trading on the day after the release of the pertinent information." When a materialization event occurred after the close of trading in Paris but before the close in New York, he extended the window from market close on the disclosure day to close on the following day.

In the context of a discussion on how the market reacted to significant news, he said that "the information starts to hit the market immediately." But he also noted that it was difficult to pinpoint when information first penetrated the market. In this case, on three dates, he found the price decline resulted from materialization events that at some point involved news-related events that produced no immediate negative price reaction in the market.

Vivendi claimed there was an "unavoidable inconsistency" between the expert's theory that markets respond instantaneously to significant news and his analysis in this case, connecting materialization events to stock price changes.

The court saw it differently. For one, his approach seemed to adhere to the academic standard. Also, the jury reasonably could have found his testimony to be "correct" as to both points: that markets respond immediately to important news and that they did not respond here to developments Vivendi mentioned because these events did not contain new information by the time they occurred. "The two are logically independent," the court said. Alternatively, the jury could have ignored the former statement; the expert's analysis only depended on the assumption that markets were efficient over a day, not on whether he believed or was correct in believing in instantaneous market reactions.

3. *Moody's downgrade.* Liberty's expert attributed the entire company-specific decline of Vivendi's share price on May 3, 2002, to Moody's downgrade even though on the record, the news was not officially released until after the stock already had experienced 60% of the total decline for that day. His general expertise in regard to trading suggested that the information was leaked into the market before the official announcement, he explained. Leaks of this type were common, he went on to say and explained how they typically unfolded.

Vivendi's expert did not offer an alternative reason for this decline.

Subsequently, Vivendi claimed the inclusion of the preannouncement declines in the loss causation and damages analysis was impermissible.

Once again, the court sided with Liberty. Its expert offered an explanation, whereas Vivendi's expert failed to present an alternative rationale for the share decline. Also, it was difficult to prove with direct evidence that trading based on leaked information took place. Under these circumstances, the jury could have found that more likely than not, news about the downgrade caused the price decline.

4. Maximum inflation date. Liberty's expert chose one day as the date of maximum inflation, that is, "the date at which the value of Vivendi's shares was most inflated by Vivendi's fraud." The inflation peaked, he found, on or before Dec. 13, 2001, the day the company's CFO wrote a private letter of reassurance to ratings agencies at a time when there had been indications that the company's liquidity risk was very high but when the indicators were not known to the market or Liberty.

Vivendi argued that the expert's choice of date was arbitrary and that he failed to consider "multiple misrepresentations" that Vivendi made from the designated day until Jan. 7, 2002, that further inflated the price. Liberty could not claim damages for inflation based any misstatements that occurred after Dec. 16, 2001, the merger agreement date. Also, the expert failed to derive the maximum inflation date from a quantitative analysis of Vivendi's concealed liquidity risk.

The court determined that the jury could have found that the letter prevented a downgrade and rejected Vivendi's "counternarrative." Further, Vivendi provided no support for its insistence on a quantitative analysis. Determining when the inflation reached its highest point did not require an absolute measure of the company's liquidity risk, just as it was "unnecessary to know the height of each mountain in a range in order to identify which is the tallest," the court said.

5. Inflation amount. Even though the plaintiffs here only alleged 25 misstatements as opposed to the 57 in the class action case, Liberty's expert determined the same inflation amount in both trials, €22.52 per share. His computation did not hinge on the analysis of the specific effects of discrete misrepresentations or omissions. Rather, he determined the growth in the inflation of Vivendi's stock price based on misrepresentations from Dec. 31, 2000, to Dec. 16, 2001. He then calculated damages resulting from the inflation by analyzing stock price declines on the nine materialization days.

Vivendi's expert did not suggest a different method, but in its motion, Vivendi claimed that no reasonable jury could have relied on a determination that arrived at the same inflation amount in trials with such disparate sets of misstatements.

This argument, the court found, would have merit if the analysis assumed that each misstatement "played a distinct and independently measurable role in inflating Vivendi's share price." But it did not; the approach Liberty's expert took was "relatively simple." For its part, Vivendi failed to present a "more sophisticated" method that computed different damages for the different sets. At the same time, "the law does not require the use of such a fine-grained quantitative method," assuming one exists. Also, the instructions to the jury made it clear that there only had to be enough evidence to make a "reasonable estimate" of damages. Liberty's expert's analysis "more than satisfied this standard," even if his approach produced the same result in both trials, the court concluded.

Why €765 million? Besides the expert's methodology, Vivendi also attacked the damages amount the jury determined. According to Liberty's expert, damages totaled €842 million, or €22.52 inflation per share. Vivendi's expert (whose methodology the court does not discuss in detail) calculated damages between zero and €175 million.

Vivendi claimed the jury's €765 million award did not align with either expert's analysis and did not correspond to the price drops Liberty's expert attributed to the corrective disclosures. In a follow-up motion, Vivendi tried "to clarify" that it did not mean to say the verdict had "to match either expert witness's damages calculation wholesale" or match the price drops the expert proposed.

The court found it "difficult to understand" on what basis Vivendi criticized the award. The verdict showed that the jury "largely but not entirely" credited Liberty's expert's computation, discounting it roughly by 10%. This modification was "within the bounds of its instructions."

But, the court continued, there was a question as to why the jury found the expert 90.86% credible, rather than 90%. It might have recognized "the many sources of imprecision" in the damages calculation at issue. Or it might have conceived of the damages Liberty's expert proposed as being roughly €850 million. Discounting that number by 10% would lead to the actual award of €765 million. In the alternative, the jury could have subtracted €2.06 per share from the €22.52 per share inflation calculation by discounting one or more of the materialization events or by incorporating one or more of the confounding events Vivendi's expert set out. Ultimately, the court concluded, it was "hopeless" to determine the deliberations the jury undertook. "There were any number of reasonable paths" for it to arrive at the damages amount, the court stated, denying Vivendi's motion and upholding the award.

Michigan Court on Double-Dipping in Divorce: 'It Depends'

Case name: *Loutts v. Loutts*
Citation: 2012 Mich. App. LEXIS 1846
Date of decision: Sept. 20, 2012
Country: US
State or Federal: State
State/Jurisdiction: Michigan
Court: Court of Appeals
Type of action: Marital Dissolution
Experts: Gary Rogow (Husband)
Judge: Per curiam
SIC: 3674

When this couple divorced in 2008, both parties asked the court to award them their Internet business, at which only the husband had worked full-time. They each also asked the court to impose a noncompete restriction against the other spouse. At trial, the court valued the company at $280,000 and awarded it to the husband, with an equalizing payment of $140,000 to the wife and a three-year restraining order on competing against the business after divorce. (Note: The appellate court opinion provides no further information on the valuation methodology or inputs.)

To determine spousal support, the Michigan family court considered the issue of the "double dip," i.e., since it had already relied on the future income of the business to determine its value, could it also use the husband's post-divorce earnings to calculate support? Finding no state precedent directly on point, it looked to an Ohio case, *Heller v. Heller,* 2008 Ohio App. LEXIS 2788 (*Heller I*) (available at *BVLaw*), which "our Court of Appeals, for whatever reason, has at least at this point, failed to undertake." Relying on *Heller,* the court concluded that principles of equity and fairness permitted it to account for the business either as an asset or as a basis for determining support, but not for both. Accordingly, it declined to use the husband's stated yearly salary of $240,000 to determine support, adopting instead the $130,000 that the husband's expert determined to be the fair market value of his compensation, and the wife appealed.

Different state, different law. At the outset, the appellate court noted that two prior Michigan cases discussed the "double-dipping" issue in the context of valuing pensions in divorce. In those cases, the trial court awarded the wife a portion of the husband's pension, with the husband retaining continuing ownership over the remainder of the plan assets. On retirement, the husband sought to modify the award, claiming that it was improper to use his retirement income for spousal support, but in each case, the appellate court found the issue turned on "*all* the circumstances of the case" as well as principles of fairness.

In line with these prior holdings, the court declined to adopt a bright-line rule regarding "excess" income in this case. Instead, it adopted a standard that allows trial courts to decide whether double dipping would lead to an equitable outcome in any particular case.

The appellate court also noted that the trial court had erred by relying on *Heller I* because the underlying Ohio statute did not mirror applicable Michigan law. Moreover, the Ohio Court of Appeals subsequently clarified that there was no "flat prohibition against double dipping applicable to every income-producing asset." *See Heller v. Heller*, 2010 Ohio App. LEXIS 5136 (*Heller II*) (available at *BVLaw*). For these reasons, the court remanded this case for a redetermination of whether its circumstances supported using the business's value for determining property division as well as support. In further findings, it also upheld the trial court's noncompete restriction against the wife.

Independent Tax Preparers Protest IRS's Regulation Efforts and Prevail

Case name: *Loving v. IRS (I)*
Citation: 2013 U.S. Dist. LEXIS 7980
Date of decision: Jan. 18, 2013
Country: US
State or Federal: Federal
State/Jurisdiction: District of Columbia
Court: United States District Court
Type of action: Federal Taxation
Experts: n/a
Judge: Boasberg
SIC: 7291 Tax Return Preparation Services

Case name: *Loving v. IRS (II)*
Citation: 2013 U.S. Dist. LEXIS 13878
Date of decision: Feb. 1, 2013
Country: US
State or Federal: Federal
State/Jurisdiction: District of Columbia
Court: United States District Court
Type of action: Federal Taxation
Experts: n/a
Judge: Boasberg
SIC: 7291 Tax Return Preparation Services

Three independent tax preparers challenged the IRS's authority to enforce a new regulatory scheme that applied to anyone who "prepares for compensation, or who employs one or more persons to prepare for compensation, all or a substantial portion of any return of tax or any claim for refund of tax." The program imposed a registration requirement that included passing a qualifying exam, paying an annual application fee, and taking at least 15 hours of continuing education courses each year.

In 2011, the IRS extended the reach of Circular 230 to cover tax-return preparers in a move to oversee an additional 600,000 to 700,000 tax professionals who are non-CPAs and nonattorneys.

The agency cited an 1884 statute (31 U.S.C.§ 330) as authority to regulate "representatives" who "practice" before it; it also claimed the increased oversight was "vital" to ensure the collection of revenue due to the United States and prevent preparers from "bungling" their clients' returns.

The plaintiffs argued the statute did not cover them and that the new requirements would threaten their livelihood. One plaintiff who worked with low-income clients said she would have to increase her prices if the new rule went into effect and would lose clients. The other two declared that they likely would close their businesses.

The court (D.D.C.) sided with the plaintiffs, declaring the IRS lacked statutory authority and enjoining the agency from enforcing the registration requirement.

'Irreparable harm'? Although it had not yet filed a notice of appeal, the IRS (with support from the Department of Justice) promptly asked the same court to stay the injunction pending a final outcome. It had established 250 testing centers, the program had cost more than $50 million to roll out, and nearly 100,000 preparers had registered to take the competency test, the IRS stated. The injunction would disrupt its tax administration and cause irreparable harm to "the public fisc"; also, the record indicated "overwhelming public support for the new regulations."

The court stated that its earlier ruling did not require the IRS to dismantle the entire scheme. The agency may wish to keep some of the centers open because some preparers voluntarily might want to take the exam, thinking that the additional credentials would distinguish them from other preparers, and also "to hedge their bets in case of appellate reversal." The court also clarified that the injunction did not suspend the IRS's requirement to obtain a preparer tax-identification number (PTIN). But it did mean that the agency could not condition PTIN eligibility on meeting the registration requirement.

The court also dismissed the agency's request for a brief suspension that would allow it to seek a stay in the Court of Appeals. "This would only lead to more confusion for preparers and their clients as the tax season gets under way," the court said.

May Expert Offer Plaintiff's Loss Calculation as His Own?

Case name: *Marine Travelift, Inc. v. Marine Lift Systems, Inc.*
Citation: 2013 U.S. Dist. LEXIS 91268
Date of decision: June 28, 2013
Country: US
State or Federal: Federal
State/Jurisdiction: Wisconsin
Court: United States District Court
Type of action: Damages (incl. Lost Profits)
Experts: Dr. Charles Breeden (plaintiff); unknown (defendant)
Judge: Griesbach
SIC: 5551 Boat Dealers

Does an expert make himself vulnerable to attack when he agrees to do nothing more than evaluate a lost profits and damages projection the plaintiff's executives made? In a *Daubert* challenge, the defendant claimed the expert was simply the plaintiff's "mouthpiece" and his failure to perform an independent analysis made his opinion inadmissible.

The plaintiff manufactured marine hoist and industrial lift equipment. In 2007, it made an agreement with the defendant providing that the latter would become the nonexclusive distributor of its marine hoist equipment in Georgia and several counties in Florida. When the plaintiff suspected that the defendant was sharing trade secrets and confidential information with customers and competitors, it terminated the agreement and three years later sued in federal court (E.D. Wis.). Its claims included breach of contract and misappropriation of trade secrets information as well as confidential and proprietary information. The defendant counterclaimed, alleging wrongful termination of the agreement.

The plaintiff retained an economist who had significant academic research and teaching experience and 30 years of experience as an independent expert on economic damages. He was to opine on the "potential lost profits and damage to goodwill" the plaintiff was "likely" to incur in the future due to the defendant's wrongful disclosure. Instead of performing an independent analysis of economic damages, the plaintiff wanted him to evaluate the principles and methods its CEO and CFO had used to calculate loss exposure and make sales projections. The plaintiff also planned to introduce the executives as experts at trial.

Loss exposure. The projections rested on the assumption that the disclosures would affect 26% of the plaintiff's worldwide sales over an 18-month period. The executives used two different methods to compute "potential lost margin" under two scenarios.

Under the first method, they assumed that the company would sell the same number of units but at a substantially discounted price for 26% of units sold worldwide. The amount of discount was based on an incident in April 2011 when the plaintiff had to give a major customer a discount of $558.25 per lifting ton on a sale of a marine lift product because of the disclosure. The executives also applied the same discount to its industrial lift products, with a multiplier of 1.5. Under the second method, they assumed the affected sales would simply be lost.

The two scenarios differed as to the number of sales they forecast. Under the first, the executives assumed the plaintiff's worldwide sales would return to the 2008 level, which, with 83 units sold, was the plaintiff's best year. When they extrapolated this number over 18 months, they arrived at 125 units; based on the 26% figure they set down, they claimed 32 units would be subject to loss.

Under the second scenario, the starting point for units was 33. This was a "rough average" of company sales from 2009 through 2011. Extrapolating this figure to 50 units left 13 units exposed to loss.

Under their "discounted sales method," the executives claimed a "potential lost margin" of $564,000 to $1.4 million; under their "lost sales" method, the range increased to between $1.6 million and $4.1 million.

Within the limits of his assignment, the economist expert concluded the projections reflected a "reasonable, accurate and reliable methodology for assessing potential business damages." He confirmed that damages could range anywhere from $564,000 to $4.1 million. Further, he stated that the plaintiff "also faces a significant risk of loss of its business goodwill." There was a threat "far into the future" that the wrongful conduct "may result in a conversion of business away from [the plaintiff] and to [the defendant] and its affiliated companies." He added that, depending on the defendant's instances of wrongdoing, "actual future business damages … may vary accordingly."

Talk of 'potential damages' is irrelevant. The defendant claimed the expert testimony was inadmissible under Fed. R. Evid. 702 for various reasons.

1. *26% loss exposure.* The expert performed no independent analysis and simply served as a "mouthpiece" for the plaintiff's executives, the defendant claimed. In his deposition, he admitted that the executives came up with the 26% loss exposure, a figure he did not independently verify. Also, even though the plaintiff claimed lost profits because of the necessity of discounts and lost sales, it actually increased its prices and elsewhere claimed an increase in unit sales and revenues since it had filed suit, the defendant stated.

The court agreed the testimony was irreparably flawed. For one, the expert only spoke to "*potential* business damages," the court stated with emphasis. While evidence that the plaintiff actually will suffer damages as a result of the alleged wrongful disclosure is relevant, "evidence that it might suffer such a loss is not."

But lack of relevance was not the only reason for exclusion, the court found. The expert also "offered no basis within his knowledge or experience" to support the 26% loss exposure. His report and deposition failed to explain "the propriety" of using the 26% figure, much less explain the figure. Appealing to his extensive "academic training" and many years of experience as an independent expert was not enough to establish the reliability of his opinions.

"The need for explanation and analysis [was] particularly strong" in this case, "where one would expect actual evidence of losses," the court said, pointing out that more than 18 months had passed since the alleged disclosures. If the executives' projections were accurate, actual damages should have revealed themselves by now. Yet, the plaintiff had not provided any evidence.

2. Discount valuation method. The defendant drew attention to the fact that the executives' discounted sales method, which the expert validated, relied on one 2011 sale. As to the sale, the plaintiff and expert failed to consider factors unrelated to the disclosures that made the one-time discount necessary.

The court agreed. Even assuming there was a causal link between the $558.25 discount and the disclosed information, which was not clear, one sale taking place more than two years ago hardly amounted to sufficient support for the assumptions underlying the executives' method. Also, the distribution agreement only covered the plaintiff's marine hoist equipment, but the expert accepted the executives' assumption that the company would have to give a $558.25 discount on 26% of its entire marine product line, along with a multiplier for its industrial lift equipment, said the court. The expert did not explain why the same discount would be available to customers in an entirely different market, purchasing an entirely different product, the court pointed out. His only rationale was that he based his analysis on the executives' representations, which proved incorrect considering the company's increase in actual sales since the 2011 transaction.

3. Goodwill. The defendant contended the statements on goodwill were inadmissible because the expert did not "outline any valuation" of the damage to goodwill arising from the alleged conduct. He simply referred to a "threat" that "exists far into the future."

The court agreed. The expert appeared not to have made any attempt "to approximate the value of the plaintiff's business goodwill much less estimate the amount of damages."

In concluding, the court dismissed the plaintiff's argument that the expert had a right to rely on the executives' calculations on loss exposure and sales projections because they themselves would testify as experts at trial. But that was not the issue here. Rather, the defendant's question was whether the expert would be able to offer the executives' projections as his own opinion. For all of the reasons the court had given, it concluded he was not.

Unequal Distribution of Family Business Stock Requires Discounts

Case name: *McCulloch v. McCulloch*
Citation: 2013 R.I. LEXIS 113
Date of decision: June 25, 2013
Country: US
State or Federal: State
State/Jurisdiction: Rhode Island
Court: Court of Appeals
Type of action: Marital Dissolution
Experts: Peri Ann Aptaker (wife); John Brough, Jr. (husband); Jay Fishman (court-appointed)
Judge: Flaherty

When three financial experts declared themselves unable to put a definite value on two closely held businesses, the trial court decided to assign an in-kind minority interest in both entities to the wife without valuing the considerable assets before distribution. The wife appealed.

At the core of "a protracted, if not epic, battle" (the court's description) for divorce were two family-owned businesses that "comprised an enormous portion of the marital estate." One entity was a manufacturer of fabric at which the husband served as president and CEO; all of the company's stock was in his name. The other was an affiliated company that owned equipment and real estate and in which the first company had a 10% interest. Sometime after 2007, the fabric manufacturer became involved in "the China venture," a plan to buy a controlling interest in a printing and dyeing company in China. Both the husband and CFO of the company testified that the project was vital to the survival of the business, which had been losing money each year.

Economic crisis thwarts valuation. At trial, in late 2008, both sides presented experts, and the court appointed a neutral, third expert to help it determine the value of the businesses. The wife's expert initially prepared a report that placed the value of the first entity as of Dec. 31, 2007, at about $126.4 million At the time, the expert stated that she "couldn't place [a] value o[n] the China investment" because she lacked the requisite data to determine its impact on the company. In later testimony, she said she had not completed an updated valuation for the company and any numbers related to the China investment were merely estimates. She concluded she was unable to "provide an opinion of value with respect to the China venture." She cautioned, however, that any valuation had to account for the state of the economy.

The husband's expert rebutted that there was no justification for the $126 million value; rather, he concluded the value was $106 million. He also said he lacked information about the China venture because at the time of valuing the company "the deal was not closed."

The court-appointed expert testified that since the December 2007 valuation date, "there ha[d] been a meltdown in the financial market." Job losses and reduced consumer spending dramatically changed the economic situation in countries to which, or in which, the company would sell. Considering the parties' experts had received incomplete information, this expert also lacked the data necessary to "place a value or an economic benefit on the China venture" at the valuation date.

The trial court took judicial notice of the global economic crisis that had taken place since the valuation date. (The opinion does not provide details on valuations, if any, for the second company.)

The trial court decided the stock of the first company was a marital asset. As to the second company, a fraction short of 50% was marital property because the husband had acquired the remainder before marriage or received it as a gift. It stated it did not have any "credible evidence upon which to base a fair and reasonable valuation of the value of the stock in th[e] corporation" because of the "extraordinary change in circumstances that could not have been contemplated by the parties" since the valuation date. The global financial crisis, the fact that the China venture had not been completed, and the fact that "[n]one of the experts had given any detailed consideration to the potential impact" of that project, the court said, made it impossible to accurately value the two businesses. For all these reasons, it ordered an in-kind distribution of the stock of the first company and an in-kind distribution of a partnership interest in the second company, instead of a sum in cash.

As to what percentage of stock to award to the wife, the court noted that it "would be completely inequitable" for her to receive the same portion as the husband considering her minimal contribution "towards the acquisition, preservation or appreciation of the corporate assets." The husband's "blood, sweat and tears and contributions by his family" were responsible for the company's past and perhaps future success. Accordingly, it gave the wife a 25% interest in the fabric manufacturer and a 25% interest of the portion that was marital property in the second business. The husband received 75% of the two assets.

A case for valuing assets. The wife appealed to the Rhode Island Supreme Court on a number of grounds, particularly because: (1) the trial court declined to value the assets before it assigned to her a percentage of them; and (2) the trial court's distribution of stock rendered her a minority shareholder in a closely held corporation.

Regarding the first issue, the husband argued that state law did not require a valuation of marital property before distribution.

The appellate court agreed with him that there was no bright-line rule imposing a valuation requirement on trial courts, and it declined to adopt one. At the same time, it decided that in this case the trial court had abused its discretion in failing to value the companies before assigning interests in them for two reasons.

First, the assets at issue made up "the vast majority of the marital estate." Experts for both sides stated a range between $106 million and $126 million as of the end of December 2007. Even assuming fluctuations in value since then, there was no question as to their importance.

Second, the law generally disfavors assigning stock in a closely held corporation in a way that makes one spouse a minority shareholder. Even if this type of distribution is not error per se, it was in this case, the appellate court continued, because the parties received unequal percentages. "[A] 25 percent minority share of a closely held corporation will likely not be the equivalent of 25 percent of the total value of the company" because that type of stock lacked liquidity considering "there is no established public market for the stock." Also, "a minority shareholder lacks control over the company, and therefore, the value of his or her stock is diluted in comparison to that of a majority shareholder."

It was true that the court itself earlier had adopted a rule not to apply a minority discount or a discount for lack of marketability (DLOM) in the context of an action for dissolution of a closely held corporation. But, the high court said, "we believe that such discounts are appropriate, and even necessary, when valuing an in-kind distribution of a minority share of a closely held corporation in a divorce action." Considering the illiquidity of the wife's asset and her lack of control over the business, it ordered the lower court on remand to apply both a minority discount and a DLOM when valuing the assigned portions. Finally, it pointed out that if the trial court had granted the wife the "cash equivalent of her equitable ownership interest in the companies" or "had crafted some other assignment, such discounts would not be necessary."

Merger-Related Projections Pass Muster With Delaware Chancery

Case name: *Merion Capital, L.P. v. 3M Cogent, Inc.*
Citation: 2013 Del. Ch. LEXIS 172
Date of decision: July 8, 2013
Country: US
State or Federal: State
State/Jurisdiction: Delaware
Court: Court of Chancery
Type of action: Dissenting Shareholder
Experts: Dr. Bernard C. Bailey (petitioners); Henry F. Owsley, Stephen M. Schiller, Gordian Group (respondent)
Judge: Parsons
SIC: 3699 Electrical Machinery, Equipment, and Supplies, NEC (other electrical industrial apparatus)

A recent ruling from the Delaware Court of Chancery in a statutory appraisal action could serve as a primer on valuation and the case law that has developed around the discipline. In a compact 29-page decision, the court (Vice Chancellor Parsons) with impressive clarity dissected the different methods the experts used and the reasoning that informed their technical analyses. One takeaway is that the court, again and again, credited the expert who was able to provide a cogent explanation for his selections and demonstrate his knowledge of the prevailing valuation literature.

The target-respondent was a biometrics company that provided fingerprint identification technology to various government agencies. From 1990 to 2004, it functioned as a private company and was profitable the whole time. In September 2004, it went public. The petitioners owned over 5.8 million common shares of the company. In 2008, the respondent retained Credit Suisse and Goldman Sachs to explore "strategic alternatives." The future buyer was a conglomerate of global technology companies, which, in 2010, made a verbal offer to the company that prompted its CFO to prepare bottom-up five-year financial projections for 2010 through 2015. Until then, the respondent had only generated projections for the current year. In December 2010, the parties finalized the merger, at a price of $10.50 per share.

The petitioners objected to the transaction and requested a statutory appraisal from the Delaware Court of Chancery to determine the fair value of the stock on the merger date.

Expert substitution. Both sides offered expert testimony as to the going-concern value of the target on the merger date. The petitioners' appraiser held a Ph.D. in management and headed a company that was a "global leader in authentication technology." He performed a DCF analysis, a comparable companies analysis, and a comparable transaction analysis but ultimately relied only on the DCF valuation. As he saw it, there were no truly comparable companies or transactions, but even assuming they existed, he still lacked the requisite data to draw comparisons, he said. He concluded that the target's fair value per share was $16.26.

The respondent presented expert testimony from two financial analysts: a partner and a managing director of a leading national investment bank. The expert team valued the target using a DCF analysis, a comparable companies analysis, and a comparable transactions analysis and assigning the same weight—one-third—to each. It concluded that the target's shares on the merger date were worth only $10.12 apiece.

The respondent's engagement of two experts became a disputed evidentiary issue. The second expert assumed the case after the first expert unexpectedly fell ill and went on medical leave. He read the first expert's partially prepared rebuttal report, spoke to other team members who worked on it, and ultimately adopted the first expert's conclusions. He said he had "independently assessed the validity of the judgments and conclusions of [the report]." The rebuttal report he submitted provided his conclusions, he stated.

At a later deposition, he admitted he did not know what factors team members considered in evaluating the companies they used for their comparable analyses. At trial, he also said he did not participate in preparing the first expert's initial report, never spoke to him about it, and was not familiar with one of the report's appendices. His testimony prompted the petitioners to claim that it was inadmissible under Delaware's Rule 702 because it lacked a factual basis. The expert was a "mere conduit of the content of an extrajudicial source," they argued.

The Court of Chancery said that in general an expert could replace another expert who had to abandon a case because of illness. Here, the second expert knew the valuation techniques the firm used and, therefore, was a "logical choice" for a substitute. At the same time, he "barely performed sufficient research to express an informed opinion" on certain topics and instead relied on the information from the first expert. Also he changed his testimony on the comparability of companies between his deposition and trial without giving notice to the petitioners. Accordingly, the court discredited his later statements and accorded the expert team's comparable analyses only minimal weight.

Comparable analyses. The Court of Chancery next reviewed the respondent's comparable analyses.

1. Comparable companies analysis. In essence, the experts selected 10 companies and then determined multiples by dividing the enterprise value for each company by: (1) the last 12 months' (LTM) revenue and EBITDA; and (2) estimated forward revenue and EBITDA derived from publicly available information. Next they applied a range of multiples to the target's LTM and estimated forward revenue and EBITDA. They arrived at an estimated enterprise value of $296.3 million.

The petitioners' expert called the analysis unreliable because of the dearth of data, the inclusion of noncomparable companies, and the lack of a consistent methodology.

At the outset, the court noted that six of the 10 chosen companies were significantly smaller than the target, with enterprise values of less than $50 million. Because "greater risk is typically associated with equity in a small company," the Court of Chancery rejected the use of companies whose size does not match the target's size, said the court. It found other flaws. Not one of those six had generated a profit, whereas the target had shown profits from 1990 until 2005. Only one of the 10 companies listed the target as a competitor in its annual report. At the same time, the respondent's experts omitted one company that, by their own account, was a direct competitor and had very positive financials. Its inclusion likely would have increased the values of the respondent's comparable companies analysis, said the court. For all of these reasons, it declared the analysis unreliable.

2. Comparable transaction analysis. For this analysis, the respondent's experts selected 18 transactions. Next, they calculated multiples by dividing the enterprise value for each company by: (1) LTM revenue and EBITDA; and (2) estimated forward revenue and EBITDA. They obtained multiple ranges by eliminating the top and bottom quartiles. Lastly, they applied a 20% discount to the obtained multiples to account for the need to exclude any control or synergy premiums.

The petitioners' expert criticized the use of revenue multiples instead of EBITDA multiples considering the target "was a very profitable cash-flow positive company operating in a robust industry." Also, the remainder of the analysis was defective because there were insufficient data points to allow for meaningful conclusions.

The court found both of the arguments persuasive. It added that the respondent's first expert in another case also had criticized the use of revenue multiples, calling them "more suspect due to their relatively higher level of variance." This contradictory approach undermined his credibility on this point. The paucity of data points undercut the reliability of the EBITDA multiples. Moreover, the high dispersion of the data points bolstered the court's conclusion.

DCF analysis. Since it found the respondent's comparable analyses unreliable, the Court of Chancery based its valuation solely on the DCF method. It noted that the rival experts used "conflicting inputs and assumptions" concerning the method's three basic components: (1) cash flow projections; (2) discount rate; and (3) terminal value. Highlights of the disputes are:

1. Cash flow projections. The petitioners objected to the use of the five-year projections the target's CFO and Credit Suisse had prepared and advocated for the adoption of their expert's two scenarios: (1) an "industry growth scenario" that assumed an industry growth rate through 2015 of

17%; and (2) a "cash deployment scenario" that assumed the target would spend $396 million of its cash on acquisitions.

The respondent urged the court to rely on the five-year projections that the CFO and Credit Suisse had prepared, allowing for minor adjustments.

The Court of Chancery generally prefers valuations based on contemporaneously prepared management projections, the court said. At the same time, in its earlier decision in *Gearreald*, the court determined that a lesser degree of deference was appropriate where "management had never prepared projections beyond the current fiscal year" and "the possibility of litigation such as an appraisal proceeding was likely." Another factor to consider was whether the projections were the work of directors or officers of the target who risked losing their jobs if the transaction succeeded. See *Gearreald v. Just Care, Inc.*, 2012 Del. Ch. LEXIS 91 (April 30, 2012) (available at *BVLaw*). Because these very circumstances were present in the case in front of it, the court agreed that the projections invited skepticism. But it also found that here the CFO had no reason to fear for his job if the merger went through and also was not involved in an alternative bid.

Moreover, the petitioners' expert's "cash deployment scenario" was too speculative. The record showed that, even though the company expressed an interest in acquiring companies, none of the 20 companies it had examined proved a desirable fit. Also, the court refused to "speculate as to the rate of return on [any] hypothetical acquisition." There also was insufficient evidence for the expert's "industry growth scenario." He used industry growth rates to assume a compound annual growth rate (CAGR) through 2015 of 17%, while the CAGR implicit in the management projections over the same period was only 12.1%. The court pointed out that from 2006 to 2009 the target fell far short of growth rates in the biometrics industry. In 2010, its management projected revenue to grow by 8% (from $129.6 million in 2009 to $140 million in 2010), but, in the first three quarters of 2010, it had earned only $78.2 million in revenues. For all these reasons, the court found the management projections a "reliable starting point" for the DCF analysis.

2. Free cash flow adjustments. Both sides' experts adjusted the free cash flows. The respondent's first expert deducted share-based compensation (SBC) from the target's projected cash flows; the petitioners' expert did not. Also, the respondent's expert increased working capital based on the assumption that the company would have working capital equal to 32.2% of revenues. The petitioners' expert assumed it would only need to retain 22.9% of its incremental revenues as working capital.

The court noted that the issue of how to treat SBC frequently came up in the cases. Its standard practice, which found support in the valuation literature, was to consider a nonqualified stock option plan cash neutral or cash flow positive. Because the respondent failed to show that SBC would in any way affect the target's actual cash flows, it did not represent a cash expense here, said the court.

In terms of computing working capital, the experts disagreed over the treatment of certain asset and liabilities categories: "prepaid expenses," "long-term inventory and contracted related costs," "accrued expenses," and "other liabilities." The petitioners' expert had included them based on an influential treatise, *Valuation: Measuring and Managing the Value of Companies,* by Tim Koller, Marc Goedhart, and David Wessels. The respondent's experts criticized this approach, but they failed to cite any valuation authority for support of their position, saying it was based on "experience in looking at many companies and many projections."

The court called the latter approach "essentially conclusory" and credited the petitioners' expert "based on the strong support for his view."

3. *WACC.* A major part of the discussion focused on the varying inputs the experts used to compute their respective weighted average costs of capital (WACC). Because in this case the capital structure was 100% equity and 0% debt, the WACC equaled the cost of equity. "In simpler terms, the cost of equity equals the risk-free rate plus an equity risk premium plus the company's beta times the market risk premium," the court explained.

a. Risk-free rate. To determine the risk-free rate, the petitioners' expert used the 20-year Treasury bond yield, whereas the respondent's experts used the 10-year one. Both sides recognized that either metric was acceptable.

According to the court, valuation literature, including statements from Prof. Aswath Damodaran, supported the use of the 10-year Treasury bond yield in this case.

b. Beta. The experts "clashed" over the calculations of beta and their diverging values were "the largest driver of the price difference in their respective DCF calculations," said the court. The petitioners' expert used a beta of 0.87, whereas the respondent's experts claimed a much higher value of 1.52 was appropriate. One issue was whether to use a one-year Bloomberg weekly raw beta or a two-year weekly adjusted beta. The petitioners' expert favored a one-year sample period to avoid the "significant noise associated with movements in the market due to ... the Global Financial Crisis through the period of 2007 through early 2009." The respondent's experts chose a two-year sample period but offered no explanation. The court adopted the petitioners' expert's one-year period.

Both sets of experts agreed that the beta required an adjustment to reflect the target's large cash position. The petitioners' expert adjusted the raw beta, whereas the respondent's experts adjusted the Bloomberg adjusted beta.

The court said it was inappropriate to "cash adjust a market-adjusted beta because it effectively cash adjusts the market." The number with which to begin the computation of beta was the one-year Bloomberg weekly raw beta, that is, 0.708, it concluded. It cited Shannon Pratt and Roger Grabowski's *Cost of Capital: Applications and Examples* (4th ed., 2010, page 203) for a description of adjusting beta estimates for excess cash.

The target's total assets were approximately $868.7 million. The issue was how much was surplus, as opposed to operating assets. The petitioners' expert considered $100 million as surplus, whereas the respondent's experts considered all the company's cash—$533.2 million—to be excess. Both sets of experts agreed that $100 million, an amount the company's board had said it would use for a share buyback, was excess cash. The petitioners' expert argued the remainder—$433.2

million—was an operating asset because the company's executives had indicated they wanted to use its cash balance for operations "to take advantage of the significant growth opportunities in the marketplace." The court found this position contradicted the Pratt and Grabowski treatise on which the expert expressly relied. The treatise defined surplus assets as "[a]ssets that could be sold or distributed without impairing company operations."

The respondent's experts used a peer group method to calculate beta. But since the court did not find their comparable companies analysis reliable, it used its own calculation of a forward beta of 1.397 to determine the appropriate WACC.

c. Equity risk premium. There was only a small difference in the competing experts' equity risk premiums. The petitioners' expert used a supply-side premium of 5.2% based on the *2010 Ibbotson Yearbook.* He cited numerous articles and treatises to support his position.

The respondent's experts used a 5.0% premium based on multiple sources, including Prof. Damodaran and Ibbotson, but beyond identifying their sources, they gave no explanation as to how they calculated the equity risk premium.

The court adopted the petitioners' expert's 5.2% rate, concluding he "demonstrated a stronger understanding of this subject and explained his methodology more convincingly." (The opinion sows some confusion as to what expert proposed what percentage but is clear as to the conclusion and the *2010 Ibbotson* states a 5.2% rate.)

d. Equity size premium. The rivaling experts also arrived at similar values when it came to the equity size premium. The petitioners' expert concluded it was 1.73% based on decile 7 of *Ibbotson's 2010 Yearbook* encompassing companies with a market capitalization between $685,129,000 and $1,063,308,000. The respondent's experts used *Ibbotson's 2009 Yearbook* and adjusted the company's market capitalization to exclude its large cash reserves. The respondent's second expert admitted, "the definition [for equity size premium] says market capitalization." But, he said, "We're not valuing [the company] in the DCF. Because the way the DCF works … we value the cash streams the company throws off and then we add the cash on top of it." They arrived at a 2.0% value.

The court pointed out that the Ibbotson table headings specifically said "market capitalization" and that the relevant treatises focused on the market value of common equity and did not recommend an adjustment to exclude cash reserves. The respondent's experts chose Ibbotson and as such adopted its underlying view that there was a relationship between market capitalization and rate of return, said the court. Also, the exclusion of cash was "counterintuitive." If the underlying rationale for the Ibbotson tables is that smaller companies are more risky than larger ones, excluding cash decreases the size of the company involved; this means the equity size premium increases. "Here, that would mean that [the target] would be more risky as a result of its cash reserves," said the court. But intuition leads one to expect that, when a company has cash reserves instead of debt, its riskiness should decrease. For all these reasons, the court adopted the petitioners' expert's 1.73% value.

Based on all the various inputs, the court concluded the company's WACC was 11.954%.

e. Terminal value. Both sets of experts rested their terminal value estimates on the Gordon growth model. Based on historical GDP and inflation data, economic analysts' projections, and the growth prospects of the biometrics industry, the petitioners' expert settled on a 4.5% perpetuity growth rate. The respondent's experts used a range of growth rates, between 2% and 5%, and "implicitly" selected the 3.5% midpoint.

The court again adopted the 4.5% value the petitioners' expert proposed because he "was the only expert who sought to justify his conclusion." Also, his final rate fit into the range the opposing experts gave.

The experts disagreed over whether to use a two-stage or three-stage DCF model. The petitioners' expert "gradually step[ped] down the company's growth rate using a linear progression … from 2016 through the terminal year, 2021" before he applied the terminal growth rate. The respondent's experts used a two-step model. At the end of management's projections in 2015, they estimated a single percentage rate that they used as a stand-in for the company's perpetual rate of growth beyond that period.

The court chose the three-stage model, referencing Prof. Damodaran's theory that a three-stage model was best suited for a company whose earnings initially grow at a very high rate but are expected to start a gradual decline toward a stable rate as the business grows and loses its competitive advantages. Thus, the court assumed that the target's earnings were expected to grow at a high rate of 11.45% for an initial period, which, with the company's eventual loss of competitive advantage, would gradually drop to a stable growth rate of 4.5%.

Court's valuation. By adjusting the model the petitioners' expert proposed and assuming a cash balance of $533.2 million for the relevant period, the Court of Chancery arrived at an equity value of about $963.4 million as of the merger date. Based on approximately 88.6 million shares outstanding, the price per share was $10.87, the court concluded.

Expert's 'Invocation' of Income Approach Does Not Save Valuation

Case name: *Metamining, Inc. v. Barnette*
Citation: 2013 U.S. Dist. LEXIS 89446
Date of decision: June 26, 2013
Country: US
State or Federal: Federal
State/Jurisdiction: Virginia
Court: United States District Court
Type of action: Contract
Experts: Roger Daugherty (plaintiff); unknown (defendants)
Judge: Jones

The plaintiff acquired a company that operated surface mines. It subsequently sued the sellers, alleging it did not obtain all the assets they had promised in the sales agreement. It presented expert testimony as to the value of the companies' various coal properties, which the defendants challenged as inadmissible under *Daubert.*

The plaintiff, a California company, bought the Virginia coal-mining business from the defendant owners, a married couple, for $5 million. The sellers' attorney prepared the sales agreement—a contract the court called "a model of impreciseness and ambiguity." Its defects led to disputes that prompted the plaintiff to sue in federal court (W.D. Va.), claiming breach of contract, fraud, and fraud in the inducement. The contract promised rights to assets the mining business owned that did not in fact materialize, the plaintiff alleged, among other things.

Lease premium, permit value, and discount. The plaintiff offered expert testimony as to the value of the assets the coal mining business owned at the time of the sale. The expert had a B.S in mining engineering and worked for coal companies in various capacities, starting as a miner and eventually becoming president and owner. He also was a certified appraiser and had prepared appraisals in the coal industry before.

The expert prepared estimates of the dollar values of the coal reserves of four sites the company owned. (The opinion does not provide the estimates.) Although it became clear in pretrial proceedings that the plaintiff did not in fact obtain the right to mine all of this coal, the plaintiff sought to use his opinion to show the value of the property it believed it had acquired by way of the sale. He repeatedly stated he used the income approach; he also explained why he did not use a comparable sales or market approach: Each property was so unique that no comparable was available. In each valuation, he said, he applied a "lease premium" and a "permit value" to the estimated reserve tonnages, as well as a discount. He wholly adopted the coal reserve numbers that appeared in a document the coal company's mining engineer had prepared.

He explained that he derived the three factors—lease premium, permit value, and discount—from nine variables: (1) royalty rate; (2) coal seam characteristics and seam thickness; (3) coal quality; (4) selling price; (5) status of metallurgical market; (6) rate of mining; (7) permitted and nonpermitted reserves; (8) difficulty of leasing comparable reserves; and (9) proximity to "loadout" facilities and buyer. But he also used his "intuition, personal experience and expertise" stemming from "years of appraising mineral assets," he said. In terms of the discount rate, he used a higher rate for a lease that he believed to be riskier to offset "the inherent dangers associated with that mine."

Despite his statements about using the income approach, the addendum to his expert report stated that his method to calculate the lease premium and permit values was related to the cost approach—measuring the amount of money necessary to replace an asset. He insisted that he arrived at his values by way of empirical data and comparisons to prior, similar transactions. At his deposition, in response to questions about how one could verify his evaluation of the lease premiums, he said it was a "judgment factor … based on 50 years of experience." Responding to requests to identify the income stream or data he used for the income approach to arrive at his conclusions, he said, "It would be the cost on a discount basis that an operator would pay for this reserve." He confirmed that his analysis did not include income data pertinent to the coal mining business at issue.

In their pretrial objection to the testimony, the defendants first claimed the expert was unqualified under a precedential state case that required an expert to be a licensed real estate appraiser to be allowed to testify in any state court proceeding about real property values.

The court quickly dismissed the argument, saying the decision subsequently lost its bite when the legislature passed an amendment that expressly left it to the court's discretion to decide who qualified as an expert in real property valuation. Also, federal law—Rule 702 and *Daubert*—controlled the issue of admissibility of expert testimony in federal court, which is where the case was.

Second, the defendants argued the testimony was inadmissible because the expert failed to provide an adequate explanation as to how he arrived at his conclusions.

The court agreed that the expert's methodology was flawed. For one thing, he provided no formula for calculating the three factors that were pivotal to his conclusions, that is, the lease premiums, permit values, and discount. Even though he listed variables he considered, the court and the defendants ultimately were left to wonder how he "conjured the precise figures he applied." Moreover, he admitted to using his intuition and some information that was "extremely sketchy." Accordingly, the court was unable to compare his method to the approaches other experts in the field use.

And although he invoked the income approach, which the court said was a widely accepted process for valuing assets, it seemed his method did not "focus purely on future streams of income." His statements about using empirical data and comparisons to similar transactions did not explain what the data were and what the relevance of the other transactions was to an income-based approach, the court continued.

An expert cannot "simply invoke the name of an accepted methodology without explaining how the expert's approach fits within that methodology," the court said. Given the weaknesses in the substance of his opinion, the court precluded the expert from testifying to the value of the coal reserves at issue.

Test Case Considers Proper Framework for RAND Royalty Rates

Case name: *Microsoft Corp. v. Motorola, Inc. (I)*
Citation: 2012 LEXIS 152244
Date of decision: Oct. 22, 2012
Country: US
State or Federal: Federal
State/Jurisdiction: N/A
Court: United States District Court
Type of action: Intellectual Property
Experts: Charles R. Donohue and Ramamirthan Sukumar (Motorola); Kevin Murphy, Matthew Lynde, and Timothy Simcoe (Microsoft)
Judge: Robart
SIC: 7371

Global organizations such as the International Telecommunications Union (ITU) and the Institute of Electrical and Electronics Engineers (IEEE) set common technological standards so that the world's various electronic products will all work together. One complication of such standards is that compliance often requires members to use another's patented technology. To protect against possible abuses of market power, the international rules require the owners of such "essential" patents to license them at "reasonable and non-discriminatory," or RAND, rates.

In this case, both Microsoft and Motorola are members of the ITU and IEEE. Motorola also owns two "essential" patents that fell within the standards, which it offered to license to Microsoft on a worldwide, nonexclusive basis beginning at a 2.25% royalty per compliant product (such as Microsoft's Xbox 360). Microsoft declined the offer and filed a complaint in federal district court (W.D. Wash.), alleging breach of contract. Of particular interest to IP appraisers and experts, Microsoft also asked the court for a judicial accounting of a RAND royalty rate for each of the two patents in suit.

Does *Georgia-Pacific* apply to RAND cases? Motorola retained a damages expert to calculate a RAND royalty as well as a consumer survey expert to examine the usage and value of certain patented features in Microsoft's Xbox 360. On the other side, Microsoft retained a team of three experts to conduct a RAND rate analysis. Prior to trial, each party challenged the other's experts under the *Daubert* standard.

In particular, Motorola's expert used a modified *Georgia-Pacific* framework to determine the RAND royalty the parties would have reached during a hypothetical negotiation. He began with the 2.25% rate in Motorola's offer and then adjusted it up or down according to his analysis of each of the *Georgia-Pacific* factors. To confirm the initial starting rate, he also looked at existing licenses involving Motorola's entire portfolio of standard essential patents—including the two at issue—as well as Motorola grants involving just one of the patents. He also consulted Motorola's technical experts to affirm how the patented technology fit into the applicable standards, i.e., its role as being essential to compliance. (Note: The court opinion does not reveal the expert's ultimate RAND rate.)

Microsoft didn't challenge the expert's use of the *Georgia-Pacific* framework. Instead, it claimed the licenses he relied on were not comparable because they broadly covered all of Motorola's standard essential patents, including those for cellular telephone technology. Microsoft also claimed the expert improperly focused on the "hold up" value of the patents at issue. That is, rather than assess the original or stand-alone value of the patented technology, he only valued it once it became "essential" under the governing standards. Finally, he improperly used the entire value of Microsoft's accused products to reach his royalty rate, Microsoft argued, in contravention of *Uniloc USA Inc. v. Microsoft Corp.*, 632 F.3d 1292 (Fed. Cir. 2011) (available at *BVLaw*).

As an initial matter—and despite the lack of any specific challenge to the expert's method—the court held that the U.S. Court of Appeals for the Federal Circuit, as "the appellate court for patent-related issues," has "consistently sanctioned the use of the *Georgia-Pacific* factors to frame the reasonable royalty inquiry" in suits concerning general utility patents. Further, federal district courts have upheld a *Georgia-Pacific* analysis in cases concerning RAND royalty rates. Academic authorities have also discussed the "obvious option" of extending the *Georgia-Pacific* factors to RAND evaluations in a standard-setting context, the court observed, in finding the method reliable, in this case, under *Daubert*.

The expert's application of past and existing Motorola licenses also provided "some indicia of the appropriate initial royalty rate," the court held. The licenses should be "subject to vigorous cross-examination" at trial, but any alleged over- or under-inclusiveness went to the weight of the expert's testimony, not its admissibility. Similarly, by expressly consulting Motorola's technicians, the expert appropriately considered the value of the patents in suit. "Here, it appears Microsoft's dispute is with the opinions of Motorola's technical professionals who found [the two essential patent portfolios] fundamental to the respective standards," the court held, in declining to exclude the expert's testimony on this ground.

The expert's application of the entire market value rule was more problematic. "On the face of the rule," the court said, it appeared that the expert improperly applied the 2.25% royalty rate to the entire price of Microsoft's end product (such as Xbox 360) without "first demonstrating that Motorola's standard essential patents create the basis for consumer demand," as *Uniloc* requires. However, even absent such proof, the entire market value rule does not act as a "*per se* bar" to using an end-product price, the court observed, citing *Lucent Technologies, Inc. v. Gateway, Inc.*, 580 F.3d 1301 (Fed. Cir. 2009) (available at *BVLaw*). In that case, the Federal Circuit held there was "nothing inherently wrong with using the market value of the entire product, especially when there is no established market value for the infringing component," as long as there is a proper apportionment of value among the patented and unpatented features of the product.

That said, the court was "skeptical" that the appropriate RAND rate in this case could rely on the full price of Microsoft's end products. By their very nature, Motorola's standard essential patents related to only a portion of these products, but since the court could not yet tell whether the expert's proposed testimony violated the entire market value rule—particularly since this depended in part on testimony from Motorola's consumer expert—it deferred any decision on this element until the RAND rate hearing.

As for the consumer survey evidence, Motorola's expert used a "conjoint" analysis by which he attempted to determine the value current Xbox owners place on its patented features, such as video decoding and Wi-Fi capabilities, in relation to and in combination with other features. From the collected data, the expert believed he could isolate the value to the consumer of one particular feature.

Microsoft claimed the questionnaire he used was "unintelligible" and used a nonrepresentative sample of the relevant Xbox "universe" because it included only owners of the product rather than potential purchasers. In addition, the survey expert failed to provide a margin of error for his results. But these criticisms went to the weight of the evidence, the court ruled, noting in particular that Xbox owners were "arguably more likely" to understand the technical terms of the survey and that the expert did in fact include a margin of error for his conclusions. Accordingly, it permitted the survey expert to testify at the RAND hearing.

Not your typical *Daubert* standard. As a final matter, the court considered Motorola's challenge to Microsoft's three damages experts, who believed the proper framework for determining a RAND royalty rate is an "*ex ante*, multilateral negotiation" involving full participation of essential-patent holders as well as all potential implementers.

Specifically, an "ex ante, multilateral 'lens'" properly addresses two key risks that arise in the licensing of standards-essential patents, the experts maintained. First, it captures any improper "hold up" value that the patentee might seek to use to leverage its monopoly over those who seek to implement the standard. Second, it analyzes any potential "stacking" of royalties by the patentee that would impose an unreasonable royalty "burden" on the implementers. Their analysis reflected a "real world form of multilateral licensing," the experts explained, because its parameters provided that "all licensors appreciate the potential impact of their individual licensing positions and recognize that the aggregate royalties must be sufficiently reasonable … to allow the widespread implementation of the standard."

In response, Motorola's expert claimed the international standards clearly state that RAND license agreements are "bilateral in nature, such that they occur between only the patentee and the implementer." Industry participants and academics also understand that a RAND license is the product of such bilateral negotiations, he said; moreover, in prior contests, Microsoft's own experts had proposed RAND rates based on a bilateral framework.

From a review of prior case law, the court could not find a decision that determined RAND rates for a block of standard essential patents. Further, although substantial scholarly authorities addressed RAND rates and their importance to industry standards, "only limited publication exists on the methodology a court should employ to determine a RAND royalty when negotiations between the patent holder and implementer break down." Given the lack of publication or peer review for Microsoft's proposed multilateral methodology, "the typical manner for establishing" its reliability under the *Daubert* standard is "not met in this case," the court said.

Nevertheless, this did not immediately disqualify the experts' testimony under the *Daubert* standard, which is flexible enough to accommodate new technical or scientific methods, the court noted. Under these circumstances, federal law simply requires the experts to explain "precisely how they went about reaching their conclusions and point to some objective source—a learned treatise, the policy statement of a professional association, ... or the like—to show they have followed the scientific evidence method, as it is practiced by (at least) a recognized minority of scientists in their field."

Here, the experts' analysis for reconstructing a hypothetical negotiation sought to respond to two "well-founded" and "widely recognized" concerns of hold-up value and stacking, the court said. Under the "unique" circumstances of this case and given the flexibility of the *Daubert* standard, it permitted Microsoft's experts to present their "multilateral" framework at the RAND rate hearing.

Editor's Note: In mid-November 2012, the court held the RAND hearing and took the issue of determining an ongoing royalty rate under advisement. According to news reports, the Seattle-based judge asked the parties to file further briefs by Dec. 14, 2012, and may render a final decision by early spring. See, e.g., www.pcworld.com/article/2015542/microsoftmotorola-trial-ends-first-phase-with-judge-to-set-fair-royalty-rate.html.

One Expert's Bad Data Undermine Another's Damages Calculation

Case name: *MyGallons LLC v. U.S. Bankcorp*
Citation: 2013 U.S. App. LEXIS 11004
Date of decision: May 31, 2013
Country: US
State or Federal: Federal
State/Jurisdiction: N/A
Court: United States Court of Appeals
Type of action: Damages (incl. Lost Profits)
Experts: Paul Seitz (plaintiff); unknown (defendants)
Judge: Niemeyer
SIC: 8699

A budding business sued for defamation, claimed $208 million in damages, and ultimately received $4 million. The defendants appealed, arguing the jury's verdict was unsupportable. If the award was based on general damages, it was excessive given the short history of the company; if it represented lost profits, it rested on inadmissible expert testimony

Plaintiff's 'relatively short existence.' The plaintiff company launched a prepaid consumer gas program. For an annual fee, members could buy a card of prepaid gas through the defendants' payment network that 95% of the country's service stations accepted and thus would insulate themselves against future price hikes. At the end of June 2008, the plaintiff's public announcement specifically mentioned the payment processor and the program immediately received wide media coverage. Within days, over 6,000 members signed up, and, even after the company subsequently was forced to turn away new customers, some 25,000 to 30,000 people tried to join. A day later, in response to media inquiries, the defendants publicly stated that there were no agreements and ongoing negotiations with the plaintiff. As a result, the plaintiff received an "F" rating from the region's Better Business Bureau and faced accusations on the Internet that it was running a "scam." It stopped accepting new members and refunded monies it had collected from existing ones. In early July, the defendants authorized a retraction.

In August, the plaintiff sued on a number of legal bases, including defamation. To show damages, it presented two experts whose testimony the defendants tried to exclude by way of a *Daubert* challenge.

The first, and most critical, expert was a professor of marketing who taught courses in advertising, marketing research, digital marketing, and consumer behavior. She admitted that she had no sales forecasting expertise and that "sales [are] not used as an effectiveness measure of advertising efforts or spending." But she believed she was qualified to testify because of her expertise in "communication effectiveness or persuasion with purchase intent."

She used a "funnel approach" to project the plaintiff's future membership and profits. Starting with the market's overall size, she used factors such as persons aware of the company's brand, traffic to its website, actual sign-ups, and a projected growth rate and attrition to narrow it to actual memberships. She benchmarked the plaintiff's growth against some of the most successful companies in the industry, including Apple, Costco, and Netflix, but failed to include startup companies among the comparables. She concluded that, over a three-year period, beginning on July 1, 2008, the plaintiff could have signed up about 3.3 million members assuming it "would have been in business as planned."

The second expert was a CPA. He relied on the first expert's membership projections to determine that the plaintiff had suffered $208 million in lost profits. (The opinion does not provide details of his analysis.)

The federal district court dismissed most of the plaintiff's claims and also denied the defendants' *Daubert* motion. Ultimately, the jury awarded the plaintiff $4 million in damages based on the defamation claim.

The defendants then unsuccessfully attacked the verdict in post-trial motions for judgment as a matter of law (JMOL) or for a new trial on damages. The court acknowledged that the award failed to specify whether the damages were general, to compensate for reputational injury, or special, to reimburse the claimant for "the loss of something having economic or pecuniary value." Regardless, it said, a reasonable jury could have concluded that the defendants' statements made it impossible for the plaintiff "to secure an alternative card processing network, which, in turn, caused the company to suffer pecuniary loss."

The court did, however, state that a $4 million award for general damages alone would be excessive considering the plaintiff's "relatively short existence." But it dismissed the defendants' renewed argument that the damages testimony was inadmissible.

Expert 'ignored business realities.' Subsequently, the defendants challenged the verdict with the 4th Circuit Court of Appeals. In their appeals, they made essentially three arguments, which the court reviewed in turn.

1. *General damages.* The defendants argued a $4 million award for reputational harm to a fledgling company that announced itself to the public only a few days before the defamation would be "so exorbitant as to shock the sense of the court."

The Court of Appeals pointed to the extensive media attention the plaintiff's startup announcement generated and the approximately 30,000 individuals who enrolled or tried to enroll in the program. But it agreed that this was a "nascent company with no capital, no financing, no customers who had yet used its planned consumer programs, and no profit." Any public reputation it had, it had developed in only a few days, from the end of June into early July. Accordingly, there was no justification for millions of dollars in reputational damage.

2. *Special damages.* Assuming the award included special damages, the defendants contended, it could not stand for two reasons: (1) the plaintiffs failed to prove causation; and (2) the underlying expert testimony was inadmissible.

As for causation, the appellate court disagreed, observing there was a "wave of bad press" and evidence that alternative payment networks refused to work with the plaintiff as a consequence. A jury could draw a reasonable inference of causation, the court concluded.

In terms of the expert testimony, the defendants specified that the marketing expert was unqualified to render an opinion because she lacked experience in forecasting sales and used an "overly optimistic and flawed method" to project membership. What's more, without her testimony, the damage expert's calculation lacked a proper basis and was also inadmissible.

The Court of Appeals did not expressly find the marketing expert unqualified but found her methodology and conclusions unsound. She used only "industry giants" as benchmarks for the plaintiff's growth without considering whether the company had the resources, financing, or experience necessary to ensure that degree of growth or "indeed, even as necessary to carry out its own business plan." She also failed to take into account "real circumstances" that affected the plan's viability. In a "puzzling omission," the appellate court said, the expert failed to consider what would happen if gas prices dropped. Under that scenario, "the whole purpose of [the plaintiff's] gas payment plan would be defeated." The expert's projections "ignored business realities and relied on sheer speculation," the appellate court concluded, and the district court erred in admitting the opinion.

Because the second expert's $208 million lost profits determination hinged on the excludable testimony, it, too, was speculative and inadmissible. In sum, the Court of Appeals said, the $4 million award was excessive if it constituted only general damages, and it was based on unreliable evidence if it represented some combination of general and special damages. For these reasons, the appellate court ordered a new trial on damages.

Inclusion of Inflated Purchase Price Does Not Doom Damages Calculation

Case name: *In re Novatel Wireless Securities Litigation*
Citation: 2012 U.S. Dist. LEXIS 181198
Date of decision: Dec. 14, 2012
Country: US
State or Federal: Federal
State/Jurisdiction: California
Court: United States District Court
Type of action: Securities
Experts: Bjorn Steinholt (plaintiffs); Dr. David Tabak (defendants)
Judge: Battaglia
SIC: 4812 Radiotelephone Communications

Investors brought a class action lawsuit against the defendants (the company and individual executives) for misrepresentations and insider trading under Section 10(b) of the Securities Exchange Act and Rule 10b-5 in federal court (S.D. Cal.). A provider of wireless broadband access, the company depended largely on two major accounts, Sprint and Verizon. Although the defendants knew in January 2007 about Sprint's planned cancellation of a company product, they neither disclosed this news to the public nor revealed the company's weakness in the market because the revelations would interfere with their ability to sell their stock for a profit. In the class period (February 2007 to November 2008), they made 62% of their sales shortly before July 20, 2007, when a business report announced the cancellation. During that time, four specific stock price declines occurred as a result of the market's learning of concealed adverse facts, the plaintiffs alleged.

Multiple control periods to assess price movements. The plaintiffs retained an expert to determine whether there was loss causation for class members who purchased before, and held or sold after, one of the four dates and to quantify damages. The defendants challenged his testimony in a pretrial *Daubert* motion.

1. *Loss causation.* To assess the fraudulent conduct, the expert performed an event study for which he analyzed both specific days that featured material misrepresentations to the public related to the stock and days that partially revealed the truth through corrective disclosures. He adjusted for market and industry factors that affected stock prices, but not for non-fraud-related company news. After the defendants' expert cited additional non-fraud-related information, he reviewed it, but ultimately disregarded it, concluding that it had no material negative effect on the stock price.

To evaluate the statistical significance for July 20, 2007, he performed a one-sided, as opposed to a two-sided, test. This was the appropriate approach, he stated, when there was independent evidence that the event either had a negative or positive effect on future cash flow, but not both. Initially, he used the common one-year control period to determine the normal historical statistical relationship between the company's price returns and those in market and industry indices.

After he learned of the specific fraud-related days that could taint the control period, he performed a more targeted analysis focusing on the 120 days prior to the relevant dates. This narrowing, he said, allowed him "to more accurately quantify the company-specific portion of a specific fraud-related price movement." He then ran a regression analysis using the price returns from the control period to develop a regression equation for predicting company price returns on the analyzed days. For July 20, 2007, using the shorter control period increased the statistical significance of the price decline from a 90% to a 95% level of confidence.

Given the price fluctuations on that day, he also conducted an intraday analysis to determine whether the movements were unusual in comparison to the company's historical maximum intraday declines and rebounds. While the stock traded at $28.37 per share the day before, it sank to $25.09 about an hour and a half after disclosure of the contract cancellation and rose to a closing price of $27.05 after an allegedly misleading company rebuttal later in the day. The expert determined an 11.6% drop in stock price in response to the cancellation report.

The defendants' expert criticized the use of the one-sided test in the event study, stating that to his knowledge, financial economists almost exclusively relied on two-sided tests. These, he explained, "allowed for the possibility of finding that a stock price movement is abnormally positive or negative." In contrast, a one-sided test assumed the result was only meaningful if it headed in one direction. As such, he believed, it doubled the error rate of finding that a price change was statistically significant.

He agreed that it was appropriate to use a control period close to the relevant event and that limiting it to a 120-day period was reasonable. He expressed concern, however, because the plaintiffs' expert appeared to resort to it after obtaining lower statistically significant results from the initial one-year period. As to the intraday analysis, he agreed that the July 20 stock price decline seemed to result from the disclosure of the cancellation.

2. *Damages.* After establishing loss causation, the plaintiffs' expert performed an out-of-pocket analysis to calculate Section 10(b) damages. The test, he said, limited recovery to the "difference between the purchase price and the value of the security at the date of purchase less the difference between the sale price and the value of the security at the date of sale," citing an authoritative law review article. The most important part of the calculation was to create a value line that represented the actual value of the stock, that is, to determine "the price the security would have traded *absent the alleged fraud*," he stated with emphasis. For this purpose, he replaced fraud-related price returns with predicted price returns, while holding all other ones constant. Moreover, he excluded damages for shares traded during periods for which he could not establish loss causation.

As he understood the statute, Section 20A damages captured: (a) the inflation per share at the time of the insider sales; or (b) the losses the defendants avoided by selling shares during the class period, as opposed to after disclosure of the truth, at the end of the period. Because he determined that in all instances, profits gained were less than losses avoided, he decided to use the profits-gained measure.

Failure to remove non-fraud-related factors? In their *Daubert* motion, the defendants primarily contended that: 1) the event study included substantial defects that made the loss causation analysis unreliable; and 2) the damages analyses did not comport with the controlling Supreme Court case.

1. *Event study.* Although the defendants did not object to the expert's methodology per se, they claimed his analysis did not sufficiently isolate non-fraud-related factors from consideration. The company's corrective disclosures contained pieces of unrelated negative information whose effect he failed to assess. Also, he should have used a two-sided test to determine the statistical significance for July 20. Moreover, they claimed his dissatisfaction with earlier results prompted him to narrow the control period to 120 days.

Finally, they argued, he speculated about the timing of events for his intraday analysis and failed to explain why much of the price decline occurred over an hour and a half after the market opened with full awareness of the adverse report.

The plaintiffs contended that the one-sided test was appropriate to evaluate price movement on July 20, because the day's early disclosure "was information that from an economic point of view could only result in a negative impact on the company's stock price." The 120-day control period was not an issue because, in the end, the expert used an intraday analysis to establish loss causation for that day. As for that analysis, the defendants' expert also found a link between the early negative report and the stock price decline.

The court stated that even though the plaintiffs' expert might have included an analysis of non-fraud-related company news in his event study, he properly had weighed market and industry factors. "Failure to consider one of the relevant variables does not dictate exclusion of the report as unreliable." Also, case law failed to provide a standard for determining the statistical significance of a stock price decline. Simply because the defendants' expert favored the two-sided test did not mean the approach of the plaintiffs' expert was unreasonable, the court said. For his intraday analysis, the expert compiled and identified the necessary evidence to approximate the disclosure of the critical reports. Given the unusual events of that day, this type of analysis was appropriate and could be helpful to the jury, the court found. The defendants could challenge details of the expert's method or conclusions during cross-examination.

2. *Damages calculation.* The defendants claimed the expert's calculation of both Section 10(b) and Section 20A damages contradicted *Dura Pharmaceuticals, Inc. v. Broudo,* 544 U.S. 336 (2005) (available at *BVLaw*). There, the Supreme Court held that a plaintiff must establish a causal connection between the material misrepresentation and the injury it suffered.

The defendants particularly objected to the expert's Section 20A analysis, claiming it led to the "absurd result that each defendant's profits are greater than their total sales proceeds less the amount each defendant paid for his or her shares." For example, they said, assuming a defendant bought a share for $18.78 and sold it for $24.00, his profit at most was $5.22 per share. In contrast, the plaintiffs' expert determined a profit of $12.47 per share based on his finding that the true value at the time of sale was only $11.53.

The court noted at the outset that *Dura* did not specify a method for calculating damages. Rather, the case warned against reliance on price inflation alone to establish either economic loss or loss causation. In this case, even though he incorporated the inflated purchase price into the overall calculation, he relied upon "much more" when calculating Section 10(b) damages, the court found.

He used a reliable event study and regression analysis, and his value line represented the actual value of the stock absent the alleged fraud. His methodology tried to minimize the risk that plaintiffs could recover for non-fraud-related losses.

Section 20A of the Securities Exchange Act limits damages to "profit gained or loss avoided," the court stated. While it appreciated the logic of the defendants' argument, it also considered the plaintiffs' expert's approach well reasoned. The court concluded that the defendants failed to point to legal authority in declaring his approach unreliable under *Daubert* and admitted the plaintiff's entire expert testimony.

Court Rejects Expert's Use of Going Concern Method for Inactive Business

Case name: *O'Rourke v. Burke and Hotchkiss, PLLC*
Citation: 2013 N.H. Super. LEXIS 4
Date of decision: March 6, 2013
Country: US
State or Federal: State
State/Jurisdiction: New Hampshire
Court: Superior Court
Type of action: Malpractice (Legal)
Experts: Earnest Tyler (plaintiff); unknown (defendant)
Judge: McNamara
SIC: 2051 Bread and Other Bakery Products, Except Cookies and Crackers

Citing an authority on the going concern methodology but failing to apply the prescribed principles was only one of several critical errors an expert made when he assessed damages for a struggling bagel company related to its legal malpractice claim. In its *Daubert* ruling, the court found the testimony unreliable.

The plaintiff, a bagel business, filed suit in state court against the defendant, a law firm, alleging it had failed to perfect the lending shareholders' security interests in the company. As a consequence, when the business filed for bankruptcy, the trustee was able to take possession of all of its assets. Had the firm performed to standard, the company shareholders would have kept the secured assets, disposed of the unsecured debt, and continued in business upon reorganization.

The company retained an expert, a CPA, who analyzed the going concern value of the business's assets, its depreciated value, and the value of other assets. The defendant objected under *Daubert*, as adopted by state law. The plaintiff claimed the opinion was admissible because any legitimate concerns went to weight and credibility.

No sustained earnings. The expert stated he chose to value the company as an "active business with future earning power as opposed to liquidation value." He said he used the "going concern methodology" James S. Queenan set forth in "Standards for Valuations of Security Interest in

Chapter 11," a 1987 law review article. It suggests that an expert consider earnings of the five previous years and refrain from making "long-range projections of substantial earnings for a business currently suffering losses or making only a small profit." The article calls them "largely speculative."

However, the expert here only considered earnings for one year in business—2009 to 2010—during which the company actually showed a loss of $238,187. Also, in a deposition, its owner stated that in years prior to bankruptcy its weekly cash flow was "basically a little over break-even."

Moreover, the expert based his analysis on the assumption that if the business had been able to continue it would have made a number of changes to increase profits. For example, he assumed it would have moved to a cheaper location, disposed of the retail portion of the business, and downsized in terms of space and menu. In line with this vision, he calculated labor costs, utility costs, and other expenses and projected income and annual net income. Ultimately, he concluded that the business's "going concern" value was $448,000.

The court found the testimony problematic. First, it noted that the expert had failed to follow the very method he referenced as authoritative. Contrary to the "Queenan methodology," he did not base his valuation on anywhere near a five-year period. Also, it was obvious, even at the time he performed his analysis, that the company was no longer "an active business," the court stated. In fact, "the business never generated sustained earnings."

Second, he based his analysis "entirely on speculation." Calculating damages based on a going concern valuation ultimately was based on lost profits, the court said. Even if the law does not require absolute certainty, it considers evidence of expected profits incompetent where operations have never begun. This was the case here because the expert's analysis was based on the business starting over, under a "substantially different business model from the old business."

Although the going concern methodology itself was reliable, it "cannot reliably be applied to the facts in issue," and it was not applied to the facts, the court concluded.

Regarding the expert's analysis of the depreciated value of the business's assets, the defendant noted that, even though the depreciated book value of an asset was meaningful for tax purposes, it "says little about the asset's current fair market value." The court agreed, finding this testimony could, in effect, mislead a lay jury. In sum, it excluded the expert's entire opinion.

Interdisciplinary Appraisal Cannot Prevent Incomplete Valuation

Case name: *Pappas v. Pappas*
Citation: 2013 Tex. App. LEXIS 280
Date of decision: Jan. 10, 2013
Country: US
State or Federal: State
State/Jurisdiction: Texas
Court: Court of Appeals
Type of action: Marital Dissolution
Experts: Unknown (wife); Unknown (husband)
Judge: Jones
SIC: 4225 General Warehousing and Storage (miniwarehouses and self-storage units)

At divorce, the husband and wife retained business valuators and a real estate appraiser to value two businesses, but the combined expertise did not forestall claims that the trial court "dramatically undervalued" the marital estate.

The businesses were a rental storage business and a carpet business and included real property and operations.

1. *Rental storage business.* The husband's interest in a rental storage business, which encompassed three blocks, began before the marriage, when he entered into a general partnership agreement with his father. The husband and wife agreed that one block was his separate property, but disagreed over the extent of his ownership interest in the business. He stated it was 49%, but she argued it was 50%.

Of the remaining two blocks, one had three buildings the couple and his parents had financed. The lots were for the exclusive use of the partnership, and tax returns showed them as partnership property. The funds to purchase the property came from storage-unit rental income the partnership had retained. The second block had two buildings; the husband's father had bought the lots before entering into the partnership, but during the marriage, his son used a loan from his father to buy a 49% interest in it. At the time of trial, some $58,000 remained unpaid.

The husband's expert valued the entire business—all lots in three blocks—under the income capitalization approach at $2.22 million. He did not allocate value to the business by building or block.

Using the same method, the wife's expert determined a value of approximately $2.23 million; however, he broke down the value, finding the buildings in one block were worth $1.1 million, those in the second were worth $411,000, and those in the block that was the husband's separate property were worth $684,000.

Both experts also performed a valuation under the cost approach, essentially agreeing that the overall value of the business was $1.9 million. But the husband's expert did not allocate the cost of miscellaneous improvements and land; the wife's expert proposed an allocation of both components of value among the buildings based on their value.

Disagreement comes down to discounts. The experts' principal disagreement centered on whether discounts applied and to what extent. The husband's expert determined his interest in the business required a 40% reduction to reflect a lack of marketability/liquidity, regardless of whether he had an undivided 49% interest or was an equal owner. As he saw it, even a 50% ownership "is still qualified as a non-controlling interest and is less marketable." But he also said that if the husband's interest were only 49%, an additional 20% discount for lack of control would be appropriate.

The husband also presented a real estate appraiser to speak to the value of the properties both businesses used. As to the storage business, he said "trying to get two people to agree" made it more difficult to sell an undivided interest in real property; therefore, "under the industry standard," it was appropriate to reduce the value by one-third.

Based on his experts' findings, the husband valued the community interest in the business at $82,125, arguing that only the buildings in the lots he bought after marriage and for which he paid with profits from the partnerships and with the loan were community property. The amount resulted from adding the building and land value ($429,000), reducing that figure by the 49% ownership interest, applying a noncontrolling interest discount of 33.3%, and deducing the outstanding loan balance ($58,000).

The wife's expert stated that, generally speaking, an equal, undivided ownership interest required no discount, whereas a majority interest carried a premium and a minority interest required a discount for lack of control. Here, no discount applied because the husband and his father held equal interests.

The trial court awarded the business to the husband, finding that one block was separate property and the value of the community portion of the business and real estate including the other two blocks was $82,125. It did not explain its methodology.

Overlooking one block. In her appeal, the wife claimed that the trial court undervalued the business for various reasons. Under the income capitalization approach, by her expert's account, the business was worth at least $2.2 million and the community's interest $1.1 million. Even if discounts applied, the "uncontroverted" minimum value for the business was $522,000, she contended.

The Court of Appeals found that her expert's calculation overstated the value because it included the value for the block that was separate property. This reduced the value to $1.5 million (income capitalization approach) or $1.4 million (cost approach). Because the experts used both methods, the trial court was free to use both for its valuation.

Even though the trial court did not explain how it arrived at the $82,125 value, the appellate court found it was reasonable to conclude that it adopted the figures proposed by the husband's experts. The trial court could "reasonably" have valued the business in this way, the appellate court found.

But several valuation errors led to significant undervaluation and demanded a new division of the assets. For one, even though the trial court seemed to use the cost approach to valuing the business, it failed to attribute any value to the $125,000 in miscellaneous improvements that both parties' experts included in their assessments. More importantly, it failed to assign any value to one block that was community property and, based on expert testimony, added several hundred thousand dollars to the value of the overall business, even assuming discounts applied.

2. *Carpet business.* While married, the husband, with a friend, also bought a carpet business that operated on two lots at the time of trial. A third lot served as storage for inventory.

Using an "income-oriented" approach, the husband's expert determined the business was worth approximately $1.3 million before adjustments and discounts. This method, he said, assumed that all assets—tangible and intangible—were indistinguishable components of the business and did not attempt to separate the values of the two. He relied on the business's adjusted balance summary sheets, which showed a fixed asset value of $1.17 million for 2010, including a $1.15 million value for "property, plant, & equipment" and "land" worth about $16,500. The expert applied a 30% discount for lack of marketability/liquidity and a 25% discount for lack of control and reduced the total by the husband's 49.5% ownership interest.

Although the wife's expert argued against applying any discount to the husband's equal ownership interest in the storage business, he applied a 10% discount for lack of liquidity to the husband's interest in the carpet business. (The opinion does not provide any further details about his valuation.)

An appraisal put the value of the two lots at $434,000 before any deductions applied.

The trial court valued the third lot at nearly $28,000 and awarded it to the husband. In addition, it gave him an interest in the business that was worth approximately $337,000. The court did not specifically mention the two lots in its final divorce decree, nor did it discuss real property, buildings, or land in valuing the business interest.

Incongruity in valuation. On appeal, the wife claimed that the trial court had failed to value and dispose of the community's interest in the two lots.

The appellate court agreed that there was an "incongruity" in the way the trial court dealt with the three lots: It valued and awarded one lot separately from the business, when the partnership acquired all lots in a similar way and used them for business purposes.

At the same time, the lower court's valuation suggested it had adopted the method and values proposed by the husband's expert for the business and, in so doing, had recognized that the value of the two lots was a major part of the business's overall value. For example, the income statement the expert attached to his report showed no expense for rent, which was consistent with the business's owning the property on which it operated. Therefore, it was reasonable to conclude that the trial court accounted for the value of the two lots when valuing the business and disposed of them in the award to the husband. However, the court noted that the remand as to the valuation of the rental storage business provided an opportunity for the trial court to "revisit" its valuation of the carpet business.

Intrinsic Value Review Precludes Inclusion of Fractional Discounts

Case name: *Patel v. Patel*
Citation: 2013 Va. App. LEXIS 110
Date of decision: April 9, 2013
Country: US
State or Federal: State
State/Jurisdiction: Virginia
Court: Court of Appeals
Type of action: Marital Dissolution
Experts: Mike Miller (wife); Michael Cummings, Larry Salzman (husband)
Judge: Humphreys

In its equitable distribution analysis, the circuit court expressly declined to apply the fractional discounts the husband's expert proposed for valuing his interest in companies owning hotels. On appeal, the husband claimed this was one of several critical valuation-related errors the court made.

The husband had varying interests in seven companies that owned and operated hotels and properties. At divorce, both parties introduced experts—three in all—to determine the value of the investments. The valuations focused primarily on two companies in which the husband had a one-third and a 40% ownership interest, respectively. The wife's expert used an income approach and calculated a value of $7.9 million for the hotel one company owned and a $4.15 million value for the hotel of the second company.

The husband retained two experts. One expert also used the income approach and valued one hotel at $6.4 million and the second at $3.5 million. But the alternate expert performed a fractional interest appraisal of the husband's shares in the companies.

To determine the net equity value of each company, he began with the real estate values of the hotels the companies owned; he then added the companies' other assets and subtracted their liabilities. Next, he multiplied this value by the husband's ownership percentage to arrive at the pro rata equity value, which he discounted to account for factors related to fractional ownership. These factors might include the ups and downs of the real estate market, the number of owners, income characteristics, lack of control, "sometimes partition ability, finance ability, and the overall marketability," he specified.

In terms of the first company, he said, the real estate value was $6.4 million, cash reserves were approximately $274,000, and debt amounted to nearly $6.3 million. The net assets equaled about $415,000. He applied a 35% minority discount and concluded the husband's shares in the company were worth $90,000.

As for the second company, its real estate valued $3.5 million, cash reserves amounted to $117,000, and debt to over $2.2 million; this meant the business owned net assets of $1.5 million. In this instance, the expert used a 40% discount and concluded the husband's interest was worth $350,000.

The parties agreed that four entities had a negative value and that the husband had made personal loans in varying amounts to them. Also, one company owned land but began construction of a new hotel after the couple's separation.

Circuit court combines approaches. In valuing the interests to arrive at an equitable distribution, the circuit court adopted the values the wife's husband proposed for the hotels themselves. It then factored into its calculations other assets the companies owned besides the hotels, specifically cash reserves; finally, it subtracted the companies' debts. Although it accepted the approach the husband's second expert took to determine the pro rata equity value of the companies, it expressly declined to include that expert's discounts for fractional ownership.

Under the "intrinsic value" review that state law required, the court explained, it was not "proper" to include the discounts the husband's expert derived by using a different valuation method. Instead, in determining the assets' intrinsic value, the court already considered the fact that the husband's partial interests were not liquid or easily transferrable.

It concluded that the first company valued $7.9 million; considering cash worth $274,000, loans totaling $6.3 million, and the husband's one-third ownership, his interest was worth approximately $648,000. As for the second company, it set the value of the hotel at $4.15 million, cash at $117,000, mortgage loans at approximately $2.15 million, and loans owed to shareholders at $561,000. Considering the husband's 40% ownership in the company, his share was worth approximately $623,000.

To the four businesses that had a negative value, it assigned a value of zero. State law governing the equitable distribution of marital property did not allow for an offset for the total value of a marital estate stemming from the negative value of one asset, the court stated. "If the subtraction of marital debt from the value of a marital asset leaves a negative total, the net value of the asset is zero."

Further, it awarded the husband notes payable to account for the personal loans to the four companies whose debts exceeded their values. Collectively, the notes were worth $1.9 million, the circuit court found.

'What if' is not part of valuation calculus. On appeal to the Virginia Court of Appeals, the husband assigned several errors to the circuit court's valuations. The appellate court dealt with the arguments in turn.

1. *Value of two companies.* The husband objected to the circuit court's combining values from the wife's expert and the husband's second expert, while declining to apply the latter's proposed fractional discounts.

At the outset of its review, the appellate court noted, with emphasis, that there were essentially two different approaches. Two experts used an income approach to value *"the hotels operated by the companies."* The husband's alternate expert, however, computed the full values *"of the companies themselves,"* before calculating the value of the husband's interests by discounting for his fractional interests. The circuit court had discretion to credit the wife's expert in deciding on the value for the hotels.

Precedent requires that "courts valuing marital property for the purpose of making a monetary award must determine … that value which represents the property's *intrinsic worth* to the parties," the appellate court stated, citing *Howell v. Howell,* 31 Va. App. 332 (2000) (available at *BVLaw*). This standard of value is "a very subjective concept that looks to the worth of the property to the parties," it continued. An asset may have no established market value, "and neither party may contemplate selling the item; indeed sale may be restricted or forbidden." Regardless, the court must translate the intrinsic value into a monetary amount.

Performing the requisite intrinsic value review, the circuit court did in fact consider the illiquid nature of the husband's interests in the companies and did not err when it rejected the discount the husband's expert proposed within the context of a different type of analysis, the appellate court concluded.

2. *Zero value.* The trial court erred when it assigned a zero value to interests in four companies that had a negative net value, the husband argued. Also, because he was personally liable for the debts of the companies, if any one of them went out of business, the debt would exceed the assets and he would need to cover the excess. Accordingly, that excess should count as marital debt.

The appellate court disagreed. It first pointed out that the applicable case calling for no value in instances where the debt equals or exceeds the asset's value failed to provide reasoning for its holding. Therefore, the court provided its own rationale. Young companies or businesses looking to expand frequently had to incur debt or leverage debt to generate profit or expand operations, it said. Yet, this fact did not mean the company had a negative value or was incapable of making a profit. Rather, "it merely shows that *at the time of valuation* the company has more debt than assets," the court stated with emphasis.

It dismissed the husband's concerns about their going out of business in the future. The calculation the lower court performed pivoted around the companies' intrinsic value at the time of the evidentiary hearing. There was no evidence that at that date they were insolvent or headed toward bankruptcy. To the contrary, several of the companies had brand-new hotels or acquired properties for the purpose of building new hotels on them. That the husband *may* be liable at some point in the future "is not properly part of the present valuation calculus," the court concluded.

3. *Loans.* Further, the husband claimed the circuit court improperly counted the notes payable as a marital asset when the related companies had no value or debt far above their value.

The appellate court rejected this argument for many of the reasons it gave regarding the zero value issue. It would be a mistake to assume that just because the companies' assets at present were worth less than the collective debt, the respective debts were worthless, the court said. At the time of the evidentiary hearing, the companies were operating and there were no signs that any one of them had defaulted on the loans. The lower court was not "plainly wrong" when it considered the loans "valid debts incurred by going concerns" and determined the companies "have the ability to make distributions to shareholders or repay the notes." The appellate court found that, within the context of equitable distribution, the circuit court could find the notes were worth their full value. For all these reasons, the Court of Appeals affirmed the circuit court's valuations and judgment.

Ignoring Accountant's Advice, Taxpayers Botch Investment Strategy

Case name: *Peek v. Commissioner*
Citation: 2013 U.S. Tax Ct. LEXIS 13
Date of decision: May 9, 2013
Country: US
State or Federal: Federal
State/Jurisdiction: N/A
Court: United States Tax Court
Type of action: Federal Taxation
Experts: N/A
Judge: Gustafson
SIC: 3669 Communications Equipment, NEC
Key words: IRA, Capital Gains, IRC Section 4975 c 1 B

A recent tax case shows how an investment strategy that used IRAs to maximize gains from the acquisition and sale of a company went awry when the taxpayer-investors disregarded their financial expert's advice concerning "prohibited transactions."

Two taxpayers decided to buy an alarm and fire safety company for investment purposes. They hired an accountant to structure the transaction and perform due diligence. He developed a multistep strategy that used IRAs to defer until retirement any income tax liability on the gain they hoped to make on the asset.

Accordingly, in August 2001, each taxpayer set up a self-directed IRA into which he rolled funds from an existing account. Ten days later, the taxpayers formed a new company (Newco), which they intended to use to buy the assets of the target company. On Sept. 11, 2001, each IRA acquired 50% of Newco stock for $309,000. The company then bought the target's assets for $1.1 million, including cash resulting from various loans and—critically—a $200,000 promissory note from Newco to the sellers that was secured by personal guaranties from the taxpayers. These guaranties remained in effect until the sale of Newco to a third party five years later.

At the time the accountant explained the strategy, he provided an opinion letter that said "the taxpayer could not engage in transactions with the IRA that the IRS would determine to be 'prohibited transactions.'" Another letter cautioned: "[A]ny actions you take on behalf of the corporation must be taken by you as an agent for the corporation and not by you personally." Whether the taxpayers had discussed the personal guaranties with the accountant was not indicated.

From 2001 until the 2006 sale, the taxpayers were the only corporate officers and directors in Newco. In 2003, they converted their IRAs into Roth IRAs, which meant that each Roth IRA owned 50% of the company's stock. The taxpayers reported the fair market values of the converted portions of the accounts as taxable income for 2003 and 2004. As a result of the 2006 sale of Newco, each Roth IRA received in total more than $1.6 million during 2006 and 2007.

When the taxpayers filed federal income tax returns for those two years, they did not include capital gains related to the Newco stock sale. The Internal Revenue Service (IRS) subsequently issued deficiency notices related to the proceeds of the company sale, and the taxpayers petitioned the Tax Court for review.

Section 4975(c)(1)(B) invites 'broad' reading. The IRS claimed that the taxpayers' original and successor IRAs stopped qualifying as IRAs from September 2001 through 2006, that is, the moment the taxpayers' made the personal loan guaranties. The latter were "prohibited transactions" under section 4975(c)(1)(B) of the Internal Revenue Code (IRC). Consequently, the IRA assets were distributed to the taxpayers, who owed income tax on the gain they made in 2006 and 2007.

The taxpayers responded that prohibited transactions could only occur "between a plan and a disqualified person." Here, the guaranties were between disqualified persons, the taxpayers, and a different entity (Newco) that was owned by the IRAs, but not the IRAs themselves. In other words, no plan participated in the transaction.

The Tax Court found the taxpayers' reading of the statute too narrow. Section 4975(c)(1)(B) prohibited "any direct or indirect … extension of credit between a plan and a disqualified person." Congress intended the phrase "any direct or indirect" to be read broadly, otherwise "the prohibition could be easily and abusively avoided simply by having the IRA create a shell subsidiary to whom the disqualified person could then make a loan."

Also, the court explained, the loan guaranties were not a "once and done transaction with effects only in 2001." Rather, they remained in effect through the sale of Newco in 2006; as such, they represented a continuing prohibited transaction, which, in turn, prevented the accounts that held the Newco stock from being IRAs. The tax liability from the gain belonged to the taxpayers as the creators and beneficiaries of the accounts that sold the Newco stock. What's more, the accountant's letters specifically discussed prohibited transactions, which put the taxpayers on notice; therefore, they were negligent when they failed to report income from the sale. Accordingly, accuracy-related penalties under section 6662(a) for 2006 and 2007 also applied, the Tax Court found.

Unclear Discount of Medical Practice Value Causes Remand

Case name: *Peltzer v. Peltzer*
Citation: 2012 N.C. App. LEXIS 1103 (N.C. Ct. App.)
Date of decision: Sept. 18, 2012
Country: US
State or Federal: State
State/Jurisdiction: North Carolina
Court: Court of Appeals
Type of action: Marital Dissolution
Experts: Mark Snell (Husband)
Judge: Stroud
SIC: 8011

The parties in this divorce case agreed that the husband should keep his medical practice, but disputed its value. At trial, only the husband presented a CPA expert, who provided pre- and post-tax estimates of the practice's stock value, in particular focusing on the negative consequences of any liquidation. He also emphasized the closely held nature of the practice and the "informal" nature of the shareholders' noncompete and consulting agreements.

Rather than a traditional valuation methodology, he applied a "rule of thumb" or "common sense" approach to value the practice. As the basis of his calculation, he averaged two years of gross annual receipts by a factor of 50% to conclude that the husband's shares were worth just over $328,000. If the husband were to sell his interest, the expert said, the value of his shares would drop to approximately $197,000 due to federal and state taxes.

The trial court acknowledged the difficulty in valuing the husband's illiquid interest and relied on his expert's valuation and approach. Given the close nature of the practice, any valuation should include a discount, the court stated. At the same time, it found the husband was unlikely to sell his shares and, without elaborating on any specific discount, adopted the expert's pretax value of $328,000.

Challenging his own expert. On appeal, the husband claimed that the trial court failed to use a reliable valuation methodology, including application of a discount, and failed to consider the adverse tax consequences from any sale of his medical practice.

As to the first issue, "you can't complain about a result you caused," the appellate court observed. The husband offered his expert as the sole witness to testify on business value; any deficiencies in the expert's evidence meant the husband failed to meet his burden of proof, not that the trial court erred by adopting the expert's value.

The court also dismissed the argument on tax effects. Under the applicable state statute, a trial court need only account for the consequences of a sale if these were "reasonably likely to occur." Here, the trial court expressly determined that, given the husband's age and vested interest in "continuing the protective and financially rewarding practice," he was unlikely to sell his shares.

At the same time, it was "unclear what 'discount' the trial court applied to determine the value of the practice," the court said. Most likely, the "discount" related to the 50% reduction that the husband's expert applied to the gross annual receipts, "but we cannot say for sure," the court said. "A better practice would have been to make a clear finding of fact ... as to the valuation of the medical practice at [$328,000] and how the court arrived at this value" it said, and remanded this sole issue for reconsideration.

IRS Gives Hybrid Business Favorable Tax Status

Case name: *Private Letter Ruling 201314002*
Citation: 2012 PLR LEXIS 1751
Date of decision: April 5, 2013
Country: US
State or Federal: State
State/Jurisdiction: Federal Circuit
Court: Departement of the Treasury
Type of action: Federal Taxation
Experts: N/A
Judge: Imholtz (Branch Chief)
SIC: 6519 Lessors of Real Property, NEC

A recent private letter ruling (not precedential) from the IRS discusses a data center's request for approval as a real estate investment trust (REIT) so that it could obtain favorable tax treatment under the Internal Revenue Code's section 856, subchapter M.

Hybrid businesses such as real estate holding companies, shopping centers, or similar entities that combine real property and operations pose special valuation challenges. This ruling provides a perspective on how broadly the IRS defines terms such as "rents" and "real estate assets" to draw the line between a REIT-qualifying entity and a standard corporation.

Under section 856, a REIT is "any corporation, trust or association that acts as an investment agent specializing in real estate and real estate mortgages." For purposes of federal taxation, a REIT may deduct dividend payments on its corporate income taxes as long as it pays out 90% of its taxable income each year to shareholders. In 1960, when Congress created REITs, a central concern was to ensure that their gross income primarily consisted of passive income from owning or leasing real estate.

Facts. A corporation that owned and leased several data centers in the U.S. and abroad planned to form a new entity, the taxpayer. It asked the IRS for a ruling on whether the new company qualified as a REIT under section 856. (The opinion does not identify the taxpayer or the related businesses.)

The taxpayer would be the general partner in an operating partnership (OP) that also included affiliates of the parent company as limited partners. The OP planned to acquire, lease, purchase, and develop data center buildings, the initial properties (IP), and lease them to unrelated and related tenants, as well as provide ordinary and necessary services to the tenants.

The taxpayer stated that the space it planned to lease ranged from a single rack to an entire floor measuring thousands of feet. The buildings included major structural components—electrical, HVAC, security, fire protection, and telecommunications infrastructure—that would remain permanently in place. Planned services would include providing humidity control, security, utilities, common area and public area maintenance, shipping and receiving, telecommunications infrastructure, and an interconnection to enable tenants to connect to carriers, their servers, and to one another. The services were not for the convenience of a particular tenant. The taxpayer also planned to provide remote hands services that did not require logical access to the tenants' equipment, including reseating, relabeling, or replacing external cables, rebooting servers, and changing backup tapes. It stated it would not repair, replace, or operate the tenant's equipment or provide network or IT management services (Smart Hands). Tenants could contract with the parent company and its affiliates separately and independently from the OP to provide customized services.

The taxpayer, through the OP, planned to have employees to perform Smart Hands or other non-customary services for a taxable REIT subsidiary (TRS), who would remain employees of the OP for administrative purposes. Both entities would share the employees, and the TRS would reimburse the OP for employee costs.

Legal analysis. In determining the new entity's qualification under section 856, the IRS considered several critical issues:

1. *Taxpayer's interest in real property.* IRC section 856(c)(3) requires that at least 75% of a REIT's gross income stem from rents from real property. Section 856(c)(4) specifies that at least 75% of the value of a REIT's total assets must be from real estate assets, cash, cash items (including receivables), and government securities.

"Real estate assets" may be real property (including interests in real property and in mortgages on real property) and shares in other REITs. "Interests in real property" include fee ownership or co-ownership of land or improvements and options to acquire land or leaseholds or improvements to them.

Real property, the IRS said, included the wiring of a building, plumbing, heating and air conditioning, elevators, and other permanent structures. Under the statute, it does not include "assets accessory to the operation of a business," such as machinery and office equipment that is not part of the structure or furnishings of a hotel. A prior revenue ruling that assessed whether components of a microwave transmission system qualified as real estate assets found the building, heating and air conditioning system, the transmitting and receiving towers, and the fence were real estate assets, but antennae, waveguides, and transmitting and receiving equipment were accessories and, therefore, not real estate assets.

In the case at issue, the initial properties and structural components were "inherently permanent structures." Accordingly, they met the definition of real property even if they facilitated the technology businesses of tenants.

2. *Real estate intangibles.* Section 1.856-2(d)(3) provides that the term "total assets" means the gross assets of the REIT derived in accordance with GAAP. Given the nature of its activities—owning and leasing data centers—the proposed REIT would generate goodwill that increased its value, the IRS stated. "Since the real estate intangibles relate solely to the OP's business of leasing and providing customary services to tenants," they were real estate assets and interests in real property for purposes of section 856, the IRS found. Accordingly, gain from the disposition of the real estate intangibles represented "qualifying income for purposes of sections 856(c)(2) and (3)."

3, *Services provided.* Under the statute, the term "rents from real property" includes charges for services the business customarily provides in connection with the rental. What is "customary" depends on the geographic market. The statute does not consider the services of an independent contractor that does not provide income to the REIT services the REIT provides. By contrast, the IRS said, payments to hotels, warehouses, or storage garages that cover the use of space and customized service to the occupant did not meet the definition of "rent." In this case, because the OP intended to provide only "usual or customary" services related to operating and maintaining the data centers, the payments would constitute rents.

4. *Employee-sharing arrangement.* In line with a prior revenue ruling, the IRS found the reimbursement and cost-sharing arrangements between the OP and the TRS indicated that the OP would not profit from them. Accordingly, reimbursements from the TRS to the OP for employee costs and other shared expenses were not gross income to either the OP or the taxpayer.

Based on all these considerations, the IRS found this particular taxpayer qualified as a REIT.

Court, Not Expert, Misses Mark on Loss Causation

Case name: *Pure Earth, Inc. v. Call*
Citation: 2013 U.S. App. LEXIS 14724
Date of decision: July 19, 2013
Country: US
State or Federal: Federal
State/Jurisdiction: Pennsylvania
Court: United States Court of Appeals
Type of action: Securities
Experts: Stephen Scherf (appellant); unknown (appellees)
Judge: Roth
SIC: 9511 Air and Water Resource and Solid Waste Management
Key words: Securities fraud, Loss Causation, Damages, Rule 702, Market Study

What's the distinction between a typical and a nontypical Section 10(b) securities fraud case? A recent appellate case from the 3rd Circuit (nonprecedential) provides valuable guidance to experts testifying to loss causation and damages.

In March 2007, the appellant reached an agreement to sell three companies he controlled to a waste-management company, which was publicly but not widely traded, in exchange for company stock. To seal the deal, the appellant received assurances from the company's CEO and CFO that no government investigations were pending against the buyer or its subsidiaries. These statements were untrue. At that time, the New York Business Integrity Commission looked into links between the company's largest subsidiary and organized crime and in November 2007 refused to renew the subsidiary's operating license. Consequently, the company's stock price fell to nearly zero. After the company sued the appellant for breach of the agreement, he countersued, claiming securities fraud under Section 10(b) of the Securities Exchange Act and SEC Rule 10b-5.

Pretrial the appellant presented a report from an experienced CPA and business valuator. The expert's opinion homed in on the misrepresentation regarding the investigation and the company's historical stock price. To control for other factors not related to the misrepresentation that could have influenced the stock price, he compared the movement in the company's stock price to the Dow Jones Industrial Average and several (unspecified) other waste-management companies. "After the market learned that [the company] had lost its license to haul waste in New York, the stock price gradually decreased to the current trading price of just $0.17," he concluded.

Exclusion under Rule 702. The U.S. district court found the report problematic under Fed. R. Evid. 702 in two respects: loss causation and damages.

As to loss causation, the court said the expert had to show that the company stock was "overvalued" and the decline in value was a "consequence of dissemination to the market of information regarding the true valuation that caused the subsequent deflation of the stock price." The expert failed to show how the downward spiral in value was attributable to the misrepresentation, the court concluded. Moreover, he did not sufficiently control for nonrelated variables. Specifically, he did not "develop a model of the normal returns in the subject stock price based on references to independent data that captures market and other developments that are independent of the events being tested."

As a result of the flawed loss causation model, the expert provided no reliable evidence to support his damages assessment, the court added. Therefore, the report was inadmissible. As a consequence, the court found that, even though the company committed fraud in connection with the stock sale to the appellant, the complainant could not prove damages and could not recover. (The court also ruled that the company had no case against the appellant.)

District court 'overcomplicates' analysis. The appellant challenged the exclusion of expert testimony in an appeal to the 3rd Circuit Court of Appeals, arguing that the district court had applied the wrong legal standard analyzing loss causation and damages.

At the outset, the appeals court stated that its review of the lower court's Rule 702 decision was "plenary," i.e., without showing any deference.

Loss causation, the linchpin of a securities case, requires a showing of a causal connection between the alleged material misrepresentation or omission and the loss. "In the Third Circuit, the loss causation analysis differs between *typical* and *non-typical* § 10(b) claims," the appellate court stated with emphasis. A typical 10(b) case involves a claim that the defendant made public announcements to inflate artificially the price of publicly traded stock. The appellate court called this "the well-known 'fraud on the market' scenario" that is at the core of most securities cases. In contrast, a nontypical 10(b) case involves a "private misrepresentation … to induce a particular individual to buy or sell securities." This was the situation in the instant case.

The type of case determines the type of proof a plaintiff—and his expert—must offer on loss causation and damages in order to prevail. "In a *typical* § 10(b) case, the plaintiff must show that his losses are related specifically to the market's discovery of the misrepresentation and the corresponding decrease in price due to that misrepresentation." But since a nontypical case does not implicate "larger market forces," the standard of proof is lower, said the appellate court.

Here, the expert's loss causation only had to "offer a reliable conclusion that the misrepresentation … negatively affected the value" of the company stock, which his report appeared to do. That other causes may have contributed to the decline in the stock's value did not matter as long as there was a showing that the misrepresentation regarding the investigation was "a proximate cause—not the sole cause—of the loss," the appeals court explained.

It went on to say that the district court correctly identified the case as a nontypical Section 10(b) case but erred when it required the expert to rule out other market factors that may have contributed to the stock's drop in value. In other words, it "conflated" the loss causation analysis with the damages analysis, the appellate court stated. It also "overcomplicated" the damages analysis. The expert merely needed to prove what the value of the company stock in March 2007 would have been if the fact about the investigation were known at that time. The expert's report could have assisted the jury in understanding the factors that go into the stock valuation to determine the amount of damages. Because the expert testimony was admissible under Rule 702, the Court of Appeals reversed and remanded for a new trial.

Correlation does not equal causation. One judge dissented. For one, she found the majority applied the wrong standard of review, which should have been abuse of discretion. By that measure, the district court's decision to exclude the report for lack of reliability under Rule 702 was appropriate.

As the dissent put it, the expert's conclusions regarding the effect of the misrepresentation were based on "correlation" not "causation." Even though the expert recognized the need to control for other market factors in tracing the company stock price, he failed to offer appropriate comparables, relying on the Dow Jones Industrial Average and businesses that participated in the same industry but had "dramatically different business models." The district court had reason to conclude that "such inapt comparisons" undermined the reliability of the opinion. And, although the plaintiff did not have to present a market study, he had to show the misrepresentation was a proximate cause of the loss and to show damages resulting from it. For this purpose, he could have offered different testimony that did not depend on the stock price. "For example, an expert familiar with waste-hauling companies might have been able to reliably assess [the company's] value both with and without a New York City hauling license," the dissent suggested.

Expert's Unconventional Method to Forecast Lost Profits Satisfies *Daubert*

Case name: *RMD, LLC v. Nitto Americas, Inc.*
Citation: 2012 U.S. Dist. LEXIS
Date of decision: Nov. 5, 2012
Country: US
State or Federal: Federal
State/Jurisdiction: Kansas
Court: United States District Court
Type of action: Contract
Experts: Marc Vianello (plaintiff); Christopher Pflaum, George McCollister (defendants)
Judge: Robinson
SIC: 3714 Motor Vehicle Parts and Accessories

The parties disputed a 2003 exclusive distribution agreement, with each asserting breach of contract as well as other claims. The plaintiff's expert, a CPA and credentialed business appraiser, prepared an initial report that assumed the contract would have remained in effect indefinitely and projected lost profits over a 70-year period. Following rebuttal from the defendants' two experts, he supplemented his report to establish the reasonableness of his theory and methodology.

In pretrial rulings, the federal district court of Kansas found the 2003 agreement expired without renewal on June 30, 2008, but its nonsolicitation provision continued for another five years. None of the experts amended their reports, but each side filed *Daubert* motions to exclude the other's testimony.

The plaintiff's expert categorized the losses stemming from the defendant's breach of the exclusivity contract in the following way:

- The defendants' sale of the exclusive product to the plaintiff's competitors from 2004-2009;
- The defendants denying the plaintiff the "most favored nation" prices for the same product, but requiring prepayment for it;
- The plaintiff's losing sales from 2008-2010, due not only to the defendants' sale to direct competitors, but also to the subsequent sale to third parties, as well as the plaintiff's inability to add the competitors' customers to its customer base; and
- The plaintiff's future losses from projected sales (2010-2080).

To quantify the diminished sales, the expert used Oracle's Crystal Ball Predictor software as well as the Holt-Winters method. Both are tools to formulate trends based on historical data and to predict future sales, he explained, and in particular, the Holt-Winters method is "a short-term moving average method for production forecasting." It was appropriate here because "it reflected the seasonal changes in the data without increasing the effects of seasonality over time."

He used it to forecast damages only through 2010; after that, he extrapolated damages due to reduced future sales growth for a period of 70 years, assuming constant amounts of increasing sales. To calculate the present value, he made assumptions based on the plaintiff's business records as well as information from its owner and discounted future damages by using the company's equity cost of capital, which he estimated to be 20.6%.

Ultimately, the plaintiff's expert determined total damages of $2.7 million, assigning $2.2 million to future lost profits and $270,000 to past losses.

The defendants offered two rebuttal experts in econometrics, who did not present an opinion as to the actual damages or critique the accounting method that the plaintiff's expert used. Instead, they criticized his use of the Holt-Winters model, which, they claimed, was not accepted in the statistical and economic community, and which (to their knowledge) no one had used to calculate damages in litigation. Instead, the plaintiff's expert should have used ARIMA, a statistical tool that uses regression analysis. Overall, his report showed a "profound ignorance of regression analysis," they concluded.

Moreover, when they ran regressions based on the defendants' alleged actions, they found the effect on the plaintiff's sales was not "statistically significant." However, when the plaintiff's expert ran his calculations under ARIMA, he found the results differed from his original conclusions by only $2,500.

Just 'plugging in' data. The defendants challenged the expert's report on several grounds, which the court considered in turn:

1. *Expiration date.* The expert's calculations were inconsistent with the court-determined 2008 expiration date, the defendants said, rendering the entire analysis inadmissible.

In response, the plaintiff pointed out the different ways to breach the agreement after the initial 2008 term, and some of the defendants' conduct caused residual, long-term effects. Since its expert simply assumed breach, the court's order required the plaintiff to prove the defendants' specific violations to the jury, but it did not disqualify his opinion, particularly since his analysis permitted the jury to reduce any future damages according to their findings on a breach and its effects.

Although its order rendered the expert's 70-year projection "untenable," the court agreed its prior order did not render his report inadmissible under *Daubert*, especially in light of its adjustable damages structure. The expert relied on historical data and statements from the plaintiff's owner and "when tested with the ARIMA program, his projections proved to be precise." As such, they complied with the reasonable certainty standard for admitting lost profits evidence, the court held.

2. *Qualifications*. The expert used forecasting tools that required a background in econometrics and statistics, which, as a CPA, he did not have, the defendants said.

This was "analogous to arguing the expert was not qualified to use a computer because he cannot explain how a computer is programmed," the plaintiff responded, and once again the court agreed. The expert was not presenting an opinion on statistics or econometrics; rather, he simply "plugged in" data to the forecasting programs, "a process he would otherwise undertake as an accountant."

3. *Statistical methods*. Instead of considering historical data and calculating lost profits using a regression analysis, the expert used a methodology that had not undergone rigorous testing for reliability, the defendants claimed. The ARIMA statistical tool, which uses regression analysis, would have been better.

The plaintiff pointed out that Holt-Winters had been an accepted model to predict future sales for some 50 years. What's more, the expert's supplemental ARIMA test results differed by only $2,500 from the original ones. Likewise, the court found that even though ARIMA might be the methodology of choice for statisticians, the defendants failed to show why accountants could not use Holt-Winters for their forecasts or why a regression analysis was the only way to forecast sales and lost profits. Considering the expert projected lost sales for 70 years into the future, the already small $2,500 difference between the two results would be even less for projections covering a shorter time frame.

Inadmissible rebuttal. In its motion, the plaintiff claimed the testimony by the defendants' experts was inadmissible because it improperly introduced new arguments on causation, instead of rebutting its expert's accounting method and actual damages determination.

The court agreed that the experts failed to "rebut," that is, "address the same subject matter identified by the initial expert." By using the regressions in their report to suggest the plaintiff's expert damages were not "statistically significant," they suggested there was no evidence of causation, a key element of the plaintiff's case. Because the plaintiff's expert did not testify on causation, but only on damages, the court struck these comments from the rebuttal report.

Unclear Valuation Date Eviscerates Expert's 'Precise' Partnership Valuation

Case name: *Rojas v. Duarte*
Citation: 2012 Tex. App. LEXIS 9923
Date of decision: Nov. 30, 2012
Country: US
State or Federal: State
State/Jurisdiction: Texas
Court: Court of Appeals
Type of action: Judicial Dissolution (incl. Withdrawal, Buy Out)
Experts: Unidentified (plaintiffs); none (defendants)
Judge: Antcliff
SIC: 3578 Calculating and Accounting Machines

A worker claimed that, in late 2002, he and his former mentor had verbally formed a partnership to buy, sell, and operate ATMs. After their relationship soured in May 2005, they agreed to separate and divide the assets and property equally. Because this division never occurred, he eventually sued on the basis of a buyout for his one-half interest. (The suit encompassed numerous other parties.)

At trial, the plaintiff's business valuation expert reviewed the partnership's federal income tax returns, general ledger reports, and financial statements from Dec. 31, 2005, through Dec. 31, 2008. Adjusting for items that did not reflect a going concern value, he normalized assets, income, and cash flow; he then applied a discount rate (unspecified) to the normalized figures and added back excess cash.

The trial court instructed the jury to determine the value of the plaintiff's partnership interest as of either May 31, 2005, or Dec. 31, 2008. (The opinion does not indicate what valuation date applied and why and on what basis the plaintiff's expert used the December 2008 date.)

The jury found that a partnership existed as of the earlier date and awarded the plaintiff $119,000. The defendant appealed, arguing there was: 1) no partnership; and 2) no rational basis to support the $119,000 award.

A right to damages. The appellate court first found that under the applicable state statute, the plaintiff had shown that a partnership existed. Consequently, "there is no doubt that the plaintiff suffered some amount of damages." But how the jury arrived at the $119,000 was problematic.

For instance, the court noted that the plaintiff's expert "did an excellent job" of identifying the financial aspects of the business that were important to determining its value. But his "relatively precise" valuation method pertained to only one date (Dec. 31, 2008). Since nothing in the expert's evidence allowed the jury to extrapolate that the partnership was worth $119,000 on May 31, 2005, the court remanded the case for a new trial on damages.

With Expert's Help, N.Y. Court Computes Deli's Fair Value

Case name: *Ruggiero v. Ruggiero*
Citation: 2013 N.Y. Misc. LEXIS 3698
Date of decision: July 29, 2013
Country: US
State or Federal: State
State/Jurisdiction: New York
Court: Supreme Court
Type of action: Judicial Dissolution (incl. Withdrawal, Buy Out)
Experts: Ronald Klein (plaintiff); Russell Glazer (defendants)
Judge: Pines
SIC: 5812 Eating Places (dinner theaters)
Key words: Fair value, Discount for lack of marketability (DLOM), Income approach, Discounted cash flow method (DCF), Market approach

The death of a kosher deli owner set in motion a fierce public fight between his widow and the surviving owner, the decedent's brother, over the value and rights to the business. To break the impasse, the court and parties turned to business appraisers.

For 25 years, two brothers ran a kosher deli in New York state in which they each owned a 50% interest. In August 2012, one brother died; by the end of the year, his widow sued her brother-in-law (and the company), claiming he tried to force her and her family out of the business and requesting the appointment of a temporary receiver and an accounting. The surviving brother countersued, alleging that the decedent had been stealing from the business and his widow had taken $25,000 from the corporate account without notice. After more charges flew back and forth, the court suggested that the parties engage expert appraisers. Based on their reports and subsequent testimony, the court would determine the business's fair value and decide which party should buy out the other. Both sides agreed to the procedure.

Both sets of experts had access to the same documents, including copies of daybooks, the restaurant's cash receipts, the general ledger, vendor cards, and cash register tapes. A witness confirmed that the restaurant's busiest period was between September and April—when the major Jewish holidays of Rosh Hashanah and Passover occurred. This period brought in the majority of revenue, which typically dropped off during the year's remaining months.

Plaintiff's expert devises market approach. The expert for the plaintiff (widow) decided to apply a market approach, using what he called a "price to revenue" method, rather than the conventional approach of looking at sales of comparable entities because of his inability to identify similar businesses. For multiple reasons he rejected the income approach (the court erroneously refers to the "cost approach"): There were inadequate sales data in the records the defendant (the surviving brother) kept and gaps in the general ledger related to cash purchases; he was unable to reconcile payroll on the company's books and records with cash payments; and the owners had used cash, American Express cards, and barter to pay vendors. The "price to revenue" approach, he said, enabled him to calculate revenues from sales from the company's daybooks both for the 12-month period before the death in August 2012 and the 12 months preceding his report on April 13, 2013.

Based on normalized revenues and operating profits for years of operation and years remaining on the lease, he valued the restaurant at 40% of annual gross revenue. He made two calculations as to the total value. First, for the 12 months ending August 2012, he determined approximately $2.67 million in gross revenue; 40% of this amount yielded approximately $1.1 million. From this figure, he subtracted $360,000 in working capital deficit and arrived at a fair value of $709,000. At the time of the decedent's death, half of this amount yielded $354,000. Second, for the period ending April 30, 2013, he found that gross revenue was $2.97 million; valuing the restaurant at 40% of revenue resulted in an amount of $1.2 million. After adjusting for working capital items, he concluded that the fair value for that period was just over $1 million; 50% of that figure resulted in a value of $501,000. He also found there was $297,000 in cash flow available to the owners from August 2012 through April 30, 2013.

At the valuation hearing, he said he determined the 40% price based on his experience in business valuations. He gave several reasons for the increase in value, including a significant pay down in accounts payable between August 2012 and April 2013, an increase in menu prices, and the addition of three new "meals on wheels" programs. He agreed that the company's existing debt affected the value of the business but said he had not been asked to include debt and outstanding loans in his calculations. Also, even though he considered the economic downturn, he believed it to have little consequence because by 2014 the economy would recover significantly. He stated that if the meals on wheels program were to account for 40% of the company's business, he might lower the 40% multiple.

The defendants' expert critiqued aspects of the plaintiff expert's valuation. The meals on wheels program had a much lower profit margin than regular items and made up about 34% of the revenue, he maintained. As for the claimed price increase, the rival expert ignored the price decrease for other items—the two factors balanced out any projected increase for 2013. Also, it was inappropriate to find a revenue increase for early 2013 since this typically was the busiest time for the restaurant. Moreover, there was no rationale for the 0.4 multiple in the competing expert's valuation since it lacked data to compare the business's performance with the debt and growth rate of similar companies.

Defendants' expert prefers income approach. The defendants' expert rejected the market approach, explaining that his research did not generate sufficient transactions with pricing multiples that were applicable to a valuation of the restaurant. He based his valuation on the income approach, using the discounted cash flow (DCF) method and considering the materials available to the experts. He was able to compute revenue from the restaurant's daybook and also determine: (1) accounts receivable balances; (2) accounts payable balances from actual purchases; (3) revenues; (4) payroll that did not appear on the tax returns; (5) cash payouts to vendors and nonvendors; (6) unpaid checks; and (7) the previous year's sales tax. He included the corporate debt and loans to shareholders in his calculation. He stated that, for nine years after the valuation date, there could be no distributions to shareholders out of the company's net income because there were nine years remaining on an installment loan to the widow and three other loans due to shareholders in the amount of $125,000. He determined a 60-month repayment term for the latter loans and subtracted about $25,000 per year for five years from the estimated net income. Once he had determined income, he used a 4.6% risk-free discount rate based on the downturn in the economy and arrived at a present value of $273,000 as of the date of death. Finally, he applied a 20% discount for lack of marketability (DLOM) and added $21,800 to account for the pass-through tax advantage the company had as an S corporation. His final figure for 50% of the company value was $120,200.

The plaintiff's expert pointed to flaws in this approach. The analysis, he said, rested on inadequate records for income, expenses, and accounts receivable and payable and the discount rate was unusually high—the risk-free rate should have been 2.55% given this was a niche business with a stable employee base.

The court adopted the defendant expert's valuation. The calculation of the plaintiff's expert was problematic for several reasons:

1. Since both sides had access to the same information, there was no support for the argument that he lacked the necessary data to compute the company's income;

2. He failed to consider that a large portion of the business came from the meals on wheels program, which had a lower profit margin;

3. Although he brought his figures forward to April 2013, his conclusion that there was an increase in business between the death and the 2013 date was not credible considering the business cycle; and

4. Most importantly, he did not account for corporate loans and debts even though he acknowledged these factors influenced corporate value.

In contrast, the defendant's expert provided a credible rationale for the 4.6% discount rate. The one flaw in his analysis was the insufficiently explained 20% DLOM, the court said. It agreed with the plaintiff's expert that the restaurant represented a "somewhat unique niche business." As a result, the court used the $273,000 value the defendants' expert determined, kept the $21,800 increase related to the favorable tax status, and removed the $54,600 DLOM deduction. The correct value for the business was almost $295,000, 50% of which yielded $147,400. The surviving brother was to continue running the business and buy out the shares belonging to his brother's estate, the court ordered.

Editor's note: New York attorney Peter Mahler in his "New York Business Divorce" blog points out that certain types of restaurants, including pizza parlors, change hands in sufficient numbers and show sufficiently uniform operations and financial metrics to allow for the market approach. The court's rejection of the methodology here had to do with the unexplained multiple and the unpersuasive claim that the company's records were inadequate. "It also strikes me that the estate's argument for using the market approach ... might have been inconsistent with its expert's contention, accepted by the court, that [the restaurant's] 'unique niche business' weighed against a marketability discount."

Valuation of Family Business Survives Expert's Deviation From Industry Standards

Case name: *Russell v. Russell*
Citation: 2013 Ark. App. LEXIS 151
Date of decision: Feb. 27, 2013
Country: US
State or Federal: State
State/Jurisdiction: Arkansas
Court: Court of Appeals
Type of action: Marital Dissolution
Experts: Joe Webb (wife); David Potts (husband)
Judge: Brown

The husband challenged the trial court's valuation of a family business, claiming there was no credible evidence to show it had a "fair market value" independent of the company's founder—his stepfather.

At divorce, the husband and wife agreed on the division of all property, but disagreed about the value of his one-third interest in his stepfather's business, which he acquired during the marriage.

Discount rate reduction. Both sides presented expert testimony, and both experts agreed that the value of 100% of the company was $3 million, but their computations of the value of the husband's interest differed greatly.

In a pretrial deposition, the wife's expert, a CPA, issued a disclaimer: his valuation did not follow the industry standard or his own practice; he intended it only for himself and his client, not for third parties. Normally, he said, he would discuss general economic conditions, industry-specific and company-specific risks, a standard value for the shares, and goodwill. In this case, he did none of these things because he had agreed with the wife what numbers and discounts to apply.

He said he "dropped the Mergerstat average control premium of 29.6% to 10%," reasoning that the husband had some control over cash flow but admitting that a willing buyer of his shares might not think that that control followed the purchase and, in fact, might discount the value by 50%. He applied a 5% marketability discount even though he agreed that a buyer might aim for a much higher rate, between 30% and 40%.

Later, in his trial testimony, he said he discounted the company's value by 10%. Since the husband and his two brothers, who each also owned one-third of the shares, were able to take money out of the company, they all had a degree of control. Although he recognized that the average marketability discount was 35%, he did not apply any. "Marketability and lack of control are not distinguishable," he stated.

To account for the risks related to the possible sale of the company's only client, he further discounted the value by 6%, which he thought was a high rate. He relied on the wife's statements that the company had retained the client despite several earlier changes in ownership and that, to her, meeting the client's requirements "was extremely important and outweighed any personal relationship." In a similar vein, the husband had stated the client seemed to like the company because it could adjust to changes more quickly than competitors.

Because the stepfather no longer owned the business, the wife's expert did not discount for the founder's personal goodwill. (The opinion does not provide the value the wife's expert computed for the husband's interest.)

The husband's expert, who also was a CPA, prepared a fair market valuation that complied with industry standards. Because the company was a going concern and because he could not find comparable businesses, he used an income approach. Assuming a total value of $3 million, the husband's interest was $1 million. He also thought that the company's only client might be downsizing due to changes in ownership. The expert applied a 30% discount for lack of control and a 35% discount for lack of marketability, reducing the value to approximately $458,000, half of which—$229,000—belonged to the wife.

He then discounted the goodwill of the company, assuming the enterprise goodwill was 50% and the personal goodwill that attached to the stepfather was 50%. The total value of the wife's share was no more than $115,000, he concluded. The expert's goodwill determination assumed that the stepfather remained with the company.

The trial court found that the stepfather was the company's owner of record, but the husband and his brothers all owned an equitable interest in the business. It determined that based on all the evidence, the wife's interest in the business was worth $273,000. To equalize the property division, it ordered monthly payments to the wife in the amount of $11,370 for 24 months. In a motion for a new trial, which the court denied, the husband objected that the order included pay for nonmarital personal goodwill.

All personal goodwill? The husband then challenged the decision at the Arkansas Court of Appeals. The wife failed to prove that the company had fair market value that was independent of the founder's goodwill, he argued. Specifically, the trial court's valuation rested on "questionable" expert opinion.

The appellate court acknowledged that the lower court knew that the expert, rather than following industry standards, used discounts pursuant to his agreement with the wife. But, the reviewing court said, both experts agreed on the value of 100% of the company. Also, other competent evidence supported the trial court's valuation. For example, it heard about the wife's commitment to meeting the business needs of the firm's only client and the husband's belief that the client liked the firm.

Further, the husband failed to present evidence that might lower the value of the company, including proof that the client had reduced the assignments it gave to the firm or that it was downsizing, as his expert claimed. For all these reasons, the Court of Appeals upheld the trial court's award to the wife.

Court Credits Expert's Cash Flow Analysis in Solvency Determination

Case name: *Samson v. Western Capital Partners LLC (In re Blixseth)*
Citation: 2013 Bankr. LEXIS 1001
Date of decision: March 28, 2013
Country: US
State or Federal: Federal
State/Jurisdiction: Montana
Court: United States Bankruptcy Court
Type of action: Bankruptcy
Experts: Joseph N. Karas (trustee); Kristina A. Cook (defendant)
Judge: Kirscher
SIC: 6519 Lessors of Real Property, NEC

"The Trustee … continues the fiction that [the debtor], one of the *Forbes' 400* wealthiest Americans in 2007, was insolvent during that very same year" is how the lender tried to defend against the plaintiff trustee's suit for a determination of insolvency. The Bankruptcy Court (D. Mont.) found insolvency was the reality.

In June 2007, the debtor and her estranged husband were in the midst of a "long, costly, and acrimonious" California divorce. The divorce court appointed the husband as manager of the community property; he, in turn, curtailed the debtor's access to all family businesses and cash flow. During that time, the debtor also entered into legal disputes related to her $18 million investment in two technology companies. In July 2007, she described her financial condition as "trying to pay $100 worth of stuff with 10 cents." She was approximately $2 million in arrears to creditors, she stated in an affidavit, even after using all her money from the sale of real estate.

Also at that time, the husband ended his financial involvement with the businesses of the debtor's son. Searching for funds to develop various projects, the son approached the defendant for money. The latter considered this "the opportunity to do a large loan, anywhere between $5 million and $15 million for a billionaire and her son." Regardless of the family's cachet, it adhered to its standard practice and required personal guarantees from the debtor and her son. Recognizing that the son's assets were all "illiquid," the lender admitted the inducement to make the loan was the debtor's guarantee. When the defendant was unable to obtain the debtor's financial statements for due diligence, it accepted a written statement from her attorney regarding her financial and legal condition. Based on a preliminary review of the assets, the letter stated, it appeared the assets of the couple's estate were community property, totaling "in excess of $1 billion." It further noted that, under California law, the wife was expected to receive assets in excess of $500 million.

The two-year loan to the debtor's son closed on June 15, 2007, for a total amount of over $13 million. The debtor's personal guarantee included an after-acquired property clause. Between May 30, 2007, and Sept. 9, 2008, directly or indirectly, she made payments of over $4.5 million to the defendant. The debtor's divorce only became final in October 2008; along the way, the couple had reached two "minisettlements" and a 42-page final agreement that awarded her several businesses that declared Chapter 11 bankruptcy in November 2008.

In January 2009, the defendant obtained a default judgment against the debtor and her son for nearly $13.3 million, after the son had failed to make payments on the loan. In March 2009, the debtor filed for voluntary Chapter 11 bankruptcy, showing a secured debt of nearly $103 million and an unsecured debt of nearly $57 million.

After conversion to Chapter 7 bankruptcy, the trustee in charge of administering the bankruptcy estate filed an adversary proceeding against the defendant, claiming in essence that the guarantee was avoidable because it was a fraudulent transfer. On the signing date, June 15, 2007, the debtor was insolvent. The defendant claimed the debtor received reasonably equivalent value and was solvent. Both sides presented expert testimony.

'The very definition of insolvency.' To avoid the guarantee, under federal bankruptcy law, the trustee needed to show: (1) that the debtor was insolvent at the time she incurred the obligation or rendered insolvent by it; and (2) that she received less than reasonably equivalent value.

1. Solvency. Both sides' experts—both CPAs—agreed that the debtor would be insolvent if she failed one of three tests: the cash flow test, balance sheet test, or adequate capital test. The trustee's expert stated the debtor was insolvent under all three, whereas the defendant's expert found her solvent under all of them.

The disparate conclusions stemmed in part from a disagreement over whether to include community property in the solvency analysis. The trustee's expert considered only the debtor's personal liabilities and the personal assets over which she had control on June 15. While he recognized that "control" of an asset was not a factor under the general balance sheet test, he nevertheless contended it was a critical element for any solvency analysis because all tests "come back to what an asset can generate in terms of cash on a forward looking basis." He considered cash flow, and specifically future cash flows, "the most important determinant as to your ability to repay debts and meet scheduled obligations."

For his analysis, he relied on information the trustee provided, reviewing about 1,000 pages of documents. Four or five of them, he said, had particular relevance, including the debtor's bankruptcy schedules. These showed that in March 2009 she had zero operating cash flow, and, based on her own reports, her liabilities then exceeded her assets by roughly $60 million. Accountants routinely perform a "subsequent event review," that is, "looking at events through the date of the report" when completing audits, he stated. He carefully reviewed a 2009 expert report from the bankruptcy proceedings related to one of the major assets the debtor obtained at divorce. It showed that by 2007 this business was highly leveraged, with insufficient capital to fund its financial plans and projections. He further reviewed affidavits and declarations the debtor had signed in the course of divorce and analyzed her general ledger activity to corroborate her statements. All this information confirmed her claim that in June 2007 her expenses amounted to $2 million and that she was borrowing to pay her daily expenses, he said. He had, the expert continued, looked hard to find assets that would generate cash from day-to-day activities. "The only form of cash generation that could occur would be through the sale of that asset, and that would essentially reduce her committed obligations."

He dismissed the letter the debtor's attorney issued prior to the loan. It conveyed expectations that had no basis in reality; the values for the community property were those the husband had assigned, and they were "pie in the sky."

The trustee's expert concluded that, on June 15, 2005, her debt was roughly $21.5 million; this amount increased to $160 million by March 2009. Her assets on the signing day were only about $16.4 million. Her ability to borrow throughout did not substitute for operating cash flows, he said. He also found that her entering into the marital settlement agreement "exacerbated" her cash flow troubles. "She was taking on assets that required cash, and she didn't have any other source to generate [it] ... other than borrowing." The debtor was "the very definition of insolvency," the expert concluded.

Lack of 'professional skepticism.' The defendant's expert rebutted the opposing testimony and made her own solvency determination. She agreed with the trustee's expert's valuation of non-contingent assets and liabilities. But she assumed, "as a matter of law," that on the signing date the debtor owned half of the marital assets. Therefore, she added assets that the debtor owned pursuant to the first minisettlement and subsequently further adjusted the debtor's balance sheet to include what she called the debtor's "vested 50 percent interest in the community property." She based the second analysis on a June schedule of assets the husband had submitted to the divorce court (the opinion here states two conflicting dates, June 2007 and June 2008).

From a balance-sheet perspective, the debtor had assets in the amount of $377 million in June 2007; their value was roughly $173 million more than her liabilities. At the same time, the debtor had about $47 million in personal assets, excluding community property, and approximately $8.5 million in liabilities, the defendant's expert concluded.

The cash flow test, she stated, centered on a debtor's intent: Did she intend to incur or believe that she would incur debts beyond her ability to repay? The debtor's statements that she planned to repay debt as it matured were "pretty good proof" that she was solvent under this test, the expert concluded.

The defendant's expert also found the debtor was solvent under the adequate capital test, which considers "whether or not the transaction left the debtor with insufficient capital to continue normal business operations." Avenues to obtain capital included operations, borrowing, or equity financing, the expert stated. In June 2007, the debtor was able to borrow money to fund her day-to-day operations.

The trustee's expert failed to use "professional skepticism" in his analysis of documents that came into existence after June 2007, the defendant's expert noted. These did not record "historical circumstances" but were "filed with the Court for the purposes of eliciting a result." Moreover, she faulted him for considering the full amount of the debtor's guarantee as liability. He did not account for the value of the primary security, that is, "the probability that the other guarantor, [the son], would not satisfy the remainder of the loan."

The trustee's expert gave his own rebuttal. The competing expert failed to perform a proper analysis under any of the tests. Without questioning, she accepted the values the husband had assigned to assets in determining one-half of the community property and then subtracted certain liabilities.

The court credited the testimony of the trustee's expert for numerous reasons:

- His choice to exclude community property that was under the control of the debtor's husband aligned with case law that stated "[a]sset valuation ... should be reduced by the value of the assets not readily susceptible to liquidation and the payment of debt."

- In her solvency analysis, the defendant's expert failed to consider whether any of the community assets generated income. She ignored the fact that "the marital asset which supposedly had the most value" was in financial straits and lacked the ability to generate any cash flow.

- While the defendant's expert criticized the trustee's expert for being insufficiently skeptical, she was the one who "applied no professional skepticism to values assigned to marital assets by [the husband]." By contrast, the trustee's expert "tested the veracity of the documents and declarations he examined."

- As to his ignoring that there were other primary borrowers (the companies the son set up for purposes of the loan) and two primary guarantors, the court pointed out that, before the promissory note matured, the defendant "was looking to Debtor for payment on the obligation," as court documents against the son and debtor showed.

- The trustee's expert "persuasively testified" that a solvency analysis should begin with an entity's operating or future cash flows to determine "the supportable level of debt." He did not fail to give proper weight to the preloan letter, considering its reliance on values the husband provided. In 2007, none of the assets the debtor ultimately received had positive cash flows.

- Regardless of whether one considered only the assets over which the debtor had control or one-half of the community assets, the debtor was insolvent on the day of signing the guarantee.

2. *Reasonably equivalent value.* The defendant tried to argue that the debtor did not need to receive reasonably equivalent value for the full amount of the $13 million loan because there were other assets that secured the loan. The court dismissed this claim, noting the defendant itself admitted that it considered the son's assets "illiquid and high-risk" and relied "almost exclusively" on the divorce settlement to ensure repayment.

The court also disposed of the claim that the debtor received "value" upon signing. "The sole value of the guarantee to Debtor was a mother's satisfaction in helping her child," the court said. There was no other value, "particularly from the standpoint of [her] creditors."

Regardless of how *Forbes* magazine portrayed her, at the relevant time, the debtor did not have sufficient assets to support her lifestyle or carry on any business. In the defendant's opinion, she was "too big to fail"; however, that opinion was based on "unreliable and untested information," the court concluded.

As a remedy, it set aside the guarantee and ordered the defendant to return property it had received from the debtor and her son and still held as well as pay the trustee $4 million for property it had received but no longer held.

Court Upbraids Expert Who Discusses Subject Outside Area of Expertise

Case name: *Securities and Exchange Commission v. Tourre*
Citation: 2013 U.S. Dist. LEXIS 87211
Date of decision: June 18, 2013
Country: US
State or Federal: Federal
State/Jurisdiction: New York
Court: United States District Court
Type of action: Securities
Experts: Dwight M. Jaffee, Ira Wagner (plaintiff); Dr. Mukesh Bajaj (defendant)
Judge: Forrest

The recent trial pitting the Securities and Exchange Commission against a former Goldman Sachs trader offered a note of caution to valuation experts: Overreach in your opinion, and risk exclusion—and the court's disapprobation—for lack of appropriate qualification under *Daubert*.

The SEC alleged in federal court (S.D.N.Y.) that a former Goldman Sachs trader, with assistance from a hedge fund, created a synthetic collateralized debt obligation (CDO) that was designed to fail. The hedge fund participated in selecting the instruments that made up the reference portfolio and then took a short position. The parties did not disclose these material facts to prospective and actual CDO investors.

To counter the disclosure allegation, the defendant offered testimony from a financial expert that the government attacked in a pretrial *Daubert* motion. The expert, a Ph.D. in business administration, directed a consulting firm for legal and regulatory matters and had worked for other consulting firms in the past. He also was a "visiting lecturer" with U.C. Berkeley's business school, where he taught graduate courses in corporate finance, investments, and financial engineering, and earlier had taught finance and business economics at the University of Southern California.

In his report, he observed, among other things, that the offering documents for the CDO at issue provided all "economically material" information and that the failure to disclose the hedge fund's role in creating and marketing the CDO caused no harm to participants in the transaction. "As a matter of economic logic," once investors knew the portfolio of securities in the reference portfolio, they had enough information to assess the credit risk and "formulate their own views of the future prospects of this portfolio," he stated.

However, as to his expertise, he acknowledged in his deposition that, aside from lecturing about CDOs in his class, he had never worked for a financial institution or "any institution with any involvement with CDOs." He never structured, marketed, or invested in a CDO. Nor did he survey CDO market participants during the relevant time period. His exposure to that industry went no further than serving as an expert after the 2007 financial crisis.

The government objected that the testimony was inadmissible under *Daubert* because the expert lacked the appropriate qualifications and aspects of his opinion invaded the province of the jury or court.

'A professional testifying expert.' At the outset, the court noted that the expert's report failed to "state the area in which he seeks to be qualified as an expert in this case." This gap left the court to assume "that defendant intends to offer him in the general field of 'financial economics.'" Above all, he was a "professional testifying expert," the court went on to say, noting "the long list of matters" on which he had opined: market efficiency, loss causation, and damages in securities cases (one CDO case), to name a few.

His opinion in this case was problematic for several reasons. Even though he lacked practical experience in the CDO industry, "he intends to opine about what information would and would not matter to CDO investors," the court said. Under *Daubert,* he was unqualified to do so. According to the court, his area of expertise—structured finance and reading and talking about finance—was not even "sufficiently proximate to the subject of his proposed testimony" to make up for his lack of experience with CDOs. Structured finance was "so broad a category as to become meaningless" in a case that centered on synthetic CDOs, "a very specific type of security."

Moreover, his statement that his conclusion about "economically material" information relied on "economic logic" was simply a form of inadmissible ipse dixit—which the law rejects because it is not a reliable methodology under *Daubert,* the court added. Further, an expert could not testify as to whether specific information at issue in a case was "material." This was a question for the jury, and inserting the word "economically" in front of "material" did not convert an inadmissible statement into an admissible opinion.

Similarly, his statements that investors who played the market had the tools to assess the credit risk and would not have behaved differently had they known about the hedge fund's short position were jury questions. Even though experts may opine on industry practice, in this case the expert had admitted that he had no knowledge of the industry and, therefore, could only base his opinion on the evidence of the case.

"Being a professional testifying expert in the financial area does not give an individual the qualifications to opine in every financial area as to every type of analysis," the court summed up its position.

It precluded all testimony related to the importance of the hedge fund's role in the disclosures and any potential loss to investors arising out of that role. However, because the government consented and because the court found his financial economics expertise less problematic in the context of providing background information on the "basic economics of structured finance," it allowed the expert to speak to the latter topic.

Expert's Valuation Method Precludes Improper Inclusion of Goodwill

Case name: *Sharp v. Sharp*
Citation: 2013 Neb. App. LEXIS 58
Date of decision: April 9, 2013
Country: US
State or Federal: State
State/Jurisdiction: Nebraska
Court: Court of Appeals
Type of action: Marital Dissolution
Experts: Luke Northwall (wife); Chris Best (husband)
Judge: Moore
SIC: 8011 Offices and Clinics of Doctors of Medicine (except mental health specialists, HMO medical centers, and ambulatory surgical and emergency centers)

One of the principal issues in this divorce case was the trial court's valuation of two medical practices in which the husband had varying interests. On appeal, the husband objected that one valuation wrongly included personal goodwill and the other a "mathematical error" as to the size of his interest.

The husband was a physician who practiced internal medicine through two venues. In the first, he was the sole shareholder of a company that contracted out his services as the medical director of a series of nursing homes and also contracted out his services to a concierge medical practice, in which members pay an annual fee, in addition to standard office visit fees, to ensure direct access to a doctor.

The second practice was more traditional. At incorporation in 2006, it had three partners, the husband included. In 2009, one of the original partners left. At trial, the husband initially stated a third partner joined in January 2010 but subsequently admitted the date actually was January 2011. A fourth partner came on board in January 2012. The husband also testified that, if he were to leave the business, he would only receive $15,000 for his interest based on the practice's "stock restriction agreement."

The parties' experts both were CPAs and experienced business valuators and used a capitalization of earnings method to value the first practice. The wife's expert noted that this method was one of three principal methods in business valuation. First, he determined that in this case it was reasonable to adjust officer's compensation upwards, from the $60,552 the 2010 income statement listed to $100,000. When he subtracted that amount from the company's earnings, he arrived at net earnings of $100,687. Applying a 26.52% capitalization rate, he obtained a "rounded" value of approximately $380,000.

Because he lacked information as to the business's receivables and payables, he decided not to perform an asset-based valuation. This method was appropriate when a business had no established earnings history, a volatile earnings/cash flow history, or when it was questionable whether the company could continue without an infusion of additional cash or could be sold as an asset-based purchase, the expert explained.

Thus the husband's 100% ownership interest in the first practice was worth $380,000, he concluded. He valued the second entity at $456,000 and concluded that, at the time he completed his report, in November 2011, the husband owned a one-half interest, yielding a value of $228,000.

In contrast, for the first practice, the husband's expert arrived at a value of approximately $104,000. He set compensation at $176,000, maintaining that this figure reflected the payment an independent contractor received who performed services similar to the ones the husband provided. He admitted on cross-examination that, had he used the $100,000 compensation figure, his valuation would have increased by some $250,000.

He also performed a net asset valuation based on the company's balance sheet for Dec. 31, 2011. This method, he decided, yielded a value of approximately $14,000. He concluded that the $90,000 difference in value resulting from his two valuations represented the market value of the business's intangible assets, including goodwill. Up to 20% of this amount was business goodwill, and the remainder personal goodwill, he decided. His investigation into the practice indicated there was some personal goodwill "due to the age of the business and the way the accounts were held." Excepting personal goodwill, the first practice was worth between $14,000 and $32,000.

He criticized the wife's expert for using pre-income-tax earnings in his valuation and failing to adjust for fixed asset replacements and additions.

He valued the second practice as of Dec. 31, 2011, assuming a one-fourth ownership interest. The entity itself was worth $400,000, and the husband's share $100,000.

At trial, the wife's expert responded. He noted that the stark disparity between the valuations under the capitalization of earnings approach stemmed from disagreement over the husband's compensation. The competing expert's $176,000 adjustment was "questionable," he said, because the business did not have enough cash "to pay that out" without borrowing. He thought the likelihood of this was small, and the husband admitted so.

Moreover, he pointed out, the first practice had a note payable for $88,000 from the husband, which his expert failed to consider in his valuation. Had the husband's expert added this amount back into the adjusted net asset valuation, "the professional practice goodwill issues would have been eliminated," the wife's expert claimed. Given the wide yearly differences in past asset purchases, he said it was impossible to confirm that the opposing expert made a proper adjustment for fixed asset replacements. To justify the adjustment, more detail was necessary; at the same time, this adjustment changed the value of the business by $40,000.

The district court adopted the valuations the wife's expert proposed for both businesses. But for the second practice, it determined that the husband possessed a one-third, not a one-half, interest. Therefore, based on the $456,000 valuation the wife's expert provided for the entity, the husband's interest was worth $152,000.

Conflicting testimony on partnership interest. The husband appealed to the Nebraska Court of Appeals as to both valuations.

Goodwill. In terms of the first practice, he claimed the trial court erred when it credited the conclusions of the wife's expert because the valuation included personal goodwill. Specifically, considering he was the sole shareholder, all income the first practice generated was the result of his own labor and the wife's expert simply valued his future labor.

In support, he cited precedent in which a wife's expert had used a "capitalization of excess earnings" approach to value the two practices in which the spouse was the sole shareholder. In that case, the district court rejected the valuation, and the state Supreme Court ultimately affirmed. The high court decided that, for goodwill to qualify as a divisible asset in a divorce case, it had to be a "business asset with value independent of the presence or reputation of a particular individual, an asset which may be sold, transferred, conveyed, or pledged." In contrast, goodwill that depended on the continued presence of a particular individual was not a marital asset. Further, the court made it clear it did not reject categorically the capitalization of excess earnings as a method to determine earning capacity. See *Taylor v. Taylor,* 386 N.W.2d 851 (1986) (available at *BVLaw*).

The appellate court here rejected the argument. This case, it said with emphasis, was not similar to the cited case because here the wife's expert did not use a capitalization of *excess* earnings method; he also did not determine a value in the form of goodwill based on the husband's presence or reputation. Instead, he used a capitalization of earnings approach based on the practice's actual earnings, albeit with an adjustment for reasonable compensation. The husband's expert used the same approach but chose a higher amount of compensation. The wife's expert plausibly explained that what the husband's expert designated as "goodwill"—the difference between the capitalization of earnings value and the adjusted net asset value—would not be there if he properly had addressed a note receivable.

Mathematical error. The husband did not challenge the district court's accepting the $456,000 value the wife's expert determined for the second business. But he claimed he only had a one-fourth interest at the time of trial. The trial court should have used that date and size of partnership interest.

Again, the reviewing court disagreed. The record showed that the husband had given confusing testimony as to when the third and fourth partner joined the practice. He admitted that he only had a one-third interest as of Dec. 31, 2011, the date when his own expert valued this practice. There was no mathematical error, the appellate court stated, adding, "for the sake of completion," that the district court did not abuse its discretion when it decided to value the business before the fourth partner joined.

Prior Deal's Royalty Formula Captures Trade Secret's Value

Case name: *Southwestern Energy Production Co. v. Berry-Helfand*
Citation: 2013 Tex. App. LEXIS 8549
Date of decision: July 10, 2013
Country: US
State or Federal: State
State/Jurisdiction: Texas
Court: Court of Appeals
Type of action: Intellectual Property
Experts: Keith Selinger (plaintiffs); unknown (defendant)
Judge: Bass
SIC: 1382 Oil and Gas Field Exploration Services (except geophysical mapping and surveying)
Key words: Trade Secret, Misappropriation of a Trade Secret, Reasonable royalty, Expert testimony, Overriding Royalty Interest

In a trade secret case centering on gas and oil exploration, the jury awarded the plaintiffs over $11.4 million in actual damages based on calculations from a reservoir engineer that were analogous to a reasonable royalty in patent infringement. On appeal, the defendant claimed the expert "did not know his case" and relied on a noncomparable third-party agreement to extract the value of the plaintiffs' proprietary material to the defendants.

Escalating litigation. The plaintiffs were two geologists who undertook what is arguably the most comprehensive study of the potential for gas production from the James Lime formation covering 2.75 million acres in five Texas counties. They identified 10 sweet spots for production, as well as multiple stacked pays (zones at different depths in the ground that are each capable of producing oil or gas). Even though the team separated, the minor contributor kept a 20% interest in the joint research and methodology. By 2004, the study's main author had begun to lease in two promising locations. Her primary goal was to sell a drill-ready prospect for cash and an overriding royalty interest to a larger exploration company with which she could develop the other identified sweet spots.

In February 2005, she approached the defendant, the fifth largest natural gas producer in the U.S. Before her presentation, the parties signed a one-year confidentiality agreement under which the defendant would not disclose her information to third parties and not acquire leases within a certain area. The defendant ultimately declined to participate in any prospect with the scientist. A short time later, the scientist reached an agreement with a third party for $1.8 million and an overriding royalty interest. The deal incorporated a prospect identification agreement covering three counties. It provided that the third-party buyer of the prospects would retain the scientist to locate prospects in three counties for $15,000 per month for six months; for any prospect in which the buyer decided to participate, she received a variable overriding royalty interest in production (on average 3%) and a 6.25% "back in" working interest. On the other hand, if the buyer found the prospect, the scientist received only the option to buy a 6.25% working interest.

In 2006, the defendant bought a large block of leases in two of the relevant five counties from Exxon and in the fall of 2007 began drilling its first James Lime well. It continued to lease land in the five-county area, with all the leases located in the area of the top 10 identified sweet spots. By the time of trial, in 2009, it had drilled in 144 wells. All were successful and clustered around the sweet spots the plaintiff had identified in her presentation; revenue amounted to some $382 million.

Starting in 2006, both scientists began to sue some 15 oil and gas operators but not the defendant, whom they only added in February 2009. Whereas most of the suits settled, this case went to trial. The jury found that the study represented a trade secret and the defendant was liable under five legal theories: trade secret misappropriation, theft of a trade secret, breach of fiduciary duty, fraud, and breach of contract. It awarded $11.4 million in actual damages, to which the trial court added nearly $24 million in disgorgement for illicit gains and $4.6 million in attorney's fees—arriving at a total of approximately $40 million.

Digging for 'the actual value' of proprietary study. To calculate damages, the plaintiffs presented expert testimony from a reservoir engineer with 45 years of experience in the oil and gas industry. The gist of his calculation was to determine the total net revenues the defendant would receive from exploiting the study, that is, the trade secret. He then considered what percentage of the total revenues should go to the plaintiffs to compensate for the value the defendant gained from the misappropriation.

The expert's pretrial calculation included 29 wells that turned out not to be related to the plaintiffs' claim. His revised report, however, solely relied on the 144 wells the plaintiffs' attorneys had designated as drilled within the sweet spots. By his computation, accrued revenues from those amounted to $382 million. To calculate the present value of the projected revenue from those wells, he relied on the production history of each well as reported to the Texas Railroad Commission and the reported prices for oil and gas. His calculation of the production decline curve for each well to estimate future production was based on a method standard in the industry for 90 years. He deducted severance and ad valorem taxes and monthly operating expenses that varied with the depth of the well, and he discounted the value of future proceeds to arrive at the present value of projected revenues.

He then determined the part of past and projected revenues that represented the defendant's gain from its misappropriation, as opposed to the revenues that referred to the defendant's own contribution of risk capital, equipment, expertise, and other elements. In doing so, he applied the percentage compensation formula that the third-party prospect identification agreement set down. Based on its overriding royalty, he calculated 3% of the total net revenues. Next, he computed the projected payout of the wells and applied 6.25% to the revenues after payout. When adding these figures, he arrived at damages from the 144 wells of $35.3 million.

His calculation included $10.65 million related to the defendant's $355 million sale of the deep rights under its Exxon leases based on his belief that the plaintiffs had a right to 3% of those proceeds. Accordingly, he concluded the total damages were nearly $46 million.

During cross-examination, the expert admitted that he had added a well that the defendant had drilled before its meeting with the plaintiff scientist. He further acknowledged that he had to correct his pretrial report. Ultimately, the plaintiffs' attorneys designated the 144 wells underlying his revised calculation, he said. He also admitted that he worked off the assumption that the plaintiffs owned a 100% working interest in all the subject wells and was unaware that they only owed 36% of one well.

Expert does know his job. The defendant challenged the award at the Texas Court of Appeals, arguing that there was insufficient evidence to find liability under any of the legal theories. Moreover, there was no support to justify the actual damages award—the trial court should have excluded the expert testimony because it represented unfounded assumptions, inconsistencies, and bald assertions.

As to liability on the various legal theories, the appellate court found there was only evidence of misappropriation of a trade secret and breach of contract. As to damages, it found the plaintiffs failed to show a loss of opportunities or sustained losses attributable to the breach of the confidentiality agreement considering they sold prospects to a third party for a considerable sum. Although the expert used the correct measure of damages for misappropriation of a trade secret—that is, the defendant's gain—this was not the proper measure of contract damages.

Concerning the damage calculation for misappropriation of a trade secret, the court explained at the start of its analysis that "courts adopt the fiction that a license or royalty was to be granted at the time of the misappropriation" to capture the value of the trade secret to the defendant. Courts "borrowed" the concept of a "reasonable royalty" from patent infringement cases, including the *Georgia-Pacific* framework. "Reasonable royalty," the appellate court pointed out, does not necessarily equate to the defendant's profits on actual sales; "instead, it is intended to measure the actual value of what has been misappropriated."

The state appeals court considered the defendant's multiple objections to the damages calculation in turn.

1. The plaintiff's expert "did not know his case" because he could not identify the wells relevant to his damages calculation, the defendant contended.

The court saw it differently. Although the inclusion of 29 wells in the expert's pretrial report necessitated a revision and he relied on the plaintiffs to identify the subject wells, there was no reason to invalidate the trial report and testimony. It was not the expert's job to designate the wells the defendant was able to locate by misusing the plaintiffs' trade secret, the court said.

2. The expert erred when he based damages on the compensation formula that appeared in the plaintiffs' earlier agreement with a third-party buyer. For one, that agreement covered only three counties, whereas the damages here related to wells in all five counties. Since the price of mineral rights varied from county to county, the expert failed to explain how the agreement's compensation formula was applicable to the wells in the two additional counties.

The court noted that the variation in price for minerals and leases was of no consequence since the expert based his calculations on revenue from actual production. The earlier agreement specified that the plaintiffs received pay only from actual revenues. If the identified prospects turned out to be unsuccessful, there was no payment. To calculate the defendant's advantage resulting from the plaintiffs' information, the expert properly applied a percentage equivalent to an established "reasonable royalty" in the industry to the present value of net revenues.

3. The expert used the wrong formula, the defendant stated. The earlier agreement specified that, whenever the buyer found the prospect, the plaintiffs only had an option to buy a 6.25% working interest. Since in this case the defendant found the prospect, the expert should have used this formula.

The court disagreed. The issue of who found the prospect was in dispute. The plaintiffs contended their research and analysis guided the defendant's exploration, and the jury agreed. This justified the expert's assumption of a 3% royalty interest and a 6.25% "back in" interest after payout.

4. The expert was wrong to assume a percentage of revenues equating to a 3% overriding royalty, since the third-party agreement provided the size of the override could vary depending on existing royalty burdens.

The court found there was evidence that the overriding royalty interest to the plaintiffs on average was 3%.

5. The expert mistakenly assumed a 100% working interest by the defendant in all the subject wells, the defendant argued.

The court said that there was no evidence that showed that the defendant owned less than all the working interest in the other wells. Therefore, the expert's mistake as to one well was "not so serious as to render the balance of his testimony unreliable."

6. The expert's calculation of 3% of the defendant's $355 million sale of deep rights demonstrated the overall unreliability of his opinion, the defendant argued. That 3% was the equivalent of a 3% overriding royalty. However, an overriding royalty owner typically receives payment only for production, the defendant went on to say. The plaintiffs never would have obtained an overriding royalty related to the sale of deep rights.

The court found this argument irrelevant. It agreed that stacked-pay potential played an important role in the plaintiffs' study. There was no real proof that the trade secret was linked to the defendant's acquisition of the Exxon leases and the subsequent sale of the deep rights. The jury's verdict made clear that the jurors did not see the requisite causal connection. They calculated 3% of the undisputed accrued revenue from the wells the Railroad Commission reported. This percentage figure was within the range of the 3% overriding royalty and 6.25% "back in" working interest that was "customary and reasonable" compensation in the industry for prospect identification, the court concluded.

For all of these reasons, the state Court of Appeals affirmed the $11.4 million award for misappropriation of a trade secret, but it reversed and remanded as to disgorgement of illicit gains and actual damages based on liability under any of the other legal theories the plaintiffs unsuccessfully had presented.

Battle of Three Experts Turns on Reliability of Third-Party Appraisals

Case name: *SnoPac Products, Inc. v. Spencer*
Citation: 2012 Wash. App. LEXIS 1585
Date of decision: July 9, 2012
Country: US
State or Federal: State
State/Jurisdiction: Washington
Court: Court of Appeals
Type of action: Dissenting Shareholder
Experts: Owen Dahl (company); Kevin Grambush (minority shareholders); Robert Duffy (court-appointed)
Judge: Spearman
SIC: 0913

Just three years after launching a fish and crab processing company, the founder sold most of his shares (70%) to his son and gifted the remainder in equal parts (10%) to each of his three daughters. With the son at the helm, the business prospered for over 20 years in Alaska waters, making hundreds of thousands of dollars in annual distributions to its passive shareholders as well as the majority owner.

A 'perfect storm' of events. Beginning in 2000, a confluence of events—including tighter industry regulation, increased competition, and even natural disaster—caused the business to flounder. The large annual distributions to the minority shareholders dried up, and they began to suspect their older brother of mismanaging operations. By 2004, the business carried $5 million in debt and either had to shut down or dramatically increase its processing capacity.

To salvage the business, the owner authorized the purchase of a single fishing vessel for $2.5 million and then spent another $6.5 million to turn it into a "floating" processing plant. In 2008, the company also bought and refurbished an onshore processing plant for $2.8 million. By this time, the owner wanted to buy out his siblings and retained an independent appraiser to value the company. For insurance purposes, it had already booked its main asset—the onboard processing vessel—at $9 million. Believing this book value was too high and "not normally a good indicator of fair market value," the company's appraiser caused it to retain another marine surveyor who—within a day of his engagement and after inspecting the boat for only two hours—concluded the vessel was worth only $3 million. Based on this value, as well as the company's current debt load, the appraiser said the minority shares were worth nothing.

At just about the same time, however, the company reapplied for insurance coverage, expressly warranting that the fair market value of the vessel was $9.1 million. The minority shareholders also commissioned their own business appraiser, who relied primarily on the $9.1 million value and, after depreciating the asset over a 15-year term, concluded the vessel was worth $7.1 million. Overall, he valued the 10% interests at $400,000 each, and the company filed suit to appraise the dissenting shareholders' stock.

Court seeks a BV lifeline. Just before trial, the company needed to obtain additional insurance and financing. Once again, it used the marine surveyor who supplied the $9.1 million value for the vessel in 2007, only this time, he said its fair market value had increased over the intervening two years to $16.7 million.

To clarify the competing valuations, the court appointed an experienced, credentialed BV expert from a national firm. This expert retained his own marine surveyor, who valued the vessel at $5.5 million, including $3 million in "crab processing rights." The court-appointed appraiser ultimately valued the fishing vessel at $2.5 million, excluding its intangible rights, and also determined that the value of the minority shareholders' interests was zero (0).

At trial, each of the three BV experts testified. The court discredited the company's expert for relying on the underlying $3 million appraisal for the vessel. In particular, the court noted that this marine surveyor had completed his report within a day of his retention, as compared to his typical practice, which required a month to compete an appraisal. Indeed, the court said it was "unclear exactly how he reached his $3 million conclusion."

The court also identified several problems with its own expert's reliance on the $5.5 million appraisal. In his market approach, the marine surveyor had relied on only one comparable transaction, the $5 million sale of an onboard fishing and processing vessel that nevertheless did not have similar costs or capacity as the company's vessel. It was also unclear whether this comparable transaction was at fair market value or liquidation value.

Ultimately, the trial court found the appraisal by the minority shareholders' expert to be the most credible. Based on this evidence, it valued the vessel at $6.25 million and the company's onshore processing plant at $2.8 million; its equipment and other tangible assets were worth approximately $790,000. After subtracting the company's liabilities from its assets, the trial court determined the net asset value of a 10% interest was just over $350,000, and the company appealed.

Company helped create its own valuation storm. On review, the appellate court noted the surveyor's rushed report sufficiently discredited the $3 million appraisal. That left the trial court with a range of credible evidence from approximately $9 million—the value of the vessel on the company's own books and from its first insurance appraisal—all the way up to $16.7 million in its most recent insurance application. Based on this range, the trial court "was entitled to value the [vessel] at $6.25 million," the appellate court held.

As a final argument, the company claimed the trial court erred by applying net asset value instead of "fair value" to the appraisal of the dissenting shareholder's stock. However, applicable state law

(Washington) does not require a court to conduct both a "fair value" and an "asset value" appraisal in dissenting shareholder actions, the appellate court ruled, and it affirmed the lower court's findings in all respects.

Assignee's Low Valuation Does Not Control Patent Damages Calculation

Case name: *SSL Services, LLC v. Citrix Systems, Inc.*
Citation: 2013 U.S. Dist. LEXIS 4275
Date of decision: April 17, 2013
Country: US
State or Federal: Federal
State/Jurisdiction: Texas
Court: United States District Court
Type of action: Intellectual Property
Experts: Brett Reed (plaintiff); Dr. Charles R. Mahla (defendants)
Judge: Gilstrap

In this patent infringement case, the defendants filed post-trial motions to overturn the jury's $10 million lump-sum award. No reasonable jury could have arrived at that sum considering the low valuation of the company holding the patent at the time of the hypothetical negotiation, they contended.

The plaintiff owned a portfolio of patents, including the patent-at-suit, which it acquired from the now-defunct assignee and which relates to technology for computer authentication and encryption. In 2008, it sued the defendant software makers in federal court (E.D. Tex.), alleging they used and sold the protected technology in their Access Gateway and Netscaler features.

In 2012, the case went to trial. Based on the court's pretrial ruling, the plaintiff was able show that, even though the defendants' violation did not begin until 2004, they became aware of the patent-in-suit as early as 2000 when they entered into a relationship with the original assignee that produced licensing and distribution agreements incorporating the patent as relevant to the technology at the center of the contracts. The original assignee's CEO stated that in 2004 the company had a valuation of only $3 million. Also, in 2005, the plaintiff bought the patent in dispute for $800,000.

The plaintiff's damages expert based the royalty rate for his damages calculation on the two agreements, providing an analysis of their comparability to the requisite hypothetical negotiation of a *Georgia-Pacific* analysis.

Although these contracts were not patent licenses, they were sufficiently comparable, he stated, because they involved the actual parties and specifically included the patent-in-suit, which was central to the technology the contracts covered. Also, he pointed out, they were important to other *Georgia-Pacific* factors, not just as "comparable licenses." Specifically, they showed the assignee's licensing policies and considerations and the competitive position of the negotiating parties. Further, they were near in date to the hypothetical negotiation. He agreed, however, that they provided the defendants with rights to an entire product that "would not be part of" a hypothetical patent license.

The defendants' damages expert admitted that these licenses were the most comparable contracts available.

The plaintiff's expert also explained that the $3 million valuation pertaining to the original assignee and the subsequent patent sale to the plaintiff were facts of little consequence to assessing patent damages. These events occurred in the context of a "fire sale," he said. He based his calculation on the actual use of the defendants' accused Access Gateway functionality, which was featured in a series of the defendants' products. Using internal documents from the defendants, he showed that the accused technology was vital to the success of the products and that the patented features within Access Gateway drove customer sales. Moreover, several documents revealed how the defendants attributed revenue to Access Gateway in terms of the products that contained them. As he saw it, this information provided a clue as to how the defendants themselves valued the accused products. By his calculation, the plaintiff's damages amounted to $10 million.

The jury found the defendants liable and awarded a lump sum of $10 million in harmony with the expert's calculation. The defendants subsequently contested the verdict in motions for judgment as a matter of law and for a new trial.

'As comparable as we're going to get.' In attacking the damages, the defendants raised several issues, which the court considered in turn. First, they said, there was no evidence to support the royalty rate on which the lump-sum award rested because it resulted from noncomparable licenses.

In fact, the trial court should never have admitted these licenses into evidence for purposes of a reasonable royalty analysis because they merely provided for rebranding and support services, not a patent license. Even the plaintiff's expert agreed that they included rights to a product that was not part of a hypothetical patent license.

The plaintiff countered that they were sufficiently comparable, as its expert's exhaustive analysis of their relevance and comparability to a hypothetical negotiation showed.

The district court stood by its earlier decision to admit them. Crediting the plaintiff's expert, it found what mattered was that they involved the actual parties to the hypothetical negotiation and the disputed technology, were made just prior to the hypothetical negotiation, and were relevant to other *Georgia-Pacific* factors. Even the defendants' expert agreed that these contracts were "as close as—to comparable as we're going to get," the court said.

Next, the defendants argued that no reasonable jury could have believed that a prudent business would have paid $10 million for rights to a single patent when the original assignee was worth only $3 million at the time of the hypothetical negotiation. Also, the plaintiff itself only paid $800,000 for the patent in 2005.

The jury carefully considered statements from the plaintiff's expert that these two events took place under "very different" circumstances and did not limit the reasonable royalty the defendants owed to the plaintiff, the court decided.

Finally, the defendants claimed the plaintiff's expert did not sufficiently link the royalty rate to evidence of actual use of the accused Access Gateway feature within certain products. The products had "many, many additional features," the defendants said and also claimed that their evidence showed that "a vast majority of purchasers" did not even use the Access Gateway functionality.

The court again disagreed. The plaintiff's expert, using the defendants' own documents, convincingly showed how critical Access Gateway was to their products and how critical the patented features were to Access Gateway. Also, their internal documents reflected the value the defendants placed on the accused technology. This evidence supported the jury's award, the court concluded, and it denied the defendants' motions.

Buy-Sell Agreement Fuels War Over Workable Stock Appraisal Method

Case name: *Sullivan v Troser Management, Inc.*
Citation: 2013 N.Y. App. Div. LEXIS 1641
Date of decision: March 15, 2013
Country: US
State or Federal: State
State/Jurisdiction: New York
Court: Court of Appeals
Type of action: Buy/Sell Agreement
Experts: Unknown
Judge: Panel
SIC: 7999 Amusement and Recreation Services, NEC (skiing facilities)

Ten years of litigation over a shareholder buy-sell agreement between parties that never agreed on the value for the shares of a closely held corporation have taken the litigants through four rounds of appeal but not close to an answer as to the appropriate valuation method.

The plaintiff served as the defendant's director of sales for the operation of a ski resort. In 1986, the parties made an agreement that promised him an 18% equity interest in the defendant's closely held corporation if he remained employed until year-end 1991. Under a contemporaneous buy-sell agreement, the defendant had the option to buy back the plaintiff's stock if, among other things, the employment ended.

The purchase price was to be "an amount agreed upon annually by the Stockholders as set forth on the attached Schedule A." If the parties failed to establish an annual value, "the value shall be the last agreed upon value except that if no such agreed upon value is established for a period of two years, the value shall be the last agreed upon value increased or decreased by reference ... the company's book value." The agreement listed the plaintiff as a "stockholder." No Schedule A exists.

In 2003, the plaintiff sued in state court (Supreme Court, Monroe County, which is a trial court) for specific performance of the stock issuance. Moreover, he requested an order that, once the stock was issued, the defendant had an obligation to repurchase it and a determination of the parties' rights and duties under the buy-sell agreement. The trial court directed the defendant to issue 18% of its shares of stock to the plaintiff, which the defendant subsequently did. The court also ordered the parties to execute the buy-sell agreement and fixed a price for the purchase. Specifically, it valued the buy-back interest at an amount that aligned with a prior buyout involving a different shareholder. Both sides appealed.

Volley of appeals. In 2005, the defendant sought dismissal of the complaint, arguing it was time-barred. The appellate court declined. At the same time, it granted the plaintiff's request to overturn the lower court's setting a price for the purchase of his shares.

In 2006, the trial court directed the defendant to repurchase the stock for approximately $110,000, based on the defendant's claim that the method to value the stock was by prorating the value of its parent corporation among that company's three subsidiaries. The plaintiff appealed, contending that the agreement required that the two stockholders of the defendant determine the value of the stock, not the owners of the parent corporation. He also provided a letter he had received from the defendant's attorney in 1999 that specified a different valuation method. The appellate court ruled for the plaintiff.

In 2009, the trial court denied the plaintiff's request for a determination that his shares "be valued on the basis of his percentage interest in the Defendant's assets" in the event that the defendant exercised its option to buy back the shares. He advocated for the use of a net asset approach that the state's highest court had approved in a case about the buyout of a law firm partner pursuant to an agreement that provided for a future agreement among partners that never came into existence.

The plaintiff appealed, contending the agreement's purchase price provision was unenforceable. The defendant presented other stock valuations. The appellate court said the plaintiff showed "as a matter of law that the stockholders have never agreed upon a value of the stock." Accordingly, there was no way to ascertain his share price in accordance with the terms of the buy-sell agreement. Evidence of stock valuations from other transactions was of no consequence because the plaintiff was not a party to them.

'No uniform rule for valuing stock.' In 2011, the trial court denied the defendant's motion to set the stock purchase price at approximately $184,000 based on its expert's calculation. The expert had used the same formula the plaintiff proposed in 2009.

The appellate court affirmed the denial. Its 2010 ruling notwithstanding, it stated it did not then require a net asset valuation, a method the High Court approved but did not mandate. The court clarified that its earlier decision established that the plaintiff's shares had to be valued "on the basis of his percentage interest." However, issues of fact as to what the appropriate method for valuing the defendants' assets remained.

The court rejected the defendant's claim that the buy-sell agreement's reference to book value dictated its use to determine the price for the plaintiff's shares. The parties never agreed on the value of the shares, and there was no adjustment to be made. "Book value does not come into play." In this vein, it also noted that, even though, under provisions of the business corporation law, the plaintiff had no right to the "fair value" of the stock, "it does not follow … that the plaintiff is entitled only to book value."

There was "no uniform rule for valuing stock in closely held corporations," the appellate court stated. A court must tailor the valuation method to a particular case, based on the evidence at trial.

The appellate court, however, agreed with the defendant that the trial court had erred in finding the defendant had exercised its option to buy back the shares. The plaintiff earlier had raised the issue in an inappropriate manner. A resolution of this question could wait until the defendant actually refused to buy the shares at the price the lower court set after a trial on the value of the shares, the appellate court concluded.

Editor's note: New York attorney Peter Mahler, in reporting on the case in his blog, notes that the parties could have avoided years of litigation had they prepared a simple schedule or certificate of value in accordance with the agreement. But no one must think this omission is a "freak occurrence." "Rather," Mahler says, "it is symptomatic of the myriad problems afflicting fixed-price buy-sell agreements."

Expert May Use Public Information for Company Valuation

Case name: *Superior Offshore International, Inc. v. Schaefer*
Citation: 2012 U.S. Dist. LEXIS 174841
Date of decision: Dec. 11, 2012
Country: US
State or Federal: State
State/Jurisdiction: Texas
Court: United States District Court
Type of action: Bankruptcy
Experts: Norman Dufour (plaintiff); Christopher M. James, Alan D. Bell (defendants)
Judge: Atlas
SIC: 1382 Oil and Gas Field Exploration Services

Before filing for Chapter 11 bankruptcy, the plaintiff provided subsea construction and diving services to the oil and gas industry. The defendants were members of the board of directors prior to its initial public offering (IPO) in April 2007. In connection with the bankruptcy, a special committee representing the plaintiff sued, alleging breaches of the duty of care and duty of loyalty and good faith, as well as self-dealing; for example, the defendants approved a $28 million special dividend to the board's chairman and awarded him the full benefit of an increased IPO that left the company undercapitalized and unable to continue its operations. Also, two defendants failed to disclose and pursue more lucrative offers for the *Achiever*, a vessel the company tried to sell.

Both sides retained experts. In its pretrial *Daubert* motion in federal court (S.D. Tex.), the plaintiff sought to exclude the testimony of the defendants' two experts regarding the company's capitalization at the time of the IPO. They used public information, including the prices at which the company's stock traded on the exchange following the IPO and the views of security analysts who worked for the underwriters that had performed due diligence on the plaintiff one year before the IPO. (The opinion does not indicate the experts' valuations.)

One of the defendants' experts also critiqued the factors and valuation methodology the plaintiff's expert used in appraising the *Achiever*. While he had valued the vessel at $100 million in 2007 in a business appraisal, he increased the amount to $135 million after the plaintiff had retained him.

***Daubert* safeguards are less critical.** Regarding the company's capitalization, the plaintiff claimed the experts used unreliable information; as to the vessel appraisal, it argued the expert lacked experience in appraising marine vessels. The court dispensed with both objections quickly.

Although reliance on publicly available information is not always the preferred methodology, the court said, "it could be an acceptable procedure when the company's stock is trading in an efficient market." This seemed to be the case here because one source of information was the securities analysts who worked for the underwriters and thus had more access to internal information than other analysts.

As to the plaintiff's second objection, the defendants' expert did not plan to testify about vessel appraisal generally, but specifically to address the plaintiff's expert's method and unexplained change in the vessel's value.

In denying the motion, the court noted that the case would be tried to the court, not a jury. In *Daubert*, the Supreme Court's main concern was guarding against jury confusion and exposure to unreliable testimony. Here the court was easily capable of determining whether the experts' testimony was helpful and how much weight to give it.

Claims Court Rules IRC Section 409A Governs Discounted Stock Option

Case name: *Sutardja v. United States*
Citation: 2012 U.S. Claims LEXIS 126
Date of decision: Feb. 27, 2013
Country: US
State or Federal: Federal
State/Jurisdiction: Federal Circuit
Court: United States Court of Federal Claims
Type of action: Federal Taxation
Experts: n/a
Judge: Wheeler
SIC: 3674 Semiconductors and Related Devices

Does liability under section 409A of the Internal Revenue Code depend on whether the taxpayer received a stock option at a discount? This issue was at the heart of the U.S. Court of Federal Claims pretrial ruling in a refund claim.

Section 409A regulates the taxation of nonqualified deferred compensation. Under the statute and the relevant regulations, specifically Notice 2005-1, nonstatutory stock options may qualify as deferred compensation and, as such, must be included in gross income. If a stock option is granted "at the money," that is, the strike price is equal to the fair market value of the underlying shares at the grant date, no taxable event occurs. On the other hand, the IRS consistently has considered a discounted option deferred compensation that falls within the purview of section 409A. Amounts includible in gross income are also subject to interest on prior underpayments, and an additional income tax equal to 20% of the compensation is required to be included.

Disagreeing with the IRS's premise. The taxpayers worked for a prominent semiconductor firm. As a senior executive officer, the husband received an option to a fixed number of shares, which vested at predetermined dates provided he continued his employment. At the time of grant, it did not have a readily ascertainable fair market value, but, during the relevant years, the underlying stock traded on the NASDAQ. The taxpayer exercised three fully vested portions of the option in 2006 during a transition period between the effective date of section 409A and the effective date of the applicable regulations. The amount in dispute was $5,282,125, plus interest.

The IRS conceded that, if the option price was set at fair market value, there was no section 409A taxation. But, in their summary judgment motion, the taxpayers disagreed with that premise, arguing that the issue of discount was not relevant to resolving the case in their favor. Even if the employer granted the option at a discount, there was no taxable event until the employee exercised the vested portions and sold the shares. They gave the following reasons, which the court considered in turn.

1. Notice 2005-1, which defines "deferral of compensation" for purposes of section 409A, conflicted with Supreme Court jurisprudence, which typically requires that a stock option be included in gross income at the date of exercise, not at the grant or vesting date.

The Court of Federal Claims found no inconsistency because the precedential Supreme Court case, which held that there was no compensation until exercise, concerned a nondiscounted stock option. Notice 2005-1, and, as such, section 409A, "preserves that same treatment" because it excludes nondiscounted options from the definition of "deferred compensation," the court said.

2. Notice 2005-1 was not legal authority because it was not a final regulation, but rather the "first part of … a series of guidance with respect to the application of § 409A."

Although it was true that the Treasury Department did not issue final regulations under section 409A until 2007, Notice 2005-1 deserved deference because its definition of "deferred compensation" was consistent with the proposed regulations and final Treasury regulations that interpreted "a relatively complex new tax provision," the court stated.

3. To determine the meaning of "deferral of compensation," the court should look to a final Treasury regulation that came out under the Federal Insurance Contribution Act (FICA) and was similar to Notice 2005-1 but specifically excluded the grant of a stock option from its definition.

The court declined, finding the FICA regulation only applied in a specified limited context.

4. Even if the option grant was discounted, under California law, which governed the option agreement, the husband did not have a "legally binding right" to compensation until exercise.

The government countered that the option itself was compensation and created a right to compensation upon vesting. If granted at a discount, there was deferred compensation from the date of vesting.

The court again agreed with the IRS. Under California law, "the vested options give the optionee the legally binding right to purchase shares at a designated price." Relevant case law recognized that "the option itself is compensation, regardless of when that compensation is measurable and realized for tax purposes."

5. Even if the option were discounted and subject to section 409A, the deferral of income fell under the short-term deferral exception.

The taxpayer's option agreement, on its face, failed to meet the requirements of a short-term deferral, the court said. Although the taxpayer exercised portions of the option within two and a half months after the vesting year, the company's stock option plan allowed for exercise up to 10 years. Also, upon vesting, the option was not subject to a substantial risk of forfeiture. Any limitation period the agreement specified was merely a grace period in which the employee could exercise the vested portions of the option following the termination of employment.

For all of these reasons, the Court of Federal Claims denied the taxpayers' motion. The case is headed to trial. As the court said, the outcome will turn on the factual issue of whether the taxpayer received an option at a discounted price below fair market value.

Fed. Circuit Affirms $95M Patent Award Based on Price Erosion Theory

Case name: *Synqor, Inc. v. Artesyn Technologies, Inc.*
Citation: 2013 U.S. App. LEXIS 5051
Date of decision: March 13, 2013
Country: US
State or Federal: Federal
State/Jurisdiction: Federal Circuit
Court: United States Court of Appeals
Type of action: Intellectual Property
Experts: Brett Reed (plaintiff); unknown (defendants)
Judge: Rader

Following trial and the district court's refusal to overturn the jury's award for patent infringement, the defendants challenged the outcome at the Federal Circuit, alleging multiple errors related to the plaintiff expert's price erosion theory and reasonable royalty rate.

The litigation revolved around high-efficiency power converter systems for large computer systems and telecommunication and data communication equipment. In late 2010, a jury found nine power converter manufacturers infringed the plaintiff's patents related to a multistage distributed power architecture, the "intermediate bus architecture." It awarded lost profits and reasonable royalty damages of $95.3 million.

The defendants appealed the verdict in motions for judgment as a matter of law (JMOL) or a new trial with the district court but were unsuccessful. (Find *Synqor, Inc. v. Artesyn Technologies, Inc.*, LEXIS 91668 (E.D. Tex. Aug. 17, 2011), at *BVLaw*).

The defendants subsequently appealed to the Federal Circuit. Their damage-related claims were similar to the ones they had presented to the district court. First, they said, damages were excessive because the plaintiff failed to support its price erosion theory. Second, the plaintiff's improper introduction of entire market value evidence justified a new trial.

Price erosion theory. At trial, the plaintiff introduced evidence that it was a major player in the power electronics industry, growing from zero revenues in 1998 to over $40 million by 2004, largely due to its becoming Cisco's number-one supplier. The company's president and CEO was a leader in the field, who developed the technology at issue, patented it, and introduced it into the market. But because of the defendants' selling infringing products at increasingly lower prices, the plaintiff was unable to benefit from the pricing exclusivity it should have had.

Within this context, the plaintiff's expert presented a damages model that included lost profits and reasonable royalty components and hinged on the price the plaintiff claimed it would have enjoyed "but for" the price erosion that the defendants' accused products caused. The "but for" prices were two to three times above the prices the defendants actually charged.

The jury heard testimony that, when the plaintiff first entered the market, it was able to sell bus converters at prices "in the 60s to as high as $110" per unit. In 2002, it sold to Hewlett-Packard and Sun for $84 per unit, and, in 2010, during a market shortage, it supplied Cisco with 18,500 converters at $70 and $81 per unit.

The defendants' expert claimed the plaintiff could not have obtained the 2010 prices over the long term because the industry eventually would have switched to a noninfringing type of converter rather than pay the plaintiff's prices for patented products.

By contrast, the plaintiff's technical expert showed that alternative converters were inferior to the patented ones and that at the time of trial the noninfringing converters were just beginning to compete with the earliest unregulated bus converters.

Also, while a Cisco representative stated his company would not have paid the 2010 price over the four-year infringement period, he agreed that the company would have had to incur significant costs to redesign its end products to make them compatible with any noninfringing converter that was not a "drop-in replacement." But those replacements did not exist as of August 2010. Another defense witness admitted he did not know of customers who actually had switched from the protected converters to any noninfringing alternatives.

In the face of this evidence, the jury adopted the plaintiff expert's damages model and awarded over $87 million for lost profits and the balance—approximately $8 million—for a reasonable royalty.

The district court, in turn, found the jury had a sufficient basis to accept the proposed model and upheld the award.

The Federal Circuit stated that its review of the entire record revealed sufficient evidence for the jury to accept the "but for" pricing the expert put forth. Damages were based on speculation and guesswork, the court concluded, and it affirmed the district court's denial of the defendants' motions.

Reference to customer end products. In their motions to the district court and Federal Circuit, the defendants claimed the plaintiff's reference to $20 billion in customer end-product sales "skew[ed] the damages horizon for the jury."

The district court held the discussion of end-product sales was not unfair or prejudicial, and the Federal Circuit agreed. The plaintiff expert's calculation rested on the "but for" sales price of the patented bus converter. The reference to end-product value supported the plaintiff's expert statement that the "the price elasticity of demand for the bus converters would be high because they enable space savings and efficiency while representing a small fraction of the end price." The district court did not abuse its discretion in denying the defendants' motion for a new trial, the Federal Circuit concluded.

Chancery Trusts DCF to Arrow in on Common Stock Value

Case name: *In re Trados Inc.*
Citation: 2013 Del. Ch. LEXIS 207
Date of decision: Aug. 16, 2013
Country: US
State or Federal: State
State/Jurisdiction: Delaware
Court: Court of Chancery
Type of action: Breach of Fiduciary Duty
Experts: William Becklean (plaintiff); Greg A. Jarrell (defendants)
Judge: Laster
SIC: 7371 Computer Programming Services
Key words: Fair value, Merger, Discounted cash flow method (DCF), Comparable companies method, Comparable transactions method, Common Stock, Liquidation Preference, Securities

In a consolidated shareholder suit, the plaintiff common stockholder was able to prove that the process by which the target company's directors drove a merger was unfair. But did the transaction result in an unfair price just because it left the common stock with nothing? This was the valuation issue the Delaware Court of Chancery recently examined in deciding whether the directors committed a fiduciary breach.

Merger-oriented. The target company developed proprietary desktop software for translating documents. By the late 1990s, it dominated the desktop market and looked to expand into the enterprise market. In 2000, it pursued venture capital (VC) that would allow it to realize its growth strategy. The VC firms received preferred stock and seats for their representatives on the company's board of directors. Even though by the end of 2003 the company had achieved a 25%-year-over-year growth and made budget, the VC backers were dissatisfied. In early 2004, difficulties related to government business prompted the then CEO to lower revenue forecasts from $33 million to $28 million for the year. Subsequently, the board terminated him and the VC directors began to look for an exit, retaining JMP Securities (JMP) as an advisor on potential buyers. At the same time, they searched for a new CEO. In July 2004, the board approved the new CEO and adopted a management incentive plan (MIP) that compensated management for achieving a sale regardless of whether the transaction would benefit the common stock. JMP presented a valuation that indicated a very broad valuation range, stretching from $20.4 million to $169.8 million.

Shortly afterward, the future buyer offered $40 million for the company—$10 million in cash and $30 million in stock; the directors declined for the time being. Around the same time, the new CEO took charge and quickly improved the situation. He was able to secure $4 million from a provider of venture debt. For the fourth quarter of 2004, the company generated "record" revenue of $8.7 million and a "record" profit of $1.1 million. Its enterprise revenue surpassed desktop revenue, which raised expectations that its repositioning plan could succeed. In February 2005, the CEO presented a stand-alone business plan for 2005-2007. He believed there was room for growth in the market's enterprise software area. He thought the company could play a dominant role in the global information solutions (GIS) field, that is, the translation aspect of the enterprise content management space. He projected revenue of $30 million in 2005, $38 million in 2006, and $50 million in 2007, assuming flat desktop revenue and growth in the enterprise and GIS segments. Under his leadership, the company achieved an operating budget of $165,000 in the first quarter of 2005 and a cash balance of over $5 million, beating budget.

Regardless, in July 2005, a third party acquired the target for $60 million in cash and stock. Pursuant to the company's certificate of incorporation, the merger qualified as a liquidation, which meant that, under the MIP, the first $7.8 million went to management and the remainder of the proceeds to the preferred stock. The total liquidation preference was $57.9 million. Without the MIP, the common shareholders would have received $2.1 million.

Duty to generate value for the common stock? The plaintiff owned 5% of common stock. In July 2005, he requested an appraisal for his shares from the Delaware Court of Chancery. Based on discovery in this action, he filed a second lawsuit in 2008 alleging that the board's approval of the merger was a breach of fiduciary duty to common shareholders. The directors should have continued to operate the company independently until it could generate value for the common stock, he argued. The court consolidated the suits and certified a class made up of the "beneficial owners of [the company's] common stock whose shares were extinguished" by the merger.

At trial, the plaintiff and the defendant directors presented expert testimony on the value of the company on the merger date.

1. Breach of fiduciary duty action. The Court of Chancery first decided the breach of fiduciary issue. The plaintiff was able to show that the board lacked a majority of disinterested and independent directors approving the merger. For example:

- Two of the directors received personal benefits from the merger, including the CEO who stood to gain $2.34 million from the MIP, plus employment with the buyer and a paid seat on the board; and
- Three of the directors were fiduciaries of the VC funds that obtained differing amounts by way of the $57.9 million liquidation preference that kicked in with the merger. They had a "dual fiduciary problem" because as holders of preferred stock they received $52 million, whereas the common stockholders not only got nothing but also lost the ability to benefit from their ownership interest in the company in the future. As the Court of Chancery put it: "It would not stretch reason to say that this is the worst possible outcome for the common stockholders."

The plaintiff's successful showing meant the directors' decision making was subject to the "most onerous" standard. To defeat the claim, they had to prove they acted with "entire fairness," i.e., "the transaction was the product of fair dealing and fair price."

a. Fair dealing. At the outset, the court said it saw no evidence "suggesting the directors set out to deal with the common stockholders in a procedurally fair manner." They pursued the merger because the company did not offer enough of a return to justify a continuing investment of their time and their funds' exposure to capital loss. That they brought on board a new CEO and rejected the buyer's first offer of $40 million did not prove they were not looking for an exit, said the court: "An owner who decides to fix up the place need not have changed her mind about what to do with the property."

The MIP, which was the brainchild of the conflicted fiduciaries, exemplified the unfairness. As designed, it required the common stockholders to pay $2.1 million and the preferred stockholders $5.7 million to fund it. Without the MIP, the latter would have received $57.9 million based on the merger and the common stockholders $2.1 million. With it, the common stockholders obtained zero. In effect, they contributed 100% of their ex-MIP proceeds and the preferred stockholders only 10%, the court pointed out. The plan's structure provided that there would be nothing for the common stockholders until the deal price surpassed the preference by more than the MIP payout. But even if the purchase price exceeded the break-even value ($66.5 million), the common stockholders still contributed disproportionately to the MIP despite its receiving some proceeds.

At trial, the directors strained to show that the board did consider the interests of the common stock, but the court was not swayed. "Conflict blindness and its lesser cousin, conflict denial, have long afflicted the financially sophisticated," it said. They "fully appreciated" the diverging interests but did nothing to ensure representation of the common stockholders—they did not even obtain a fairness opinion to analyze the merger from the latter's perspective. An outside opinion would have improved the record on fair dealing, the court noted.

Also, the directors never considered making the merger contingent on approval by a majority of the common stockholders. In fact, Microsoft, one of the largest common stockholders, abstained from voting "because it could not stomach ... the fact that it would receive nothing," the court stated. In toto, the evidence on fair dealing "decidedly favored" the plaintiff.

b. Fair price. At trial, the defendants "adopted aggressive positions" to show that the common stock had no value and the merger price was fair. According to the court, even though their statements had a grain of truth, they "exaggerated to the point of caricature." The crux of their argument was that the company could not have self-funded its business plan, would have run out of cash within three or four months, and would have filed for bankruptcy.

There was a counterargument, said the court. The emergence of a new CEO in 2004 quickly improved the picture. Before his arrival, the company budgeted a third-quarter loss of $1.4 million; with only one month left in the quarter, he cut the loss to $0.9 million, and for the last quarter the company achieved a "record profit" of $1.1 million. "There was a realistic possibility that it could self-fund its business plan." The court also dismissed the defendants' attempts to disavow the business plan itself, particularly the GIS component, which several directors suddenly dismissed as "invented" or "fantastical." But the future buyer saw value in it because, when it hired the target's CEO, it insisted on a noncompete to ensure he would not take the plan and obtain funding elsewhere to implement it; the buyer also pursued the GIS. Finally, the defendants claimed the company could not grow because it was part of a stagnant niche market. But, said the court, documents showed that an independent market research firm was less pessimistic. It indicated that worldwide revenue for translation/globalization software tools was $147 million in 2002 and that the market might increase to $247 million in 2007. In a business presentation to Microsoft, the company talked about a market potential of $250 million from translation departments and service providers. Even the CEO's less-rosy picture of a $65 million addressable market did not spell doom but held the promise of some room for growth. All these factors indicated risks but not "mortal crises," the court found.

This is not a valuation. Ultimately, the decision on fairness hinged on valuations. The court considered three.

1. *JMP valuation.* The plaintiff argued that the July 2004 JMP valuation showed the company had value and that JMP's subsequent tweaking of the comparables signified the defendants' attempt to manipulate the valuation to justify the merger.

JMP performed both a comparable company and comparable transaction analysis. The comparable company analysis generated a median multiple of 2.0 times last-12-months (LTM) revenue and suggested an enterprise value of approximately $55 million. The comparable transaction analysis examined seven acquisitions from July 2003 through February 2004 involving "selected content management and search companies" and generated a median multiple of 2.8 times LTM revenue. This implied an enterprise value of approximately $75 million.

JMP did not make another presentation but in January 2005 provided the company CEO with a better set of comparables that yielded a median transaction multiple of 2.2 times LTM revenue. It also broke out the comparable companies into a "content" set and a "language translation services" set, resulting in a median trading multiple of 1.6 times LTM revenue and 1.5 times LTM revenue, respectively. Subsequently, JMP provided yet another cut of the trading multiples that resulted in a median of 1.3 times revenue.

In the court's words, the JMP valuation with July 2004 stand-alone values from $55 million to $75 million presented a problem for the defendants because subsequently the company's performance improved significantly. The defendants' response "was more strained testimony." Although the two analyses were titled "Valuation Considerations" and "Valuation Summary," the responsible JMP executive claimed the document was not a valuation at all. "This was sad," said the court.

But the court went on to say that the valuation was problematic. Both analyses included a broad spectrum of comparable companies and transactions, implying a range of value from $20.4 million to $169.8 million. Although this spread might be fine for a first draft, it called out for refining. What's more, the company's parallel-running efforts to attract interested buyers indicated no one was interested in paying from $55 million to $75 million for it.

The court found the revised multiples did not indicate improper manipulation but suggested the company did not have any true peer companies. The most appropriate comparables were the language translation services companies, which traded at 1.6, 1.3, and 0.6 times LTM revenue. Before the company could achieve a higher multiple, it needed to carry out its business plan and successfully transition to a primarily enterprise-driven business—which was not a guaranteed outcome.

2. *Defendants' expert.* The defendants' expert also prepared comparable company and comparable transaction analyses but found the comparables inadequate for a reliable valuation. Therefore, his opinion relied solely on a discounted cash flow (DCF) analysis based on the February 2005 business plan. The starting point for his projections were the February 2005 projections to which he then added a second stage of more moderate growth. Management's projections assumed that: (1) revenue would grow at a compound annual growth rate of 24% from 2004-2007 (the historical rate from 2001-2004 was 18%); and (2) EBITDA margins would average 15.4% from 2005-2007 (in contrast to negative historical EBITDA margins in 2001, 2002, and 2004 and a positive historical EBITDA margin of 2% in 2003). The starting point for the second stage was management's projected revenue growth rate of 31.6% in 2007, which he then lowered evenly across each year of the five-year secondary period to arrive at a perpetuity growth rate of 7%. This meant that between 2004 and 2012 revenue would grow annually at a rate of 21%. For his second-stage EBITDA margins, the expert began with management's projected margin of 19.4% in 2007, then lowered the margin evenly across each year to ultimately settle at 15% in 2013. As a result of these assumptions, he projected net cash flow of negative $483,000 in 2005 and increasing to $9.3 million in 2013.

In sync with the long-term growth rate of the U.S. economy, he used a 7% perpetuity growth rate. He arrived at an 18.5% discount rate using the WACC method. The sum of all these figures yielded a value of $48.6 million, which increased to $51.9 million once he included cash on hand. As he saw it, this value represented a best-case scenario.

3. *Plaintiff's expert.* The plaintiff's expert prepared valuations based on three alternative methods. First, he used LTM revenue multiples stemming from the comparable companies JMP produced in early 2005. He obtained an implied value of $43.0 million, to which he added a 25% control premium for a total value of $53.7 million. Second, he used LTM revenue multiples stemming from a survey of transactions in the Capital IQ database; it included companies in the "enterprise software industry" whose deal values ranged from $50 million to $250 million. This method yielded an implied value of $68.2 million. Third, he did a comparables-of-comparables analysis for which he created a list of comparable transactions from lists investment bankers had produced in fairness opinions for target companies that the expert considered comparable to the target. The LTM revenue multiple resulting from this method produced an implied value of $85.4 million. Finally, he developed a modified version of the defendant expert's DCF using an exit multiple from his comparable company analysis to calculate the terminal value. This method resulted in an implied value of $77.8 million.

The court credited the defendant expert's DCF valuation, finding that it successfully addressed the central issue of fairness. The expert made "reasonable and plaintiff-friendly assumptions." For example, his 7% perpetuity growth rate was generous in light of many Delaware decisions that applied lower growth rates. Also, his discount rate was lower than the 21.82% discount rate an Ibbotson report suggested, the court pointed out. Nevertheless, the value emerging from his valuation was less than the $60 million merger proceeds.

The court saw numerous problems with the work the plaintiff's expert performed. For example, for the two comparable transaction analyses that yielded values greater than the merger price, he failed to adjust for synergies. Also, he "gamed" the relative weightings of his three methodologies. Originally, he weighted the three methods equally, seeing no reason to emphasize one over another. After a critique of his valuations from the defendants' expert, he submitted a revised report in 2011 adopting some of the competing expert's suggestions and generating lower valuations. But by giving a 60% weight to his comparables-of-comparables approach and 20% weightings to the two others, he managed to increase the overall value again to $75.6 million. He called this adjustment a "feels right sort of thing." Weighting all three analyses equally would have shown a value of only $69.1 million, said the court. In general, he failed to demonstrate that the comparable companies and transactions he used were in fact comparable.

His modified DCF analysis "came closest to the mark," the court said. "When valuing a VC-backed portfolio company, using an exit multiple could make sense, because this technique recognizes that VCs often exit through trade sales." But there were two fatal defects. In terms of method, he did not use the same set of 17 comparable companies for his exit multiple that he used in his comparable companies analysis. Instead he first reduced the original 17 to 12 and then to eight; these adjustments compromised the integrity of the three sets. Factually speaking, his analysis assumed the company could be sold for 1.3 to 1.7 times revenue. But reality was different. There was a dearth of suitable buyers, but no shortage of targets. If the company had declined the buyer's offer, the latter could have gone elsewhere. And, even though the 2005 business plan included a repositioning strategy that might enable it to "merge up" at a higher multiple, this approach presented the greatest risk because it required a successful transition, capital, and a buyer willing to credit the company's greater value. To assume an exit through sale at the end of the projection period and use the same 18.5% discount rate that the defendants' expert used for stand-alone cash flows underestimated the uncertainty embedded in that strategy.

The defendant expert's DCF showed conclusively that the company could not grow at a rate that would generate value for the common stock, even if it likely could self-fund and stay in business, the court concluded. Thus, despite the conflicts of interest and unfair process, the directors proved that the transaction was fair because the price was fair.

2. *Appraisal action.* The outcome for the fairness case and the appraisal proceeding was the same, said the court: If "the common stock had no economic value before the merger, then the common stockholders received the substantial equivalent in value of what they had before"—zero, in this instance.

DE Chancery Court's Appraisal Puts Focus on Precrisis Projections

Case name: *Towerview LLC v. Cox Radio, Inc.*
Citation: 2013 Del. Ch. LEXIS 139
Date of decision: June 28, 2013
Country: US
State or Federal: State
State/Jurisdiction: Delaware
Court: Court of Chancery
Type of action: Dissenting Shareholder
Experts: Dr. Samuel Kursh (petitioners); Rajiv Gokhale (respondent)
Judge: Parsons
SIC: 4832 Radio Broadcasting Stations (networks)
Key words: Discounted cash flow method (DCF), Delaware Court of Chancery, Statutory Appraisal

In the wake of the 2008 economic meltdown, what kind of rebound did the management of a radio broadcaster expect in May 2009 when it merged into one of its parent company's entities? According to the Delaware Court of Chancery, the answer to this question was the key to determining the fair value of the petitioners' shares in a statutory appraisal action.

The petitioners were shareholders of the respondent, a radio broadcasting business that owned, operated, and serviced 86 stations in 19 markets. In March 2009, its parent company announced a tender offer to buy its stock for $3.80 per share and consolidate it with a wholly owned subsidiary. A month later, the buyer increased the offer price to $4.80. Certain stockholders—distinct from the petitioners—filed a class action suit alleging breaches of fiduciary duty against the company, its board, and the related businesses. The merger took place on May 29, 2009. The shareholders, over the objections of the petitioners, ultimately agreed to a settlement, which the court approved. Subsequently, the petitioners requested an appraisal of their shares. For this purpose, the court conducted a bench trial during which it heard expert testimony on the stock's fair market value on the merger date.

The projections. Every year, company management prepared bottom-up five-year financial projections, which represented the company's long-range plan (LRP). It considered the first year's forecast a "budget," including monthly numbers, and the other four years "out-years," which were "done at a very high level." Further, management routinely created monthly forecasts for the current year, which provided new estimates for several of the following months of the current year. In December 2008, the company's board of directors approved the 2009 LRP covering the years 2009 through 2013. In hindsight, the LRPs were "consistently over-optimistic," particularly with regard to the out-years.

The issue in the case was how relevant and reliable the 2009 LRP remained to management in the wake of the national financial crisis in the second half of 2008 and its dramatic effect on company revenues. In fact, departing from normal practice, in January 2009 management generated another forecast for the year, not just the next few months. It updated the current-year forecasts again in February, March, April, and May. The most recent forecast before the merger was the May 20, 2009, forecast. By early 2009, management expectations were decidedly less optimistic than the 2009 LRP reflected. The January 2009 forecast lowered projected revenues and operating cash flow (OCF) by 14.7% and 37.6%, respectively, compared to the 2009 LRP. By May 2009, projected revenues were 16.8% lower and OCF was 40.1% lower than the 2009 LRP indicated.

But management did not entirely abandon the 2009 LRP. It sent the projections to various parties, including outside appraisers whose enterprise valuation of the company as of Dec. 31, 2008, considered the projections one of numerous sources with which to create their own cash flow projections, based on historical performance and industry trends. Also a May 2009 company memo claimed that the 2009 LRP to some extent already took into account "the deteriorating environment" and shrinking revenue. "[F]uture years' growth is attainable due to recovery in the industry," it said.

The contentions. The parties and their experts had differing views on how meaningful the 2009 LRP was for valuation. According to the petitioners, in May 2009 industry participants, including the company, expected the industry to climb out of the slump it was in in early 2009 and return to form at some point in the foreseeable future. As the radio industry's star, the company was in the best position to achieve a recovery, once the latter "inevitably occurred." Evidence that management continued to rely on the 2009 LRP in early 2009 meant it believed in the eventual return to the plan's projections. The only question was how long it would take for the "cyclical" recovery to take place. The petitioners said their valuation expert's analysis provided the correct answer and urged the court to adopt his conclusion as to the fair value of the stock in May 2009.

In contrast, the company claimed that, at the time of the merger date, company management and radio industry observers understood that the industry was undergoing a "secular" change, which had begun before the 2008-2009 collapse. The recession simply established a new baseline. The company's management realized the plan was obsolete and did not expect a return to its financial projections. Accordingly, the company advocated in favor of adopting its expert's valuation, based on historical data from the recent 2000-2001 recession.

The experts. Both parties presented industry and valuation experts.

Petitioners' expert. The petitioners' valuation expert only performed a discounted cash flow (DCF) analysis. He used the May 2009 forecast to project cash flows for 2009 and used the 2009 LRP to project cash flows for 2010 through 2013. He also assumed that the company would return to the 2009 LRP after 18 months, in late 2011.

Based on an equation that considered inflation, population growth, and increased productivity, he chose a terminal growth rate of 2.5%, which he said was conservative, considering an inflation rate of 2%, an assumed long-term growth rate of 1.7%, and productivity of about 1.0%. These inputs, he explained, supported a "generally regarded historical growth rate of 4% to 6%." He dismissed the rival expert's claim that this rate was unsupportable because it assumed that "for every one percent of revenue growth, [the company's] free cash flow will grow by two percent into perpetuity." His assumption rested on the company's operating leverage, the petitioners' expert responded. If revenues simply aligned with inflation, "the fall to the bottom line would be a little bit higher because of operating leverage, the fall of the free cash flow."

He used an 8.1% discount rate. As a result of these inputs, the expert obtained a fair value of at least $11.05 per share. He maintained that certain adjustments to the 2009 LRP, including the company's retained cushion and omitted deferred taxes, added to the value. For example, a statement from the company's CFO that the company had decreased revenues by $2 million and increased expenses by $2 million each year to manage expectations meant that the final calculation should reflect this additional $4 million, he believed. But he did not adjust his DCF analysis to specify the changes he suggested in regard to the two items. Instead, he simply increased the per-share value by $1.07 and arrived at $12.12 per share.

Company's expert. The company's expert also based his valuation on the DCF—only he performed two. He also undertook a comparable companies analysis but found the latter less meaningful because market values of debt were only available for one comparable. Moreover, in light of the 2008 economic meltdown, the book values of debt were a poor proxy for market valuation. As he saw it, the multiples emerging from the comparable companies analysis were unreasonably high and would overstate the value of shares.

For the first DCF analysis, the expert used the May 2009 forecast to project 2009 cash flows using the actual EBITDA compound annual growth rate (CAGR) the company recorded in the four years after the 2000-2001 recession. Specifically, he used the forecast's 2009 OCF projections and grew them at a rate of 4.6% each year until 2013. The rate was in line with the 2009 LRP in which management had projected OCF values for 2010 to 2013 with annual growth rates in the range of 3.4% to 4.1% and EBITDA with annual growth rates from 1.4% to 2.7%. Also a J.P. Morgan report projected a 2010 EBITDA growth rate of 5.1%.

For the second DCF analysis, he generated projections for 2009 through 2010 based on a combination of consensus analyst EBITDA estimates for the company; to project cash flow for 2011 through 2013, he used the actual EBITDA CAGR for the three years following the 2000-2001 recession.

He reasoned that there was no justification to use the 2009 LRP because at the time of the merger the company's management and industry analysts had reduced projections for 2009 and subsequent years significantly. Some inputs from the 2009 LRP—depreciation and costs for the long-term incentive plan (LTIP)—did make it into his DCF. He computed the weighted average cost of capital (WACC) using the capital asset pricing model (CAPM) to determine the cost of equity. He arrived at a range from 5.81% to 7.65%, excluding a small stock premium, and 7.03% to 9.2%, including the premium. He used an 8.0% WACC to discount the company's unleveraged free cash flows. Further, he chose a terminal growth rate of 1.25% based on analyst statements ranging from -1% to +2%.

He concluded that the fair value of the shares was in the range of $3.40 to $5.29 and proposed a midpoint, $4.28 per share, as the correct price on the merger date.

The court. The court acknowledged that the disparity in the experts' conclusions stemmed primarily from the differing cash flow projections they selected. Premerger management projections are "an appropriate starting point from which to derive data in the appraisal context," the court said at the outset. But here the changes in the economy and radio industry that took place between the creation of the 2009 LRP in October 2008 and the merger in May 2009 severely undermined the plan's reliability. Management acknowledged this much when it considerably reduced projections for 2009 in the months preceding the merger.

The principal issue, the court declared, was "how quickly, if at all, the radio industry in general and [the company] in particular, would have been expected to recover to pre-recession expectations." The court was "wary" of accepting the petitioners' argument that a May 2009 valuation anticipated a return to the 2009 LRP's 2011-2013 cash flow projections in the near future. The expectations of company management for the immediate future "had plummeted." Also, it rejected the proposition from the petitioners' expert that the steep recession in the radio industry in 2008 and 2009 would be followed by a steep recovery. This theory relied on a correlation between real gross domestic product (GDP) and advertising revenue in the radio industry that the expert had failed to prove.

Cash flow projections. The May 2009 forecast, which reflected the possibility of a "limited cyclical recovery," was the appropriate starting point for projecting the company's free operating cash flows after December 2009, the court found. Accordingly, it accepted the May forecast DCF analysis the company's expert performed as a "general framework." It decided the petitioner expert's model, which predicted a return to the 2009 LRP by the end of 2011, was "too optimistic."

In a footnote, the court added that the company expert's valuation was "more reliable generally." Not only did his report explain the calculations in his DCF analyses, but it also included the formulas supporting his conclusions. Because the opposing expert did not "explain clearly his calculations or how he arrived at his results," the company's expert could not replicate the analysis precisely.

As to the court's adjustments to the general framework, it found that, even though there was support for the 4.6% growth rate in the record, this number failed to account for any significant recovery from the "depth of the recession," which compelled management to adjust the 2009 EBITDA downward by 41%. In other words, the company's expert assumed the 2008-2009 recovery would have no "cyclical aspect" to it. However, following the 2000-2001 recession, on which the expert drew, the company's OCF grew by 9.28% in 2002, 0.44% in 2003, 5.18% in 2004, and 4.06% in 2005. Despite evidence that the radio industry had secular concerns, cyclical factors and the general economy played a role in the 2008-2009 recession, said the court. Therefore, it was plausible that there were expectations in 2010, the year following the recession, that there would be a "bump in growth" similar to 2002. Although an "imperfect model," the court adopted a 2010 OCF growth rate of 9.28% and a 4.6% rate for the years 2011 through 2013. At the same time, it found that there was no support for an increase of 37.6% in 2010 and 27.3% in 2011, as the petitioners' expert proposed.

Terminal growth rate. The court pointed out that both analysts expected inflation to be around 2% to 2.5%. It first dismissed the company's argument in favor of a growth rate below the inflation rate because the company "was not a mature, stable company." Even if the company faced certain secular challenges, there was no evidence that it risked insolvency, the court said; moreover, the company's expert "projected a stable future for the Company." Although it was unwilling to adopt the petitioner expert's rate of 2.5%, the court recognized the company's operating leverage and applied a 2.25% rate.

Discount rate. The experts' discount rates varied only by 0.1%, the court pointed out. Because it adopted the analyses of the company's expert, it accepted his 8.0% discount rate, which, it noted, actually favored the petitioners.

Retained cushion and deferred taxes inputs. Adding the $4 million to the final calculation, as the petitioners' expert suggested to account for the cushion, would represent an additional value of $0.62 per share at the expert's 8.01% discount rate. But there was insufficient evidence that the OCF of the May 2009 forecast was low by $4 million. Moreover, the record did not support an adjustment for the omitted deferred taxes.

Based on the Court of Chancery's modifications to the company expert's framework, it concluded the appropriate price for the petitioners' stock was $5.75 per share on the day of the merger.

No Taboo Against Marketability Discount in Shareholder Suit

Case name: *Tutunikov v. Markov*
Citation: 2013 N.J. Super. Unpub. LEXIS 1935
Date of decision: Aug. 1, 2013
Country: US
State or Federal: State
State/Jurisdiction: New Jersey
Court: Court of Appeals
Type of action: Dissenting Shareholder
Experts: Unknown (plaintiff); unknown (defendants)
Judge: Per Curiam
SIC: 7379 Computer Related Services, NEC (except computer systems consultants and disk conversion services)
Key words: Marketability discount, Minority discount, Dissenting Shareholder Action, Balsamides

In calculating the fair value of the plaintiffs' interests in a dissenting shareholder suit, the trial court said an investment proposal from a third party presented a "more realistic" value of the target company than the parties' expert valuations. At the same time, the court made a 35% upward adjustment to account for the proposal's embedded marketability discount. The defendants and the dissenting shareholders challenged the court's valuation.

In 1997 four partners "anticipated" that they would form a corporation that would provide software applications and consulting services for financial institutions. To this end, they prepared a final draft and a resolution setting down the share allocation. The plaintiffs were two minority partners, who left the corporation before the filing of a certificate of formation to work elsewhere. A subsequent operating agreement, which was to override all prior agreements, listed all four men as members. Some seven years later, the minority partners learned that the majority partners had given themselves a 100% salary raise and made other adjustments to their advantage and requested a buyout of their interests. The majority owners offered $10,000 per share, admitting this amount bore no relationship to the value of the company but saying it was what the company could afford to pay. The plaintiffs believed it was worth $10 million and wanted $1.8 million for their shares.

Third-party investment proposal. At the end of November 2004, a global accounting software company outlined a "proposal investment" in the company. The defendants informed the plaintiffs that the proposed financing made it reasonable to buy out their interests for $500,000. In fact, the proposal valued the company at $5 million. The investor would infuse $500,000 in cash and obtain a 9.09% equity interest in a newly formed LLC. The investor reserved the right to make further cash infusions and thus increase its equity interest. The plaintiffs did not accept the offer and instead filed suit in the New Jersey Superior Court. The investor never exercised its option to invest further. Subsequently, the company merged with another company. In a premerger buyout proposal, it offered one plaintiff $350,000 and the other $262,500. The interests of all partners in the company were worth a total of $3.5 million.

The main issues at trial were: (1) whether there was oppression of the minority interest holders; (2) what precisely the plaintiffs' ownership interests in the company were; and (3) what the fair value of the two ownership interests was.

Both sides presented valuation experts. The plaintiffs' expert concluded that the company was worth $35.5 million. In contrast, the defendants' expert valued the company at $3.5 million. (The opinion does not give details on the calculations.)

Expert valuations too biased. The trial court found there was oppression, which translated into an award for the plaintiffs for attorney's fees and costs. It set the ownership interests at 10.45% for one plaintiff and 7.84% for the second.

As to valuation, it discredited both expert opinions and instead turned to the third-party "proposal investment" for information leading to a "more realistic value of the company." The experts' data, the court said, was "subject to the prejudices of the party experts." The $500,000 investment indicated that the value of the company prior to the investment was $5 million, it concluded

But, the trial court continued, that price represented "a non-marketable interest since the company was a non-publicly traded company. Even though "discounts generally should not be applied in … an oppressed shareholder action absent unusual or extraordinary circumstances," in this instance an upward adjustment was appropriate. "[T]he $5 million value derived from the … transaction which contains a marketability discount must be removed to reconstitute the fair value of the shares." Accordingly, the court added 35% and arrived at a total company value of $6.75 million.

At the same time, it denied the plaintiffs' request to adjust for a minority discount, which they claimed the offering price also included. This modification would "pay [the plaintiffs] for rights in the company that they do not enjoy."

Embedded minority discount or premium? Both sides challenged several of the trial court's findings at the appellate division. Regarding the valuation, the defendants made two arguments. First, the $5 million valuation implicit in the "proposal investment" did not include a minority discount. Based on their expert's calculation, the company's actual value was $3.5 million. The $1.5 million difference between the two values reflected the investor's willingness to pay more for other benefits, including a seat on the board of directors and a liquidation preference, than it would have paid for just an equity interest. Second, even if the market value of the company were $5 million, the trial court should have used a marketability discount to reduce the value to $3.25 million to adjust for the implied premium.

The plaintiffs also presented two objections. First, the lower court erred when it did not adjust for an embedded minority interest in the $5 million offering price. Second, the trial court made a mathematical error in adjusting for the implied marketability discount. The proper calculation required the court to divide $5 million by 65 because the offer only represented 65% of the company's total value. Accordingly, the total value was about $7.7 million.

At the start of its analysis, the appellate court pointed out that, even though the trial court's factual findings in valuation disputes require deference from the reviewing court, no such deference applied to findings as to "what discounts or premiums the determination of fair value may include, or must exclude, since they are questions of law."

The appellate court went on to explain: "A majority discount adjusts for lack of control over the business entity, while a marketability discount adjusts for lack of liquidity in one's interest in an entity" (citing *Balsamides v. Protameen Chemicals,* 160 N.J. 352 (1999)) (available at *BVLaw*). In terms of the minority discount, the court agreed with the defendants that the offering price did not contain a minority discount. The investor received benefits beyond an equity interest in the company. But, said the court, the offer also did not embed a premium for preferred membership in the LLC, as the defendants tried to claim.

As to the marketability discount adjustment, the appellate court agreed with the trial court that, generally speaking, this discount was inappropriate within the context of a dissenting shareholder action. But, the appellate court continued, in this case the trial court "utilized the marketability discount in valuing [the company], not in valuing the plaintiffs' particular interests." This was a significant distinction. "Discounting at the corporate level may be entirely appropriate if it is generally accepted in the financial community in valuing businesses" (citing *Balsamides*).

Considering that both experts applied a marketability discount of 35% in valuing the investor's offer, the trial court's adjustment was appropriate—even if it declined to adopt either expert's valuation of the company.

Lastly, the appellate court agreed with the plaintiffs that the lower court erred when it applied the discount factor to the company value. The fair value was $7.7 million. Considering one plaintiff's interest was 10.45%, his share in the company was worth about $804,000; given the other plaintiff's interest was 7.84%, his portion valued $603,000, the court concluded.

Flawed Market Reconstruction Ends Lost Profits Claim

Case name: *Tyco Healthcare Group LP v. Ethicon Endo-Surgery, Inc.*
Citation: 2013 U.S. Dist. LEXIS 43992
Date of decision: March 28, 2013
Country: US
State or Federal: Federal
State/Jurisdiction: Connecticut
Court: United States District Court
Type of action: Intellectual Property
Experts: Dr. Keith Ugone (plaintiffs); Dr. Gregory Bell (defendant)
Judge: Arterton
SIC: 3841 Surgical and Medical Instruments and Apparatus (except tranquilizer guns and operating room tables)

In this patent infringement suit in federal court (D. Conn.), the plaintiffs claimed lost profits, in addition to reasonable royalty damages, but their expert stumbled when he tried to show causation to lost sales by calculating the market share allocation the plaintiffs would have had "but for" the defendant's infringing products. His reasonable royalty analysis gained better traction in the court.

Both parties produced "advanced energy" surgical products for laparoscopic and minimally invasive procedures. The plaintiffs claimed the defendant violated three of its patents for ultrasonic surgical devices—instruments that use ultrasonic energy to cut and coagulate vessels in surgery. In a bench trial, the court found infringement as to all patents in suit.

Entire value of devices. In terms of damages, the parties stipulated that the plaintiff only had a right to a reasonable royalty for the defendant's initial six-year infringement, from 2004 to January 2010. At the same time, the plaintiffs requested lost profits and royalty damages for violations from 2010 to the present. Both sides presented expert testimony.

Under the Federal Circuit's "functional unit" test, the plaintiffs' expert calculated damages based on the entire market value of the patented products. The rule states that the damages calculation may include in the compensation base unpatented components of a device "when the unpatented and patented components are physically part of the same machine." See *Rite-Hite Corp. v. Kelley Co.*, 56 F.3d 1538 (Fed. Cir. 1995).

The defendant objected, but the court agreed with the expert's approach. The patented features of the accused devices were physically connected to and part of the instruments, and, besides, the defendant's damages expert used the entire market value of the infringing products in his own calculations.

Lost Profits. The plaintiffs had to prove a right to lost profits by passing the four-part *Panduit* test, showing: (1) there was demand for the patented product; (2) causation to lost sales, through evidence that there was no noninfringing substitute for the protected products or that the plaintiffs had an established market share; (3) a manufacturing and marketing capability to exploit the demand;

and (4) the amount of profit they would have made absent the infringement. *Panduit Corp. v. Stahlin Bros. Fibre Works, Inc.*, 575 F.2d 1132 (6th Cir. 1978).

They satisfied the first part and sought to meet the second requirement by way of a model their expert developed to reconstruct the market and show the plaintiffs' share absent the infringing products. The relevant market was one of advanced-energy-based cutting and coagulating devices in which the plaintiffs competed with two different types of products, those using ultrasonic energy and others using radiofrequency (RF), the expert said. The litigants dominated the market and competed directly with each other. The defendant's marketing and R&D materials showed that it considered the plaintiffs' RF energy products competition, and witnesses for both sides stated that surgeons used both types of instruments for the same type of surgeries. This proved that these devices functioned interchangeably, the expert stated.

In the "actual market" in 2010, when the infringing products were available, the plaintiffs had a 24% market share, he determined. In the "but for" market of 2010, the plaintiffs would have had a 54.2% market share, notwithstanding the defendant's access to "immune" ultrasonic products (not subject to liability under a 1999 settlement agreement between the two parties) and its own line of RF products, as well as the presence of a small number of other competitors.

For 2011, the plaintiffs' actual market share was 27.5%, but, under the expert's reconstruction, it would have been 60.2%. This increase was due to the steady rise in the use of RF technology, he said, relying on a 2010 report from the Millennium Research Group (MRG) on vessel-sealing instruments. The analysis projected that by 2014 the two energy sources would have something akin to a 50-50 market share. In a world without the infringing products, the plaintiffs would achieve a higher share, he concluded.

The defendant's expert painted a different picture, claiming primarily that the "immune" products would fill in the "hole" the market experienced once the infringing devices were unavailable. In 1999, those products had an 86.9% market share. But, by his account, in the actual 2010 world, it was at most 0.2%.

The plaintiff's expert disagreed with this line of thinking. There was documentation that surgeons disfavored some attributes of the immune products; moreover, he said, "you can't just say in the year 2000 the immune products had a certain market share and ... put it down in 2010." At most, these products would claim 7% to 9% of the market, taking into account that the defendant would market them more aggressively and might lower their price to compete with available inferior products.

The court rejected the model the defendant's expert proposed but found the market reconstruction of the plaintiffs' expert also problematic. For one, the MRG document included information that found the two product types had "separate strength," a point that "undercut" the expert's argument. Also, the defendant produced evidence that showed the plaintiffs were pursuing a separate path to market another ultrasonic product. Documents showed that they believed that market segment was "currently led by [the defendant.]" Speaking about the 2008 market, the plaintiffs divided the vessel-sealing market into two segments, finding the ultrasonic component owned 60% of it and the RF energy component roughly 40%. Surgeons preferred the ultrasonic tools for cutting and the RF energy ones for sealing.

There was insufficient evidence from which to infer that "RF technology would have taken over the advanced energy market to the extent [the plaintiffs' expert] claimed," the court concluded. Because the plaintiffs failed to prove causation, they could not claim lost profits.

Cooperators versus competitors. Next, the court considered the experts' rival reasonable royalty testimony based on the *Georgia-Pacific* factors.

Reasonable royalty. Both experts agreed on the starting date of a hypothetical negotiation but disagreed over the significance of a series of licensing agreements between the plaintiffs and outside parties and the defendant and third parties.

Ultimately, the plaintiffs' expert concluded the royalty rate would fall between 12% and 15%, whereas the defendant's expert put it between 1.5% and 5%, recommending a 2.6% rate.

The agreements included a 1996 contract in which another company granted the plaintiffs a license for one of the patents in suit at a 5% royalty rate. The plaintiffs' expert found it not probative because the parties were "cooperators," instead of direct competitors—thus, in a relationship unlike that of the litigating parties. Under the agreement, both sides would develop technology to build an ultrasonic device.

He also rejected a second agreement involving the plaintiffs and showing a 5% rate because it centered on technologies that were not sufficiently related to the technology at issue. The fact that the plaintiffs had not granted any other licenses for the patents in suit would drive up the rate.

The defendant's expert used the first agreement to set a 5% upper limit for his royalty range, but the court agreed with the plaintiffs' expert. There were substantial dissimilarities, such that the 5% rate did not "necessarily indicate an upper ceiling of the reasonable royalty rate."

An agreement the defendant made with a third party in 1995 covered components with which to assemble a licensed instrument—an ultrasonic handpiece design. It limited the defendant's right to operate in a "licensed field" and required it to pay a lump sum of $200,000, plus a royalty of 1.5% of net sales. Based on this rate, the defendant's expert set the lower limit of his range at 1.5%.

The plaintiffs' expert pointed out that the contract "significantly predated" the date of the hypothetical negotiation and was irrelevant to the success of the ultrasonic technology that factored into a 2000 negotiation. The court agreed this rate was not probative.

A 1998 agreement between the defendant and another company built on the parties' earlier 1992 contract. The parties cross-licensed their patents at a zero percent royalty rate; they specified there would be negotiations for any patents either side wanted to add and that the rate would not exceed 3%. If one side wanted to add a second patent to the same product, they could negotiate a rate up to 5%.

The defendant's expert found those rates to be "ceilings." The plaintiffs' expert focused on the contract's last clause, stating that, in the event of termination of the agreement, "the royalty rate for any patent licensed by such terminating party … shall be doubled for the remaining term of the license." This provision, he contended, was critical because it showed what would happen if the relationship between licensing parties changed from cooperative to competitive.

Under another agreement, the defendant granted a third party a license to a patent that covered ultrasonic surgical technology for a $66-per-unit royalty payment. This contract was "highly relevant," the plaintiffs' expert stated, because it revealed the value the defendant placed on this very type of technology. Considering the sales price for the defendant's best-selling ultrasonic surgical instrument—between $376 and $624—the per-unit royalty payment would equal 11% to 18% of the per-unit revenue of that product, he calculated.

The defendant's expert dismissed it as not comparable because it was a collaborative agreement. The court disagreed, noting that the defendant's expert, himself, had described the patent at the heart of the contract as "one of the foundational patents … of ultrasonic." The agreement was relevant in that it showed the defendants required a relatively high royalty rate "for a technology that shares some common features with the ultrasonic patents in suit."

Considering several other factors, the court concluded that the appropriate royalty rate was 8%. It was sufficiently higher than the 5% rate the 1996 agreement specified for cooperating parties. And, on one hand, it accounted for the fact that the defendant had its own ultrasonic technology in the form of the "foundational" patent and its immune products; on the other, it considered that the defendant's accused products were far more successful than its immune products.

Applying the 8% rate to $1.75 billion of infringing sales, the court awarded the plaintiffs royalty damages of nearly $141 million.

Expert's 'Unsupportable' Inputs Undermine DCF Analysis and Credibility

Case name: *U.S. Bank N.A. v. Verizon Communications Inc.*
Citation: 2013 U.S. Dist. LEXIS 8521
Date of decision: Jan. 22, 2013
Country: US
State or Federal: Federal
State/Jurisdiction: Texas
Court: United States District Court
Type of action: Bankruptcy
Experts: Carlyn Taylor (plaintiff); Mark Hopkins (defendants)
Judge: Fish
SIC: 2741 Miscellaneous Publishing (shopping news and advertising periodical publishing or publishing and printing except Internet)

A 10-day bench trial in federal court (N.D. Tex.) focused on a single factual issue: What was the enterprise value of a directories business on the day Verizon spun it off?

Prior to Nov. 17, 2006, the entity was a wholly owned subsidiary of Verizon. Subsequently, it operated for two years as an independent company that was traded on the New York Stock Exchange, before filing for Chapter 11 bankruptcy in early 2009. The plaintiff was the litigation trustee, which, in the context of reorganization, pursued a variety of claims against Verizon and related entities.

Business in for 'secular change.' The plaintiff's chief arguments were that the transaction was a fraudulent conveyance and the defendants had misrepresented the company's value to the market. Verizon's key executives recognized that its directories business was undergoing a "secular" change. Publicly they portrayed the subject as having the potential for significant growth, while secretly they considered it a "dying harvest business" that they needed to sell off.

Under the divestiture, the subject incurred $9.1 billion in debt in exchange for Verizon's domestic print and electronic directories. To structure the transaction as a tax-free event, the parties entered into a tax sharing agreement (TSA) that allocated liability should the IRS later determine that the event did not qualify as such.

At the time of the spin-off, there was significant investor interest in directories companies because of their high and stable cash flow. Verizon's directories business historically produced more than $3.4 billion in annual revenue and its EBITDA margins were about 50%. But while stand-alone directories companies traded at as much as 10 times EBITDA, Verizon's was trading at only 5 to 5.5 times EBITDA.

Also, Verizon's and the subject's SEC filings indicated declining revenues from 2001 through 2006, and industry analysts projected future revenue declines in the incumbent print business. The management forecasts that Verizon provided only to private-side investors showed a flat EBITDA from 2006 through 2010; free cash flow forecasts for the subject showed declines from $459 million in 2006 to $437 million in 2010.

Three private-side investors undertook their own valuations. Morgan Stanley concluded that on the day of the spin-off, the subject would have a total enterprise value of $12.5 billion and an equity value of about $3.4 billion. Citibank determined an enterprise value of $11.7 billion to $14.4 billion, and Goldman Sachs calculated a value of $12.5 billion, with an equity value of approximately $3.4 billion. In November 2005, the Verizon board received a "strategic update" that indicated a valuation range of $10.5 billion to $15 billion resulting from a discounted cash flow (DCF) analysis, based on "plan of records" forecasts for the previous five years, 2005-2009.

In contrast, an internal Verizon document from summer 2005 suggested a value of only $6.5 billion. This was the result of a "downside case" DCF analysis evaluating a worst-case scenario for the print business alone, a company executive explained. He subsequently "refined" the analysis, using a lower discount rate and correcting earlier analytical flaws. The final valuation, he said, "was what it was when the transaction was completed," that is, $12.8 billion.

Not all calculations count the same. At trial, the plaintiff presented a valuation expert and the defendants a rebuttal as well as a tax expert. The plaintiff's expert was a CPA, who was also a certified insolvency and restructuring accountant, a credentialed business valuator, and held licenses from the Financial Industry Regulatory Authority (FINRA). To determine the value on the spin-off date, she made three separate calculations using: 1) the "market multiple method"; 2) the "comparable transaction method"; and 3) the DCF method.

Under the market multiple approach, she used the same five directories companies and multiples that the investment bank Houlihan Lokey had used when it performed a valuation analysis for a solvency opinion for the subject in fall 2006. She determined the value ranged from $11.7 billion to $13.2 billion, but only weighted the outcome at 15%. Verizon's directories business performed worse than the comparables, she said. Also, the selected companies were not truly comparable: Only one was, like the spin-off, an incumbent print company doing business in the U.S. However, that company received significant tax benefits related to the purchase of another directories company—benefits not available to the subject.

Under the comparable transaction method, she again drew on data—in this instance, 17 company transactions—Houlihan Lokey had used for its solvency opinion. Ultimately, she arrived at a value range of $13.4 billion to $15.8 billion, but again she only assigned 15% weight to the result, reasoning that the 17 transactions did not involve sufficiently comparable companies and the TSA prevented the subject from accessing the transactions market. This restriction, she found, conflicted with the premise of the comparable transaction method—that the subject is able to access the market.

For the DCF valuation, she made three different calculations based on three different projections of the subject company's free cash flow for the projection period. For one projection, she adjusted a "base case" projection that Verizon had prepared in 2006; for a second, she used a stress-test projection Houlihan Lokey had made before presenting its solvency opinion; and for a third projection, she used a mathematical extrapolation of the trend of the actual historical performance of Verizon's directory business from 2003 to 2006. She derived her terminal growth rate from the Gordon growth model, assuming an annual rate of EBITDA decline in perpetuity.

She determined a discount rate of 9.75% using the standard weighted average cost of capital (WACC) formula, which she applied to the three sets of projected cash flow in the projection period and the terminal value. Moreover, she applied a 2% company-specific risk premium in calculating the company's cost of equity. As a result, the overall discount rate was 1% higher than it would have been without the premium. The adjustment was appropriate, given certain disadvantages that were specific to the subject, she explained, including its operating in lower-growth, highly competitive urban markets, lagging behind competitors in terms of performance, having inexperienced management, and facing restrictions in the strategic and financial options it could pursue because of the TSA.

She concluded that the value ranged from $5.4 billion to $6.3 billion and that the midpoint—$5.85 billion—most accurately reflected the enterprise value under the DCF. She stated that she "looked deeply" at any potential flaws in her analysis, given that the result deviated sharply from the other valuations, but ultimately decided to weight the result at 70%.

The weighted calculations produced a value range of $7.5 billion to $8.8 billion. The midpoint—$8.15 billion—was the enterprise value on the day of the transaction, she concluded; this meant the company was insolvent after, including its spin-off debt.

Finally, although she agreed that a valuation professional normally would consider the price at which the company stock traded as "a prime indicator" of its value, she thought in this case it was "completely unreliable" and chose to disregard it. Because of Verizon's misrepresentations and omissions, investors were prone to inflate the subject's equity value by at least $4 billion. She also asserted that Verizon had not disclosed the significant differences in EBITDA margins from the incumbent print and electronic businesses; concealed the steady annual declines in revenue in specific Northeastern urban markets; and failed to disclose consistent missed management projections, as well as a consulting group's pessimistic forecast about the future of the directories business.

Accusations of 'double counting.' The defendants' rebuttal expert focused most of his critique on his counterpart's DCF analysis. Under accepted valuation principles, it was "incorrect" to use a purely historical average for a projection, as she did in her third projection, he noted. It also was inappropriate to use the Houlihan Lokey stress-test projection because that originally was for a sensitivity analysis, not for the purpose of valuation. And she made inappropriate adjustments to Verizon's base case projection. For example, Verizon's incumbent print revenue projection was already more conservative than industry reports suggested; similarly, there was no reason to downward adjust projections of independent market growth because the company historically had seen strong growth in this revenue segment and its projections were again more conservative than industry expectations.

As for the terminal value, to assume an annual rate of EBITDA decline in perpetuity was "commercially unreasonable and inappropriate in a DCF valuation." Most analysts would assume that management would take drastic steps to assure such steep declines did not occur, he said. In fact, the subject had planned for an annual $200 million dividend from which it could withdraw if projected revenues were not on target.

Her discount rate was too high. For one, it assumed a capital structure of 44% debt, 56% equity, which he said was common in European companies, but inappropriate for a U.S. business. The one comparable most similar to the subject had a capital structure that was weighted much more heavily toward the debt side, which most analysts would "mimic" in their calculation. He also objected to the 2% company-specific risk premium. Those risk premiums generally were disfavored because they allowed analysts to improperly inject subjective hindsight; moreover, their use in this case led to "double counting," since the plaintiff's expert already had assumed "drastically" lower cash flows than contemporaneous analysts.

As the defendants' expert saw it, merely correcting for the errors in her discount rate and terminal value calculations would have led to a DCF value that was $4.3 billion higher. The result would have been a range of $9.7 billion to $10.6 billion even before weighting it and adding it to the weighted results of the market-based valuations.

He asserted that the plaintiff's expert's DCF analysis produced "a significant outlier" in relation to the calculations she achieved under the other methods and noted that Shannon Pratt's authoritative treatise prescribed ways of how to handle this type of irregularity. An expert might disregard the outlier, assign more weight to the consistent valuations, or more closely examine the model that produced the irregular result to determine what went wrong.

The defendants' tax expert stated that TSAs were typical in spin-off transactions; they provided an incentive for the spun-off company to use diligence before entering into post-spin transactions that might undermine the tax-free status of the earlier event. The agreement here did not impose onerous burdens on the subject to repay or refinance its debts following the transaction.

Reliance on market evidence. The court found the defendants' valuation expert convincing. "For nearly every step of the DCF analysis, [the plaintiff's expert] selected inputs that forced [the company's] value lower," it said, producing a valuation "that is low in the extreme and that implied an incredibly low trading multiple for [the subject]."

It further agreed that numerous instances of double counting "infected" the DCF analysis and the expert's overall conclusions. She not only applied an unjustified company-specific risk premium, but also weighted the market multiple method at 15%, ostensibly because the companies Houlihan Lokey had selected were not sufficiently comparable. But the bank, in its earlier analysis, had already applied a multiple discount to account for any dissimilarity.

It was beyond dispute that the plaintiff's expert's valuation under the DCF method "produced an extreme outlier even within her own analysis," the court stated. But rather than disregard or assign low weight to this valuation, she did the opposite: assign low weight to the consistent valuations. Consequently, the court dismissed the valuation.

All credible evidence indicated that the subject company was solvent on the spin-off date, it noted. Also, there was no misrepresentation. Verizon's and the subject's public filings contained comprehensive risk disclosures informing the market of a general decline in the use of print directories.

Relying on market evidence, the court found that the value "implied by trading on the NYSE was no less than $12.8 billion." But choosing to "remain agnostic" about the precise final figure, it held that the value on the spin-off date was "at least $12 billion."

Does Apportionment Rule Extend to Trade Secrets Cases?

Case name: *Versata Software, Inc. v. Internet Brands, Inc.*
Citation: 2012 U.S. Dist. LEXIS 145020
Date of decision: October 9, 2012
Country: US
State or Federal: Federal
State/Jurisdiction: Texas
Court: United States District Court
Type of action: Intellectual Property
Experts: Alan Ratliff (defendant)
Judge: Bryson
SIC: 7371 Computer Programming Services

Both the plaintiff and defendant sold software to large automobile manufacturers that permitted customers to comparison-shop for cars online. After the plaintiff lost its contract with Chrysler to the defendant, it sued for patent infringement related to the software technology. In response, the defendant countersued for theft of trade secrets and breach of contract, claiming it owned the critical comparison-enabling components of the software and calculating damages based on the plaintiff's continuing contracts with Toyota.

Damages based on all of the plaintiff's profits. In assessing damages for a jury trial, the defendant's expert reviewed various documents related to the plaintiff's work for Toyota, including the contracts as well as financial and business records related to income from the contracts and licenses for the software. He also looked at industry research that both parties had conducted, including market and consumer studies, and drew on his prior experience working with automobile manufacturers and service providers, including Toyota. (For example, he noted one document "highlighted" the plaintiff's need for the comparison component of the software.) Further, an additional technical expert for the defendant testified how the plaintiff used the component in preparing its software products for Toyota

Based on this review, the damages expert testified that the comparison functionality was the basis for Toyota's purchase of the plaintiff's software and that the defendant was entitled to all of the profits from contracts, which amounted to $2 million. If the jury was not prepared to accept the proposition, he still believed that "*not less* than 50%" of those profits was attributable to the plaintiff's theft. Notably, the plaintiff cross-examined the expert, but did not present its own expert to calculate damages for the alleged trade secret theft. After the defendant vigorously contested the patent infringement claims on the basis of invalidity and anticipation, the jury returned entirely in the defendant's favor of $2 million, and the plaintiff appealed.

As a preliminary matter, the plaintiff argued that the defendant's expert incorrectly applied all of its revenues from the Toyota contracts, in violation of the entire market value rule (EMVR). Borrowing the rule from federal patent law, which permits recovery of damages based on the entire value of the accused product if the patented feature drives consumer demand, the plaintiff claimed the expert's evidence "was not up to the task." That is, he never showed that the basis for Toyota's interest in the plaintiff's software was the trade secret component, and he failed to prove that all of the profits from the Toyota contract were attributable to the same. At a minimum, the plaintiff maintained the expert should have apportioned the amount of profits that were due directly from the stolen technology.

Sidestepping the issue. Importantly, the plaintiff did not cite any legal authority or case precedent for its argument to apply the EMVR to trade secret cases. "In any event," the court said, "all that is at issue here is whether the evidence supports the jury's finding that [the defendant's] trade secrets were of sufficient importance to [the plaintiff's] work on the Toyota project" so that their award of all of the profits is appropriate.

To determine this narrower issue, the court acknowledged generally the financial documents and market/industry surveys that the defendant's expert relied on, noting in particular that the plaintiff was free to explore any of their shortcomings on cross-examination. Similarly, the plaintiff had "ample" opportunity to point out any flaws in the expert's calculations as well as any alleged inconsistencies in his offering a lesser amount. Finally, the plaintiff could have had an expert offer an alternative measure of misappropriation damages, but chose not to do so. The court said, "At the end of the day, the jury apparently chose to believe" the testimony of the defendant's expert, "which it was entitled to do," and affirmed the $2 million award.

Fed. Circuit Chides Defendants for 'Improper' Admissibility Challenge

Case name: *Versata Software, Inc. v. SAP America, Inc.*
Citation: 2013 U.S. App. LEXIS 8838
Date of decision: May 1, 2013
Country: US
State or Federal: Federal
State/Jurisdiction: N/A
Court: United States Court of Appeals
Type of action: Intellectual Property
Experts: Neeraj Gupta, Chris Blackwell, Roy Weinstein (plaintiffs); Michael Wagner (defendants)
Judge: Rader
SIC: 7372 Prepackaged Software (mass reproduction of software)

A patent infringement suit involving software for product pricing resulted in two jury trials and a failed post-trial challenge by the defendants to the $345 million award. In their most recent appeal, the defendants contended that the plaintiff expert's lost profits theory should never have been admitted and there was insufficient evidence for the award.

New damages law, new trial, no resolution. The patented technology concerns the computerized pricing of products. In 1995, Versata (plaintiffs) introduced a hierarchical pricing engine and "breakthrough" commercial software called "Pricer" that it sold to "Tier 1" companies, including IBM, Lucent, Motorola, and Hewlett-Packard. Between 1995 and 1998, Versata had an average of $5 million in revenue and $3 million in profit stemming from the product. Before SAP (defendants) entered the market, the company made at least 61 sales of Pricer, and, for at least 21 sales, Pricer was the only product the customer bought from Versata. Accordingly, the plaintiffs' win rate was 35%.

Once SAP, the market leader in business software, bundled the technology into its full enterprise software, Pricer sales slipped and Versata's win rate dropped to 2%. In 2001, Versata stopped selling Pricer to anyone, even non-SAP customers, and, from 2003 to 2011, the damages period, it made no sales.

But internal SAP documents from 2007 confirmed that demand for the patented functionality remained. In the documents, SAP stated that there was "customer need for hierarchical access" and that the key to its business was to have "capability."

In 2007, Versata sued for infringement. Following the first trial, the jury awarded it over $138 million, but the trial court granted SAP's motion for a new trial on damages based on decisions from the U.S. Court of Appeals for the Federal Circuit that changed or refined the determination of patent damages.

On retrial in 2011, the jury assessed two theories: lost profits and reasonable royalty. In terms of lost profits, Versata's expert focused on Pricer sales the company lost to Tier 1 customers. He concluded the initial pool included 435 customers. Based on the company's historical 35% win rate, he then determined that Versata would have been able to sell its product to 152 of the lost customers. He acknowledged that Versata would not in 2003 simply have been able to make sales at the rate it did in 1998. There would have been a ramp-up period. He also discounted the pool of lost customers, concluding that, during the eight-year damages period, Versata lost 93 sales to SAP. This decreased the win rate to 21%. In his sales value calculation, he considered both "the direct costs of making those sales" and related "general and administrative expenses." As for price elasticity, he explained that, pursuant to the principle that a lower price results in greater demand, his using a lower price when valuing the lost sales would have resulted in an offset by additional lost sales.

He determined that the base value of each lost sale was approximately $1.8 million. When he factored in the additional revenues from each sale, including maintenance and consulting deals, he arrived at $3 million in profit per sale lost to SAP. Considering the pool of lost sales, the total lost profits amounted to $285 million, he concluded. The jury awarded $260 million.

As for royalty damages, the district court precluded Versata's expert from presenting his analysis, leaving only SAP's expert to testify. He conducted a hypothetical negotiation using the *Georgia-Pacific* factors. He noted that there was a comparable license for software similar to Pricer and that SAP had sold it to 12 customers. He then stated that the reasonable royalty rate here should be a $2 million lump-sum payment.

On cross-examination, he elaborated on the comparable license. The average sales price per customer for the product was $333,000. An appropriate royalty rate of that amount would have been 40%, that is, $133,200 per customer. SAP had made approximately 1,300 infringing sales. If the customer rate were applied to those sales, the damages would be $170 million, he stated.

The jury awarded $85 million, raising the total damages amount to $345 million.

SAP subsequently challenged the award in motions for judgment as a matter of law (JMOL) or for a new trial, which the trial court denied. In terms of the lost profits amount, the court found the final number "was not a product of speculation, but was based on sound economic proof confirmed by the historical record." As for the reasonable royalty, it noted that SAP "cannot legitimately challenge the comparability of its own comparable." (An extended discussion of the district court's ruling and the opinion are available at *Business Valuation Update* and *BVLaw*.)

Defendant says no sales equals no demand. SAP then appealed the trial court's findings and the verdict at the Federal Circuit, claiming, among other things, that the district court erred when it refused to overturn the lost profits and royalty awards.

Specifically, Versata's expert developed a "but for" model that was inconsistent with sound economic principles, SAP stated. The trial court erred by admitting the fatally flawed testimony. The jury "could not have had" sufficient evidence to award lost profits.

The Federal Circuit dismissed the argument that the expert's lost profits theory was "legally defective" and thus unreliable and inadmissible as "improperly raised." Any questions as to the admissibility of the expert's opinion were subject to the framework of *Daubert* and the Federal Rules of Evidence, it said. SAP was not appealing a *Daubert* ruling but now tried to introduce those issues "under the guise of sufficiency of the evidence." This, the court said, "is the improper context" for deciding admissibility questions.

Second, SAP argued the expert did not follow the *Panduit* analytical framework. For one, considering that Versata stopped selling the product in 2001, Versata had no evidence of demand during the damages period, which began in 2003.

The Federal Circuit disagreed. Versata showed demand before SAP entered the market. This evidence was especially probative, the court said, because it gave a picture of a world in which Versata enjoyed market exclusivity—a state similar to the hypothetical "but for" SAP's infringement world.

Even though the market for Pricer disappeared once SAP bundled hierarchical pricing into its software, SAP's 2007 documents confirmed that customers continued to want the patented functionality.

SAP was wrong to equate the lack of sales of Pricer with a lack of demand. "The act of 'selling' an item does not necessarily mean the item must be 'sold,'" the court stated. For the purpose of lost profits, the *Panduit* factors did not require proof that there was demand for a "particular embodiment of the patented functionality," i.e., Pricer. Also, SAP's expert had an opportunity to present his alternative lost profits model to the jury but declined to do so.

Moreover, SAP argued that Versata failed to satisfy *Panduit* factor 4. The expert's "but for" model made assumptions about demand and price elasticity that were inconsistent with the real world, and he failed to account for market forces not related to infringement that could have caused the losses.

This argument also was persuasive, the court said. The plaintiffs' expert specifically adjusted for market and economic pressures, discounting the win rate to account for the time Versata would need to ramp up its sales and discounting his sales value calculation to reflect costs related to making the sales. He also accounted for price elasticity when calculating the number of lost sales. Versata made a prima facie showing of lost profits, but SAP subsequently failed to meet its burden to show that a different amount would have been more reasonable, the court concluded.

EMVR 'never triggered.' SAP attacked the royalty award by claiming that its expert intended his calculation to be a $2 million lump sum that covered all of the infringing sales. The jury improperly "extrapolate[d] a per customer royalty from the royalty estimate." Also, the award "violated the entire market value rule" (EMVR).

In line with the trial court, the Federal Circuit dismissed SAP's attempts to disavow testimony from its own expert regarding the comparable license. He never disputed that he proposed a 40% royalty, and he never questioned the number of SAP's infringing sales, the court observed. "The jury used common sense and merely applied SAP's proposed royalty to a larger number of infringing sales than SAP desired." It was free to reject the maximum proffered award and choose an intermediate rate.

The EMVR never came into play, the court continued. SAP's expert did not apply his 40% royalty rate to the entire value of the infringing products but only applied it to the value of the comparable software sales. Therefore, he only accounted for all of the infringing sales. For all these reasons, the Federal Circuit affirmed the award.

Expert's Anemic Analysis Imperils Damage Calculation

Case name: *Wallace v. Kalniz*
Citation: 2013 Ohio App. LEXIS 2987
Date of decision: July 5, 2013
Country: US
State or Federal: State
State/Jurisdiction: Ohio
Court: Court of Appeals
Type of action: Damages (incl. Lost Profits)
Experts: Dr. Malcolm Cohen (plaintiff); unknown (defendants)
Judge: Jensen
SIC: 8021 Offices and Clinics of Dentists
Key words: Business Loss, Damages, Expert testimony, Rule 702, Discounted cash flow method (DCF)

An economist expert who failed to do rigorous research to support his loss calculation got caught in the litigation crossfire when the defendants defeated the plaintiff's tort claims in pretrial motions, including a motion to strike his report and affidavit. After the trial court disqualified the expert testimony, there was no triable issue as to damages. The plaintiff tried to salvage the case on appeal.

The plaintiff was a dentist desirous of selling his practice, and the defendants were dentists owning and practicing in a larger group that sought to expand. In mid-2007, the parties pursued negotiations and preparations, culminating in the plaintiff's handing the defendants his client list and demographics. But a few months later, the defendants changed key terms of the draft agreements, and the deal fell apart in early 2009. The defendants reorganized and opened but without the plaintiff. The plaintiff sued, alleging breach of contract, deceptive trade practices, business interference, conversion, and fraudulent misrepresentation.

The trial court first granted the defendants' summary judgment motion on the breach of contract claim. They then filed another motion on the tort claims, requesting that the court strike the opinion of the plaintiff's damages expert under the state's evidentiary Rule 702 and accordingly find there was no material issue as to damages.

Gap between actual and projected revenues. To determine economic losses, the plaintiff retained an MIT-educated economist who served as president of the Michigan Employment Research Corp. and whose work focused on labor market issues, new hires, and labor shortages.

He reviewed a host of materials, including financial information for the plaintiff and select financials for the defendants, an American Dental Association practice survey, an analysis of the plaintiff's practice, information resulting from an interview with a dental consultant, federal bond rates, and an article on the increment-decrement model of labor force activity.

He prepared several discounted cash flow (DCF) analyses using three different periods—end of 2011, 2027, and 2042—and also three different scenarios. Under the first scenario, the plaintiff continued with his existing practice; under the second, the plaintiff upgraded his office in 2008, as initially planned; under the third, the plaintiff updated his office *and* added 10% additional collected income in 2009, representing assumed lost income due to the defendants' entering the market.

He first issued an expert report in 2009 whose calculations were based on his projected revenues for 2009 and 2010. As the case moved along and the actual revenues surfaced, they exceeded his projections by about 20% to 25%. His updated November 2011 report reflected the actual numbers for 2009 and 2010. When the discrepancy came up at his deposition, he explained that economic science did not enable him to provide exact estimates and that, in light of the dire economy at that time, he did not believe there would be any growth.

He projected that the plaintiff's collections would have been 10% higher had the defendants not entered the same market based on the assumption that a competitor inevitably took business from the plaintiff. But he agreed that there could have been overall growth in the area that benefitted both the plaintiff and the defendants. As to how an office 10 miles away from the plaintiff's practice would decrease the latter's business, he admitted he had not done research to verify his assumption. Ultimately, he said, he had "a lot more questions" and would want to discuss the issue of why the plaintiff's practice increased with the plaintiff before trial.

He predicted no growth in the plaintiff's practice for 2009 and 2010, pointing to the 2008 recession. As he saw it, the loss of jobs and attendant dental insurance, "maybe" would lead people to postpone dental treatment and tooth cleaning. But he admitted he had not specifically researched this issue to support his hypothesis and had no independent information on the relationship between dental insurance and the individual's decision to get dental care or the performance of dental practices in a recession.

He predicted a 12% growth starting in 2011 for three years, followed by a 5% flat rate. He agreed that the growth could result from charging patients more or from obtaining new patients. At his deposition, he stated that he did not investigate whether the plaintiff had gained or lost patients and again said he "would want to" research a number of issues before testifying in court, including: trends related to the plaintiff's practice, the business's fee structure, and any change in the nature of the practice and its marketing.

To discount cash flow to present value, he used a 4.4% rate.

Based on his assumptions, he estimated that the economic loss ranged between $251,000 and $2.6 million.

Also at his deposition, he explained that his calculation resulted from applying the formula that had appeared in a business valuation the plaintiff had obtained at the time he had bought his practice from a retiring dentist in 2005. Although the expert believed his own calculation was accurate, he could not vouch for the methodology because he did not have all the information the earlier business valuator had. He said he did not perform any independent investigation to support his conclusion as to the business value at work life expectancy. But assuming the earlier formula was valid, he said, "discounting to present value would give a valid estimate at the time [the plaintiff] would retire."

The trial court gave two reasons for striking the opinion. One, even though the expert was "a highly qualified economics and econometrics expert," he was not qualified "to act as a business valuation expert." Two, "although the methods used to calculate the amounts [the plaintiff] allegedly lost appear accurate and appropriate," the calculations were based on speculative and unreliable assumptions. Notwithstanding the expert's review of numerous documents, he never explained how "the sources impacted the figures he used." Ultimately, his calculations were "only as good as the assumptions on which they were based," the trial court concluded.

Expert speaks in generalities. The plaintiff appealed to the Ohio Court of Appeals on various grounds, including the trial court's decision to disqualify the expert. The appellate court reviewed both aspects of the lower court's findings.

1. *Qualification.* The expert explained that when he performed his calculations, he merely applied a formula a different business valuator had used in the earlier valuation, the appellate court noted. Therefore, he did not perform a business valuation he was not qualified to do. Accordingly, the trial court erred when it struck the opinion based on qualification concerns.

2. *Assumptions.* On the other hand, the appellate court agreed with the trial court that the expert's calculations were merely speculative. "He reviewed no data to inform his opinions and listed a number of items that he wanted to—but did not—review in calculating [the plaintiff's] economic loss." If he had done the things "he said he wanted to do," he might have been able to state a basis for his assumptions, said the reviewing court. Without doing so, he was left to argue the overall state of the economy and to rely on his untested beliefs about people's dental care practices in hard economic times. Consequently, the trial court did not abuse its discretion in striking his damages testimony.

Bankruptcy Court Wary of Asset Approach in Solvency Analysis

Case name: *Whyte v. C/R Energy Coinvestment II, L.P. (In re SemCrud)*
Citation: 2013 Bankr. LEXIS 2351
Date of decision: June 10, 2013
Country: US
State or Federal: Federal
State/Jurisdiction: Delaware
Court: United States Bankruptcy Court
Type of action: Bankruptcy
Experts: M. Freddie Reiss (debtor); Michael Lederman (defendants)
Judge: Shannon
SIC: 1389 Oil and Gas Field Services, NEC (except construction of field gathering lines, site preparation and related construction activities performed on a contract or fee basis)
Key words: Bankruptcy, Chapter 11, Solvency, Asset approach, Income approach, Market approach

Five months before it filed for Chapter 11, the debtor made partnership distributions to the defendant equity interest owners for over $29 million, which the plaintiff trustee sought to avoid and recover. The Bankruptcy Court considered expert testimony on the issue of solvency at the time of the distributions.

The debtor primarily serviced the energy industry, moving oil and gas products via trucks and pipelines and storing them; its revenues for 2007 were about $13.2 billion. But it also had a marketing business that was trading in derivatives on the New York Mercantile Exchange (NYMEX) and the over-the-counter markets. Ultimately, these activities caused a liquidity crisis and the debtor's Chapter 11 bankruptcy filing in July 2008.

The defendants were equity owners in the debtor and as such received equity distributions, including over $29 million in February 2008. In challenging the distributions, the litigation trustee claimed that the debtor's CEO had engaged in speculative derivatives trading in violation of the company's loan agreements. Also, the debtor allegedly had moved millions of dollars into a company the CEO owned to enable him to do his own commodities trading.

Agreement on valuation basics. In trial in Bankruptcy Court (D. Del.), the trustee argued the transfer was avoidable because the debtor received no value for the distributions considering they were equity distributions. The defendants tried to claim that the debtor's status as a limited partnership allowed for taxes to pass through to the individual partners, which meant there was a value. The court dismissed that claim, pointing out that the Bankruptcy Code and case law taught that equity distributions did not confer "value" on the transferor.

To succeed on its fraudulent transfer claim, the trustee next had to show the debtor was insolvent on the distribution date. For the solvency analysis, both sides presented expert testimony to determine the debtor's fair value.

The experts agreed—and so did the court—that the debtor should be valued on a going-concern basis because liquidation in bankruptcy was not "clearly imminent" on the distribution date. Rather, the business was fully functioning, with plans to continue operations. The experts, and the court, further agreed that there were three standard approaches to valuing the company—the income approach, the market approach, and the asset-based approach—and that the income approach was the preferred method for valuing a company on a going-concern basis.

Trustee's expert advocates asset approach. But when it came to choosing the appropriate method for *this* case, the experts disagreed. Accordingly, their conclusions as to solvency diverged considerably.

Specifically, the trustee's expert claimed the asset approach was the only reliable approach here. It alone accounted for the speculative trading activities. He used Jan. 31, 2008, as the valuation date and analyzed the company's consolidated financial statements for 2007 and the unaudited financials for January 2008. He made several key adjustments to the balance sheet line items. For one, he reduced the receivables for the CEO's company from $263.4 million to zero, reasoning it was "very unlikely" that the debtor would be able to collect on the money owed. The records showed a lack of documentation for that company's receivables and "lackluster" collection efforts on the debtor's part. An informed buyer would have assigned little or no value to the receivables, he argued. He explained that "debt issuance costs" were the "upfront costs a company pays when issuing debt and it is capitalized as an asset on the company's balance sheet and amortized over the life of the debt issued." He decided to reduce the debt issuance balance from $28 million to zero, he said, because "there is no value of this 'asset' to a third party." The asset only reflected the costs the company previously had incurred, he continued. He reduced "the investment in affiliates" item by $13.5 million because of the sale of one entity.

He made no adjustment for "goodwill," stating that the balance sheet already took it into consideration. The same logic, he said, applied to "customer relations," which was "an intangible asset created through the acquisition of a business." Even though it was appropriate to make downward adjustments for items related to the CEO's speculative trading and concomitant significant unrealized losses, he found it unnecessary to do so for his report.

He also described certain limitations the income approach and market approach showed in this case. The income approach was inappropriate here, he found, because of "the lack of reliable, detailed financial projections and corresponding assumptions with which to create a discounted cash flow (DCF) valuation." He acknowledged that a Goldman Sachs valuation from June 2008 used both the income and market approaches (see below) and, specifically, the DCF. But, he said, that analysis relied on financial projections whose assumptions Goldman Sachs did not provide; therefore, he was unable to assess their reasonableness. He also believed the Goldman valuation rested on the "incorrect premise" that the debtor was not involved in speculative trading.

He concluded that the market approach was inapplicable because the company's "risk profile was materially different" from other companies in the same industry. Accordingly, he could use no comparable companies to obtain a transaction multiple. He noted that Goldman, under the market approach, resorted to an "adjusted EBITDA" figure as a multiple metric. As he saw it, that metric was inappropriate because of significant unrealized derivative losses and the incorrect assumption that the debtor's trading activities had physical inventory behind them.

He concluded that only the asset approach applied, and it showed the debtors were insolvent by at least $429 million as of Jan. 31, 2008.

Defendants' expert opts for income approach. The defendants' expert relied primarily on Goldman's June 2008 valuation, which, he reasoned, was close to the distribution date. Further, Goldman valued the debtor on a going concern basis, using the income and market approaches. It prepared the valuation in the context of an actual 144A securities offering, which, again, ensured reliability, the expert believed. Moreover, Goldman had substantial access to the debtor's due diligence documents, including projections, and to management. The valuation, he said, was easily adjustable for "any negative economic impact that [the debtor's] trading activities may have had on the Company's value and its solvency cushion."

Goldman's valuation indicated a range of value from $4.3 billion to $6.1 billion. The defendants' expert adjusted those values to account for market multiples from February to June, adding $384 million to $543 million in value. He also increased the value by $206 million to account for "construction-in-progress," which he said would have value to a buyer. Goldman's valuation was for a securities offering rather than a mergers and acquisitions transaction. He decreased the value by $14 million to account for the sale of the affiliate entity. Next, he subtracted "net long-term debt" from the adjusted value to arrive at "net equity," which, he concluded, ranged from $3 billion to $5 billion. After subtracting other balance sheet liabilities totaling $2.2 billion, as well as $143 million related to "net trade book deficiency" from the net equity, he determined there was a "solvency cushion" ranging from $670 million to $2.7 billion.

The defendants also presented a trading expert to calculate the net trade book deficiency so as to measure the negative economic impact the debtor's trading activities had. He maintained that $143 million was a "conservative risk premium" the debtor had to pay.

For his part, the defendants' valuation expert criticized several aspects of the competing expert's asset approach. For one, he disagreed with the latter's decision not to adjust "goodwill" for fair value by distinguishing between book value based on accounting principles and value. He also objected to eliminating the $263.4 million receivables, relying on statements from the trading expert that they were not a credit risk as of March 2008. The company had paid $102.4 million in January and February. Lastly, he pointed out that the item "minority interest" that appeared as a liability on the balance sheet in the amount of $320.3 million represented the value of the equity ownership of minority shareholders and was not in fact a liability. He concluded that, if he adjusted the asset approach accordingly, he was able to show the debtor was solvent even then, from anywhere between $183 million to $250 million.

Court rejects receivables valuation. The court said it was "not convinced by the trustee's arguments against adopting the income approach in this case." They were based on the expert's unsupported contention that there was a lack of reliable financial projections and accompanying assumptions. Even though neither expert had access to the debtor's financial forecasts and assumptions, or to management, there was the Goldman valuation, which relied on them and which the court found reliable. It was contemporaneous and not generated "in anticipation of litigation." Because Goldman prepared the valuation in connection with a 144A securities offering, it did significant due diligence; preparations included sessions with debtor management throughout 2008 and access to a data room that stored documents going forward from 2005 when the debtor's credit agreement originally was drafted. It was appropriate for the defendants' expert to apply the income approach and use the Goldman valuation as a starting point.

As to the criticism that Goldman did not know about the speculative trading and, therefore, could not produce an accurate valuation, the court said the defendants' expert adequately quantified and adjusted for the activity's effects by relying on the analysis of the trade expert and applying a $143 million risk premium.

The asset approach was problematic, said the court. Even if one acknowledged the "insider nature of these transactions," it was impossible to conclude the receivables from the CEO's company were uncollectible. There were the $102.4 million payments at the beginning of 2008. Considering that the trustee's expert determined that insolvency amounted to $429 million, decreasing the value by $263.4 million—that is, the full amount of the receivables—amounted to a significant portion of the calculation and was not necessarily accurate. For all these reasons, the Bankruptcy Court held the trustee had failed to prove the debtor's insolvency at the date of distribution.

Nash Bargaining Solution Survives *Daubert* Challenge, Royalty Analysis Does Not

Case name: *VirnetX Inc. v. Cisco Systems, Inc.*
Citation: 2013 U.S. Dist. LEXIS 28223
Date of decision: March 1, 2013
Country: US
State or Federal: Federal
State/Jurisdiction: Texas
Court: United States District Court
Type of action: Intellectual Property
Experts: Roy Weinstein (plaintiff); unknown (defendant)
Judge: Davis
SIC: 4899 Communications Services, NEC (except ship to shore broadcasting, satellite communications, pay telephone concession operators)

The plaintiff's expert presented two models to capture infringement damages: a reasonable royalty emerging from a hypothetical negotiation and the Nash bargaining solution (NBS). In its *Daubert* motion, the defendant claimed neither approach yielded a reliable result.

In 2010, VirnetX Inc. sued multiple leading technology companies in federal court (E.D. Tex.), including Cisco and Apple, alleging infringement of several patents for creating secure protocols for virtual private networks. The technology allows a website owner to interact securely with a customer or an employee working from home to have protected access to the employer's electronic files. The court severed the cases, and in November 2012 a jury awarded VirnetX $368.2 million against Apple. In February 2013, the same court upheld the verdict.

'Math trick.' At issue in the plaintiff's case against Cisco were the defendant's routers, software, and phones with virtual private-networking functions. For damages, VirnetX's expert first calculated a reasonable royalty. Even though he believed that the patented features were not the basis for demand for Cisco's products—and even though Cisco sells components and software separately from its larger devices, including servers and towers—he used Cisco's sales figures without separating out the noninfringing elements.

Starting with the total revenue from the accused products, he made various adjustments. For one, he removed U.S. government sales from the revenue base; he also removed the cost of ancillary items such as power cables, batteries, and extra memory. He then multiplied the adjusted revenue base by 70% to arrive at an "adjusted royalty base." This apportionment factor emerged from one customer survey that indicated that 70% of customers bought the products for security reasons, he stated. Finally, he multiplied the adjusted revenue base by a reasonable royalty rate of 1%. (The opinion does not provide the total amount of reasonable royalty he determined.)

In challenging the expert's methodology, Cisco contended he violated the entire market value rule because he considered the entire revenue from infringing products, even though he conceded that the protected technology did not substantially create the value of the component parts. The 70% apportionment factor was an impermissible "math trick," Cisco said—a way to apply a lower royalty rate to the entire market value.

VirnetX countered that, in establishing his royalty base, the expert "apportioned out" several components. Also, his analysis relied on the best data Cisco provided; any analytical flaws stemmed from Cisco's inadequate sales information. Further, in making his 70% adjustment, the expert justifiably relied on a relevant customer survey.

The court found the expert made "no sincere attempt" to link the damages to the requisite "smallest salable patent-practicing unit," as the Federal Circuit required in *LaserDynamics, Inc. v. Quanta Computer, Inc.*, 694 F.3d 51 (Fed. Cir. 2012) (available at *BVLaw*). He did not consider using the smaller components or software Cisco sold, and his 70% apportionment factor was a "poor substitute for the type of analysis one should undertake when parsing an alleged infringer's profits for patented versus unpatented features."

Accordingly, VirnetX would only be able to use his reasonable royalty testimony if the expert amended his report by recalculating his royalty base, the court ruled.

Next, the court considered the expert's application of the NBS. The method received notoriety in *Oracle America, Inc. v. Google Inc.*, 798 F. Supp. 2d 1111 (N.D. Cal. July 22, 2011). In that case, the court said:

> The Nash bargaining solution is a mathematical model that purports to define the most mutually beneficial outcome of a two-party bargaining scenario. After identifying the profits each party could expect without a deal and the surplus created by their cooperation, the Nash model allocates the value of the deal in two steps: each party first receives the same profits it could expect without a deal, and then the remaining surplus is divided evenly between them.

It barred the plaintiff's expert from testifying to it because its "complex mathematical formulas and equations ... would surely be incomprehensible to the average juror." (A digest of that case and the opinion are available at *BV Update* and *BVLaw*.)

In the case at issue, VirnetX's expert applied NBS to Cisco's gross profit margin without specifically showing how the profits were related to the patents in suit. He determined that, under this model, there would have been a 45%-to-55% profit division between the plaintiff and the defendant.

Cisco claimed VirnetX's expert wrongly applied the model because he failed to calculate the incremental profits that stemmed from the use of the patented invention. Also, he failed to explain his deviation from the 50-50 split the model prescribes.

The court quickly disposed of these objections, finding Cisco had no basis to complain since both parties' experts considered the same incremental profits that accompanied the incremental revenue the patents in suit generated. Also, VirnetX's expert gave some explanation for his adjusted profit split (which the opinion does not provide). Accordingly, his NBS testimony was admissible.

Note: The case subsequently went to trial under supervision of the same judge who had presided over VirnetX's trial against Apple. But, in this case, on March 14, 2013, a different jury found no liability and rejected VirnetX's $258 million damages claim.

Minority Shareholder's Conduct Warrants Marketability Discount

Case name: *Wisniewski v. Walsh*
Citation: 2013 N.J. Super. Unpub. LEXIS 724
Date of decision: April 2, 2013
Country: US
State or Federal: State
State/Jurisdiction: New Jersey
Court: Court of Appeals
Type of action: Dissenting Shareholder
Experts: Gary R. Trugman (plaintiff/seller); Roger J. Grabowski (defendants/buyers)
Judge: Per Curiam

An 18-year-long suit featured two credentialed valuation experts and their divergent approaches for determining the fair value of the selling shareholder's interest in a closely held company. The trial court used a modified version of the discounted cash flow (DCF) method, but its valuation prompted each side to claim discount-related errors.

Three siblings—two brothers and a sister—each owned a one-third interest in a company their father built. What started as a one-truck operation in the early 1950s grew over decades into a successful business providing freight consolidation, line-haul, and dedicated fleets for certain retail stores. For much of the expansion, the older brother led the company, but during an enforced absence the younger brother took charge. The sister never worked there, but her husband also served as an officer.

Several of the younger brother's actions caused his sister to sue. This litigation spawned other suits, including a 1996 oppressed shareholder action in which the younger brother alleged his two siblings attempted to oust him. In the first phase of findings, the trial court determined that in fact it was the younger brother—the plaintiff—who was the oppressing shareholder and that his conduct harmed the other shareholders—the sibling defendants—but not the company. The court also found that the defendant older brother uniquely contributed to the success of the company, such that it performed poorly during his absence and grew again after he retook control of it.

Accordingly, it ordered the younger brother to sell his interest back to the company at fair value based on expert valuations. For this purpose, both the plaintiff seller and the defendant buyers, i.e., the sister and the older brother (who died in 2009), retained experts.

In 2002, in the second phase of the proceedings, the court considered the parties' expert reports on valuation but failed to conduct a hearing. It set the fair value of the younger brother's interest at $12.4 million. The parties appealed, and the reviewing court reversed and remanded for a new valuation based on an evidentiary hearing. In 2007 and 2008, the trial court issued decisions explaining its valuation of the interest at $32.2 million based on a 2000 valuation date (the valuation date was another issue of contention). After the trial court had entered final judgment in 2010, both the seller and the buyers—the sister and the late older brother's estate—appealed anew.

DCF versus market approach. The seller's expert used a discounted cash flow analysis, which calculates the value of a company as the present value of its expected future cash flow. In a nutshell, he determined the company's projected revenues by extrapolating from data indicating the growth of key clients, normalized the company's expenses to delete unusual costs such as excess officer compensation, and applied a discount rate to the resulting figure to arrive at the present value of the company's income stream.

In extrapolating, he followed the guidelines of the American Society of Appraisers. He also reviewed the older brother's deposition and the company's historical financial data but said he was not able to obtain any of the company's internal projections. The data, he concluded, indicated that the company was mature, its operations consistent, and growth during the five years that preceded the valuation date steady: 12.4% in 1996, 8.5% in 1997, 4.1% in 1998, 10% in 1999, and 8.5% in 2000. Accordingly, he set the long-term growth rate at 5%.

Because company expenses during the valuation year were unusually high compared with prior years, he said he decided not to use actual expenses but instead calculated an average of normalized expenses over the preceding three years.

He used the build-up method to calculate his discount rate, first considering the long-term Treasury bond yield as of the valuation date. He determined a 7% equity risk premium, a size premium of approximately 3.5%, and a company-specific risk premium of 4%. The latter captured the risk from being invested in the company at issue, including the fact that the business relied greatly on the older brother for its success. All things considered, the final discount rate was 12%, he decided. Further, he calculated a 40% equity-to-60% debt ratio, which, he said, justified the discount rate.

He acknowledged that his DCF analysis made some control-level adjustments to account for factors such as excessive officer compensation. But he noted that there was justification to add an independent control premium to the value of the company because it was plausible that a third-party buyer would run the company with an efficiency that exceeded the adjustments his valuation had made.

The buyers' expert used a market approach, estimating the value of the company through extrapolation from data related to sales of comparable businesses.

In critiquing the seller's expert's determinations, he maintained that the very sources the latter used to set the equity-to-debt ratio supported a 70% equity-to-30% debt ratio and a significantly higher discount rate of 16.5%.

The buyers' expert also contended that, in consolidating the company's financial statements, the competing expert had double counted the company's income and had included income from a property the company strove to develop, without accounting for operating expenses, decreasing the expense ratio, and increasing the resulting value of the company accordingly. He maintained that the valuation-year expenses accurately represented the company's current operations and should serve as a benchmark.

Moreover, he decided that, given the older brother's critical role in the company's success, any buyer would demand a key person discount to account for the effect of his death. He suggested that 15% would be an appropriate figure.

(The opinion does not provide the experts' valuation figures.)

Qualified acceptance of DCF method. The trial court found weaknesses in both testimonies, but on the whole preferred the approach the seller's expert used. Under the circumstances, the DCF methodology was "more consistent" with the applicable legal standard and "more conducive" to computing the "intrinsic value" of a company for which there was no ready market, the court said. While it did not dismiss the market approach as inherently incompatible with the fair value standard, it questioned the decision of the buyers' expert not to also perform a DCF valuation to corroborate the results from the market valuation. At the same time, the court credited several critical elements of his analysis.

In terms of the seller's expert, the court faulted his failure to meet with company representatives to verify his revenue projections but also recognized the company's unwillingness to make internal projections available. Ultimately, it found the 5% long-term growth rate reasonable.

But the court rejected his calculation of the company's expenses and instead adopted the general approach the buyers' expert proposed: using data from the valuation year, instead of an average of the prior three. It noted, but dismissed, the latter expert's claims that the competing valuation contained miscalculations, including double counting. If there were an inaccuracy in the calculation of the expense ratio, it would disappear by using the method of the buyers' expert, the court seemed to say.

It decided the 12% discount rate the seller's expert computed was consistent with industrywide data on which even the buyers' expert relied. Moreover, the resulting 40% equity-to-60% debt ratio estimate fell well within the range a source on which the buyers' expert relied determined for a sampling of trucking companies, the court concluded.

The trial court decided a marketability discount was inappropriate and rejected statements from the seller's expert that there was justification for an independent control premium. The expert's DCF approach produced a fair value of a controlling interest in the company that eliminated any need for a special premium, the court stated. Suggestions that the company's management was somehow deficient were without basis considering the evidence that the older brother had run the business efficiently.

Finally, based on evidence that the older brother's singular efforts had been responsible for the company's success, the trial court "quite strongly" supported the use of the 15% key-person discount the buyers' expert proposed to account for his death.

In the final analysis, it valued the selling shareholder's interest at over $32 million.

Discounts at the heart of appeals. Both parties challenged the trial court's new valuation at the New Jersey Superior Court's appellate division. The salient arguments centered on the lower court's application of, or decision not to apply, discounts.

Buyers' appellate claims. The buying shareholders contended:

(1) For his DCF valuation, the seller's expert calculated a discount rate based on an incorrect equity-to-debt ratio.

The appellate court deferred to the trial court's finding that the rate was within the range of values appearing in a source of data that the buyers' expert used.

(2) The trial court erred when it refused to apply a marketability discount.

The appellate court stated that a marketability discount, which adjusts for "the understanding that demand for such a relatively illiquid interest is limited and its value consequently diminished," was only applicable under "extraordinary circumstances" in forced buyout circumstances. Whether such circumstances existed hinged on considerations of fairness and equity.

For guidance, the reviewing court looked to precedent, which states that, "where the oppressing shareholder instigates the problems, ... fairness dictates that the oppressing shareholder should not benefit at the expense of the oppressed." *Balsamides v. Protameen Chems.*, 160 N.J. 352 (1999) (available at *BVLaw*). This principle, the court found, was directly applicable to the case at issue despite the difference in degree of oppressive conduct. Although, unlike in *Balsamides*, the seller here was the minority shareholder and his oppressive actions did not actually harm the company, "the fact remains that [he] should not be rewarded when his conduct not only harmed the other shareholders but necessitated this forced buyout."

Accordingly, the trial court erred in not applying an appropriate marketability discount. In remanding, the appellate court pointed out that its decision did not exclude the possibility that such a discount might already be implicit in the discount rate of the DCF valuation the court adopted. But absent a clear understanding of whether that was the case, the trial court should reconsider the award through application of an appropriate marketability discount.

Seller's appellate claims. The selling shareholder argued:

(1) The trial court failed to apply a control premium.

A valuation seeks to establish the fair value of a shareholder's proportional interest "in the entire entity as a going concern," the appellate court explained. It went on to say that a control premium represented the "added amount an investor is willing to pay for the privilege of directly influencing the corporation's affairs." Because New Jersey courts infrequently have dealt with the use of the control premium, state courts have looked to Delaware jurisprudence for guidance. "Delaware courts have usually rejected application of the premium in a discounted-cash-flow analysis," the appellate court observed.

It found that the trial court's decision not to use an independent control premium aligned with the applicable legal principles and the record. There was no reason to believe that the DCF valuation the seller's expert performed in this case did not produce the value of a controlling interest in the company. Also, there was no basis for the expert's claim that the older brother's management of the company was not as efficient as it might be under a third-party buyer.

(2) The trial court erred when it applied a key-person discount.

A key-person discount factors into the valuation the risk of holding an interest in a company that depends to an unusual degree on one executive or a small group of executives, the appellate court noted. The court itself had not previously addressed the applicability of this discount in a fair valuation, it stated. But other jurisdictions frequently have rejected its use. Ultimately, the applicability turned on "what equity demands in a given situation." In this case, the trial court had reason to believe the older brother was a key person in the company, based on testimony about his unique contributions to the company's success.

It dismissed the seller's argument that, even if that was the case, ultimately the older brother's death proved to have little effect on the company's success. Because that result was unknowable as of the valuation date, the appellate court said, it would be inappropriate to consider it at this point. Also, the seller's expert accounted for the company's dependence on the older brother by increasing the discount rate in his DCF analysis, without objection from the seller. Accordingly, the appellate court affirmed the trial court's decision in favor of the discount.

In remanding "for the fixing and application of a marketability discount," the appellate court also ordered the trial court to determine whether, in adopting the calculations of the seller's expert, it also adopted any inaccuracies as the buyers' expert had alleged.

Excess Earnings Method 'Better Isolates' Business Goodwill

Case name: *Wright v. Wright*
Citation: 2013 Va. App. LEXIS 53
Date of decision: Feb. 19, 2013
Country: US
State or Federal: State
State/Jurisdiction: Virginia
Court: United States Court of Appeals
Type of action: Marital Dissolution
Experts: Robert Raymond (wife); Gregory Lawson (husband)
Judge: Beales

This divorce case represents another challenge to the use of the excess earnings methodology to value a spouse's professional practice, including personal and business goodwill for equitable distribution purposes.

The husband was an equity partner in a leading law firm. At divorce, his earnings were in the third-highest compensation level for equity partners, out of 16.

Under state law, only goodwill that was attributable to the business entity, the husband's law firm, qualified as community property, whereas goodwill resulting from the individual's efforts qualified as the owner spouse's separate property.

To derive the marital share of the value of the husband's practice, the wife retained an expert who used the excess earnings method—which the court called "bottom up" method—to calculate the value of his professional goodwill. Both sides and the court acknowledged that the same expert, using the same method, had testified on behalf of the prevailing party in a precedential divorce case that also involved an equity partner's interest in the same law firm. See *Howell v. Howell*, 523 S.E.2d 514 (2000) (available at *BVLaw*).

The court does not provide details about the analysis the expert performed in this case but refers to *Howell* to explain the methodology. There, the expert compared the husband's average income for three years to that of a peer group. The difference between the two reflected the excess earnings stemming from the husband's association with the law firm, not from his personal efforts. "It was the additional income he received from being associated with his law firm." He then projected excess earnings over the husband's expected career with the same firm and used the discounted future earnings method to calculate the present value of the husband's total future excess earnings.

In the instant case, the expert testified that this approach was preferable to other methods and was the "approach that I've used in valuing virtually every professional practice, large or small, certainly for the last 10, 15 years." The marital value of the husband's interest here was almost $1.5 million, he concluded. His assessment did not include a value for the husband's personal goodwill.

The court also does not provide details about the valuation the husband's expert performed, but notes that he made adjustments and applied discounts based on testimony that his client was subject to a reduction in income and planned to retire at age 61. He found that the marital value of the husband's interest was $503,000, that is, roughly a third of the value the wife's expert's determined.

The trial court accepted the valuation of the wife's expert, calling his opinion "better reasoned and more credible" than the competing testimony. His approach showed a "better focus on intrinsic value," and his estimation of goodwill was more persuasive because he "better isolated institutional goodwill by determining what an attorney's law firm interest value with husband's skill, knowledge, and experience value would be if he was in a firm that lacked the attributes of husband's law firm." The court found the various adjustments and discounts the husband's expert applied "arbitrary."

Although the court did not discuss the husband's personal goodwill, its final decree stated that it could "only take cognizance of *institutional* goodwill" (emphasis in original)

Available financial data. In his appeal to the Virginia Court of Appeals, the husband claimed the trial court erred in crediting the wife's expert's defective valuation. Specifically,

- There was no justification for using the excess earnings method in this case. Unlike in the earlier *Howell* case in which the expert resorted to it because he did not have access to partnership financial data, here, the husband provided the relevant financial data;
- The expert neither valued nor accounted for the husband's personal goodwill;
- His valuation did not "tax-effect for accounts receivables and work in progress";
- The comparison group of firms and attorneys was not comparable to the husband and his practice;
- The valuation assumed an increase in the husband's income, including post-separation earnings; and
- It failed to consider testimony regarding a reduction in income and early retirement.

The appellate court disposed of the arguments quickly. It agreed that the testimony of the wife's expert "strongly suggests" that he had more financial information at his disposal than was the case in *Howell*. But, it continued, there is no controlling authority that instructs trial courts to limit the use of the excess earnings method to cases in which pertinent financial information is unavailable. Whether to accept the approach is a factual issue "within the sound discretion of the trial court."

The Court of Appeals also agreed that the wife's expert did not compute a value for the husband's personal goodwill. But given the trial court's explanation in its final decree, the appellate court determined "that no part of husband's *personal* goodwill was included" in the distribution award calculation. Finally, as the fact finder, the trial court had no obligation to give weight to the early retirement testimony. For all these reasons, the appellate court affirmed the $1.5 million marital value of the law practice interest.

www.ingramcontent.com/pod-product-compliance
Lightning Source LLC
LaVergne TN
LVHW062156300926
849161LV00010B/2682